Searching the Scriptures

Andrews University Seminary Emerging Scholars Pay Tribute to Their Professors

Richard M. Davidson
Jiří Moskala
Roy E. Gane
Paul Z. Gregor
Ranko Stefanović
Thomas Shepherd

Slaviša Janković, Editor

Department of Old Testament
Seventh-day Adventist Theological Seminary
Andrews University
Berrien Springs, MI 49104-1500

Contents

PART 1: OLD TESTAMENT

PART 2: NEW TESTAMENT

PART 3: PSEUDEPIGRAPHA

PART 4: BIBLICAL ARCHEOLOGY

PART 5: SYSTEMATIC THEOLOGY

INDEX

Contributors

Janković, Slaviša is a PhD Candidate with an emphasis in Old Testament Exegesis specializing in ritual and legal texts. He is adjunct professor at the Seventh-day Adventist Theological Seminary at Andrews University, Berrien Springs, Michigan, USA.

McGuire, Amanda J. is a PhD Candidate with an emphasis in Old Testament Exegesis, specializing in angelology and ancient calendar systems and languages. She is adjunct professor at the Seventh-day Adventist Theological Seminary at Andrews University, Berrien Springs, Michigan, USA.

Morrow, Laura is a PhD Candidate with an emphasis in the Old Testament Exegesis, specializing in the book of Daniel. She is adjunct professor at the Seventh-day Adventist Theological Seminary and the Department of Religion and Biblical Languages at Andrews University, Berrien Springs, Michigan, USA.

Orellana, Michael is a PhD Candidate with an emphasis in Biblical Archeology, specializing in Iron Age Palestinian Archaeology. He is adjunct professor at Peruvian Union University, Lima, Peru.

Rivas Santini, Abelardo is a PhD Candidate with an emphasis in Biblical Archeology, specializing in ancient religions and Iron Age Transjordan. He is adjunct professor at the Seventh-day Adventist Theological Seminary at Andrews University, Berrien Springs, USA and Peruvian Union University, Lima, Peru.

Rodrigues Milli, Adriani holds a PhD in Old Testament Exegesis and the title of his dissertation is *Toward a Priestly Christology: A Hermeneutical Study of Christ's Priesthood*. His area of expertise is Christology. He is assistant professor of Systematic Theology in Unasp University, São Paolo, Brazil.

Rojas, Ronald holds a DMin and is a PhD Candidate with an emphasis in Old Testament Exegesis, specializing in the book of Daniel. He is associate professor of Religion at Atlantic Union College, Lancaster, Massachusetts, USA.

Sciarabba, Davide is a PhD Candidate with an emphasis in Systematic Theology, specializing in Theological Ethics. He is assistant professor at the Department of Religion and Biblical Languages at Andrews University, Berrien Springs, Michigan, USA.

Sigvartsen, Jan A. holds a PhD in Old Testament Exegesis and the title of his dissertation is *The Afterlife Views and the Use of the Tanakh in Support of the Resurrection Concept in the Literature of Second Temple Period Judaism: The Apocrypha and the Pseudepigrapha*. His areas of expertise are Second Temple period Literature and Resurrection Beliefs. He is adjunct professor of Department of Religion and Biblical Languages at Andrews University, Berrien Springs, Michigan, USA and an Old Testament Lecturer at Friedensau University, Germany.

Sigvartsen, Leanne M. holds an MA in Counseling. Her interest is in the area of Gender studies, women's issues, and sexism studies.

Skinner, Jerome holds a PhD in Old Testament Exegesis and the title of his dissertation is *The Historical Superscriptions of Davidic Psalms: An Exegetical, Intertextual, and Methodological Analysis.* His area of expertise are Wisdom Literature, Historical Books, Hebrew Language and Literature. He is adjunct professor at the Seventh-day Adventist Theological Seminary at Andrews University, Berrien Springs, Michigan, USA and Spring Arbor University, Spring Arbor, Michigan, USA.

Wetterlin, Cory is a PhD Candidate with an emphasis in Systematic Theology, specializing in the subject Divine Indwelling. He is adjunct professor at the Seventh-day Adventist Theological Seminary at Andrews University, Berrien Springs, Michigan, USA.

Acknowledgments

A project such as this is rarely brought to fruition through the efforts of one person. The completion of this volume, through its multiple stages of preparation and refinement, has been a collaborative effort. I have been blessed to have been a part of this collaboration.

The purpose of this project is simple. In writing these essays each author wishes to offer a tangible expression of appreciation and gratitude to those professors who have invested their time in teaching them the value of studying Scripture. Each one of the professors represented has greatly influenced the authors' understanding of the Biblical text, and for this they are forever indebted to them. This festschrift recognizes the scholarship of the following professors: Drs. Richard M. Davidson, Jiří Moskala, Roy Gane, Ranko Stefanović, Paul Gregor, and Thomas Shepherd.

It is impossible to acknowledge all of those who have assisted me in this project. However, first and foremost, I would like to thank Dr. Jiří Moskala for his constant support and encouragement, without which this project would never have been initiated. Next, I would like to thank all of the contributors who have invested their time and talent. I am grateful for their patience and persistence. I am also indebted to my colleague Laura Morrow for proofreading most of the essays and offering her insights as well. The expertise of Averil and Dr. Laren Kurtz in performing the final proofreading and copy-editing is inestimable. Finally, I would like to acknowledge the initial editing of Dr. Riemar Vetne and his substantial suggestions for some papers.

Additionally, I would like to offer a special word of thanks to Amy Rhodes for formatting the book, Adelina Alexe for taking photos for the cover pages, Jan and Leanne Sigvartsen for printing suggestions, helpful pieces of advice and cover page, and Dorothy Show for her administrative assistance.

My warmest gratitude goes to my family, my wife Maria and children Jakov, Ruta Maria and Aron. Because of the demands of this project they were bereft of my full attention for the last two years. Maria took upon herself some of my duties and I am deeply grateful. In addition, she has been my source of constant support, love, and encouragement. Maria is my true ʿēzer kĕnegdô and I am immensely grateful to God for her.

Finally, I would like to express my sincere and deepest gratitude to God, our Creator and Redeemer, who is the source of all we need for a meaningful and abundant life. I firmly believe that He was the source for all the courage, encouragement, patience, diligence, guidance, enthusiasm, focus, originality and creativity which were needed so that this Festschrift could be brought to fruition. Soli Deo Gloria!

Slaviša Janković, Editor
Andrews University,
Berrien Springs, MI
January 2018

A Tribute to Dr. Jiří Moskala

Jiří Moskala was born in Cesky Tesin in what is now the Czech Republic. He later met and married his wife Eva and then had five children. Remarkably, Moskala grew up as a Seventh-day Adventist Christian and later became an ordained minister of the Seventh-day Adventist Church under the Communist regime of the former Czechoslovakia, serving as pastor in the Czecho-Slovakian Union for over a decade. He received his Master of Theology in 1979 from the Comenius Faculty of Protestant Theology (presently the Protestant Theological Faculty of Charles University) after the Adventist Bible Seminary was closed after only one year. Subsequent to the peaceful end to Communist rule in his native country during the Velvet Revolution of 1989, Moskala established and became principal at the Seventh-day Adventist Theological Seminary in Prague where Adventist pastors were trained for ministry. In addition to his pastoral and pedagogical ministry, he also served in the Health and Education departments of the Czecho-Slovakian Union. Ultimately, his thirst for knowledge and his interest in biblical studies led him to further his education and complete a Doctor of Theology (ThD) at the former Comenius Faculty of Protestant Theology in 1990.

He continued to pursue his interest in biblical studies in the United States at the Seventh-day Adventist Theological Seminary at Andrews University where he completed a Doctor of Philosophy (PhD) in Old Testament Studies. In 1996, he joined the faculty of the Seminary as Associate Professor of Old Testament Exegesis and Theology. After some years, he became chair of the Old Testament department, a position in which he supported and advocated for both students and faculty. Shortly thereafter, in 2013, he accepted the position of Dean of the Theological Seminary, a position he currently holds.

As author of over 50 articles, chapters, and books, Moskala has greatly influenced the interpretation and understanding of the Hebrew Bible and its theological underpinnings, especially for the Seventh-day Adventist Church. For example, his first dissertation on the challenging theories of authorship concerning the book of Daniel was so persuasive that he was able to convince faculty members at the former Comenius Faculty of Protestant Theology of the certainty of his conclusions. However, Moskala's convincing analysis not only successfully supported his dissertation thesis, but also supported the prophetic paradigm of Adventism. Furthermore, his second dissertation, *The Laws of Clean and Unclean Animals in Leviticus 11*, clearly explained the rationale and theology behind Leviticus 11. While this topic has historically been challenging and its rationale, elusive, Moskala's adept analysis produced significant insights into a topic that holds an important place in the religious practices of the Seventh-day Adventist Church and in its theological conception of biblical law.

Moskala has served the Seventh-day Adventist Church in several capacities and has devoted his talents and time to enriching and supporting the work of the Church. He has worked as pastor, teacher, and administrator. His work has spanned several continents, where he has made innumerable presentations at theological symposia, Bible conferences, and Church committees across 13 divisions. He works tirelessly to elucidate the message of the Church and explain the meaning of the biblical text for both clergy and laity. Today, his work continues to enrich the study of God's Word and to further the mission and message of the Church throughout the world.

Laura Morrow

A Tribute to Dr. Richard M. Davidson

Dr. Richard Melvyn Davidson is a fourth-generation Seventh-day Adventist Christian from Glendale, California. He attended Adventist schools in Glendale for his primary and secondary education. At Glendale Adventist Academy, he served as class pastor for three years. His desire to know God intimately led him to enroll in the Theology department at Loma Linda University from 1963 to 1968. During this time, he spent one year in Hong Kong as a student missionary. He was the first student from LLU to serve in this capacity. In addition, he met and later married the former Jo Ann Mazat. Davidson's theological studies challenged his understanding of the Bible, especially the application of the historical-critical method to the Biblical text. This would later lead him to search the Scriptures so that he could better understand God's word and the Seventh-day Adventist message.

After completing his degree at LLU, Davidson was hired by the Arizona Conference. After one year of pastoring, Davidson felt the need to augment his knowledge of the Bible, so in 1968, he enrolled in the Theological Seminary at Andrews University in Berrien Springs, Michigan, where he completed his Master of Divinity. Afterwards, he resumed his pastoral ministry from 1970-1976. During this time, he attended a Bible Conference where he began to develop a better understanding of the appropriate use of Scripture within a faith-based setting.

Eventually, he returned to Andrews University to complete his doctoral studies under the supervision of Dr. Gerhard Hasel. Davidson's expertise as a student was recognized and he was later asked to become part of the faculty in the Old Testament department. During his tenure as part of the faculty at Andrews University, Richard and his wife Jo Ann were blessed with two children, Rahel and Jonathan.

His expertise in Old Testament studies is unique and wide-ranging. In addition, his passion and advocacy for Old Testament research is known outside of and within Adventism. Outside of Adventism, his dissertation (1980) *Typology in Scripture: A Study of Hermeneutical τύπος Structures*, is still being reprinted and is considered a major contribution on the topic. Furthermore, his magnum opus, *Flame of Yahweh: Sexuality in the Old Testament*, is the most comprehensive study on biblical sexuality.

He has written 36 chapters on various topics of biblical studies and 25 articles for scholarly and professional journals. In addition, Davidson has presented 94 scholarly papers at various professional meetings, such as the Society of Biblical Literature, the Evangelical Theological Society, and the Adventist Theological Society.

Within Adventism, Davidson has contributed many years of service. He is the recipient of several teaching awards, including the prestigious J. N. Andrews Award as Professor of Old Testament Interpretation in 1995. He also served as the president of the Adventist Theological Society from 1996-1998. Finally, throughout the course of his distinguished teaching career, he has presented countless lectures and sermons in various seminars, Bible conferences, and symposiums around the world.

Even though Davidson is devoted to his research, he likes to stay in touch with nature. He earned the mountaineering "title" of fourteener, which means that he has climbed all 54 mountains in the state of Colorado with an elevation of at least 14,000 feet. Besides mountaineering, he also enjoys canoeing and skiing.

Concerning her husband, Davidson's wife JoAnn comments that "he can fix everything, both people problems and household appliances, and even cars. He has great common sense. He is full of wisdom and has a warm personality. When I come home with problems and tell them to him, he thinks about them for a minute, analyzes them and suggests possible solutions. He has the ability to see the many different sides of any problem. He is a great friend."

My friendship with Dr. Davidson began in 2003 when I was finishing the 3rd year of my undergraduate studies in Theology at a small seminary in my home country of Serbia. When I was considering graduate studies, Dr. Davidson was a visiting professor at the school. He encouraged me to come to Andrews. In addition, he asked some of his students and staff from Andrews University to send me current material not available in my country for my final research project. I am greatly indebted to him for his kindness.

When I was finally able to attend Andrews University, I had the opportunity to take several classes from Dr. Davidson that helped to shape my theological perspective. I have also had the pleasure of his expertise as chair of my doctoral committee. He has been a profound spiritual and academic mentor, as well as a sincere friend. His example of combined academic skill and Christ-like ministry will always be the paradigm that I will strive to emulate.

Jo Ann Davidson and Slaviša Janković

A Tribute to Dr. Roy E. Gane

Roy E. Gane was born in Sydney, Australia to Erwin and Winsome Gane. His family moved to the United States when he was a child, and he spent much of his time in Lincoln, Nebraska, where his father taught theology at Union College. He was a bright young man, who took college-level Greek courses as a teenager.

He did his undergraduate work at Pacific Union College, where he double-majored in theology and music. It was here that he met the love of his life, Constance E. Clark. The two married in 1980, and together they have a daughter, Sarah Gane Burton.

Roy's graduate work was done at the University of California, Berkeley under the supervision of the renowned late Jacob Milgrom. Gane completed his dissertation in 1992. His dissertation, "Ritual Dynamic Structures," was hailed by his professor as thought-provoking and important. Gane later published it as *Ritual Dynamic Structure* with Gorgias Press in 2004.

After his graduation, Roy taught at his *alma mater*, Pacific Union College (1992-1994), before taking a position at the Seventh-day Adventist Theological Seminary at Andrews University in 1994. During his years of service at the Seminary, he has served as PhD/ThD/MTh director (2003-2008) and is currently Professor of Hebrew Bible and Ancient Near Eastern Languages.

During his tenure as PhD/ThD director and in his continuing career as a teacher, Roy has been a wonderful mentor. He challenges his students to strive for academic excellence and he encourages them to enter into scholarly dialog. His students appreciate the timely, detailed feedback on their writing projects and the mentorship he provides in getting articles published. He has served on numerous dissertation committees as both chair and committee member. During the 2004-2005 school year, he received the Daniel A. Augsburger Excellence in Teaching Award.

Gane is a prolific scholar, and has thus far, has published seven books and more than 60 articles and 30 book chapters. He also served as the primary translator for the book of Leviticus in the *Common English Bible* (2011). Two of his books, *NIV Application Commentary: Leviticus, Numbers* (Zondervan, 2004) and *Cult and Character: Purification Offerings, Day of Atonement, and Theodicy* (Eisenbrauns, 2005) have become indispensable works on the subject of the Israelite ritual system. He is one of the top Levitical scholars in the discipline today and is active in scholarly circles both within the church and within the larger community of Biblical scholarship. Andrews University recognized his scholarship when he was awarded the Siegfried H. Horn Research Award in the 2013-2014 school year.

Roy Gane has been an inspiration to both myself and to other students in the Seminary. His classes are truly a place for both spiritual enrichment and intellectual engagement. As a professor, he is remarkable in that he encourages his students to develop their own theories when solving a problem; he is never afraid to allow his students to debate with him on a topic. As a result, students leave his classes more well-rounded and grounded in their theology and in their progress as scholars of the Word.

J. Amanda McGuire-Moushon

A Tribute to Dr. Paul Z. Gregor

Paul Gregor was born in Croatia. At the early age of 15, he moved away from his family to attend a newly established Adventist boarding academy, now Adriatic Union College, in Marusevec, Croatia. To the surprise of many, he chose to study theology to become a pastor. He never looked back in thinking that he had made a wrong decision.

After completing his undergraduate work at Adriatic Union College and serving mandatory military training, he started working as a pastor and married his lovely wife Helena, whom he met at Adriatic Union College. They have one son Samuel and two grandsons, Luka and Nikola.

While working as a pastor, he felt the need to further his education, and so his academic journey took him to Newbold College, England. There he completed his Bachelor of Arts and his Masters of Arts in Religion. A visiting professor from Andrews University encouraged him to pursue a doctoral degree at the Theological Seminary. It was then that he made the decision to pursue Old Testament Studies, with an emphasis in Archaeology and Ancient History. He defended his dissertation the same week his wife defended her doctoral dissertation, and so graduation was very special to him.

He received a call to serve as professor at the Adriatic Union College and after a year, became its President. However, he felt a calling to go to the mission field and after much prayer and pleading with the Lord, went to Northern Caribbean University in Jamaica. There, he became professor and later Chair of the School of Religion and Theology department. Those were the most exciting years of his life, because missions shape one's Christian life and it is where one witnesses God's working on a daily basis. His students at NCU appreciated the love and patience he showed them and the impact of his teachings on their ministry. Thus, in 2005, he received an Award of Scholarship and Recognition and again in 2007, he received an Award for Significant Contribution to Scholarship at Northern Caribbean University.

In 2007, he received the call to teach in the Old Testament Department of the Seminary at Andrews University and since 2013, he has chaired the Department.

Dr. Gregor is a prolific scholar and has authored and co-authored books, participated in different symposiums, and written numerous articles in academic and professional journals. Some of his books are entitled *Issues Concerning the History of Ancient Israel; Toward Understanding God; Israel's Cousins: Moab and Edom during the Time of Exodus*. His latest chapters published are "Geography of Esau/Edom: History, Geography, and Archaeology in Genesis" in the *SDA International Bible Commentary*, "Creation Revised: Echoes of Genesis 1 and 2 in Pentateuch" in *The Genesis Creation Account, and its Reverberations in the Old Testament* and "Water Systems in the Levant: Newest Discoveries from Tall Jalul" in *Research of the History and Culture on Ancient Near East in Croatia*.

Dr. Gregor is also a seasoned field archaeologist, excavating in Jordan. He has been in the field for almost 30 years, where he served as co-director and director at Aqaba, tell Jalulu, and Khirbet Safra. In addition, Dr. Gregor has traveled around the world giving seminars related to his field of expertise. He has been an inspiration to both myself and other students in the Seminary. His ability to simplify difficult material so that every student can understand it is valued among students. Students respect a professor who practices what he teaches.

Michael Orellana and Helena Gregor

A Tribute to Dr. Ranko Stefanović

Ranko Stefanović was born in Croatia, part of the former Yugoslavia. He started his academic studies at the SDA School of Theology in Belgrade where he graduated in 1970. In 1972, he married Estera with whom he has 2 children, a son and a daughter, and now 3 grandchildren. Subsequently, he served for eighteen years as an ordained minister in Bosnia and Croatia. After several years of pastoral experience, he went to AIIAS, Philippines, where he obtained first a BTh (1989) and then an MA in Religion (1990). The following academic year, 1996, he went to Andrews University, Michigan, where he pursued a PhD in Religion in the area of New Testament.

Stefanović started his academic career at Canadian University College, Alberta, Canada, where he taught and chaired the Department of Religious Studies from 1996-1999. He then moved back to Andrews University, Michigan, where he served from 1999-2009 as professor in the Department of Religion, and from 2006-2009 also as a chair. In 2009, he moved to the SDA Theological Seminary, also at Andrews University, where he is currently teaching in the New Testament Department.

An amazing teacher, Ranko is loved by students and colleagues. He has received several awards for his extraordinary teaching. In 1999, he received the Henry and Harriet Johnson Award For Excellence in Teaching from Canadian University College. In 2003, he received the Daniel A. Augsburger Excellence in Teaching Award and the Teacher of the Year Award, presented respectively by the College of Arts and Sciences of Andrews University and the Andrews University Student Association. Among the different classes that Dr. Stefanović teaches, Matthew and Romans have a privileged position in his heart, while Revelation is simply his passion and area of expertise.

Stefanović is also an influential New Testament scholar, distinguishing himself as an expert in the book of Revelation. In 2013, he was awarded the J. N. Andrews Medallion for excellence in teaching, scholarship, and service by Andrews University. Dr. Stefanović is the author of several scholarly papers published in numerous academic journals and editor of several books. His most notable work is *Revelation of Jesus Christ* (2002), a 670-page commentary on the book of Revelation, which is the standard textbook in many SDA colleges and universities. Given the success of the book, in 2009 Andrews University Press published a second revised and updated edition. This commentary, intended for both scholar and lay person, contains rich backgrounds of Old Testament, New Testament, and extra-biblical material and gives depth to Dr. Stefanović's analysis and interpretation of the text. Other publications are worthy to be highlighted: *The Background and Meaning of the Sealed Book of Revelation 5* (Andrews University Press, 1996) and his most recent book, *Plain Revelation: A Reader's Introduction to the Apocalypse* (Andrews University Press, 2013).

Ranko had and still has a deep impact on Adventism not only through his teaching and publications, but also for his commitment to the mission of the church. In fact, he is a sought-after speaker and lecturer at seminars, camp meetings, and churches across the globe. He has presented many programs on 3ABN Television, including a 26-program series on Matthew and a 26-one-hour-program series on the book of Revelation.

I am pleased to offer this personal tribute to Dr. Ranko Stefanović, to his ministry, to his teaching, to his scholarship, and to his contributions to the Adventist Church. He has been an outstanding teacher and also a great mentor, but moreover a man of God in my academic journey.

Davide Sciarabba

A Tribute to Dr. Thomas Shepherd

Thomas Shepherd was born in Van Nuys, CA, the middle child of five siblings. His father, Allen Shepherd, was a Loma Linda University-trained physician and his mother Irma "Tawni" Herwick Shepherd was a homemaker. He grew up in a happy Christian home, attending Adventist schools from elementary through graduate school. Following graduation from San Fernando Valley Academy, he attended Pacific Union College. He was a theology, pre-med major, torn between his love of ministry and medicine. Following graduation from PUC in 1973, he was accepted into the Loma Linda University School of Public Health where he first completed a Master of Public Health with an emphasis in Nutrition and then a Doctorate of Public health. While there, he met and married Sherry Bom Shepherd, a Loma Linda medical student.

Following completion of their respective graduate programs, Tom received a call to the Illinois Conference to work first as an associate pastor in the Northside Church in Chicago and later in the Joliet/Bolingbrook district while Sherry began a residency program at Rush Presbyterian Hospital.

Tom and Sherry have always had a deep sense of mission and when the opportunity arose in 1979, they accepted a call to serve in Malawi, Africa. Tom worked as the Health & Temperance Director and ADRA Program Coordinator for the Malawi Union while Sherry worked as a physician at the Adventist Health Center in Blantyre until their children, Amy and Jonathan were born in 1980 and 1982. They remained in Malawi until 1985 when Tom felt a pull to return to the ministry of the Word. The Shepherd family returned to the United States where Tom enrolled in the Andrews University Theological Seminary to complete his masters and PhD in New Testament Interpretation. Following completion of his PhD in New Testament, the Shepherd family returned to the mission field in Sao Paulo, Brazil where Tom taught New Testament at Instituto Adventist de Ensino Central Campus.

The Shepherds returned to the United States in 1994 and Tom taught in the Religion Department of Union College from 1994 to 2008, when he joined the faculty of the Adventist Theological Seminary at Andrews University as a professor of New Testament Interpretation. In 2011, Dr. Shepherd added the role of the Director of the PhD/ThD programs to his responsibilities at the Adventist Theological Seminary. Shepherd continues to grow the PhD/ThD program each year in quality and opportunities for students to make professional connections.

Thomas Shepherd has been active in leadership within the Society of Biblical Literature, writing proposals establishing the Mark and Methodology Consultation, the Mark Group, and the Sabbath in Text, Tradition and Theology Consultation. He has also presented scholarly papers at the annual meetings of the Society of Biblical Literature. He was co-convener of the international conference, *Resurrection of the Dead: Biblical Traditions in Dialogue*, held in Louvain-la-Neuve in Belgium in April 2010. He is a past president of the Adventst Theological Society. Dr. Shepherd has taught Revelation for 10 years at the undergraduate and graduate levels since coming to the Seminary. Shepherd's expertise in NT interpretation has also included his published dissertation, *Markan Sandwich Stories: Narration, Definition, and Function*, and his current project of writing commentaries on both Mark's Gospel and Peter's Epistles for the new SDA International Bible Commentary series.

Tom is passionate about exercise and he enjoys playing his cello with the Seminary String Quartet. For 6 years he was the head elder of the Eau Claire Seventh-day Adventist Church, where he is now the Sabbath School Superintendent. He is husband of one, father of two (both of whom he was privileged to baptize), and proud grandfather of six.

Amy M. McHenry and Cory D. Wetterlin

PART 1: OLD TESTAMENT

Nature of the Covenant with Noah in Genesis 6:18[1]

Ronald Rojas

Of all God's covenants with humans explicitly mentioned in the Scriptures, God's covenant with Noah in Gen 6:18 has been the most disregarded by scholars.[2] When it is not, just a passing comment is commonly offered.[3] As a result, God's covenant with Noah has not been seriously taken into account when biblical covenants are defined or examined to find criteria to establish which characteristic binds the biblical covenants all together. The irony of this neglect is that Gen 6:18 has the first occurrence of *běrît* ("covenant") in the Bible,[4] and therefore, it is the pivot text for quarreling on behalf of the unity of the covenants.[5]

---

1. I dedicate this paper to my mentor Roy Gane who introduced me to and inspired me to have passion for the subject of biblical covenants. This paper was presented at the 9th Annual Seminary Scholarship Symposium, SDA Theological Seminary, Andrews University, Berrien Springs, Michigan, February 8, 2013.

2. It is significant that John Walton, in his commentary on Genesis, avoided commenting on Gen 6:18. John H. Walton, *Genesis*, NIVAC (Grand Rapids, MI: Zondervan, 2001), 313. Likewise Carl F. Keil and Franz Delitzsch, *Commentary on the Old Testament*, 10 vols. (Peabody, MA: Hendrickson, 1996), 1:91; Rolf Rendtorff, *The Covenant Formula: An Exegetical and Theological Investigation*, trans. Margaret Kohl (Edinburgh: T&T Clark, 1998); John H. Sailhamer, "Genesis," in *Genesis, Exodus, Leviticus, Numbers*, vol. 2 of *The Expositor's Bible Commentary*; ed. Frank E. Gaebelein (Grand Rapids, MI: Zondervan, 1990), 84; Gerhard von Rad, *Old Testament Theology*, trans. D. M. G. Stalker, 2 vols. (New York: Harper, 1962).

3. See, for example, Walter Brueggemann, *Genesis* (Atlanta, GA: Knox, 1982), 79; John J. Davis, *Paradise to Prison: Studies in Genesis* (Grand Rapids, MI: Baker, 1975), 122; Derek Kidner, *Genesis*, TOTC 1 (Downers Grove, IL: InterVarsity, 1967), 96; John Skinner, *A Critical and Exegetical Commentary on Genesis*, ICC (New York: Scribner, 1910), 162–63; E. A. Speiser, *Genesis*, AB 1 (Garden City, NY: Doubleday, 1964), 52; Gerhard von Rad, *Genesis: A Commentary*, rev. ed., OTL (Philadelphia: Westminster, 1972), 127; Claus Westermann, *Genesis 1–11*, trans. John J. Scullion, CC (Minneapolis, MN: Fortress, 1994), 423.

4. In relation with Noah, *běrît* occurs seven more times in the covenant ratification after the Flood (Gen 9:9, 11, 12, 13, 15, 16, 17). Accordingly, the covenant with Noah has the second major number of occurrences of *běrît* in Genesis, being surpassed only by God's covenant with Abraham.

5. Some interpreters see the covenant with Noah as the foundation of the other covenants. See, for example, Roger T. Beckwith, "The Unity and Diversity of God's Covenants," *TynBul* 38 (1987): 107; Steven L. McKenzie, *Covenant* (St. Louis: Chalice, 2000), 8; Edward P. Meadors, *Creation, Sin, Covenant, and Salvation: A Primer for Biblical Theology* (Eugene, OR: Cascade, 2011), 51.

It is the interest of this paper to determine the nature of the covenant with Noah in relation to its continuity and discontinuity in God's overall covenant plan. For that, it will be examined in terms of the factors that motivated the covenant, the structure of the passage, and a close reading of the Hebrew syntax and vocabulary.

Historical Context

After sinning, Adam and Eve did not realize the consequences of their actions. It was with their progeny that they started to experience them. Their firstborn became the first criminal by killing his brother Abel (Gen 4:8). Then Genesis 4 describes how Cain's lineage went from bad to worse (see Gen 4:24).[6] In this way, the biblical account highlights the fact that sin was not restrained; it did not stop with Adam and Eve. On the contrary, it passed on from generation to generation and spread throughout the earth to such an extent that God declared that "all flesh have corrupted their way" (Gen 6:12 ESV).

Due to God's curse upon the land (Gen 3:17), Lamech expected that his son Noah could give rest (*nāḥam*) to humankind (Gen 5:29). However, unfortunately, it was at that time that God started to regret (*nāḥam*) his creation (Gen 6:6–7). The use of the same verb for Lamech's expectations of his son is parodied by God's feeling. Instead of rest, destruction will come upon the earth.[7] God's original creation will be cleansed. Thus, a reversal of the creation is in view here.[8]

The verb used to describe the situation of the earth and humankind is *šāḥat* ("to spoil," Gen 6:12), the same used to describe the purpose of the Deluge (v. 17).[9] This wordplay suggests that God will grant to humankind what they actually want. In other words, God will spoil them because they already decided to be spoiled. Thus, so to speak, God's sentence cannot be seen as a punitive act. This idea is reflected in the following text: "Then hear in heaven and act and judge Your servants, condemning the wicked by bringing his way on his own head and justifying the righteous [*ṣaddîq*] by giving him according to his righteousness" (1 Kings 8:32 NAS; cf. Deut 25:1).

The principle of the *lex talionis* is also implied.[10] By using the term *kî* ("because," "for"), Gen 6:12 states openly that the reason the earth has been spoiled is the human race. They are responsible for the corruption of the earth. That the earth does not spoil itself is also indicated by the passive voice (*niphal*). Having this clear, it is understood why the destruction of the earth ultimately means the

---

6. Von Rad, *Old Testament Theology*, 1:154.

7. Since "all flesh have corrupted" (Gen 6:12), "all flesh" will be destroyed (Gen 6:13, 17). The phrase "all flesh" indicates universality. However, the fact that a group of people and animals were saved indicates that God preserved a remnant. For details concerning the universality of the Flood, see Richard M. Davidson, "The Genesis Flood Narrative: Crucial Issues in the Current Debate," *AUSS* 42 (2004): 49–77.

8. So Meadors, *Creation*, 52; Sailhamer, "Genesis," 80.

9. In v. 17, the verb is prefaced by the preposition *lĕ*. Such construction is used to indicate purpose. See Thomas O. Lambdin, *Introduction to Biblical Hebrew* (New York: Scribner, 1971), 129; Paul Joüon and T. Muraoka, *A Grammar of Biblical Hebrew* (Rome: Pontificio Istituto Biblico, 2006), 405; Bruce K. Waltke and Michael P. O'Connor, *An Introduction to Biblical Hebrew Syntax* (Winona Lake, IN: Eisenbrauns, 1990), 606.

10. Gordon J. Wenham, Genesis 1–15, WBC 1 (Waco, TX: Word, 1987), 172; Keil and Delitzsch, *Commentary on the Old Testament*, 1:90.

cleansing of the human race (v. 13).[11] Just as humankind spoiled the earth, God will spoil humankind. God, then, is making justice to the earth.

However, the following section opens with a positive element:[12] "But Noah found favor in God's eyes" (v. 8). The *waw-disjunctive* with which this verse begins indicates that Noah is introduced as an individual who is the exception.[13] Thus, God is portrayed as wanting to destroy the earth while at the same time, wanting to save Noah. How God will deal with this awkward situation (of being just) is expressed in the pericope of the establishment of the covenant (vv. 13–22).[14] It is in this historical context that God made a covenant with Noah. Accordingly, Noah's covenant background was a divine judgment.[15]

Structure of Genesis 6:13–22

It is in Gen 6:13 that God makes known to humans what the problem with the earth is and what his plan is to solve it. The preceding verses (Gen 6:5, 11–12) present God's evaluation of humankind situation: God sees the earth.[16] However, starting with Gen 6:13, God's actions change from seeing to speaking. That is why commentators agree that Gen 6:13–22 forms a segment[17] which depicts two divine speeches: God's instruction to build an ark (Gen 6:13–16) and God's promise to deliver Noah and his family, as well as a group of animals (Gen 6:17–22).[18] Within this unit, several elements such as syntax and word repetitions reveal the cohesion of the verses.

---

11. Although it is said that "all flesh" will be destroyed (e.g., Gen 6:13, 17), a remnant from both people and animals was left. Therefore, God's original creation was not undone, as commonly believed; it was just simply cleansed (Slaviša Janković, personal communication to the author, March 8, 2015).

12. Umberto Cassuto, *A Commentary on the Book of Genesis: Part 1, From Adam to Noah (Genesis I/VI 8)*, trans. Israel Abrahams (Jerusalem: Magnes, 1961), 307.

13. So, Wenham, *Genesis 1–15*, 345; John Goldingay, *Old Testament Theology*, 3 vols. (Downers Grove, IL: InterVarsity Press, 2003), 1:173. By overlooking the historical context, Walton has considered the covenant with Noah as *general* (universal) in contrast with the others, which were *specific*. See John H. Walton, *Covenant: God's Purpose, God's Plan* (Grand Rapids, MI: Zondervan, 1994), 61. While the covenant with Noah has a universal impact due to the fact that he and his house were the only survivors, the covenant itself was specfic for Noah and his descendants: "I will make a covenant with *you* [Noah]" (Gen 6:18).

14. See Craig G. Bartholomew, "Covenant and Creation," CTJ 30 (1995): 23.

15. Arthur W. Pink, *The Divine Covenants* (Grand Rapids, MI: Baker, 1973), 66; Chun Sik Park, "Theology of Judgment in Genesis 6–9" (PhD diss., Andrews University, 2005), 209.

16. According to Sarna, the phrase "the Lord saw" has juridical overtones in Gen 6:5 due to the fact that God is presented as investigating facts and being ready for action. Nahum M. Sarna, *Genesis* (Philadelphia: Jewish Publication Society, 1989), 47.

17. See Umberto Cassuto, *A Commentary on the Book of Genesis: Part 2, From Noah to Abraham (Genesis VI 9/XI 32)*, trans. Israel Abrahams (Jerusalem: Magnes Press, Hebrew University, 1961), 55–71; David A. Dorsey, *The Literary Structure of the Old Testament: A Commentary on Genesis-Malachi* (Grand Rapids, MI: Baker, 1999), 51–52; Victor P. Hamilton, *The Book of Genesis: Chapters 1–17*, NICOT (Grand Rapids, MI: Eerdmans, 1990), 279–85; Kenneth A. Mathews, *Genesis 1–11:26*, NAC 1A (Nashville, TN: Broadman & Holman, 1996), 361–70; Speiser, *Genesis*, 54; Bruce K. Waltke, *Genesis: A Commentary* (Grand Rapids, MI: Zondervan, 2001), 135–37.

18. Herman Gunkel, *Genesis*, trans. Mark E. Biddle (Macon, GA: Mercer University Press, 1997), 143.

The verb *šāḥat* ("to spoil") occurs in both Gen 6:13 and 17, having God as the subject. It is used to describe what God will do to the earth because of the depravation of humankind (see also Gen 6:12). The repetition of the verb "to spoil" in v. 17 serves to repeat the thought of v. 13, either as an *inclusio* (to close) or as a resumption (to continue). Since the unit does not end here, the most obvious is that the latter is in view.

The repetitive use (five times) of the verb *'āśāh* ("to do") delimits vv. 14–16. In fact, the verb is found both at the beginning of v. 14 and at the end of v. 16, forming thus an *inclusio*. God's specific instruction to Noah for building the ark is enclosed in these verses. In this way, it is obvious that Gen 6:14–16 should be seen as a unit.

Then, v. 17 starts with a *waw-disjunctive*, whose function is to break the line of thought to provide further information of what is being spoken. God is again the subject of the verbs. In fact, Gen 6:17 repeats the idea of Gen 6:13.[19] Then again, in v. 18b the subject of the verb changes from God to Noah. This reveals that, in some way, there is a break in v. 18a. Both v. 17 and v. 18a have a *Hiphil* verb. The former has the earth as the direct object; the latter has Noah as the direct object. Since v. 17 refers to God's destruction in contrast to God's saving of Noah, it indicates that the *waw* in v. 18a should be taken as conveying an adversative nuance.[20] That means that the covenant must be seen as the redemptive God's solution from the Flood[21] and as a matter of life or death.[22]

This is also reinforced by comparing Gen 6:5–8 with Gen 6:11–18. Verses 5–6 describe the corruption of the entire earth, while v. 7 states God's decision because of it. Then, v. 8 introduces an exception, namely, Noah. The meaning is that humankind is spoiled, but not Noah. The same pattern is found in Gen 6:17–18a: because the earth is spoiled (Gen 6:11–12), God will destroy it (Gen 6:13, 17); however, he will establish his covenant with Noah. Just as the positive side of Gen 6:5–8 is not found until the destruction of the earth is stated, the positive side of Gen 6:11–18 is not found until the flood is affirmed.[23] Therefore, Gen 6:18 should be seen as a turning point in this narrative.

Verses 19–20 form a perfect parallelism. Both verses mention the animals and then the expression "two of every sort...to keep [them] alive" (שנים מכל תביא להחית). They reveal that the purpose of entering into the ark is to preserve the life (see also 7:3).[24]

In this context, it is significant to notice that God is acting passively. Noah is the one who has to build the ark (v. 14), to enter with his family into it (v. 18b), to bring animals into it (v. 19), and to get enough edible food for himself, his family, and the animals (v. 21). It seems that Noah has to save himself.[25] Apart from

---

19. So Mathews, *Genesis 1–11:26*, 365.

20. The action cannot be sequential, because it would imply that Noah and his family would enter into the ark just *after* the flood.

21. Bartholomew, "Covenant and Creation," 23; Goldingay, *Old Testament Theology*, 1:173; John H. Stek, "'Covenant' Overload in Reformed Theology," CTJ 29 (1994): 27.

22. Park, "Theology of Judgment in Genesis 6–9," 209.

23. Wenham, *Genesis 1–15*, 174.

24. Davidson, "The Genesis Flood Narrative," 63.

25. See Sarna, *Genesis*, 52.

declaring the coming flood and how to be saved from it, the only action that God does on behalf of Noah is the establishment of the covenant (v. 18a). This suggests that the covenant plays an important role in this narrative.

Although this pericope is understood as having most verbs in imperative mode, the truth is that imperative verbs are found only in Gen 6:14 and 21. Since a discontinuity is introduced in Gen 6:17, Gen 6:17–20 should be understood as predictions, not commands.[26] Finally, it should be observed that the subject of the verbs goes back and forth from God to Noah. Only when Noah is the agent is the term "ark" (*tĕbāh*) mentioned.

A. God (v. 13)
  B. Noah (vv. 14–16)
A'. God (v. 17–18a)
  B'. Noah (vv. 18b–22)

All the above observations show that Gen 6:13–22 are tightly connected. They can be outlined in the following way:

A. God decides to destroy humankind and the earth (v. 13)
  B. God commands Noah to build an ark (vv. 14–16)
    C. God will cause to bring [*bô'*] a flood to destroy everything (v. 17)
      D. God makes a covenant with Noah (v. 18a)
      D'. Noah and his family shall enter in the ark (v. 18b)
    C'. Noah will cause to bring [*bô'*] animals to keep them alive (vv. 19–20)
  B'. God commands Noah to victual the ark (v. 21)
A'. Noah obeys God (v. 22)

The Meaning of Qûm in Gen 6:18

An examination of covenants in ancient Near Eastern texts has revealed that כרת ברית ("to cut a covenant") is the standard formula for covenant-making.[27] However, in the Old Testament, many examples of covenant-making are lacking this formula (e.g., Gen 6:18; 9:9, 11, 15, 17; 17:7, 19, 21). In fact, in the book of Genesis, כרת ברית is used once for God's covenant with Abraham (15:18) and four times for covenants among humans.[28] It is absent in the covenant with Noah (6:18; 9:9, 11, 17) and Isaac (17:19, 21), where instead, הקים ברית ("to establish a covenant") is found. The ratio of these two formulas in Genesis is 5 (כרת ברית) to 7 (הקים ברית); when God is involved, the ratio is 1 (כרת ברית) to 7 (הקים ברית).

26. Wenham, *Genesis 1–15*, 172. Although no imperative is found in vv. 17–21, Gen 7:9, 16 interprets vv. 18a–20 as God's commands. "Then Noah and his sons and his wife and his sons' wives with him entered the ark because of the water of the flood. Of clean animals and animals that are not clean and birds and everything that creeps on the ground, there went into the ark to Noah by twos, male and female, as *God had commanded Noah*" (Gen 7:7–9 NAS).

27. M. Weinfeld, "*bĕrît*," *TDOT* 2:257–59. For a list of the 57 treaties currently extant from ancient Near Eastern texts, see John H. Walton, *Ancient Israelite Literature in Its Cultural Context: A Survey of Parallels between Biblical and Ancient Near Eastern Texts* (Grand Rapids, MI: Zondervan, 1989), 95–100.

28. In Genesis, כרת ברית occurs four more times, but they refer to covenants made between people: Abraham-Abimelech (21:27, 32), Isaac-Abimelech (26:28), Jacob-Laban (31:44).

Thus, from a statistical perspective, it can be said that in Genesis, כרת ברית is not the standard expression to make a covenant.[29] Besides, it shows that unlike כרת ברית, הקים ברית is never used for covenants among humans.[30]

In Gen 6:18, הקים ברית is used for the covenant-making with Noah. This is its first occurrence out of seven in Genesis. Its usage in this passage is still debated. For some, הקים ברית is just a synonym of כרת ברית.[31] They argue that its incidence is due to the different sources used, namely, the Priestly source (P) and the Yahwist source (J): Where כרת ברית occurs, J is in view; and where הקים ברית, P is in view. This approach (source criticism) solves the problem based on the preference of the covenant formula by different biblical authors. This solution is an easy way to alleviate the problem. Even if these interpreters are right about P and J sources, they do not offer any reason why the P source departs from the standard usage of covenant-making formula (כרת ברית) by using הקים ברית.[32] Consequently, the "documentary thesis," even though it tries to give the cause, is deficient in presenting a rationale for the different covenant formulas in P and J sources, which is essentially what matters.

To date, the best study of הקים ברית in relation to כרת ברית comes from William J. Dumbrell.[33] He has proposed that הקים ברית is consistently used for the continuation of a relationship, rather than its initiation (Gen 26:3; 38:8; Deut 8:18; Jer 34:18).[34] In this way, he saw the covenant with Noah as formalizing a previous covenant arrangement. This implies, then, that there was already a preexistent covenant. For Dumbrell, the preexistent covenant was the covenant with Adam.

---

29. Dennis McCarthy saw three common elements in all OT covenants: (1) preamble with its historical prologue, (2) promises and obligations, and (3) blessing-curse formula. Dennis J. McCarthy, *Old Testament Covenant: A Survey of Current Opinions* (Richmond, VA: Knox, 1972), 1–10.

30. Köhler noted that in the Scriptures, כרת (plural) + ברית is used for covenants between equals, while כרת (singular) + ברית + ‫את־ or ‫עם־ ("with") is used for covenants granted *only* by a superior. Likewise, he observed that הקים ברית is used for covenants initiated by God because he is sure to make it stand up. Ludwig Köhler, "Problems in the Study of the Language of the Old Testament," *JSS* 1 (1956): 4–5.

31. Beckwith, "The Unity and Diversity," 99 n. 23; Matthews, *Genesis 1–11:26*, 367; Paul R. Williamson, *Sealed with an Oath: Covenant in God's Unfolding Purpose* (Downers Grove, IL: InterVarsity Press, 2007), 73; Weinfeld, *TDOT* 2:260.

32. John Day, to my knowledge, is the only one who has made an effort from a Source Criticism approach to find a reason for the use of הקים ברית rather than כרת ברית in the P source. He proposes that the P writer has הקים ברית "because for him the only major covenants were those with Noah and Abraham (Gen 9:8–17; 17:1–21)." John Day, "Why does God 'Establish' Rather than 'Cut' Covenants in the Priestly Source?" in *Covenant as Context: Essays in Honour of E. W. Nicholson*, ed. A. D. H. Mayes and R. B. Salters (Oxford: Oxford University Press, 2003), 92.

33. William J. Dumbrell, *Covenant and Creation: An Old Testament Covenantal Theology* (Nashville, TN: Nelson, 1984); idem, *The Faith of Israel: A Theological Survey of the Old Testament* (Grand Rapids, MI: Baker, 2002), 25; idem, "The Covenant with Noah," *RTR* 38 (1979): 1–9.

34. Dumbrell's main argumentation has been preceded and followed by many interpreters. See, for example, Peter J. Gentry and Stephen J. Wellum, *Kingdom through Covenant: A Biblical-Theological Understanding of the Covenants* (Wheaton, IL: Crossway, 2012), 155–61; Bartholomew, "Covenant and Creation," 26; Gerhard F. Hasel, *Covenant in Blood* (Mountain View, CA: Pacific Press, 1982), 31; L. DeQueker, "Noah and Israel: The Everlasting Divine Covenant with Mankind," in *Questions disputées d'Ancien Testament: Méthode et théologie*, ed. C. Brekelmans, BETL 33 (Leuven: Leuven University Press, 1989), 128; Umberto Cassuto, *Genesis VI 9/XI 32*, 67–68; Wenham, *Genesis 1–15*, 175; Mathews, *Genesis 1–11:26*, 367; Gordon J. McConville, "běrît," *NIDOTTE* 1:748–49.

The Meaning of "My Covenant"

The covenant with Noah is called "my covenant." According to grammarians, the possessive "my" means possession or relation.[35] Since the covenant is something abstract, the sense here is that of possession. In this way, the covenant could be seen as belonging to God. If this is the meaning of "my" here, the covenant is not something new; rather it is being shared with Noah. This is also supported by the direct object marker *ēt*, which is almost always used with a definite noun,[36] implying that God is not speaking of any covenant, but of *his* covenant. Thus, it should be conceded that the covenant with Noah refers to an already-existent covenant that God is freely passing to Noah.[37] For William. J. Dumbrell, this was "the most natural interpretation"[38] of the phrase "my covenant."

Paul R. Williamson, on the other hand, has challenged this interpretation by calling attention to Exod 19:5, where "my covenant" is used for the establishment of the covenant with the Israelites at Sinai.[39] The significance of this passage for the understanding of "my covenant" lies in the fact that unlike the covenant with Noah, the verb *kārat* is the one used for its ratification (Exod 24:8). If, as Dumbrell insisted, the verb *kārat* is always used to initiate a covenant, then "my covenant" cannot refer to an already-existent covenant here.[40] Williamson suggested that the expression "simply underlies its *unilateral* character," that is, "God describes his covenant as 'my covenant' because he initiated it and he alone determines its constituent elements" (emphasis supplied by the author).[41]

While Williamson was right on arguing that *kārat* presents a problem concerning the continuity of the covenant at Sinai with the previous ones and the unilateral character of the covenant, his interpretation does not preclude Dumbrell's interpretation that the phrase "my covenant" refers to an already-existent covenant. Why? First, the initiation of a covenant with the Israelites does not necessarily indicate that the covenant is distinct from previous ones. The verb *kārat* may be used to refer to the initiation of the covenant with a new group of people, or simply that God is adding a new phase to the covenant already known by their forefathers.

---

35. Waltke and O'Connor, *An Introduction to Biblical Hebrew Syntax*, 303; Ronald J. Williams and John C. Beckman, *Williams' Hebrew Syntax* (Toronto: University of Toronto Press, 2007), 48.

36. Waltke and O'Connor, 162; Jouön and Muraoka, 415; Williams and Beckman, 168.

37. Gunkel commented that the possessive pronoun "my" expresses the notion that God grants to Noah his covenant in free grace. Gunkel, *Genesis*, 145.

38. Dumbrell, *Covenant and Creation*, 24.

39. Williamson, *Sealed with an Oath*, 72.

40. Williamson, 73.

41. Williamson, 74.

Second, the expression "my covenant" in Exod 19:5 seems to resemble Exod 6:3–5[42] rather than Exod 24:7–8.[43] At least three details seem to aim in that direction. (1) The keeping of "my covenant" is presented as the condition to enjoy the benefits offered. The people together accorded God's proposal (Exod 19:8). Their response suggests that they already knew[44] the conditions implied in the expression "my covenant." In this way, "my covenant"[45] must refer back to something. Moreover, (2) the *raison d'être* for the Israelites' liberation from Egypt to possess the land was God's covenant with Abraham, Isaac, and Jacob (Exod 2:24; 6:2–8). Therefore, the covenant at Sinai should be understood under the umbrella of the covenant with Abraham.[46] Finally, (3) the expression "my covenant" is not found in Exod 24:8.

Gen 6:18 in Relationship with Gen 9:9–17

By rendering Gen 6:18 and 9:9 "I will establish my covenant with you," English translations seem to suggest that the same group of people is in view in both passages. Nevertheless, it is quite clear in Hebrew that the covenant made with Noah before the Flood (Gen 6:18) is not addressed to the same group to whom it is addressed after the Flood (Gen 9:9). The Hebrew text says that the covenant in Gen 6:18 was made "with you [singular]," whereas in Gen 9:9, it was made "with you [plural]." The ambiguity comes from the fact that modern English language does not distinguish the second person singular ("you") from the second person

---

42. Terence E. Fretheim, *Exodus*, IBC (Louisville, KY: Knox, 1991), 209.
43. S. R. Driver, *The Book of Exodus*, CBSC (Cambridge: Cambridge University Press, 1911), 170. Joe M. Sprinkle has elucidated a chiastic structure in Exod 19–24, which allows one to see how Exod 19 is related to Exod 24. Joe M. Sprinkle, "Law and Narrative in Exodus 19–24," *JETS* 47 (2004): 242.
A. Narrative: Covenant offered (19:3–5)
   B. Law (general): Decalogue (20:1–17)
      C. Narrative: People fear (20:18–21)
   B'. Law (specific): Body of the covenant (20:22–23:33)
A'. Narrative: covenant accepted (ratified) (24:1–11)
44. A Jewish legend found in Pesikta Rabbati Piska 21 says that God went to Esau, the children of Ammon and Moab, and the children of Ishmael, and he asked them: Will you accept the Torah? All of them asked God for the content of it before giving an answer. However, when God went to Israel and asked them to accept the Torah, they immediately answered: We will do and hearken (Exod 24:7). W. G. Braude, *Pesikta Rabbati: Discourses for Feasts, Fasts, and Special Sabbaths*, trans. William G. Braude, 2 vols., YJS 18 (New Haven: Yale University Press, 1968), 1:417. This legend presents the Israelites as promising action even before the content of the Torah is known. It should be noticed, anyhow, that the legend is based on Exod 24:7, and not Exod 19:5.
45. Richard J. Sklba sees a full covenant-making in Exod 19:1–8, thus dividing the relationship with Exod 24. Richard J. Sklba, "Redeemer of Israel," *CBQ* 34 (1972): 3–4.
   1. Preamble: a summons by God (v. 3b)
   2. Historical prologue (v. 4)
   3. Stipulations (v. 5a)
   4. Blessings (vv. 5b–6a)
   5. Acceptance in a solemn assembly (vv. 7–8)
46. Fretheim, *Exodus*, 209.

plural ("you"). Hence, modern English translations are misleading in these two texts.[47]

In chapter 6, God only addresses Noah (Gen 6:13), while in chapter 9, he addresses both Noah and his sons (Gen 9:1, 8). However, the fact that entering the ark is seen as the reason for the covenant indicates that the covenant was implicitly made with all those who entered the ark, including the animals.

It is interesting to notice how those who will enter the ark are described: "And you [Noah] shall come into the ark: you, and your sons, and your wife, and your sons' wives, with you" (Gen 6:18b).[48] This text depicts those who will come into the ark besides Noah. But while the second person (Noah) is included in the verbal form (ûbā'tā), the second personal pronoun ("you") is added as part of the group accompanying Noah. Thus, the pronoun "you" referring to Noah is superfluous.

However, several details suggest that the pronoun "you" should be detached from the second clause ("and you [Noah] shall enter in the ark"). First, its placement at the end of the clause does not permit it to connect *directly* with the verb "to enter," which appears at the beginning of the clause. If this were the meaning intended, the author would have put the pronoun next to the verb.[49] Furthermore, the use of the *waw* with several subsequent nouns indicates that the *waw* is connecting those appositional nouns with "you" by way of a list of people. In this way, the simple subject becomes a compound subject.

According to grammarians, when several nouns are to be added appositionally to the main simple subject, the resumptive pronoun is repeated (e.g. Gen 7:1; 13:1; 17:9; Exod 20:10).[50] This means that the first mentioned person (Noah) is representative of the subsequent ones (Noah's sons, Noah's wife, and Noah's sons' wives). Thus, when it says that Noah shall enter into the ark, it is clarified that those belonging to Noah's house should enter as well (Gen 6:18; 7:7, 13; 8:16, 18).[51] A similar example is found in Gen 13:1 where it says that Abraham went up [singular] to Egypt (Gen 13:1a), but then it is made clear that his wife Sarah and his servants went up with him as well (Gen 13:1b).

This representative function suggests, then, that when God was making a covenant with Noah, he was implicitly making it with his family as well. That such is the case may be confirmed by reading Gen 9:9, 11, where the plural "you"

47. Old English translations (e.g., ASV, DBY, DRA, ERV, GNV, KJV, YLT) keep the difference between the second person singular and plural by using the archaic pronoun "thou" for the singular and "you" for the plural.

48. Note that in Gen 6:18, males are listed first, then females. Noah's family list is mentioned several more times in this narrative (Gen 7:7, 13; 8:16, 18). Only in Gen 8:16 does Noah's wife precede Noah. Sarna says that because husband and wife are not listed together, Midrashic sources inferred that sexual intercourse was prohibited in the ark (Genesis Rabba. 31:12; 34:7). Sarna, *Genesis*, 58. However, Gen 8:18 is after 8:16 and the males-females order is resumed.

49. Joüon and Muraoka, *A Grammar of Biblical Hebrew*, 507.

50. Joüon and Muraoka, *A Grammar of Biblical Hebrew*, 508; Waltke and O'Connor, *An Introduction to Biblical Hebrew Syntax*, 295; Frederic C. Putnam, *Hebrew Bible Insert: A Student's Guide to the Syntax of Biblical Hebrew* (Quakertown, PA: Stylus, 2002), 10. This is also done in order to avoid confusion since the verb (which is singular) will not agree in number with the nouns.

51. The pronoun "you" used in Gen 6:18 has been replaced by the proper noun "Noah." Both are governed by the verb bô' ("to enter"). The same pattern ("you," then "Noah") is found after the flood: "You" occurs in 8:16 occurs and "Noah" occurs in 8:18. However, now they are governed by the verb yaṣa' ("to get out"). A closer look reveals that when God is the speaker "you" is used, but when the narrator is the one who describes the events "Noah" is used.

('*ittkem*) is found in the making of the covenant with Noah and his sons. When Gen 6:18 is compared with Gen 9:11, it is evident that the singular '*ittāk* ("you") has been replaced by the plural '*ittkem* ("you"). However, one wonders why the writer was not consistent in this matter. Does the author have different nuances in view?

Whereas God speaks only to Noah in Gen 6 (v. 3), God speaks to both Noah and his sons in Gen 9 (vv. 1, 8). This simple recognition helps one to understand why the covenant in 6:18 is made only with Noah ('*ittāk*);[52] yet in 9:9, 11, it is made with both Noah and his sons ('*ittkem*). Although this can suggest that distinct covenants are in view, the above argument indicates that they are the same. However, it is not clear why the recipients vary if both texts refer to the same covenant.

A plausible reason is that Noah's sons were not born when God established his covenant with Noah.[53] According to Gen 5:21, Noah begot his sons after he was 500 years old.[54] Concerning Shem, it is said that he was 100 years old two years after the Flood (Gen 11:10). If Noah was 600 years old when the Flood came (Gen 7:6) and Shem was 98 years old (100 − 2 = 98), it indicates that Shem born when Noah was 502 years old. The significance of this chronological recognition is that God spoke to Noah 120 years before the Flood (Gen 6:3).[55] According to the narrative, Noah was 600 years old when the deluge came (Gen 7:6). This means that God spoke to Noah 120 years before he was 600 years old. Thus, Noah was 480 years old when God promised to establish a covenant with him. Since Noah became a father after he was 500 years old, at the age of 480 he was childless. Accordingly, it is comprehensible why God did not speak to both Noah and his sons in Gen 6:18, namely, Noah's sons were not yet born.

Therefore, Noah had to practice faith, not only in believing that a deluge was ready to come, but also in believing that he would have children. Faith in having descendants is not only found in the covenant with Noah, but also permeates the covenant-making in Genesis. Adam, Abraham, Isaac, and Jacob did not have children when God made a covenant with them. They had to believe that a seed would come from their own bodies.

As to the animals, although they were part of the covenant (9:10–12), they were not mentioned in the covenant before the Flood either. The same that was said for Noah's sons may be said for the surviving animals, namely, they were not

---

52. Morphologically, the suffix *kě* refers to a feminine, not a masculine person. This would imply that the covenant was not made with Noah, but with a female figure. However, whenever *kě* is found in pausal form, as it is in this case, it may also refer to a masculine person. Friedrich W. Gesenius, *Gesenius' Hebrew Grammar*, trans. A. E. Cowley (Oxford: Clarendon, 1910), 330 §103b.

53. In Genesis the covenant-making seems to include the promise of a seed (Gen 3:15; 15:4–6).

54. Although pre-Flood people lived long lives, they became fathers at a relatively early age. For example, according to Genesis 5, Mahalalel became the youngest recorded father at the age of 65 (Gen 5:15), whereas Methuselah, who had the longest life, became the oldest recorded father at the age of 187 (5:27). Thus, the fact that Noah was 500 years old (more than 300 years older than his predecessors) when he first became a father is striking in the narrative. So Gunkel, *Genesis*, 138.

55. Josephus understood the 120 years as the life-span of humankind. Josephus, *Ant.* 1.75. Today many commentators believe likewise. For example, Mathews, *Genesis 1–11:26*, 335; Wenham, *Genesis 1–15*, 142; Cassuto, *Genesis VI 9–XI 32*, 297–98; Skinner, *A Critical and Exegetical Commentary on Genesis*, 144–45; Sarna, *Genesis*, 46; Sailhamer, "Genesis," 77; Walton, *Genesis*, 296. However, because most people lived more than 120 years even after the flood (see Gen 11:10–31), it is preferable to see the 120 years as a reference to the period ending with the beginning of the Flood. Hamilton, *Genesis 1–17*, 269; Keil and Delitzsch, *Commentary on the Old Testament*, 1:86; Speiser, *Genesis*, 46.

mentioned because they were not there yet (6:19). However, when God made his covenant after the Flood (9:1–17), Noah and his family and the animals were all together, possibly next to the ark (cf. 8:15–20).

Two Covenant Phases

Based on the previous discussion, it is clear that covenant-making had at least two phases: one before and one after being delivered. The first phase is called the promissory covenant.[56] In this phase, God promises to give some benefits to humans for nothing. Humans are only expected to say either yes or no. No stipulations are mentioned. Thus, it is based on God's grace. The second phase is the covenant ratification.[57] It focuses more on the conditions of the covenant. It is in this phase where the covenant is approved and sanctioned formally by a sacrifice (e.g. Gen 15:9–11; Exod 24:4–8; Heb 9:18–20).

An obvious question emerges from these two phases. Why does God first promise and then ratify his covenant? Taking into account that stipulations are not explicitly mentioned in the first phase in contrast to the second phase, Gane implied that the laws or stipulations are for people who are *"already* saved by grace" (my emphasis).[58] In this way, unlike humans who make covenants based simply upon promises, God establishes his covenant on the basis of what he has already done on behalf of his people. What Gane suggested is that the first phase is necessary in order to assure his people that he will fulfill his promises and that they may accept God's covenant by love only. T. Desmond Alexander, however, claimed that the reason is to concede a probationary time to the beneficiaries so that they can show their loyalty to God.[59] While Alexander was right in seeing the subjective side of the covenant, he overlooked the fact that stipulations are lacking in the first phase. Moreover, in so saying, he was implying that after the ratification, there was no turning back.[60] Nevertheless, the history of the covenants reveals that benefits can be lost at any time.[61] Consequently, Gane's proposal should be favored.

---

56. For details see, Walter Vogels, *La promesse royale de Yahweh préparatoire à l'alliance: Étude d'une forme littéraire de l'ancien testament* (Ottawa, ON: University of Ottawa Press, 1970), 45–75, 133–152; idem., *God's Universal Covenant: A Biblical Study* (Ottawa, ON: University of Ottawa Press, 1979), 2.

57. George E. Mendenhall, "Covenant Forms in Israelite Tradition," *BA* 17.3 (1954): 50–76. See also Klaus Baltzer, *The Covenant Formulary in Old Testament, Jewish, and Early Christian Writings*, trans. David E. Green (Philadelphia: Fortress, 1971); 9–18.

58. Roy Gane, "The Role of God's Moral Law, Including Sabbath, in the 'New Covenant'" (2003), 5, http://adventistbiblicalresearch.org/sites/default/files/pdf/Gane%20Gods%20moral%20 law.pdf

59. T. Desmond Alexander, "Genesis 22 and the Covenant of Circumcision," *JSOT* 25 (1983): 21.

60. Gordon J. Spykman affirmed that the covenant is one-sided (unilateral) in its origin, but two-sided (bilateral) in its continuation. Gordon J. Spykman, *Reformational Theology: A New Paradigm for Doing Dogmatics* (Grand Rapids, MI: Eerdmans, 1992), 263–264.

61. Walton has identified four types of jeopardy in God's covenant with his people: Benefit jeopardy, abortive jeopardy, circumstantial jeopardy, and revelation jeopardy. Walton, *Covenant*, 94–107.

Why with Noah?

The most obvious detail in the covenant with Noah is that God is the initiator.[62] In the narrative, God is the active agent while Noah is passive. God is the one who decides both to reveal his intention concerning the earth to Noah and to make a covenant with him (Heb 11:7).

In this way, God is presented as offering the covenant as a favor, that is, an undeserved gift.

Therefore, Noah's salvation depended completely on God (see 2 Pet 2:5). That is why only one reason is given in the narrative as to why God saved Noah: "But Noah found grace in the eyes of the Lord" (Gen 6:8). The expression "to find grace in the eyes of" occurs forty-three times in the OT.[63] It means that a good disposition is granted upon someone (Gen 32:5; 39:4; Deut 24:1).

This does not mean that God's grace upon Noah was a divine caprice. In the very next verse (v. 9), three details are given that seem to provide the rationale for Noah's election:[64] "Noah was a righteous [ṣaddîq] man, blameless [tāmîm] among the people of his time, and he walked [hālaq] with God" (Gen 6:9 NIV).[65]

A survey of the phrase "to find grace in the eyes of" seems to suggest that the grace can be gained (Gen 32:5; 39:4; Deut 24:1; Ruth 2:10; 1 Sam 25:8; Prov 3:4). For example, Jacob sent his servant to speak to Esau so that he might "find grace" in Esau's eyes (Gen 32:5, MT 6). The use of the preposition lĕ suggests that "to find grace" is the expected result of something previously done.[66] The same construction appears in Gen 33:8. Because of it, a few English versions (NEB, NJB)[67] prefer to translate the verb māṣa' ("to find") as "to win." In doing so, they understand that Noah gained God's grace. They see an effect-cause pattern in vv. 8–9. Such a pattern is not uncommon in Hebrew thinking.[68] The idea would be, then, that Noah found favor by virtue of his character.

This concept is also found later on in Scripture. In Ezek 14:14, 20, Noah is presented as being saved because of his own justice (ṣādaq). The same word occurs in Gen 6:9 to describe Noah's character.[69] In the same way, Noah is presented in the NT as being saved because of his piety. 2 Pet 2:5 says that God did not forgive Noah's contemporaries, but saved Noah and his house. Then, 2 Pet 2:9 says that just as God knows how to save the godly (eusebeîs), he punishes the ungodly

---

62. Hasel, *Covenant in Blood*, 19.

63. Edwin Yaumachi, "*ḥēn*," *TWOT*, 303.

64. Hamilton, *Genesis 1–17*, 276; Mathews, *Genesis 1–11:26*, 346, 368.

65. Hans K. LaRondelle equated the covenant relationship with "walking with God." Hans K. LaRondelle, *Our Creator Redeemer: An Introduction to Biblical Covenant Theology* (Berrien Springs, MI: Andrews University Press, 2005), 18. Nevertheless, it should be noted that Enoch "walked [hālak] with God" (5:22, 24), and God did not make a covenant with him. John H. Stek is against seeing the God-human relationship as fundamentally covenantal. Stek, "'Covenant' Overload," 40.

66. The combination of the preposition lĕ + infinitive construct is used to indicate purpose or result. See Joüon and Muraoka, *A Grammar of Biblical Hebrew*, 405; Waltke and O'Connor, *An Introduction to Biblical Hebrew Syntax*, 606.

67. Although the NET Bible has "to find favor," it argues in its note that in Gen 6:8, divine grace is earned.

68. See Jacques Doukhan, *Hebrew for Theologians: A Textbook for the Study of Biblical Hebrew in Relation to Hebrew Thinking* (Lanham, MD: University Press of America, 1993), 193.

69. Unlike Gen 6:9, ṣādaq in Ezek 14:14, 20 is feminine because the noun that accompanies it is feminine.

(*adíkous*).[70] The parallelism between these two verses implies that Noah was saved because he was a godly person. Later in the narrative of the destruction of Sodom and Gomorrah, it is made clear that God does not destroy the godly [*ṣdq*/ *eusebeîs*] with the ungodly [*rāšā'*/*asebēs*] (Gen 18:23).

Moreover, Jewish literature corroborates this view.[71] The book of Jubilees says that Noah was saved "for his heart was righteous in all his ways" (Jub 5:19),[72] and Sirach says that a remnant was left because "Noah was found perfect and righteous" (Sir 44:17). Other documents only present his blameless character without suggesting that as the reason Noah was saved (Sibylline Oracles 1.125).[73]

In addition, Alexander has noticed that the covenant with Noah has the same structure as the covenant with Abraham in Gen 17.[74] For example, the divine command to "walk (*hālaq*) before me, and be perfect (*tāmîm*)" (Gen 17:1) resembles Noah's description in Gen 6:9:[75] "Noah was a just man, perfect (*tāmîm*) in his generations. Noah walked (*hālaq*) with God" (NKJV). Of interest, here is that Alexander observed that in the Hebrew verbal sequence imperative + cohortative, the second clause expresses the purpose or result.[76] Since this pattern is found in Gen 17:1–2, where v. 1 has the imperative and v. 2 has the cohortative, he concluded that the covenant of v. 2 is conditional to the command stated in v. 1.[77] In this way, he proposed two phases in the covenant-making. The first phase is the promissory covenant and the second phase is the covenant ratification, in which the latter is subordinated to the former.

This pattern (imperative + cohortative) is also found in Gen 12:1–3. Verse 1 has the verb in imperative and vv. 2–3 have most verbs in cohortative. The implication is that Abraham should first obey (depart from Ur to the Promised Land) in order to enjoy the covenant benefits of vv. 2–3. The same can be said of Noah. He should build the ark and enter into it in order to enjoy the covenant benefits. The parallel between these two covenants suggests seeing Noah's character as the reason why he was chosen.

All of these reveal that in the covenants, certain conditions were imposed upon the beneficiary. However, the conditions were not with the goal of earning the benefits but of keeping them.[78] Walton suggested that the covenant benefits can

---

70. The adjective *ádikos* literally means "unrighteous." Thus the fact that *eusebeîs* is in contraposition to *adíkous* in this passage indicates that the "godly" are those who are not only devout, but also righteous.

71. For the references, I am indebted to Jacques Van Ruiten, "The Covenant with Noah in Jubilees 6.1–38," in *The Concept of the Covenant in the Second Temple Period*, eds. Stanley E. Porter and Jacqueline C. R. De Roo, JSTSup 71 (Leiden: Brill, 2003), 167–90.

72. Robert H. Charles, *The Apocrypha and Pseudepigrapha of the Old Testament*, 2 vols. (Oxford: Clarendon, 1913), 2:20.

73. Charles, *The Apocrypha and Pseudepigrapha*, 1:338.

74. See T. Desmond Alexander, *From Paradise to the Promised Land: An introduction to the Pentateuch* (Grand Rapids, MI: Baker, 2012), 180; Alexander, "Genesis 22," 19–20. Williamson saw an ethical obligation as prerequisite of the covenant with Abraham by looking back to the covenant with Noah. Paul R. Williamson, *Abraham, Israel, and the Nations: The Patriarchal Promise and Its Covenantal Development in Genesis*, JSOTSup 315 (Sheffield: Sheffield, 2000), 174–176.

75. Significantly, the word "perfect" (*tāmîm*) is found only in these two occasions in Genesis.

76. See Lambdin, *Introduction to Biblical Hebrew*, 119.

77. Alexander, "Genesis 22," 19.

78. Here is found the two-sided (bilateral) elements of the covenant, which Spykman noted. For details, see footnote 53.

be endangered if disobedience is found. Thus, a tension is found between faith and works, the same one found in the New Testament (Eph 2:8; Jas 2:26), where works are seen as a result of faith (Gal 5:6).[79]

On the other hand, it should be noted that the biblical account presents Noah as coming from a faithful lineage (Gen 5) in contrast to an unfaithful lineage (Gen 4:17–24). The interesting fact about this division is that the faithful lineage seems to be presented as the chosen one through whom the promised "seed" (Gen 3:15) would come.[80] This lineage is defined as those who commenced worshiping the Lord's name publicly (4:26).[81] Consequently, it should not be overlooked that God made a covenant with Noah because he was part of the chosen lineage. The same can be said of Abraham. This indicates, then, that God's election did not originate in Abraham, as is commonly argued, but with Seth.[82]

This passage may suggest the reason why the word *bĕrît* was absent in the covenant with Adam.[83] According to Gen 4:26, being recognized as those who invoke the Lord's name was not necessary until the time of Seth's son, probably to make clear that throughout Seth's descendants there was always a faithful descendant.[84] Thus, Noah's genealogy seems to suggest that God never runs out of followers, an unbroken line, as promised in Gen 3:15.[85]

The implication of this is that since the covenant with Noah was made at a time when everyone was found being evil in God's eyes, its purpose was primarily to preserve God's people in a critical situation[86] "so that God's promise of redemption could be realized."[87] This perception also sheds light on the fact that God's covenant with Noah was based only on grace. God saved Noah from the Flood for the same reason he saved the Israelites from Egypt's slavery, namely, because of his promise to their fathers (see Gen 6:18; Exod 2:24; 6:5–8). When this concept is appreciated, it is understandable why God is interested in making a covenant

79. Roy Gane, "Covenant of Love," Syllabus for GSEM 538 Covenant, Law, Sabbath, Andrews University, 1997, 84.

80. Sailhamer, "Genesis," 69.

81. The phrase "to call upon God's name" (לקרא בשם יהוה) is found later in Genesis in relation to God's worship (12:8; 13:4; 21:33; 26:25). See Hamilton, *Genesis 1–17*, Mathews, *Genesis 1–11*:26, 292; Westermann, Genesis 1–11, 340–41. Since it is very clear that this is not the first time people worshiped the Lord, Gordon Wenham contended that it is better to understand Gen 4:24b as referring to the beginning of public worship. Wenham, *Genesis 1–15*, 116. Moskala, nevertheless, insisted that public worship results in public preaching. Therefore, he suggested, like Luther, that the verb *qāra'* means "to proclaim" here. Jiri Moskala, "The Concept and Notion of the Church in the Pentateuch," in *"For You Have Strengthened Me": Biblical and Theological Studies in Honor of Gerhard Pfandl in Celebration of His Sixty-Fifth Birthday*, ed. Martin Proebstle (St. Peter am Hart, Austria: Seminar Schloss Bogenhofen, 2007), 13–14.

82. Walton did not take into consideration the covenant with Noah because he did not find the concept of election, which he believed was the feature that binds all the covenants. See Walton, *Covenant*, 47. However, a close reading reveals that the covenant with Noah indeed included "election."

83. For the biblical basis for the covenant with Adam, see O. Palmer Robertson, *The Christ of the Covenants* (Phillipsburg, NJ: Prebysterian & Reformed, 1980), 93–108.

84. T. Desmond Alexander, "Genealogies, Seed and the Compositional Unity of Genesis," *TynBul* 44 (1993): 265.

85. For further study regarding the family tree in Genesis, see T. Desmond Alexander, "From Adam to Judah: The Significance of the Family Tree in Genesis," *EvQ* 61 (1989): 15–19; Alexander, "Genealogies" 255–70.

86. Cf. Stek, "'Covenant' Overload," 25, 39. Walton has argued very well that the establishment of a covenant is often followed by a dark period of spiritual history. Walton, *Covenant*, 63–81.

87. LaRondelle, *Our Creator Redeemer*, 19.

with his people and why his covenant/promise is unconditional, that is, because he will fulfill what he promised in Gen 3:15. Consequently, it is understandable why this promise became "foundational for the covenants to follow."[88]

Conclusion

An examination of the historical context has revealed that the covenant with Noah was motivated by God's judgment upon humankind.[89] However, while scholars concede that the covenant was essentially made in order to preserve Noah and his family from the flood,[90] they overlook the fact that their preservation was essential to uphold the promise of Gen 3:15 and that God's covenant with Noah involved the promise of a seed, just as in other covenants (e.g. Abraham, David).[91] In this manner, the covenant with Noah should be understood as being offered unilaterally, in the sense that God initiated it and he alone determined its constituent elements, and upholding a previous covenant, possibly that of Gen 3:15.

In addition[92], a careful look at the larger context (Gen 4:26) seems to suggest that the word *běrît* is not present before Gen 6:18 because the term is possibly used to distinguish the faithful ones in a critical situation. If this is the case, it is understandable why Noah's righteous character is highlighted in the narrative.

With regard to the definition of the covenant, Gen 6:18 reveals that many covenant definitions are found faulty when they are applied to the covenant with Noah.[93] For example, neither the so-called "Immanuel principle"[94] ("I will be your God, and you will be my people") nor the taking of an oath[95] is found in this covenant. Thus, these covenant-formulas cannot be taken as an essential element of God's covenant with his people. On the other hand, this study showed that the

---

88. Paul R. Williamson, "Covenant: The Beginning of a Biblical Idea," *RTR* 65 (2006): 6; Williamson, *Sealed with an Oath*, 58. Spykman affirms: "At the heart of the covenant is the divine promise." Spykman, *Reformational Theology*, 259. Cf. also Richard M. Davidson, "Interpreting Old Testament Prophecy," in *Understanding Scripture: An Adventist Approach*, ed. George W. Reid, BRIS 1 (Silver Springs, MD: Biblical Research Institute, 2005), 197.

89. Bartholomew, "Covenant and Creation," 23; Stek, "'Covenant' Overload," 27.

90. Scott Hahn, *Kinship by Covenant: A Canonical Approach to the Fulfillment of God's Saving Promises* (New Haven: Yale University Press, 2009), 97; Rolf Rendtorff, "'Covenant' as a Structuring Concept in Genesis and Exodus," *JBL* 108 (1989): 387; Rolf Rendtorff, "Noah, Abraham and Moses: God's Covenant Partners," in *In Search of True Wisdom: Essays in Old Testament Interpretation in Honour of Ronald E. Clements*, JSOTSup 300 (Sheffield: Sheffield, 1999), 133.

91. Roger T. Beckwith affirmed that all covenants point forward to Christ. Beckwith, "The Unity and Diversity," 107.

92. James Barr, "Reflections on the Covenant with Noah," in *Covenant as Context Essays in Honour of E. W. Nicholson*, eds. A. D. H. Mayes and R. B. Salters (Oxford: Oxford University Press, 2003), 12–13.

93. This is one of the reasons why the covenant with Noah is left out when theologians deal with the covenants. Another reason is that in recent decades, the interest has been in making connection with ANE treaties, and the covenant with Noah seems to have no relationship at all with those treaties.

94. Robertson, *The Christ of the Covenants*, 46.

95. Gordon Hugenberger has argued that the failure to mention an oath does not mean that it was absent in practice. Gordon P. Hugenberger, *Marriage as a Covenant: A Study of Biblical Law and Ethics Governing Marriage Developed from the Perpsective of Malachi*, VTSup 52 (Leiden: Brill, 1994), 11. In fact, Beckwith has shown that the oath elements is found in only two or three covenants (with Abraham, the Israelites, and David). Beckwith, "The Unity and Diversity," 103–107. Niehaus, in the same line, affirmed that the covenant with Noah is the exception to this rule. Jeffrey Niehaus, "Covenant: An Idea in the Mind of God," *JETS* 52 (2009): 234.

promise of a "seed" plays a paramount role in all covenants.[96] Therefore, more attention should be given to it in covenant theology studies.

---

96. Davidson, "Interpreting Old Testament Prophecy," 197.

The Dawn of the Battle of the Sexes – Genesis 3:16

Leanne M. Sigvartsen and Jan A. Sigvartsen

The book of Genesis is the book of beginnings. It functions as the introduction chapter to the Bible since all major biblical themes are introduced in this book, with the following biblical books expanding and exploring these themes. Richard M. Davidson[1] noted that "Gen 1-3 has been increasingly recognized as set apart from the rest of the Bible, constituting a kind of prologue or introduction. These opening chapters of Scripture are now widely regarded as providing the paradigm for the rest of the Bible."[2] Based on a close reading of these three chapters, Davidson found a seven-faceted theological center,[3] which, he suggested, are components of the Great Cosmic conflict concerning God's character, the grand metanarrative of the Bible.[4] However, Genesis 1-3 contains more than these seven facets and this chapter proposes that these creation accounts also reveal the dawn of the battle of the sexes. This chapter will briefly consider the origin of sexism as it appears in the creation account, and then more extensively review modern empirical research relating to sexism not only toward women, but also toward men.

---

1. Many examples used in this paper pertain to the Seventh-day Adventist faith community as this publication has been written to honor several of its scholars, thus, making this article more applicable for that context.

2. Richard M. Davidson, "Back to the Beginning: Genesis 1-3 and the Theological Center of Scripture" in *Christ, Salvation, and the Eschaton: Essays in Honor of Hans K. LaRondelle*, eds. Daniel Heinz, Jiří Moskala, and Peter van Bemmelen (Berrien Springs, MI: Old Testament Department, Seventh-day Adventist Theological Seminary, Andrews University, 2009), 11. Davidson continued by referring to the following four scholars who have made a similar observation: Phyllis Bird ("Bones of My Bones and Flesh of My Flesh," Theology Today 50 [1994]: 525, 527); Lilian Calles Barger (*Eve's Revenge: Women and a Spirituality of the Body* [Grand Rapids, MI: Brazos, 2003], 128), John Rankin ("Power and Gender at the Divinity School," in *Finding God at Harvard: Spiritual Journeys of Thinking Christians*, ed. Kelly Monroe [Grand Rapids, MI: Zondervan, 1996], 203); and Deborah F. Sawyer (*God, Gender and the Bible* [London: Routledge, 2002], 24, 29).

3. These seven facets are (1) creation and the divine design for this planet, (2) the character of the Creator (with implications for theodicy), (3) the rise of the moral conflict concerning the character of God, (4) the Gospel covenant promise centered in the Person of the Messianic Seed, (5) the substitutionary atonement worked out by the Messianic Seed, (6) the eschatological windup of the moral conflict with the end of the serpent and evil, and (7) the sanctuary setting of the moral conflict (Davidson, "Back to the Beginning," 19).

4. Davidson, "Back to the Beginning," 29.

The Dawn of the Battle of Sexes

In the first creation story (Gen 1:1-2:4a), God creates humans, both male and female, in His image and likeness to possess the earth and become caretakers of His creation (Gen 1:26-28). However, in the second creation story, the Eden Narrative (Gen 2-3), man is created first, he receives God's commandment regarding the forbidden tree, he names all the animals, and only then does the woman enter the story, as the man's helpmate and mate. The author of Genesis 2 concludes that the marriage custom, that the man should leave his parents in order to start a new family unit with his wife, has its origin in the creation itself (Gen 2:23-24). The chapter ends on a very positive note: they were both naked but were not ashamed (v. 25), emphasizing the perfect harmony and innocence experienced in the first marriage—they were indeed "one flesh" and carrying God's image and likeness. In Genesis 3, the narrator gives the account of how this perfect harmony between the first couple, the first man and woman, breaks down and reveals the ultimate consequences of their open rebellion against God.

The apparent discrepancies between these two versions of the creation account have given rise to multiple views regarding the pre-fall relationship between men and women or husband and wife (God's intended plan), how the fall affected this relationship, and finally, God's post-fall plan for male/female or husband/wife relationships. Davidson, in his major work on sexuality in the Old Testament,[5] listed six major views regarding man-woman relationships in Genesis 1-3. The first three views are hierarchical in nature, where God intended the woman (or wife) to be subordinate to male (husband) supremacy/leadership, and the fall was caused by a violation of this God-ordained hierarchy or ruptured relationship. Genesis 3:16 records God's divine pronouncement concerning Eve; however, interpreters who adhere to this hierarchical God-given view understand this statement differently (as a description, prediction/prescription, or reaffirmation of the original hierarchical view), see Table 1 below. It should be noted that all three views consider male-female hierarchy as still valid in the post-fallen world.

---

5. Richard M. Davidson, *Flame of Yahweh: Sexuality in the Old Testament* (Peabody, MA: Hendrickson, 2007). I was privileged to work as Davidson's research assistant when he was concluding this publication and enjoyed many hours immersed in the manuscript and our many conversations regarding the content of his book.

Table 1. Man-woman relationships (ranking) in the beginning (Gen 1-3): Hierarchical views.

		Creation (Gen 1-2)	Fall (Gen 3)	Divine Pronouncement concerning Eve (Gen 3:16)
Hierarchical Views	1	Subordination/submission of woman to male supremacy/leadership	Violation of male-female hierarchy and/or ruptured relationship	*Description* of the perversion of hierarchical relationships (woman seeks to control man and/or man exploitively subjugates woman)
	2	Submission of woman to male leadership	Violation of male-female hierarchy and/or ruptured relationship	*Prediction* that woman would desire to get out from under man's authority, and *prescription* that man must exercise his "godly headship" to restrain her urge to control him
	3	Subordination/submission of woman to male supremacy/leadership	Violation of male-female hierarchy and/or ruptured relationship	*Reaffirmation* of original hierarchical roles as a continued divine blessing, or a statement of continued subjugation of woman by man

In a careful reading of Genesis 1-2, paying close attention to the literary structures of the two creation accounts, the words and word clusters used, and inter- and intratextual connections, it becomes difficult to find textual support for a God-ordained hierarchical pre-fall view (views 1-3).[7] Instead, there is ample support for a pre-fall egalitarian view, where God intended full equality between human beings, male and female, husband and wife. This is one of the many implications of God's decision:

Genesis 1:27

So God created earthling in His image;

in the image of God He created him;

male and female He created them.

וַיִּבְרָא אֱלֹהִים ׀ אֶת־הָאָדָם בְּצַלְמוֹ

בְּצֶלֶם אֱלֹהִים בָּרָא אֹתוֹ

זָכָר וּנְקֵבָה בָּרָא אֹתָם:

---

6. Tables 1 and 2 are both a modified version of Davidson's table listing the six major views on man-woman relation in Genesis 1-3, however, I have added Davidson's personal view, as stated in the book, as the seventh view; see Davidson, *Flame of Yahweh*, 64-65, 76.

7. See e.g., Davidson's discussion on "Equality of the Sexes without Hierarchy," in Flame of Yahweh, 22-35; Jan A. Sigvartsen, "The Creation Order – Hierarchical or Egalitarian?" *Andrews University Seminary Studies* 53.1 (2015): 127-142.

It is important to keep in mind that the noun "man" (*'ādām*) in Genesis 1 is not a proper name as is the case in Genesis 2, but a generic term for a human, or earthling, and is defined in the text as a combination of the two sexes, זכר ונקבה, *male and female* (Gen 1:27).[8]

Table 2 below outlines the major egalitarian views with Davidson's personal view highlighted as the seventh view. They all hold a God-ordained pre-fall egalitarian view in which there is full equality between the sexes, with no subordination or submission of woman to male supremacy or leadership; however, these four views vary in what happened to the relationship at the fall, and the meaning of the divine pronouncement concerning Eve in Genesis 3:16. The fourth view considers God's pronouncement as predictive, stating the natural consequences of sin upon the marital relationship and, by extension, in society at large—sexism, where men consider themselves as superior and should therefore usurp authority over women, is a result of sin and not ordained by God. The fifth view considers God's pronouncement as a permanent prescription, a post-fall hierarchical reality instituted by God to preserve harmony in the home. The sixth view considers God's pronouncement as a blessing. It should, therefore, be understood as God upholding the pre-fall egalitarian ideal even in the post-fall world. As becomes clear from Table 2, the seventh view, describing Davidson's personal view, attempts to present the middle ground by combining the fifth and the sixth views. Thus, God's pronouncement should be understood as prescriptive in the sense that the wife should voluntarily submit[9] herself to her husband's leadership as a result of sin in order to provide harmony in the home, but the pronouncement should also be understood as a "promised blessing of divine grace" in the sense that God

---

8. This emphasis that humanity as a whole, and not each individual, is the image or likeness of God, is crucial since this speaks against sexism, racism, and elitism, the main –isms that appear in most societies. This is also a reminder that everyone has worth, since each individual reflects a part of God's image, and that all have a common origin, God himself. Moreover, in a religious community who worships a common Creator, it becomes important to listen to each member's religious experiences, since each member has a different experience and picture of God, and each member carries a different aspect of God's image. Only by taking these different perspectives into consideration will the community get a better picture of who the Creator God is. Paul, in Galatians 3:28, makes a similar argument in support of equality, interestingly covering the same three isms – racism, elitism, and sexism: "There is no Jew or Greek, slave or free, male or female; for you are all one in Christ Jesus" (CSB).

9. The term "voluntary submission" is an idealized application of והוא ימשל־בך, *and he shall/will rule over you*. Robert D. Culver noted that the word "*māshal* usually receives the translation 'to rule,' but the precise nature of the rule is as various as the real situations in which the action or state so designated occur. It seems to be the situation in all languages and cultures that words for oversight, rule, government must be defined in relation to the situation out of which the function arises" ("מָשַׁל," *TWOT* 1:534). Philip J. Nel observed that this verb could have both a positive and a negative connotation, and that the control a person has over another can be abusive as attested in Proverb 28:15 (CSB): "A wicked ruler over a helpless people is like a roaring lion or a charging bear" ("משל," *NIDOTTE* 2:1137). Thus, the subject of the verb, the male in Genesis 3:16, determines if this relationship will be abusive. A "voluntary submission" would only make sense in a society where women have been given the freedom to make their own independent choices and carry the same value as men. However, this was not the reality for women in biblical times, nor in most cultures up to the present day. Even if a woman is provided the opportunity to submit herself voluntarily to her husband's dominion, what will happen if she no longer feels comfortable in submitting to her husband? Is the word "voluntary" used to sanitize a submissive relationship as something beautiful? If the wife is no longer submitting, would she be doubly judged, as her submission is no longer voluntary either? Would her husband's benevolence turn to hostility?

will empower the husband-wife team to strive for the God-intended egalitarian pre-fall relationship.[10]

Table 2. Man-woman relationships (ranking) in the beginning (Gen 1-3): Egalitarian views.

		Creation (Gen 1–2)	Fall (Gen 3)	Divine Pronouncement Concerning Eve (Gen 3:16)
Egalitarian Views	4	Full equality with no subordination/submission of woman to male supremacy/leadership	Ruptured relationship between the sexes	*Predictive* description of the consequences of sin – man usurps authority over the woman – which "curse" is to be removed by the gospel with return to egalitarianism
	5	Full equality with no subordination/submission of woman to male supremacy/leadership	Ruptured relationship between the sexes	*Permanent prescription* of divine will in order to preserve harmony in the home after sin: wife's submission to her husband's leadership
	6	Full equality with no subordination/submission of woman to male supremacy/leadership	Egalitarian relationship continues	*Blessing of equality* (no hierarchy of leadership/submission) in the midst of a sinful world and its challenges
	7	Full equality with no subordination/submission of woman to male supremacy/leadership	Ruptured relationship between the sexes, but Egalitarian relationship should continue	*Qualified prescriptive* divine sentence announcing the voluntary submission of the wife to her husband's servant leadership as a result of sin; However, *promised blessing* of divine grace designed to lead back as much as possible to the original plan of harmony and union between equal partners without hierarchy.

Davidson concludes his discussion on "Sexuality and the Fall: Genesis 3" by suggesting a balancing act between a hierarchical and an egalitarian post-fall view:

With egalitarians (and against hierarchicalists) it can be affirmed that Gen 1-2 presents God's divine ideal for men and women at creation to be one of equality in both nature and function, with no superiority or leadership of the male and no inferiority or submission of the female. With hierarchicalists (and against egalitarians) it can be affirmed that God's prescription for harmony and unity after the fall does include the wife's submission to the servant leadership of her husband. Against the hierarchical position, however, the evidence in 3:16 already seems to point to the implication that the servant leadership principle is limited to the relationship between husband and wife or at least should not be seen as barring women from roles of leadership over men in the believing community or society at large. Also against the hierarchical position, the evidence of this text points

---

10. It should be noted that Jacques Doukhan suggested an altogether different reading of the divine pronouncement given in Genesis 3:16 in light of Genesis 4:7, demonstrating that this pronouncement was given to both Adam and Eve, thus arguing that God's statement points beyond the mere male-female relationship. Rather, Genesis 3:16 gives the explanation to God's promised salvation in the preceding verse (Gen 3:15), which had become necessary due to Adam and Eve's failure to control the temptation in Genesis 3:6, when evil was "desiring" them (this parallels Cain's failed attempt to control the evil which caused him to kill his brother Abel). See, Jacques Doukhan, "From Subordination of Woman to Salvation by the Woman: An Exegesis of Genesis 3:16 in the Light of Genesis 4:7 and Genesis 3:15" (paper presented at the annual meeting of the Adventist Society of Religious Studies, Chicago, IL, 16 November 2012).

toward a prescription qualified by grace, a prescription representing God's less-than-the-original ideal for husbands and wives, thus implicitly including both a divine redemptive call and enabling power to return as much as possible to the pre-fall total egalitarianism in the marriage relationship, without denying the validity of the servant leadership principle as it may be needed in a sinful world to preserve unity and harmony in the home.[11]

It should be noted that only two of the seven views (views 1 and 4) presented in the above two tables consider the subjugation of woman as a natural consequence of sin.[12] With the exception of view 6, which sees God upholding the egalitarian view, the four remaining views (views 2, 3, 5, 7) consider the supremacy of the male sex in the post-fall world as God-ordained.[13]

This brief overview of the various views on God's pronouncement in Genesis 3:16 demonstrates the difficulties in determining how to understand God's

---

11. Davidson, *Flame of Yahweh*, 80.

12. Davidson found this position unsatisfactory as the context of Genesis 3:16 is a legal trial (Gen 3:8-13), which is concluded by a legal sentence (Gen 3:14-19), thus, he argued, God's words to the woman should be considered executive—a part of God's prescriptive punishment on the woman. This conclusion, according to Davidson, is further supported by "the use of the first person singular 'I'" referring "to the Lord, who is pronouncing the judgment, and the Hebrew infinitive absolute followed by the finite verb implies 'the absolute certainty of the action,'" therefore, "God is not merely informing the woman of her fate; God is ordaining the state of affairs announced in 3:16. God is the Judge announcing his personal sentence for Adam and Eve's guilt" (*Flame of Yahweh*, 67-70). If, as Davidson suggested, Genesis 3:16 is God's divine sentence in response to Eve's transgression, it would also follow that the physical pain and potential mortality experienced in the context of childbearing and birth is also a part of God's prescriptive punishment on all women, in addition to her "desire" (for a discussion on the meaning of the word *t'shûqâ*, desire, see Joel N. Lohr, "Sexual Desire? Eve, Genesis 3:16, and תשוקה," *JBL* 130.2 [2011]: 227-246). Thus, would a woman who consents to an epidural during her labor or undergoes a c-section violate a divine sentence? And should maternal prenatal and postnatal health be ignored, as any intervention for both the mother and child would violate God's curse? This is not a hypothetical question as Nicholas Kristof and Sheryl WuDunn observed: "In most societies, mythological or theological explanations were devised to explain why women should suffer in childbirth, and they forestalled efforts to make the process safer. When anesthesia was developed, it was for many decades routinely withheld from women giving birth, since women were 'supposed' to suffer" (*Half the Sky: Turning Oppression into Opportunity for Women Worldwide* [New York: Vintage Books, 2009], 116). A predictive interpretation would leave room to utilize technological and medical advances that could preserve the health and lives of both mother and child. An executive judgement suggests that the lives of both mother and child are not worth saving because to do so would transgress God—a concerning position indeed, especially for religious people who also espouse a prenatal prolife position.

13. Matthew Henry, although considering female submission as a part of the creation order (hierarchical – View 3), made the issue clear: "This sentence amounts only to that command, *Wives, be in subjection to your own husbands*; but the entrance of sin has made that duty a punishment, which otherwise it would not have been. If man had not sinned, he would always have ruled with wisdom and love; and, if the woman had not sinned, she would always have obeyed with humility and meekness; and then the dominion would have been no grievance: but our own sin and folly make our yoke heavy. If Eve had not eaten forbidden fruit herself, and tempted her husband to eat it, she would never have complained of her subjection; therefore, it ought never to be complained of, though harsh; but sin must be complained of, that made it so. Those wives who not only despise and disobey their husbands, but domineer over them, do not consider *that they not only violate a divine law, but thwart a divine sentence*" ("Gen 3:16," *Matthew Henry Commentary* on Gen 3:16, www.biblestudytools.com/commentaries/matthew-henry-complete/genesis/3.html; emphasis added). Umberto Cassuto argued for an egalitarian pre-fall view, however, he considered the post-fall women submission as God's divine sentence (View 5): "Measure for measure: you influenced your husband and caused him to do what you wished; *henceforth, you and your female descendants will be subservient to your husbands*. You will yearn for them, but they will be the heads of the families, and will rule over you" (*A Commentary on the Book of Genesis*, 1:165-166; emphasis added).

statement addressed to the woman. Does God introduce a hierarchical structure for male-female relations after the fall to reintroduce harmony and unity in a post-fallen world—as an antidote to the effect of sin—or is God only describing the effect sin will have on all human relations, an effect already seen in the blame-game between Adam and Eve upon eating the forbidden fruit? Is it possible to entertain a voluntarily hierarchical structure in which a wife submits to the servant leadership of her husband without creating a potential abusive relationship,[14] or to keep this voluntarily hierarchical structure purely within the context of the home? Should a wife be submissive to her husband's every whim? Or should she only submit to his leadership if it is in line with God's instructions, her conscience, and her critical thinking? Or should she only have to submit to a God-fearing and righteous husband? If a woman's voluntary submission is prescribed by God, then it becomes easy to argue that a wife who is not willingly submitting to her husband's will in any situation not only disobeys her husband, but also God's instructions or command, as her husband serves as her "god."[15] Is it even possible to condone a hierarchical structure without running the risk of also condoning various types of sexism, and by default, racism or elitism? To state it plainly, should the ultimate goal for a married couple be to recreate the pre-fall harmonious egalitarian relationship in their home, or should the goal be for the wife to become perfectly willing to submit herself freely to her husband's will to preserve and sustain their marriage in this post-fallen world?[16]

Assuming that God has the best interest of humans in mind and given that the meaning of God's words spoken to Eve in Genesis 3:16 are not completely clear, as they have been understood as descriptive (view 1), reaffirmation (view 3), predictive (view 4), prescriptive (view 5), blessing (view 6), a combination of predictive and prescriptive (view 2), or a combination of prescriptive and blessing (view 7) by interpreters, a biblical exegete needs to show some caution before promot-

---

14. By most western ethical standards, Abraham's treatment of Sarah (Gen 12:11-20; 20:1-18), Lot's willingness to hand his daughters over to the people of Sodom (Gen 18:8), Laban's scheming involving his two daughters (Gen 29:22-30), Judah's treatment of his daughter-in-law Tamar (Gen 38:1-26), and the David and Bathsheba incident (2 Sam 11) are some examples of sexual exploitation, disempowerment, and abuse of women even by some God-fearing men who attempted to safeguard their own best interest and desires.

15. Interestingly, in Modern Hebrew, the word for husband is ba'al and women would refer to their husbands as הבעל שלי, literally "my god."

16. If the latter, it becomes easy to blame the woman for her husband's extramarital affairs, incest, and divorce, all sentiments insinuated in *Seventh-day Adventists Believe: An Exposition of the Fundamental Beliefs of the Seventh-day Adventist Church*, 2nd ed. (Silver Spring, MD: Ministerial Association and General Conference of Seventh-day Adventists, 2005), in the exposition on Fundamental 23, Marriage and the Family (329-346). Regarding the issue of incest, the commentary states: "Often this results when the normal husband-wife relationship has been neglected and one of the children has been chosen to play the role of the spouse," placing the blame on the person who did not fulfill their partner sexually (337). Regarding divorce, pressure is placed on the injured spouse to forgive as "adultery need be no more destructive to your marriage than any other sins" and "when you are ready to forgive and let go of your negative attitudes," God will mend the relationship (337-338), thus suggesting the divorce is due to lack of a forgiving heart by the injured spouse.

Anecdotally, a female friend of the authors expressed that in a presentation by her Seventh-day Adventist conference president's wife (at a gathering for ministerial spouses), it was stressed that as pastors' wives, it was their responsibility to dress attractively to ensure their pastor-husband did not commit adultery with one of the female members of his congregation, essentially placing some fault/responsibility on wives if this were to happen.

ing a certain interpretation to make sure that he/she does not cause more harm than good when applying God's words to modern times. Athalya Brenner raised a valid point regarding Genesis 3:16 when she stated: "Any interpretation of this utterance—as a curse, aetiological statement of fact, blessing or otherwise—is largely dependent on the reader's gender position and may vary considerably."[17] Joel N. Lohr expanded on the "gender position" aspect by noting: "Clearly there are a variety of factors in play, not the least of which is one's religious or theological persuasions, or one's place in history, society, and culture. All of this, to be sure, contributes to one's 'gender position,' but we need to be clear. The effects of one's wider presuppositions are truly far-reaching and profound in reading this verse."[18] Thus, the second half of this chapter will consider empirical behavioral research, which may add some further insight into the ramifications of viewing female submission as a God-given prescription, blessing, or both. This consideration should in no way be considered as an attempt to change the meaning of the biblical text, as multiple views already exist among biblical scholars of how to understand Genesis 3:16. However, the empirical behavioral research presented may give some additional factors to take into consideration when deciding which view of God's pronouncement may be both the most plausible and contextually consistent with God's character.

Empirical Research Relating to the Subordination of Women

This section will first consider empirical research relating to the subordination of women, giving a brief description of *hostile sexism* and *benevolent sexism* before briefly considering *benevolent sexism* in religious groups. This chapter will conclude by considering *ambivalent sexism* and the Lindy Chamberlain case. Some readers may question how recent empirical research can provide any valid insight for a biblical exegete regarding human behavior due to the great timespan and cultural differences between biblical time and the present. Modern psychology and behavioral science is a fairly recent scientific discipline. However, it follows a transparent, empirical research and publication standard as stipulated by the *Publication Manual of the American Psychological Association* and has thus come a very long way from how it was practiced, and condemned, in the 19th century by some religious leaders.[19] These standards assure transparency and replicability in an endeavor to ensure that the findings and conclusions are sound and to determine if the findings are only culturally or regionally specific. Małgorzata Mikołajczak and Janina Pietrzak suggested the questionable belief

---

17. Athalya Brenner, *The Intercourse of Knowledge: On Gendering Desire and 'Sexuality' in the Hebrew Bible*, Biblical Interpretation Series 26 (Leiden: Brill, 1997), 53.

18. Lohr, "Sexual Desire? Eve, Genesis 3:16, and תשוקה," 227.

19. In 1862, Ellen G. White warned against the danger of psychology: "The sciences of phrenology, psychology, and mesmerism are the channel through which he [Satan] comes more directly to this generation and works with that power which is to characterize his efforts near the close of probation" (Ellen G. White, "Phrenology, Psychology, Mesmerism, and Spiritualism," *Review and Herald* 19.12 [February 18, 1862]: 6), however, Merlin D. Burt noted: "When Ellen White used the terms 'psychology' and 'science,' she was speaking of these spurious and erroneous movements and not the modern definitions of these terms" ("Ellen G. White and Mental Health Therapeutics," *Dialogue* 21.1 [2009]: 12-15).

of "essential differences between men and women, making each more or less adequate to fill particular roles in society, appear to be relatively universal. The ambivalence this division entails for both men and women has been observed in a number of countries."[20]

Sexism research throughout the 20th century concentrated mainly on investigating sexist attitudes towards women, often without investigating sexism towards men. These studies primarily focused on overtly hostile forms of sexism, which for a long time was the only aspect of sexism that was considered relevant.[21]

In 1996, however, sexism research took a new direction when Peter Glick and Susan Fiske[22] empirically identified that there existed two distinct forms of sexism: a proverbial good cop/bad cop, where one seemingly hostile form (bad cop) punished those who rejected a stereotypical traditional gender role, and a seemingly benevolent form (good cop) rewarded those who did. Unlike previous research, which only focused on sexism by men towards women, these two forms of sexism were applicable to both men and women, by both men and women, and reinforced gender hierarchy and inequality among the sexes.[23]

Hostile Sexism

The first type of sexism was, unsurprisingly, *hostile sexism*, which most readers would agree should be avoided. *Hostile sexism* endorses antipathy, resentment, and overtly hostile behavior towards individuals who cast off traditional gender stereotypes. This sexism perpetuates gender inequality as well as dangerous and even unlawful behaviors towards men and women. For example, men of definite marriageable age who choose not to get married or are unable to find a female spouse with whom they would like to spend their lives are perceived as rejecting a traditional gender role that men should marry and have children (Gen 1:28) because it is "not good for man to be alone" (Gen 2:18). Thus, they can be subjected to treatment such as social ostracism from other male groups, accusations of homosexuality regardless of whether they are or not, or overt exclusion from

---

20. Małgorzata Mikołajczak and Janina Pietrzak, "Ambivalent Sexism and Religion: Connected Through Values," *Sex Roles* 70 (2014): 387.

21. Peter Glick and Susan T. Fiske, "An Ambivalent Alliance: Hostile and Benevolent Sexism as Complementary Justifications for Gender Inequity," *American Psychologist* 56.2 (2001): 109-118.

22. Some readers not familiar with behavioral scientific research may find it strange that this section seems to refer to the work of primarily two academics. However, this is not the case. Ambivalence theory comprising of *hostile and benevolent sexism* has been explored in many hundreds of peer reviewed papers published in scholarly behavioral scientific journals and is currently a premiere theoretical model for sexism. The journal articles cited in this chapter concentrate on those written by Glick and Fiske because they developed the initial theoretical model and were the lead researchers of a number of papers written regarding this empirical research. Subsequent research has taken place, particularly by Fiske, who heads the Fiske Lab at Princeton University – a research lab which studies intergroup relations, social cognition, and social neuroscience. See http://www.fiskelab.org.

23. Peter Glick and Susan T. Fiske, "The Ambivalence Towards Men Inventory," *Psychology of Women Quarterly* 23.3 (1999): 519-536; and idem, "The Ambivalent Sexism Inventory: Differentiating Hostile and Benevolent Sexism," *Journal of Personality and Social Psychology* 70.3 (1996): 22-48.

certain professions or positions which give preference to males who are married.[24] If they pursue a non-gender stereotypical career, they can also be subject to social penalties, mockery, and social ostracism, even violence. Should they pursue a career which does not earn sufficient funds to wholly support a family, they can be treated with disdain by others, have limited or no influence among their male peers, and be overtly rejected by women regardless of their personal merit. Should they be homosexual, rejecting marriage to a woman altogether, they may be subjected to exclusion from societal groups, hostile discrimination, violent behavior, and in some societies, even death.

Hostile sexism also affects women in that those who reject the traditional gender role of making marriage and motherhood their sole career may be subject to discrimination and poor treatment, regardless of whether they submit to their husband's servant leadership. A woman who has a child out of wedlock can be treated badly by both men and women who endorse traditional gender roles because she has rejected a traditional (sometimes religious) mandate that sexual relationships and children should only exist within the context of marriage. Her child may also be subject to this hostility and labeled illegitimate, which is then justified by some because this derogative term is a consequence of his/her mother's rejecting the prescribed gender role of women having children within marriage.

Not very long ago, maternal mortality was very high, but medical advances have significantly decreased death as a result of childbirth. However, in a number of developing countries that do not have access to this medical care, becoming a mother can still be deadly. A woman who chooses not to marry or have children for this reason may be subjected to hostile sexism by those around her because a traditional gender role requires women to be married mothers. Thus, a woman is left no choice but to marry and risk death by having children. In addition, because of the biblical mandate "I will greatly increase your pains in childbearing; with pain you will give birth to children" (Gen 3:16), traditional religious communities that endorse this belief can discourage the provision of medical attention to women giving birth, which may result in complications and death for both mother and child.[25]

A woman who chooses to pursue a career may also be subjected to a range of hostile behaviors in the workforce and in her community. She may be labeled as being a bad mother who puts her financial needs ahead of her children. She may be paid less than her male counterpart because it is perceived that she has a husband who can support her (or should have a husband to support her if she is unmarried, widowed, or divorced) and that her wages are merely pocket money

---

24. On the topic of selection criteria for the office of elders and deacons, the New Testament writer Paul makes it a requirement for the candidate to be both married to one wife and have children (1 Tim 3:2-5, 12). Interestingly, this passage is often used by those who oppose the ordination of women, as this list seems to suggest that females would not qualify for the job as they are "not married to one wife."

25. Kristof and WuDunn, *Half the Sky*, 93-108.

and not essential income that she and her family relies on.[26] If she questions this, her contribution can be downplayed, her position misclassified or mislabeled to justify lower wages, and she can be subjected to unfavorable treatment or even dismissal. She may experience bullying, sexual harassment, and discrimination in the workplace, which is justified by the hostile belief that if she were at home where she belonged, this would not be happening. The extreme end of *hostile sexism* towards women is, of course, rape, sex trafficking of women, and domestic violence,[27] where the traditional gender role of male rulership and women's submission to men and their needs is exploited or used to punish women perceived as not endorsing a traditional gender role. In this case, it is justified by the underlying belief that she was, in some way, deserving of it.[28]

Benevolent Sexism

The second type of sexism identified by Glick and Fiske is a more subtle, gentler sexism that often slips under the interpersonal radar and has been named

---

26. Merikay Silver's lawsuit against Pacific Press in the early 70s regarding equal pay for equal work between male and female workers serves as an example that this issue is not unknown to the Seventh-day Adventist Church. At that time, the SDA Church followed the head-of-household rule, which paid a person a higher wage if he/she was supporting a family. In this case, Merikay, who was the sole breadwinner of her family, did not receive this extra pay as she was a woman and not a man. The last of the four lawsuits regarding this issue ended in December 1983, ten years after Silver brought the issue to the attention of the courts on January 31, 1973. Pacific Press settled their case involving Silver (April 1978), lost the other three cases, and was required to reimburse 140 female employees who were a part of a larger lawsuit. This summary of the case is based on "The Merikay Silver Case," http://www.sdadefend.com/MINDEX-M/Silver.pdf. For further reading, see: Merikay McLeo, *Betrayal: The Shattering Sex Discrimination Case of Silver Vs. Pacific Press Publishing Association* (Austin, TX: Mars Hill Publications, 1985) and Richard H. Utt, Pacific Press Lawsuit: The Other Side of the Story (Rialto, CA: The Author, 1988). Some may ask how far this denomination has come since this very public wage issue and if wage discrimination has morphed into a job description issue where certain positions are intended for women and are classified as mere secretarial positions while their day-to-day responsibilities are fairly similar to that of their "boss" who receives a significantly higher wage. The gender pay gap is also a problem in the larger society. In the United States, the wage of a woman working full time typically is 79% of the wage of a man. Although great progress has been made since 1979 when women earned only 59% of the wage of a man, there is still a long way to go. The District of Colombia has come the furthest in closing the gender pay gap by reaching the 90% mark, while the state of Louisiana has only reached the 65% mark. This information is sourced from a report entitled "The Simple Truth about the Gender Pay Gap," http://www.aauw.org/files/2015/09/The-Simple-Truth-Fall-2015.pdf, published by the *American Association of University Women* (AAUW).

27. For more real stories relating to women who have experienced this type of *hostile sexism*, see Kristof and WuDunn, *Half the Sky*, 93-108. See also Jimmy Carter, *A Call to Action: Women, Religion, Violence, and Power* (New York: Simon & Schuster, 2015), who aptly wrote: "Some selected scriptures are interpreted, almost exclusively by powerful male leaders within the Christian, Jewish, Muslim, Hindu, Buddhist, and other faiths, to proclaim the lower status of women and girls. This claim that women are inferior before God spreads to the secular world to justify gross and sustained acts of discrimination and violence against them. This includes unpunished rape and other sexual abuse, infanticide of newborn girls and abortion of female fetuses, a worldwide trafficking in women and girls and so-called honor killings of innocent women who are raped, as well as the less violent but harmful practices of lower pay and fewer promotions for women and greater political advantages for men" (*A Call to Action*, 3-4).

28. Most of these examples were compiled from the qualitative responses of 142 Seventh-day Adventists who participated in a study investigating sociocultural attitudes of individuals within this religious organization. See Leanne M. Sigvartsen, *Religious Verbal Fluidity: What Nice Christian Folk Really Think...*, Religious Verbal Fluidity 1 (Berrien Springs, MI: ClergyEd.com, 2015), 28-49.

benevolent sexism.[29] Unlike *hostile sexism, benevolent sexism* is motivated by genuine feelings of affection and concern where individuals are judged favorably and receive favorable treatment because of their endorsement of traditional gender roles. These traditional gender roles are similar to those mentioned in the Eden Narrative after the fall (where Adam is the provider and protector of Eve, the subordinated child bearer, Gen 3:16-19). On the surface, this type of benevolence may seem innocent and something one should strive for—even a fulfillment of the "promised blessing" portrayed in view six of Davidson's list of six views of man-woman relationships as described earlier in this chapter. However, a closer look at benevolence reveals that it can have some negative consequences for both sexes,[30] thus, questioning its place as a "promised blessing" or a divinely mandated ideal, rather than a consequence of sin.[31]

Benevolent sexism becomes problematic because it can place unreasonable expectations on individuals who may not be in a position to endorse such a traditional gender role. For example, a man working to support his stay-at-home wife who raises their children may seem the ideal, but what if his wage is insufficient

29. Glick and Fiske, "The Ambivalent Sexism Inventory," 22-48.

30. This is a complex issue, thus, for the purpose of this chapter we found it necessary to simplify the discussion so it would be easier for the general reader to comprehend. For a more detailed discussion/description of the theory of *ambivalent sexism*, see Glick and Fiske, "An Ambivalent Alliance," 109-118.

31. The recently translated manifesto on women by the Al-Khanssaa Brigade, the all women police/religious enforcement unit of the ISIL (Islamic State of Iraq and the Levant), better known as IS (Islamic State), provides a fascinating insight into their ideology. The main goal of the *Islamic State* is to reinstitute the Caliphate and Sharia law, idealizing the time and culture of Prophet Mohamed. This document idealizes traditional gender roles, noting that women's main responsibility is the home, marriage, and childbearing: "The greatness of her position, the purpose of her existence is the Divine duty of motherhood. Truly, greatness is bestowed upon her, and it is God's will that her children honor her. The Righteous were distinguished from the others, 'And [made me] dutiful to my mother, and He has not made me a wretched tyrant' (Quran 19:32), and the Prophetic ruling was 'Paradise is under the mother's feet', narrated by Ibn Majah, authenticated by al-Albani" (page 18). This manifesto also outlines the failure of the western model of women – feminism (pages 19-23), the ideal model for Muslim women (pages 24-26), and concludes with several case studies (pages 27-40). For the full text, see www.quilliamfoundation.org/wp/wp-content/uploads/publications/free/women-of-the-islamic-state3.pdf. This idealized view is, however, a far cry from the many reported cases of abuse of women in the territory under the rule of *Islamic State*, which, interestingly, is perpetrated by women committed to the cause. See e.g., www.clarionproject.org/analysis/isis-points-sharia-law-justify-slavery-women#; www.al-monitor.com/pulse/security/2014/03/isis-enforces-islamic-law-raqqa-syria.html; fortune.com/2015/05/05/isis-women-recruiting/. Although most Evangelical Christians are horrified by the ideology and methods of *Islamic States*, many conservative Evangelical Christians would agree that women should stay in the home and are critical to the many achievements of modern feminism, as noted by Samuel Koranteng-Pipim: "Though many are not aware of it, the most powerful ideology driving the campaign for women's ordination is feminism. This ideology is very seductive because it is rooted in the pervasive thinking of egalitarianism, which holds that full equality between men and women can be achieved by eliminating gender role distinctions in the home and in the church" (www.adventistsaffirm.org/article/141/women-s-ordination-faqs/4-feminism-s-new-light-on-galatians-3-28). The idealization and promotion of traditional gender roles also appear in the official exposition of the 28 Beliefs of Seventh-day Adventism, which gives the following statement on Fundamental 23, Marriage and the Family: "Motherhood is the closest thing on earth to being in partnership with God....God created the mother with the ability to carry the child within her own body, to suckle the child, and to nurture and love it. Except for the extenuating circumstances of severe financial burdens or being a single parent, if she will accept it, a mother has the unique privilege of remaining with her children all day; she can enjoy working with the Creator in shaping their characters for eternity" (*Seventh-day Adventists Believe*, 340). The promotion of traditional gender roles is also a part of the ministry of the *Focus on the Family*; See: www.focusonthefamily.com/marriage/gods-design-for-marriage.

to cover the cost of their legitimate expenses? He must sacrifice his own personal wellbeing by working more, or take a high-paying position he may not enjoy, or that could even be dangerous. In pre-industrialized societies, a husband was often able to work from home, on the farm, or within a short walking distance, thus being able to be involved in the family or having children work alongside him. However, due to industrialization, the husband often has to remove himself from the family for most of the day (or months at a time in military or offshore mining positions), returning at night exhausted to a group of people who have bonded in his absence.[32] This may result in a male feeling like a stranger in his own home, where the children prefer and feel closer to their mother. It can also produce tension with his wife, who may have an expectation that now that he is home, it is his turn to care for the children, allowing her to have a break from them, regardless of whether he is exhausted (or suffering post-traumatic stress in the case of some military families).

A man may have to pursue a career which allows him to make more money, even though he would have preferred or held significant talent in a career choice that had less earning capacity. A risky venture such as starting a small business may also be less of an option for him too. He may have to turn a blind eye to behaviors or practices in his workplace that he finds morally questionable or illegal simply because he needs his income.

His earning potential, rather than his merit as a person, may become a large factor in what type of woman he is able to attract and how he will be treated by other males. Those associated with his wife may judge him unfavorably if his income does not meet their expectations. If he should lose his income, this highly vulnerable system collapses as there is no backup income for the family to rely on until another income can be secured, placing unnecessary stress on a family unit. In times gone by when employment opportunities were more plentiful, this may not have been a problem, as another position would be readily available. However, increased competition for positions can make long-term unemployment a reality in the current age. He may even have to take a significant pay cut in order to secure another job. A man who fails to find a position quickly or has to accept lower wages may be perceived as somehow lacking, rather than a victim of global economic forces.

Conversely, *benevolent sexism* can affect women too, even though there are significant rewards for women who endorse a traditional gender role. She will not be required to earn an income or pursue a difficult career path in a competitive job market, but she is wholly dependent on her husband's being able to do this, which, as mentioned previously, can be problematic. In addition, after working at great personal and emotional cost to earn a living, the expectation that a man is going to hand over his entire income to a woman to do with as she sees fit or include her in financial decision-making may not be consistent with reality in many families. Thus, income a woman has access to will be largely determined by her husband,

---

32. For further reading regarding the social impact of the industrial revolution, see Richard D. Fitzgerald, "The Social Impact of the Industrial Revolution," in *Science and Its Times: Understanding the Social Significance of Scientific Discovery*, eds. Josh Lauer and Neil Schlager (Detroit: Gale, 2000), 4:376-381.

and she will also have to defer to his final decision-making on all matters if she is to endorse a traditional gender role and continue to receive the financial benefits of it.

Benevolent sexism that idealizes the joy of motherhood and believes all women are innate mothers creates a very difficult environment for women who cannot have children or do not want to because of genetic predispositions. *Benevolent sexism* by nature creates an environment where women without children are automatically perceived as not endorsing this gender role and may be treated as though they are deliberately rejecting it, thus subjecting them to *hostile sexism*. If they do choose to pursue a career, they may be subjected to *hostile sexism*, similar to that outlined in the previous section, as they are again perceived as rejecting the stereotypical traditional female gender role of mother and homemaker. Women who suffer from postnatal depression may also be subject to hostility and lack of sympathy from others who believe motherhood is innate to all women. Thus, a woman may hide her depression or allow it to go untreated, resulting in significant stress to herself, her husband, and child/children.

As a homemaker, a woman may be required to meet certain expectations such as keeping the house clean, serving dinner at a particular time, fulfilling her husband sexually in spite of illness, work overload, or unexpected demands of children. Failure to do this is questioned by her husband and the all too familiar argument over whether her contribution is sufficient may manifest itself. In addition, a man who has worked all day and comes home to find his wife sitting on the couch reading a book or watching television because she has completed her tasks for the day may view her as lazy or that her contribution is not equal to his own, which may result in resentment toward her.

Benevolent sexism may also have negative consequences among women because when women are not encouraged to seek their own income or success, but rather, seek it through aligning themselves with a male who will do this for them, they can become competitive with other females as they seek to secure the scarce males who will provide significant income and high social status.[33] When motherhood becomes the measure of the success and worth of a woman, achievement and perceived achievement of their children may become evidence of a wom-

---

33. The theme of barrenness plays an important role in the Old Testament. This theme demonstrates the importance of the role of childbearing and how it related to the status a woman in, especially, a polygamous setting within Old Testament society. The theme is first introduced in Genesis 11:30, when the narrator reveals that Sarah is barren, a crucial element to keep in mind in order to fully appreciate the Abraham narrative. The association of childbearing and status becomes a central element in the relationship between Sarah and Hagar, her surrogate, who treated Sarah with contempt upon realizing that she had become pregnant with Abraham (Gen 16:4-6). Competitiveness among subordinated women reveals itself with Leah and Rachel, who even used surrogates Zilpah and Bilhah (Gen 29-35) in their battle to win favor in their husband's eyes and secure status within the family and also with Hannah who was barren and Peninnah who had several sons and daughters (1 Sam 1-2); Peninnah provoked her (1 Sam 1:6-7), again suggesting not only contempt and competition, but also that ridicule from peers was strongly associated with being childless. Even women who were still the favorite wife of their husband (e.g., Rachel and Hannah) had a strong desire to have a child of their own. Curiously, when a barren woman mentioned in the biblical text does eventually have a child, this child often becomes the next important character in portions of the biblical narrative (Isaac, Jacob, Joseph, Sampson, Samuel, John the Baptist).

an's success. Thus, they may push their children into activities[34] or exaggerate their children's abilities, placing enormous pressure on them to perform. This may even result in a "soccer mom" mentality, where humiliation and questioning adults who hold a contrary view of their children's abilities arises. They may also minimize the accomplishments of other children to reinforce their own children's performance and success. Women who have children with disabilities are at a distinct disadvantage and may be erroneously perceived as bad mothers, particularly if their children's disability is associated with challenging behaviors.[35]

Benevolent Sexism in Religious Groups

Benevolent and *hostile sexism* do not exist independently. *Benevolent sexism* rewards those who adhere to these traditional gender roles and reinforces gender hierarchy and inequality while utilizing hostile sexism to punish those who cast off traditional gender roles. The original researchers, Glick and Susan Fiske, named the theoretical model describing the relationship between *hostile* and *benevolent sexism* the *"ambivalent sexism"* theory because of the seemingly polar opposite motivations of these two complimentary sexisms.[36] Over the past two decades, a wealth of research has been undertaken investigating *benevolent* and *hostile sexism* in both men and women with regard to a range of issues.

---

34. Mothers promoting, positioning, or pushing their sons is also a biblical narrative element. Rebekah was the main character in the plot of stealing the birthright blessing from her older son Esau for her favorite younger son Jacob (Gen 27:1-28:5). According to the prophecy mentioned earlier in the narrative (Gen 25:23), her older son (Esau) would serve the younger (Jacob). It could be argued that she loved Jacob above Esau not only because he stayed home among the tents and his temperament (Gen 25:27-28), but also due to the prophecy that he would become the founder of the greater nation (Gen 25:23). It was Rebekah who discovered Isaac's plan to bless Esau (Gen 27:5), who made the plan of deception (Gen 27:6-13), who prepared the needed food (Gen 27:14), who dressed Jacob in Esau's clothes (Gen 27:15), who covered parts of Jacob in goatskin (Gen 27:16), and who sent Jacob to complete the plan (Gen 27:17-29). After this act, Rebekah also orchestrated Jacob's escape (Gen 27:42-46) following the death threat voiced by her older son Esau (Gen 27:41).

Bathsheba excelled in harem politics in King David's court. Rather than an innocent victim, it would seem she was successfully able to trade her Hittite husband for King David and became a part of his harem. While in the harem, she was able to successfully position her son Solomon, who was not in direct line, by using her skills to manipulate King David. With the help of Prophet Nathan (1 Kings 1:11-40), she was able to place her son on the throne of Israel, becoming the reigning monarch's mother, and sitting on a throne on the right side of King Solomon (1 Kings 2:19). For further reading, see Beverly W. Cushman, "The Politics of the Royal Harem and the Case of Bat-Sheba," *Journal for the Study of the Old Testament* 30.3 (2006): 327-343.

The mother of Zebedee's sons (Matt 20:20-28) was also involved in promoting and positioning her sons. She approached Jesus and asked him to promise her that her two sons, James and John, would be seated on his right and left in his kingdom, the two most honorable and exalted positions. D. A. Carson notes "what the sons of Zebedee want and their mother asks for is that they might share in the authority and preeminence of Jesus Messiah when his kingdom is fully consummated" ("Matthew," in *Expositor's Bible Commentary* 8, 1st ed. [Grand Rapids, MI: Zondervan, 1984], 431). Jesus responded that she did not know what she was asking and added that it was not his decision to make, as it would be up to his Father. The narrative reveals that the other ten disciples became indignant by this request and Jesus needed to calm down the situation.

35. Most of these examples from this and the preceding sections were compiled from the qualitative responses of 142 Seventh-day Adventists who participated in a study investigating sociocultural attitudes of individuals within this religious organization; see Sigvartsen, *Religious Verbal Fluidity*, 28-49.

36. Glick and Fiske, "An Ambivalent Alliance," 109-118.

Very few studies, however, have investigated the predictability of *benevolent* and *hostile sexism* within a religious context and how religiosity can impact measures of *benevolent* and *hostile sexism*. Three studies, two conducted on Christian faiths in the United States[37] and one on Catholics in Spain,[38] all found that religiosity was able to predict *benevolent sexism* but was unable to predict *hostile* attitudes. Put simply, these studies show that a person's religiosity is not a good indicator of the presence of *hostile sexism*. This does not imply that religious individuals cannot be *hostile sexists*. Further study is required to identify what other factors may be influencing *hostile* sexist attitudes in a religious person. A fourth study conducted on Catholics in Poland[39] reached the same conclusions regarding hostile attitudes. However, religiosity was only a predictor of *benevolent sexism* among the female participants. These researchers suggested that cultural influences embedded within religious practice, rather than religious belief, may have been an extenuating factor in this study with a relatively small participant pool (n = 189). A similar study undertaken on Turkish Muslim students,[40] however, identified a positive relationship between *benevolent sexism* and religiosity for both men and women. However, unlike its Christian counterpart, this study identified a positive relationship between religiosity and *hostile sexism* in men only. In other words, the presence of religiosity in Turkish Muslim men was an indication of the likelihood of *hostile* sexist attitudes. This difference may be indicative of a culture that strongly endorses the traditional hierarchy and authority of men.

A recent study undertaken on a Jewish population in Israel identified again that religion predicted benevolence; however, there was a negative association between religiosity and hostile attitudes, particularly among men. Put simply, as religiosity increased, the likelihood of expressing *hostile sexism* towards both men and women actually decreased. The author, Ruth Gaunt, suggested that in "the Jewish tradition, derogatory speech about other people is strictly forbidden . . . where slander in all its forms is subjected to the strongest moral disapproval."[41]

A major study of over 600 participants investigating the theory of ambivalence with regard to Seventh-day Adventists in Australia and New Zealand who identify as Protestant Christians, but unlike other mainstream Christian faiths observe a Saturday Sabbath much like the Jewish faith, is currently being concluded and results were not available at the time of publication.[42] Seventh-day Adventism is an interesting case study not only because of its Sabbath observance, but also

37. S. M. Burn and J. Busso, "Ambivalent Sexism, Scriptural Liberalism and Religiosity," *Psychology of Women Quarterly* 29 (2005): 412-418; E. L. Maltby, et al., "Religion and Sexism: The Moderating Role of Participant Gender," *Sex Roles* 62 (2010): 615-622.

38. Peter Glick, M. Lameiras, and Y. R. Castro, "Education and Catholic Religiosity as Predictors of Hostile and Benevolent Sexism Toward Women and Men," *Sex Roles* 47 (2002): 433-442.

39. Mikołajczak and Pietrzak, "Ambivalent Sexism and Religion: Connected Through Values," *Sex Roles* 70 (2014): 387-399.

40. N. Tasdemir and N. Sakalli-Ugurlu, "The Relationships Between Ambivalent Sexism and Religiosity Among Turkish University Students," *Sex Roles* 62 (2010): 420-426.

41. Ruth Gaunt, "'Blessed Is He Who Has Not Made Me a Woman': Ambivalent Sexism and Jewish Religiosity," *Sex Roles* 67 (2012): 477-487

42. Leanne M. Sigvartsen, "Sex and Sensibility: Hostile, Benevolent and Ambivalent Sexism of Seventh-day Adventists Living in Australia and New Zealand," (Ph.D. diss., pending).

because it is one of the few worldwide Christian religions that was largely shaped and influenced by a cofounding female church leader, Ellen G. White. It is also currently debating whether to ordain female clergy in a manner equal to their male counterparts. It is interesting to note that the countries previously investigated all have a dominant religion or a historically dominant religion, and it was that specific religion which was explored in the context of the corresponding study. The Australian and New Zealand study may prove interesting as Australia is considered a highly secularized, post-colonial country that does not have a dominant historical religion. With approximately 70,000 members,[43] Seventh-day Adventism in this region is also far from being a major religion. It would seem, from the findings mentioned above, that *benevolent sexism* does, for the time being, exist within religious organizations, but the full extent of how it interacts with hostility is yet to be determined.

Ambivalent Sexism and Lindy Chamberlain

Benevolence and its association with *hostile sexism* produces a conundrum for religious populations who endorse a traditional gender role for women (particularly populations where women are subordinated to males either by mandate or by choice) as a theological ideal. While this type of attitude may not be perceived as too damaging within the context of religion and a religious community, the endorsement of such roles for women perpetuates it in the greater society, resulting in unexpected consequences that religious organizations could never have predicted.

In 1980, the Seventh-day Adventist Church in Australia came under intense national and international attention when Lindy Chamberlain (now known as Lindy Chamberlain-Creighton), the then wife of a Seventh-day Adventist minister, was accused and charged with murdering her infant daughter.[44] An enormous amount of media attention was given to the story and millions of people followed the case as it unfolded over subsequent years, particularly when Lindy Chamberlain was released from prison in 1986 when new evidence was provided to the court. The case was, understandably, a public relations crisis for the Seventh-day Adventist Church, and the question was asked repeatedly why the case drew so much public attention for so long and if this sort of situation could be repeated in the future,[45] particularly to other individuals in the Seventh-day Adventist Church.

The findings of a study by G. T. Viki, K. Massey, and B. Masser,[46] which investigated the part *ambivalent sexism* may play regarding women who are accused of committing counter-stereotypical crimes, may shed some light on why

43. For membership data relating to the South Pacific Division of the Seventh-day Adventist Church, see www.adventiststatistics.org/view_Summary.asp?FieldID=D_SPD.

44. K. Hansen, "The Chamberlain Case: A Tragedy for Justice," *Spectrum* 17.5 (May 1987): 55-56; L. Tarling, "Who Killed Azaria? Adventists on Trial in Australia," *Spectrum* 15.3 (March 1984): 42–59.

45. J. Craik, "The Azaria Chamberlain Case and Questions of Infanticide," *Australian Journal of Cultural Studies* 4.2 (1987): 123-150; D. Johnson, "From Fairy to Witch: Imagery and Myth in the Azaria Case," *Australian Journal of Cultural Studies* 2.2 (1984): 90–107.

46. G. T. Viki, K. Massey, and B. Masser, "When Chivalry Backfires: Benevolent Sexism and Attitudes Toward Myra Hindley," *Legal and Criminological Psychology* 10.1 (2005): 109–121.

the Chamberlain case proved to be so popular with the public and media and may provide evidence of a harsher consequence of seemingly benign *benevolent sexism*. Previous research had identified that women accused of crimes were often not dealt with as harshly as men accused of a similar crime. For example, when a man murdered his wife, there was a public outcry; however, when a woman murdered her husband, it was generally felt that he, in some way, deserved it. It was identified that benevolent chivalry played a large part in this phenomenon, that there was a benevolent attitude towards women that suggested they were not a serious threat, were motivated to commit the crime because of psychological distress, and were not deserving of harsh punishment. Thus, female crimes are less likely to rate a mention in local news media bulletins and are often underrepresented in published crime statistics.[47]

There is, however, an exception to this, and that is when a woman commits a counter-stereotypical crime—or a crime that defies what we would traditionally believe a woman capable of committing. A perfect example of a counter-stereotypical crime is a woman killing a child, as traditional stereotypes consider women innate mothers who care for and nurture all children. However, benevolence still influences this perception, particularly if she is deemed to have had a good reason for it, such as being psychologically unwell. However, if she is of sound mental health, the punishment and public attention given to this crime is profoundly harsher and more public than to a male offender for the same or comparable crimes.[48]

Viki, Massey, and Masser found that negative public perceptions of females accused of counter-stereotypical crimes were strongly linked with attitudes of *benevolent sexism*.[49] Thus, when a society endorses *benevolent sexism* and advocates that women are idealized and special nurturers of children, incapable of harming them, this society (or church) runs the risk of having individuals accused of crimes that deviate from this gender role come under unrelenting, hostile public attention.[50]

Given this finding, it is perhaps understandable why Lindy Chamberlain and her legal battle became such a public issue for so many years. Not only was she accused of an extreme counter-stereotypical crime like the murder of not just a child, but her own biological infant child, she was also the married wife of a clergyman at the time, had two other children, was not a victim of domestic violence, and was considered psychologically sound at the time of the alleged crime.

This finding is thought provoking, and the authors believe that more investigation into the influence *benevolent sexism* has on the legal and public

---

47. C. A. Sanderson, A. S. Xanna, and J. M. Darley, "Making the Punishment Fit the Crime and the Criminal: Attributions of Dangerousness as a Mediator of Liability," *Journal of Applied Social Psychology* 30 (2000): 1137-1159.

48. Viki, Massey, and Masser, "When Chivalry Backfires," 109-121.

49. Viki, Massey, and Masser, "When Chivalry Backfires," 109-121.

50. This study investigated benevolent attitudes using the case of Myra Hindley to illustrate counter-stereotypical crimes. Hindley was charged for murdering two children (not her own) and was an accomplice in a third murder. She was psychologically well at the time of her crimes. She spent 36 years in prison and was never considered for parole due to strong public opposition to her release. She died in prison.

treatment of women who are accused of counter-stereotypical crimes is certainly warranted. It provides valuable insight into how public opinion is influenced by *benevolent sexism* and the ramifications for other women accused of similar crimes, regardless of whether they committed them or not. This research also suggests that the continued endorsement of *benevolent sexism* by church organizations like the Seventh-day Adventist Church, particularly with regard to women being innate mothers, could perpetuate this phenomenon in society, a phenomenon that potentially puts members like Lindy Chamberlain at risk and brings unwanted negative public attention to a church organization. Mikołajczak and Pietrzak made a very salient observation when noting that most perpetrators and targets of *benevolent sexism* are unaware of its negative consequences due to "their indirect influence," adding that "if churches and other trusted and powerful social institutions are unwittingly fostering discrimination...we can hardly expect imminent societal change." They concluded "that one indirect effect of promoting tradition, stability, and security is the perpetuation of an unequal status quo."[51]

Conclusion

The first half of this chapter briefly considered the origin of sexism as it appears in the creation account, outlining seven views regarding God's words recorded in Genesis 3:16. The first three views (the pre-fall hierarchical views) find no exegetical support in the two creation stories which, instead, support an egalitarian creation order. Thus, the crucial issue is as follows: Should the subjugation of women be considered a natural consequence of sin and, as such, that an egalitarian pre-fall marital relationship should be considered the gold standard, or is this subjugation a result of God's prescriptive punishment on all women and the antidote which will help reintroduce harmony and unity in a post-fallen world? The second half of this chapter considered empirical behavioral research relating to the subordination of women to introduce additional factors to take into consideration when determining which view may both be the most plausible and contextually consistent with God's character.

In light of the discussion about the two forms of *sexism*, *hostile* and *benevolent*, it becomes clear that male headship and an associated hierarchical view (voluntary or involuntary), although, on the surface, it may seem good, can often have some serious consequences both within a marriage and within a faith group or a larger society. Thus, instead of viewing God's statement "And he will rule over you" (Gen 3:16) as a God-given ideal and blessing in a post-fallen world—endorsing and perpetuating a relationship that seems to be caused by sin and is a direct result of sin—it may be better to view this statement as predictive (view 4), revealing that male headship and women's submission is an additional new reality caused by sin. The creation narrative provides the answer to why the world is the way it is: sin causes death (Gen 2:16-17; 3:2-3 ‖ Gen 3:19, 22); sin causes shame of being naked (Gen 2:25 ‖ Gen 3:7, 10); sin causes disharmonious relationships—

---

51. Mikołajczak and Pietrzak, "Ambivalent Sexism and Religion: Connected Through Values," 396.

38

between humans and God (Gen 3:8-10) and in human relationships (Gen 2:25 ∥ Gen 3:7, 12-13); sin causes pain in childbearing (Gen 3:16a); sin causes tension between good and evil (Gen 3:15); sin causes hardship in survival (Gen 2:16; 3:2 ∥ Gen 3:17-19); sin causes thorns and thistles to grow. As such, the pre-fall egalitarian relationship between the sexes should be considered the creation ideal which a faith community should strive towards and replicate in their marital relationships. It can effectively close the door to "sinful" adverse behaviors like the abuse and exploitation of women—again, something one would expect a faith community to condemn.

Israelite Ritual Law Concerning the Menstruant in Context: Embodiment and Meaning in Ancient Mesopotamia and Ancient Israel

Laura Morrow

Several studies have stated that, across diverse religious traditions, concepts and practices related to the menstruant have engendered at the most, gender disparity and discrimination, and at the very least, a negative view of this common and healthy biological process.[1] Such religious concepts and practices found within the Judeo-Christian tradition invariably lead back to Leviticus 15 and the ritual purity laws of the menstruant. As a result, it has been suggested that these ritual purity laws intentionally promote gender disparity. Therefore, it would be helpful to ascertain the nature of these laws and to understand the rationale behind their inclusion in the biblical law taxonomy to determine whether such suggestions are warranted.

To this end, this study seeks to look at parallels within the ancient Near Eastern context. Specifically, this study will analyze the contemporaneous religious and cultural context in which similar customs were practiced. First, this paper will describe the background of these Biblical prescriptions by describing the Biblical law(s) regarding the menstruant, the arguments and conclusions surrounding the rationale behind it, and the general contemporaneous practices and/or laws of the ancient Near East. Then, the nature of impurity in the context of the religious structure found in ancient Mesopotamian society will be discussed. Next, this study will address a less commonly-approached subject with respect to ritual purity laws—the perception of the human body within this religious and cultural

---

1. M. Guterman, P. Mehta, M. Gibbs, "Menstrual Taboos Among Major Religions," *IJWHSP 5* (2007): 1-7, http://ispub.com/IJWH/5/2/8213; See also Anne Jensen, *God's Self-Confident Daughters: Early Christianity and the Liberation of Women* (Louisville, KY: Westminster John Knox Press, 1992), 70; Kristin De Troyer, "Blood: A Threat to Holiness or Toward (Another) Holiness," in *Wholly Woman, Holy Blood*, eds. Kristin De Troyer et al. (Harrisburg, PA: Trinity Press International, 2003); Janice Delaney, Mary Jane Lupton, and Emily Toth, *The Curse: A Cultural History of Menstruation* (New York: E. P. Dutton, 1976); Kathleen O'Grady stated that "many biblical commentators throughout history have viewed the Levitical menstrual prohibitions as divine punishment for the sinful nature of woman, which, through the actions of Eve, effected the fall of humankind. Menstruation becomes the divine 'curse' of women." Kathleen O'Grady, "The Semantics of Taboo: Menstrual Prohibitions in the Hebrew Bible," in *Wholly Woman, Holy Blood*, 5.

context. Finally, a contextual study comparing and contrasting these Mesopotamian concepts with Israelite practices and perceptions will be offered.[2]

Background to Old Testament Laws Regarding the Menstruant

Menstrual impurity is understood within the context of ritual impurity. Ritual impurity is defined as that "which is a threat to or opposes holiness, and hence must be kept separate from that sphere."[3] (Impurity in a general sense may be a result of naturally occurring physical conditions or from sinful actions.) It is also explained by at least four recognizable aspects:

> [First] it is generated by a physical substance or condition, ... second, incurring it does not constitute a sin – that is, a violation of a divine command... third, its purpose is to avoid defilement of the holy sphere centered at the sanctuary, and fourth, it has a ritual remedy, such as ablutions and sacrifice.[4]

David P. Wright separates impurities into two categories, namely permitted and prohibited impurities. Leviticus 11-15 and Numbers 19 constitute Source P or the Priestly literature, wherein one finds lists of permitted impurities and prohibited impurities.[5] Permitted impurities are "natural and necessary occurrences" that are allowed, but limited and restricted.[6] The source of the impurity is usually human and includes occurrences such as death, sex, and disease. Wright categorizes permitted impurities into four classes related to (1) death, (2) sex, (3) disease, and (4) the cult. Within each class are main impurities that can propagate secondary and even tertiary impurity.[7]

The second category, prohibited impurities, refers to controllable occurrences that are not natural or necessary and may relate to sin or a failure to rectify an impure situation. This includes sexual transgression, idolatry, and murder. Punishments are appended to or replace sacrificial requirements and, while the locus of pollution may be the person, the sanctuary and the land may also be polluted as well.[8]

---

2. William Hallo suggested that the contextual method of comparing and contrasting the culture of Israel with its neighbors is more favorable than the comparative method, in which similarities between Israel and its neighbors are highlighted. William Hallo, "Biblical History in Its Near Eastern Context: The Contextual Approach," in *Scripture in Context: Essays on the Comparative Method* eds. Carl D. Evans, William W. Hallo, and John B. White (Pittsburgh: Pickwick, 1980).

3. David P. Wright, "Unclean and Clean," *ABD* 6:729.

4. Roy Gane, "Prohibitions of Homosexual Practice in Leviticus 18 and 20: Moral or Ceremonial," *Reflections* 47 (July 2014), 2.

5. Wright, "Unclean and Clean," 6:731. Some authors do not include Lev 11 as part of the ritual purity laws. See Jiri Moskala, *The Laws of Clean and Unclean Animals in Leviticus 11: Their Nature, Theology, and Rationale – An Intertextual Study* (Berrien Springs, MI: Adventist Theological Society Publications, 2000); Hyam Maccoby, *Ritual and Morality: The Ritual Purity System and its Place in Judaism* (Cambridge, UK: Cambridge University Press; 1999), vii.

6. Wright, "Unclean and Clean," 6:730.

7. Wright noted that the main impurities are known as "fathers of uncleanness" in rabbinic terminology. Wright, "Unclean and Clean," 6:730.

8. Wright, "Unclean and Clean," 6:730.

Description of Three Explanations for the
Rationale Behind Old Testament Ritual Impurity Laws

Many explanations have been suggested to explicate the rationale for ritual impurity laws, but three authors have been most influential in the study of the topic.[9] First, Mary Douglas' anthropological approach gives insight into how impurity is understood within cultural contexts and demonstrates the social and cultural connection between ritual impurity and the overarching social order of a society. She formulated her theory around the idea that pollution is synonymous with "dirt," which she defined as "disorder." Rituals of pollution or "dirt" avoidance are public symbols, which she stated represent the social and cosmological order of a primitive society.[10]

Second, Jacob Milgrom looked at ritual purity in the context of the distinctive beliefs found in the biblical and rabbinic texts, especially in contrast and comparison to the surrounding ancient Near Eastern context. He saw the use of ritual in the worship of Yahweh as an excising of demonic forces and magical practices. These rituals of avoidance concomitantly direct the worshippers toward life and away from death and decay.[11]

Third, Hyam Maccoby's analysis of the Biblical and rabbinic texts with regard to the relationship of and distinction between ritual and morality concludes that the prohibition of ritual impurity is a factor of several related ideas. Essentially, the ritual purity system replaced the magical apotropaic practices used in polytheistic worship and was also understood to be a kind of protocol, explaining how one may approach the temple and its king (this system was exclusively for the Israelites, who had the privilege of living in proximity to the king). However, Maccoby suggested the overriding and overarching idea that such laws represented a prohibition of the cycle of generation and death from the divine sphere.[12]

The conclusions of Douglas and Milgrom have become standard interpretations in this area of study. In addition, Maccoby's explication of the rationale behind the ritual purity system, especially as it relates to impurity/mortality as a polar opposite to holiness/life, has its adherents as well.[13] While each one of the three propositions adds to the overall picture regarding the rationale behind the inclusion of menstruation in the purity/impurity laws, none of them adequately addresses the physicality inherent within such laws. The relationship between the physical (embodiment) and the ritualistic has yet to be thoroughly approached within the context of purity and impurity by the previous explications. Therefore,

9. See Deborah Klee, "Menstruation in the Hebrew Bible," (PhD diss., Boston University, 1998) for a comprehensive study of menstruation in the Old Testament. Also see R. K. Harrison, *Leviticus: An Introduction and Commentary* (Downers Grove, IL: InterVarsity Press, 1980) for an alternative view to the three mentioned above.

10. Mary Douglas, "Sacred Contagion" in *Reading Leviticus* (Sheffield: Sheffield Academic, 1996), 86-106; *Purity and Danger: An Analysis of the Concepts of Pollution and Taboo* (London: Routledge, 1966); "Couvade and Menstruation: The Relevance of the Tribal Studies" in *Implicit Meanings* (London: Routledge, 2003), 170-179.

11. See Lev 17:10-14, Deut 12:23. Jacob Milgrom, *Leviticus 1-16*, AB (New York: Doubleday, 1991), 767ff.

12. See Maccoby, *Ritual and Morality*, ix.

13. See Roy Gane, *Leviticus, Numbers*, NIVAC (Grand Rapids, MI: Zondervan, 2004), 227; Richard M. Davidson, *Flame of Yahweh: Sexuality in the Old Testament* (Peabody, MA: Hendrickson, 2007), 330-332.

further study on the contextual background of laws concerning the menstruant in the context of ancient perceptions of the body and its religious and societal meanings may enhance our understanding of this topic.[14]

Description of Similar Customs and Practices in the Ancient Near East

Although the Biblical taxonomy of ritual impurities is unique to the Hebrew Bible, it was common in ancient societies to observe rules regarding ritual impurity, with rules regarding the menstruant obtaining in a variety of ancient cultures. For example, the Babylonians believed the man who touched a menstruant or impure woman as he passed by her was impure for six days.[15] In Mesopotamian texts, the words *musukkatu* and *haristu* are used interchangeably to refer to a parturient or menstruant.[16] The Akkadian dictionary defines a *musukkatu* as "a woman in the period after she has given birth when she is in a tabooed state until she has taken a ritual bath; it may also refer to a menstruating woman."[17] A *haristu* is "a woman in confinement (mother)" or "a menstruating woman."[18]

Similarly, during the Middle Assyrian period, an edict was promulgated that stated wives of the king were not to approach him while they were menstruating. The reason was that this contact would jeopardize his cultic purity and disqualify him from bringing offerings to the gods.[19] The material evidence from ancient Egypt is inconclusive with respect to the impurity of the menstruant, yet,

---

14. Douglas' analysis begins to address the issue of the meaning of the body in society, yet she primarily used "primitive" modern societies as the source of her data, rather than comparative ancient texts or iconography that are indicative of the ideologies and practices of chronologically ancient societies.

15. Hennie J. Marsman, *Women in Ugarit and Israel: Their Social and Religious Position in the Context of the Ancient Near East* (Boston: Brill, 2003), 487. See also Karel van der Toorn, *From Her Cradle to Her Grave: The Role of Religion in the Life of the Israelite and Babylonian Woman* (Sheffield: JSOT Press, 1994). For an opposing view see Tarja S. Philip, *Menstruation and Childbirth in the Bible: Fertility and Impurity*. (New York: Peter Lang, 2006).

16. Milgrom, *Leviticus 1-16*, 951.

17. "musukkatu," *CAD* 10 II: 239-240.

18. "haristu," *CAD* 6: 104. Tarja Philip questioned the standard definitions for *haristu* and *musukkatu* and suggested that it is difficult to ascertain the context in which these words appear. She also proposed that the Assyrian Dictionary has made concrete decisions regarding these matters without definitive evidence from the respective texts. Philip, *Menstruation and Childbirth*, 5. Philip also questioned van der Toorn's assessment of menstruation within the Babylonian context and concluded "that the use of these sources (Mesopotamian texts) for a better understanding of the biblical texts is very problematic. The sources are few, diverse, and broken, and one has to be very careful not to suppose that the better-known Israeli beliefs and practices have a lot in common with their ancient Near Eastern parallels, and thus enter into circular argument." Philip, *Menstruation and Childbirth*, 7. Yet, while Philip advised caution, she did not suggest what role these texts should play, if any, in the analysis of this issue.

19. Marsman, *Women in Ugarit and Israel*, 487. Hennie J. Marsman noted that "those who were impure were not to appear before the gods, for this would offend them. The deities and their sanctuaries belonged to the realm of the pure and holy, which should not be polluted by substances or persons from the realm of the impure." Marsman cited Karel van der Toorn and E. J. Wilson as sources for this conclusion. For a more comprehensive treatment of the separation between the earthly and the heavenly realm from a priestly and architectural perspective see Michael B. Hundley, *Keeping Heaven on Earth: Safeguarding the Divine Presence in the Priestly Tabernacle* (Tübingen: Mohr Siebeck, 2011) and *Gods in Dwellings: Temples and Divine Presence in the Ancient Near East* (Atlanta: Society of Biblical Literature, 2013).

menstruation was referred to as a "time of purification," which may imply a state of impurity.[20]

This data points to the idea that various ancient societies shared a common perspective regarding menstruation, and by extension, its role in ritual impurity. This shared common perspective is apparently a factor of two concurrent and commingling phenomena within these societies: (1) the nature of impurity in the context of the religious structure found in the society and (2) the perception of the human body within this religious and cultural context.

This study will next look at these two phenomena, the nature of holiness, purity/impurity, and the perception of the human body within Mesopotamian society. The treatment of the first topic will include a brief description of the religion of ancient Mesopotamia, attendant Mesopotamian terminology for "holiness" and "purity," and finally ascertain the nature of the concept of holiness within this religious system. The treatment of the second topic will include discussions on the importance of the perception of the body in ancient society, significant terminology, the perception of the body and social position, and the perception of the body in religious practice.

The Nature of Holiness, Purity, and Impurity in Ancient Mesopotamian Religion

Ideas of holiness and purity were developed and understood within the matrix of ancient Mesopotamian religion. Leo Oppenheim's caveat aside, a clear and organized structure can be deduced from the literary, iconographic, and epigraphic material that has been discovered over the centuries.[21] Both Jean Bottero and Thorkild Jacobsen identified a distinct development over time that culminated in a parallel structure between the religious and socio-political spheres.[22] Bottero stated, "Their religion only adapted their native habits of thinking, feeling, and living to the supernatural."[23] This projection produced a religion that mimicked the civilization in its origin and development. In a similar vein, Jacobsen denoted a pattern of parallel projection in Mesopotamian religion and civilization, but expressed this idea as three metaphors: (1) gods as spiritual cores in phenomena, (2) gods as rulers, and (3) gods as parents.[24]

20. See Barbara Watterson, *Women in Ancient Egypt*, (Stroud: UK: Sutton, 1991), 84.

21. Oppenheim was convinced that "a systematic presentation of Mesopotamian religion cannot and should not be written." Leo Oppenheim, *Ancient Mesopotamia: Portrait of a Dead Civilization* (Chicago: University of Chicago Press, 1964), 72.

22. Jean Bottero, *Mesopotamia: Writing, Reasoning, and the Gods*, Translated by Zainab Bahrani and Marc Van De Mieroop (Chicago: University of Chicago Press, 1992), 203; Thorkild Jacobsen, *The Treasures of Darkness* (New Haven: Yale University Press, 1976). For a succinct introduction to Mesopotamian religion see Tammi J. Schneider, *An Introduction to Ancient Mesopotamian Religion* (Grand Rapids, MI: Eerdmans, 2011). Schneider concurred with Bottero and Jacobsen that Mesopotamian religion was intimately related to its political shifts since she noted, "Here, attention is focused not so much on the reasons for or background of historical shifts, but on the components that may have, in this author's opinion, either heavily influenced why a religious change occurred or highlighted such things as influxes of new people to the area or language shifts that influenced religious practice as we understand it." Schneider, *An Introduction to Ancient Mesopotamian Religion*, 17-18.

23. Bottero, *Mesopotamia: Writing, Reasoning, and the Gods*, 203.

24. Jacobsen, *The Treasures of Darkness*, 20.

Bottero enhanced and extended Jacobsen's second metaphor—gods as rulers—and suggested that the "monarchical principle" is the framework for ancient Mesopotamian religion.[25] Specifically, the royal hierarchical political institution was an analogy for and a foundational or guiding principle of religious awareness and conception. In essence, the religion of ancient Mesopotamia can be viewed as an organized and comprehensive system through which religious sentiment was expressed and experienced. Thus, contact with this system mirrored the forms and protocols corresponding to the monarchical system.

Within this monarchically-defined system of the divine, purity and holiness are expressed using rites and conceptions that correspond to those practiced in the realm of the king. Therefore, conceptions of purity associated with an encounter with royalty were carried over to conceptions of purity associated with an encounter with the divine. Essentially, the god was treated as a king, but one who existed in a higher realm—that of the divine.

The Terms "Holiness" and "Purity"
Within Ancient Mesopotamia

Terminological correspondences for holiness and purity give further clarity concerning these conceptions within the religious system of ancient Mesopotamia. Wilson proposed that the Sumerian term KU3 should be translated as holiness and primarily defined as "pertaining to the realm of the divine."[26] He identified at least four items or persons who are related to this realm: (1) the temple, (2) holy objects—temple utensils and accessories, (3) holy beings—Inanna and certain body parts of the gods, and (4) sacred acts and times—holy festivals.

The concept of purity (or impurity) in Sumerian is denoted by multiple words, which usually refer to the qualities of cleanness, brightness, or radiance. Words such as *shen*, *dadag*, *zalag* and *sikil* are used to represent the concept of purity, which is distinct from the concept of holiness or pertaining to the realm of the divine.

In Akkadian, the term *ellu* is used to translate KU₃ in various texts; however, it is used in contexts that suggest it should be defined as "purity" or "freedom from

---

25. Bottero, *Mesopotamia: Writing, Reasoning, and the Gods*, 212-215. Joan Oates stated, "Temple and court ritual were closely related. We read, for example, of the god Nabu going into the game park, like the king, to hunt...A ritual text from Uruk describes also a morning ceremonial reminiscent of the European *lever du roi*, perhaps equally a feature of the Babylonian court." Joan Oates, *Babylon* (London: Thames and Hudson, 1986), 175. Amelie Kuhrt also noted, "The one aspect (of kingship) that stands out clearly is the kings' close involvement in the cultic foundations of Babylonia and their frequent personal participation in the New Year Festival in Babylon." She continued, "In cult, the king was central in all respects: he was the chief builder and provider of essential resources; he participated in rituals and authorized the offerings to be made." Amelie Kuhrt, *The Ancient Near East, c. 3000-330*, 2 vols. (London: Routledge, 1997), 2:604, 605.

26. E. Jan Wilson, *"Holiness" and "Purity" in Mesopotamia*, Alter Orient und Altes Testament 237 (Neukirchen-Vluyn: Butzon & Bercker, 1994), 65. See also Judith Roberts Paul, "Mesopotamian Ritual Texts and the Concept of the Sacred in Mesopotamia," (PhD Diss., University of California, Los Angeles, 1992).

pollutants."[27] Its primary definition is purity, while it only secondarily refers to holiness. Wilson identified at least four contexts in which *ellu* is used: (1) places—purification of the temple (the New Year Festival); (2) objects—used frequently in relation to water; food, wood (cedar), and lapis lazuli; (3) beings—persons purified from magic spells; *baru*-priests purified before approaching Shamash; and (4) substances—water (most important), date palm, and salt.

The Sumerian word KU3 and the Akkadian word *ellu* enhance our understanding of the context for the concepts of holiness and purity. In particular, the Sumerian definition of holiness (pertaining to the realm of the divine) and the items associated with this concept (temple, temple appurtenances, Inanna, sacred festivals) suggest that the temple and its accompanying utensils and festivals were considered to be part of the realm of the divine, as opposed to the realm of mortals, and indicates a delineation and a demarcation between the two spheres. In addition, the definition of the Akkadian term *ellu* (purity—freedom from pollutants) and those things associated with it (purification of the temple, purifying substances, and purified persons) suggest that purity refers to the elimination of pollutants from cultic (or non-cultic) spheres.[28]

Holiness and Impurity within the Religious System of Ancient Mesopotamian

The foregoing discussion points to the concept that within the religious system of ancient Mesopotamia, the realm of the divine was rigidly delineated from the realm of human society. Furthermore, the divine realm was restricted from coming in contact with substances that were considered not pure (impure) or not clean (unclean). Thus, the realm of the divine had to be assiduously protected from coming in contact with such substances because they were a threat to its integrity.[29] With an eye to maintaining this order, cultic rites were conscientiously followed. These rites enabled specially appointed persons to participate in an

---

27. Wilson, *"Holiness" and "Purity" in Mesopotamia*, 94. Judith Roberts Paul stated, *"Ellu,* 'pure,' is an epithet often applied to gods, the parts of their bodies, and their property. Indeed, this term is so closely associated with divinity that it is often translated as 'sacred' or 'holy,' although it never lost its primary meaning." Paul, "Mesopotamian Ritual Texts," 124.

28. Paul noted, "Impurity is perceived as a substance which can be transferred from one object to another and which can be removed by some of the same means which can be used to remove dirt. It is thus not surprising that water, with or without additives, is one of the most common ritual detergents." Paul, "Mesopotamian Ritual Texts," 143. This cleansing was part of a complex of ritual acts that signaled that the act was more than common washing or bathing.

29. The realm of the divine was also considered to be a threat to humans. It was a common understanding in the ancient Near East that "the sacred is dangerous...One of the purposes of ritual is to provide a controlled environment in which human beings could approach the sacred in relative safety." Paul, "Mesopotamian Ritual Texts," 151.

encounter with the realm of the divine, which mainly included the temple complex and its appurtenances.[30]

In this framework of maintaining the integrity of the realm of the divine, certain rules were created to fulfill this purpose. Van der Toorn called such regulations "rules of decency or etiquette," which are "founded on the ethical command to worship the god in a proper manner."[31] This concept is similar to Maccoby's rationale, which suggests that laws of ritual purity were equivalent to temple protocol. Van der Toorn distinguished these rules from ethical or moral rules of conduct, which he considered to be of a higher order, and identified them as "small ethics."[32] Such rules delineate what is "seemly and unseemly" and deal with matters of cultural "taste."[33] He gave several examples of "rules of decency," specifically, lists of sacred or tabooed animals and prohibitions against persons affected by tabooed states caused by physical occurrences such as skin disease, menstruation, or sexual activity.

Like both Bottero and Jacobsen, van der Toorn also concluded that such rules are similar to those followed when approaching the king and denote matters of courtesy or convention in relation to that sphere. Thus, since the monarchical sphere is an analogy for the divine sphere, such rules of etiquette or convention would naturally transfer over to conventions for the divine.

However, he further extended this analogy and suggested that such rules of behavior were built upon societal customs and principles. This analogy presupposes the importance of the ancient Mesopotamian worldview about the interaction between the spiritual and physical realms, which did not separate the material world from the spiritual. Essentially, religious experience was grasped phenomenologically, rather than through a dichotomous conception of the spiritual and the physical. This fact is best expressed by the visible and material presence of the deity, represented by a physical statue within the temple, and by the care and feeding of this physical representation of the god. The external was representative

---

30. Some scholars have concluded that the primary origin or source of ritual impurity in Mesopotamia was demonic in nature. See David P. Wright, *The Disposal of Impurity: Elimination Rites in the Bible and in Hittite and Mesopotamian Literature* (Atlanta: Scholars Press, 1987), 248. Paul disagreed with this argument and suggested that sources of impurity were generally omitted from purification rituals. She stated, "Indeed, many of the references to sources of impurity appear in lexical lists or omen texts, with no indication of the ritual actions required for purification." Paul, "Mesopotamian Ritual Texts," 142. It appears that the sources of impurity were too numerous and the purification rite was a generic attempt to remove impurity in any form. This is in contrast to the laws found in Leviticus, which point to specific sources of ritual impurity (Leviticus 12-15). However, she did admit that Mesopotamians shared some sources of impurity with the Israelites, like bodily secretions (menstruation). Paul, "Mesopotamian Ritual Texts," 139.

31. Karel van der Toorn, *Sin and Sanction in Israel and Mesopotamia: A Comparative Study.* (Assen: Van Gorcum, 1985), p. 21-23, 12; For a succinct discussion on proper temple protocol in the Ancient Near East see Hundley, *Keeping Heaven on Earth*, pp. 119-134. He suggested that "although the ANE gods possess great power and are shrouded in considerable mystery, they are part of the created world, and thus subject to its vicissitudes...In Mesopotamia, the rule of the gods is especially contested beyond the nation's borders by such inimical forces as demons, monsters, rebellious mountains, dangerous seas, and barbarians...Humans...may influence the divine sphere primarily through the cult." Hundley, p. 122. Hundley's *Gods in Dwellings* gives a more comprehensive treatment of this subject.

32. Van der Toorn, *Sin and Sanction in Israel and Mesopotamia*, 21-23.

33. Van der Toorn, *Sin and Sanction in Israel and Mesopotamia*, 21-23.

of the inner spiritual reality, so great attention was given to its maintenance and estimation.

Moreover, ancient Mesopotamians believed the gods positively or negatively influenced the external, visible world in every aspect of life. Stefan Maul noted, "The theistic world view of the ancient Orient did not allow for chance or hazard...everything was an expression of the divine, creative will which manifested itself in the world again and again."[34] The physical world was a manifestation of the will of the gods and therefore, has to be understood within this context.

Summary

The ancient Mesopotamian religious system was a projection of the monarchical political system that predominated in that society. In this setting, ideas of holiness and purity were construed to delineate the realm of the divine and effect the removal of pollutants from this realm. Consequently, rules and regulations maintaining the integrity of this sphere were developed. These rules were predicated upon the beliefs and customs of a society that grasped religious experience through the external, visible world, which was inexorably influenced by the gods.

The Perception of the Human Body in Ancient Mesopotamia

For a variety of reasons, it is difficult to ascertain fully how Mesopotamians understood the human body within its society. Ancient texts rarely provide philosophical and sociological analyses of society and merely offer fragments of ritual practices and mythology. Nevertheless, according to Maria Wyke, "the body has become a central analytic tool in ancient Mediterranean studies."[35] It is a fruitful topic through which to investigate differences in society and to ascertain a society's structure and expressions of power.

Moreover, Julia Asher-Greve has noted that the body is essential in Mesopotamian thought, in which the duality of mind and body prevalent in Western thought is absent. These two entities make up one vital whole that is inseparable, forming a unity that expressed meaning and understanding or that "embodied" meaning and understanding.[36] This ideology was manifested, among other aspects of cultural life, in the areas of language, social position, and religious practice.[37]

---

34. Stefan M. Maul, "Divination Culture and the Handling of the Future," in *The Babylonian World*, ed. Gwendolyn Leick (New York: Routledge, 2007), 362. For further information on the religious worldview in Babylon see Takayoshi Oshima, "The Babylonian god Marduk," 348-360 and Brigitte Groneberg, "The Role and Function of Goddesses in Mesopotamia," 319-331 in *The Babylonian World* (Leick).

35. Maria Wyke, "Introduction," in *Gender and the Body in the Ancient Mediterranean*, ed. Maria Wyke (Malden, MA: Blackwell, 1998), 2.

36. Julia M. Asher-Greve, "The Essential Body: Mesopotamian Conceptions of the Gendered Body," in *Gender and the Body in the Ancient Mediterranean* (Wyke), 8.

37. Christopher Hallpike noted that "external manifestations of inner states" were of particular interest to ancient societies. Therefore, the external, or the body, was able to reveal inner states of thinking or feeling thereby giving significance to the state of the physical body. Christopher R. Hallpike, *The Foundations of Primitive Thought* (Oxford: Clarendon, 1979), 390.

Terminology of the Body

Sumerian terminology communicates the significance of the human body in various ways. For example, there is no specific term for mind or the human brain, while there are several terms for the body, namely, *su* or *su-bar*, which refer to the body as a collective group or people; *sha* which refers to the external and internal body; and (*me-*) *dim₂*, which primarily means limbs and/or creation or creature. The Sumerian word for intelligence is *geshtu*, which is written using the sign for ear. This may indicate that intelligence was linked to the sense of listening, which is an idea common to several cultures in which "understanding, thinking and knowing (are) associated with hearing."[38] *Sha* can mean body or heart and represents the same meaning for heart found in ancient Egyptian texts, where the heart is the seat of the will, thought, and feeling. Linguistically, ancient Near Eastern thought located psychological processes in physical organs, thereby manifesting a holistic concept of heart, body, and mind.

The Body and Social Position

This manner of thinking made the body important for the development of meaning within society. The social meaning that was invested in the physical body is indicative of this development. For example, physical perfection was related to royalty or kingship, while physical imperfection was an indication of a lower social status. Kings were depicted as heroic figures with strength and vigor comparable to that of the gods.[39] In a statue inscription for King Ishme-Dagan (1953-1955 BCE), he is described as, "Ishme-Dagan, the strong young man with muscles and the body of a lion, mighty youth, who possesses fearsome splendor."[40]

This concept of physical perfection and strength was expressed in the common motif of the "nude heroic man combating wild animals," found in the Early Dynastic period (c. 2800-2350 BCE),[41] which became one of the most popular motifs on cylinder seals in the Akkadian period (c. 2350-2150 BCE). This singular motif developed concomitantly with the advance of royal ideology and is mimicked in

---

38. Asher-Greve, "The Essential Body," 10.

39. The image of the "strong man" is notably expressed on the stele of Naram-Sin. His form is powerful and imposing and he is depicted with muscular arms and legs. He is also wearing a helmet with horns that indicates divinity. See Marc Van de Mieroop, *A History of the Ancient Near East, ca. 3000-323 BC* (Malden, MA: Blackwell, 2007), 70.

40. "One of the most common royal epithets is 'strong man' (*nita kala-ga*)." Asher-Greve, "The Essential Body," 20. For a discussion of the social constructions of power in Mesopotamia see Petr Charvát, "Social Configurations in Early Dynastic Babylonia (c. 2500-2334 BC.)," 251-264 in *The Babylonian World* (Leick). Some scholars suggest that city-states were once ruled by priest-kings who were supplanted by strong men who arose during threats from external forces. These strong men later became central political figures and dominated and centralized the government. Marc Van de Mieroop noted that "the head of the temple administration served as leader in the city...With the expansion of the city-states' zones of influence, competition for the remaining open areas developed and soon led to intercity wars over agricultural land. A leader's military rather than his cultic role became of primary importance in such situations." Van De Mieroop, *A History of the Ancient Near East*, 45-47. In contrast, Nicole Brisch suggested that the evidence for the existence of a priest-king is unclear. Nicole Brisch, "History and Chronology," in *The Sumerian World*, ed. Harriet Crawford (London: Routledge, 2013), 115.

41. Asher-Greve, "The Essential Body," 19.

motifs depicting the gods fighting nude, which was the only context in which gods were represented as such. Possibly, the lack of clothing enhanced the physical feat of battle, since the god completely lacked external protection.

The Body and Religious Practice

The body was also significant in the religious sphere and was a locus of meaning and religious expression. Divination used the body as a text to be "read" using a complex system of observation and interpretation. The practice of divination in ancient Mesopotamia was the predominant form of communication with the divine realm that was based on the identification of omens. An omen can be defined as, "a clearly defined perception understood as a sign pointing to future events whenever it manifests itself under identical circumstances."[42] The most prominent forms of divination were extispicy and astrology, whereas other forms, such as signs of time, the earth, and the human form, were less common.

Physiognomic omens were ascertained on the basis of observations of the human body or of human behavior and shared common principles and practices with divination for the evaluation and treatment of physical diseases.[43] Texts were compiled that included examples of omina analyses, which may have served as textbooks for initiates. The corpus, entitled *Alandimmu* was "an amalgam of ideas, beliefs, and customs that, having received the sanction of tradition, was systematically established, documented and copied."[44]

Furthermore, physical perfection was commensurate with the priestly caste and any physical imperfection disqualified a potential candidate. The position of *baru*-priest, one of the primary actors in the rituals pertaining to an encounter with the divine, required physical perfection in his "appearance and his limbs."[45] Van der Toorn also noted, "A person who is 'cross-eyed' or who has 'chipped teeth' was not allowed to approach 'the place of the (divine) judgment.'"[46]

Specific maladies such as severe skin diseases (possibly leprosy: Akkadian— *saharshubbu*) were listed as "defiling diseases" that would not only disqualify a person from the sacerdotal office, but also subject the person to divine rejection. Van der Toorn concluded that the reasons behind this extreme reaction to leprosy-like diseases may be its "conspicuousness" and its resistance to treatment.[47] Here again, one can recognize the importance of the external, physical attributes

---

42. Stefan M. Maul, "Divination Culture and the Handling of the Future," in *The Babylonian World* (Leick) 361. Alen Lenzi stated, "Divination is...a point of contact for the two bodies (the royal secret council and the divine assembly) via the person of the diviner, for within the personnel of the royal council, only the diviner had the authority to set the king's plans before the gods via an extispicy and to read the judgment of the gods..." Alen Lenzi, *Secrecy and the Gods: Secret Knowledge in Ancient Mesopotamia and Biblical Israel* (Helsinki: The Neo-Assyrian Text Corpus Project, 2008), 55.

43. Frederick H. Cryer, *Divination in Ancient Israel and its Near Eastern Environment: A Socio-Historical Investigation* (Sheffield: Sheffield Academic, 1994), 163.

44. Barbara Bock, "Physiognomy in Ancient Mesopotamia and Beyond: From Practice to Handbook," in *Divination and Interpretation of Signs in the Ancient World*, ed. Amar Annus (Chicago: Oriental Institute Seminars, 2010), 212.

45. Van der Toorn, *Sin and Sanction*, 29.

46. Van der Toorn, *Sin and Sanction*, 29.

47. Van der Toorn, *Sin and Sanction*, 30.

of the human form and their influence upon ancient Mesopotamian society. He continued, "This instinctive emotional response of loathing and inordinate fear, shared by many other societies all over the world, is the soil in which the cultic rejection of the leper is rooted."[48]

Finally, male and female bodies, as a unit and in each of their respective spheres, also had their own idiosyncratic forms of physical impurities at the nexus of this intersection between the realm of the divine and the human sphere. After physical disease and defectiveness, human sexuality posed a considerable threat to the divine sphere. This concept is somewhat puzzling, since ancient Mesopotamia viewed fertility and virility as conspicuously important within society. Mesopotamian society's apprehension of the sexual act even reached to the coupling of the gods, which is demonstrated in the Myth of Nergal and Ereshkigal, where the latter had intercourse with Erra and stated, "I am sexually defiled, I am not pure, I cannot execute the judgment of the great gods."[49]

Separately, male and female bodily functions could also cause apprehension within society and by extension, threaten the realm of the divine. The impurity of male genital discharges, whether healthy or pathological, while less commonly documented than that of female genital discharges, could be considered a threat to the purity of the divine sphere. Men who were found in this state could not participate in cultic rituals or battle and were even prohibited from entering the place of commerce.[50]

Female genital discharges are more frequently characterized as impure, although the texts are fragmentary, diffuse, and difficult to translate. The parturient incurred a thirty-day period of impurity and was called *musukkatu*, an Akkadian term for a woman in the period after giving birth, after sexual intercourse (without bathing), and during menstruation (see footnote 17). Her impurity could be transmitted by touch, so in some texts she was thought to be unapproachable during these periods, especially by cultic officiators.[51]

Summary

The human form externalized ideas of intelligence, power, and religious perfection. Mesopotamian terminology vividly expressed the connection between the body and meaning and understanding. Furthermore, the perfect human form transmitted concepts of power and authority within the social hierarchy. Finally, in the religious realm, physical perfection and purity delineated carefully protect-

---

48. Van der Toorn, *Sin and Sanction*, 31. Thomas Kazen posited the benefits of a psycho-biological approach in the study of ritual purity, which attends to the psychological bodily experience that is expressed through feelings of fear and disgust. In his analysis of impurity in relation to fear, he identified several rites within the Israelite ritual system that exhibit vestiges of apotropaic characteristics (which connote a fear of demonic forces), such as the purification rite in Lev. 14, the red heifer ritual, and the Day of Atonement ritual featuring the goat for Azazel. Thomas Kazen, *Issues of Impurity in Early Judaism*, (Winona Lake, IN: Eisenbrauns, 2010), 25-31.

49. Wilson, *"Holiness" and "Purity" in Mesopotamia*, 74.

50. Van der Toorn, *Sin and Sanction*, 32.The Akkadian word *musukku* may also refer to male impurity in regards to male genital discharges.

51. Van der Toorn, *Sin and Sanction*, 33. For a critique of Van der Toorn's analysis concerning menstruation and of the standard definition of the word *musukkatu* (noted above) see Philip, *Menstruation and Childbirth*, 5-7.

ed and defined boundaries that maintained the integrity of the divine realm.

The previous study of the nature of holiness, purity/impurity, and the perception of the human body within Mesopotamian society demonstrates an integral and interrelated relationship between the two concepts. Furthermore, this relationship adds shape and meaning to specific ancient rituals and practices. Therefore, it may be helpful to compare and contrast these ideas and concepts with ancient Israel's religious ideology and ritual practice to ascertain whether a similar meaning could be discerned therein. Specifically, two topics will be addressed in this analysis: (1) Yahwism and concepts of holiness and purity and (2) the perception of the body within concepts of cultic perfection and purity.

A Contextual Look At Ancient Israel's Concepts Of Holiness And Purity In Relation To Its Perception Of The Human Body

The religious system in ancient Israel was distinct from that of Mesopotamia in that rather than being centered on the pantheon of gods and echoing the development of its civilization and political structure, it was completely centered and influenced by the person of Yahweh. Therefore, concepts of holiness and purity were understood in connection with the attributes and person of Yahweh. However, Wright's explication of the meaning of holiness in the Old Testament shares some commonalities with Wilson's definition of Sumerian and Akkadian concepts of holiness and purity.

Wright noted that the concept of holiness, based on the Hebrew term *qodesh* (apartness, sacredness, holiness), revolves around Yahweh who is considered the source of holiness and its "ideal manifestation."[52] Comparably, the Sumerian term KU3 also relates to the divine, but is specifically defined as things pertaining to the divine realm. Both meanings denote concepts that specifically relate to deity, whether Yahweh or the pantheon of gods. Furthermore, Wright concluded that things, persons, or places characterized as holy are invariably connected to Yahweh. Humans considered holy include priests, Levites, Nazirites, prophets, and Israel as a nation. All of these groups are holy because of their connection to Yahweh and not as a result of inherent holiness. In addition, objects such as offerings, sanctuary furniture, and priestly clothing all receive their holiness from their association with the sanctuary, which is ultimately the sphere of Yahweh.

Places associated with the divine presence and times allocated to the worship

---

52. David P. Wright, "Holiness," ABD 3:237. *Qodesh* can refer to places set apart as sacred by God's presence, such as God's heavenly dwelling place or the tabernacle. It can also refer to things consecrated at sacred places, such as temple furniture. In addition, it can refer to people and sacred times. F. Brown, S. R. Driver, and C.A. Briggs. *A Hebrew and English Lexicon of the Old Testament*. (Oxford: Clarendon, 1906; repr., 2010), 871. This discussion does not negate the multifaceted definition of "holiness" proposed by Richard Davidson, who suggested there are three facets to the "holiness rationale:" (1) separation, (2) wholeness, and (3) health. See Davidson, *Flame of Yahweh*, 329-332. Davidson saw the rationale of separation in the context of sexuality and the temple. He stated, "God radically separates sexuality from any ritual activity in the cultus. As part of a polemic against the divinization of sex in fertility cults, God makes a clear and distinct separation between sex and the sanctuary." Davidson, *Flame of Yahweh*, 329. This implies that menstruation was viewed as sex-related, possibly because blood flowed from the sex organ.

of Yahweh were deemed holy. Several prohibitions preventing access to Mt. Sinai were imposed upon the Israelites because of its association with the divine presence. On earth, the primary place associated with Yahweh's presence was the sanctuary and its environs, understood to be his dwelling. By extension, the city in which Yahweh's sanctuary was located—Jerusalem—was considered holy. In addition, the Sabbath and the cyclic festivals associated with Yahweh were also holy.

Wright stated that impurity (in Hebrew—*tame*) "is a state opposed and detrimental to holiness," yet it is not the terminological antonym to holiness.[53] States of impurity are rectified by purgation offerings or ablutions and washing. These rituals denote that the concept of purity (in Hebrew—*taher*) in the Bible has some correspondence to the Akkadian word *ellu* and the concept of the removal of pollutants.[54] Nevertheless, the idea of exorcism or the removal of evil spirits is absent.

The Perception of the Body and Ideas
of Cultic Perfection and Purity

The religious practices of ancient Israel were intentionally distinct from those of Mesopotamia because of the nature of Yahweh's holiness. Thus, practices such as divination and polytheism were vehemently proscribed. Perceptions of the body in ancient Israel do, however, demonstrate some parallels with Mesopotamian thought.[55] Most notably, physical perfection was prescribed for priests and the animal sacrifices attached to the worship of Yahweh. To a lesser degree, the officiants presenting an offering were expected to be in a state of physical purity.

Leviticus 21:16-20 enumerates regulations proscribing physical imperfections for priests.[56] No male with a defect was allowed to officiate as a priest. This included blindness, physical disability (lameness), and facial disfigurement, as well as deformed limbs. Males with broken hands or feet were also similarly disqualified. The list concludes with the inclusion of hunchbacks, dwarfs, those suffering from skin disease (possibly eczema) or who have a defective eye, and

---

53. Wright, "Holiness," ABD 3:246. Tame means unclean or impure, usually (1) sexually, (2) religiously with idols, and (3) ceremonially. Brown, Driver, and Briggs. *A Hebrew and English Lexicon*, 379. Beyond matters of impurity, in the context of the Holiness Code (Leviticus 17-26), it has been observed that the concept of holiness "is first and foremost of the God of Israel." In addition, holiness is defined as separation and as association with God and belonging to God. Joann M. Dupont, "Women and the Concept of Holiness in the 'Holiness Code' (Leviticus 17-26): Literary, Theological and Historical Context," (PhD Diss., Marquette University, 1989), 87-88.

54. *Taher* – pure, clean. Brown, Driver, and Briggs. *A Hebrew and English Lexicon*, 372.

55. Aubrey Johnson described ancient Israelite thinking about the individual as "synthetic." Man is seen as a "psychical whole" in which his "soul-substance is perceived, not only in the various members and secretions of the body, but also in a more extended form in whatever bears traces of contact with him." He continued: "This class may include former secretions such as blood, spittle, and sweat; the shadow, reflection, and similar reproductions." Aubrey R. Johnson, *The Vitality of the Individual in the Thought of Ancient Israel* (Cardiff: University of Wales Press, 1964), 2-3. See also Thomas Staubli and Silvia Schroer, *Body Symbolism in the Bible* (Collegeville, MN: Liturgical Press, 2001). For a discussion of how kingship is viewed through a bodily perspective see Mark W. Hamilton, *The Body Royal: The Social Poetics of Kingship in Ancient Israel* (Leiden: Brill, 2005).

56. Roy Gane explained, "The priesthood constitutes the Lord's corps of special servants, who must be in harmony with his holy, immortal, perfect sphere to the greatest extent possible. Only in this way can they properly represent the nature and character of God to the people." Roy Gane, *Leviticus, Numbers*, 374. See also Kerry H. Wynn, "The Normate Hermeneutic and Interpretations of Disability within the Yahwistic Narratives in *The Abled Body: Rethinking Disabilities in Biblical Studies*, eds. Hector Avalos, Sarah J. Melcher, and Jeremy Schipper (Atlanta: Society of Biblical Literature, 2007), 91.

males with crushed testicles.[57] These regulations are similar to the Mesopotamian physical restrictions for priests, which also promote physical perfection.

Analogous to priestly physical perfection, the animal sacrifices were supposed to be free from physical defects. Any animal sacrifice that had a defect defiled the altar and in essence, Yahweh, according to Malachi 1:8. Defects found in animal sacrifices include blindness, lameness, and sickness, which are similar attributes found in relation to the priest.

Physical perfection was not imposed upon ordinary officiants, but ritual purity was a requirement. The laws of ritual purity in Leviticus 12-15 refer to physical states that are comparable to the laws of etiquette described by Van der Toorn. Ritual laws for the parturient (Lev 12), for scaly skin disease (Lev 13 [14]), and for male and female discharges (Lev 15) refer to physical states that apparently threaten the divine realm. Therefore, such laws in some ways exhibit similar (but distinct) underlying concepts as those found in Mesopotamia.[58]

Conclusion

This study suggests that the ancient Mesopotamian religious and cultural context in which regulations of ritual purity were followed was constructed upon the understanding of holiness and purity. Moreover, this ancient society's perception of the human body in relation to their conception of holiness and purity in the context of their religious system also influenced their practice of ritual purity laws. In addition, this study found that ancient Israel's conception of ritual purity laws might also have been influenced by its conception of holiness and purity within the religious system of Yahweh and its perception of the body in relation to its religious system.

Thus, suggestions that Biblical ritual purity laws regarding the menstruant inherently promote gender disparity may not fully take into account the ancient context behind the generation of such laws. This study suggests that the Biblical laws regarding the menstruant are parallel to Mesopotamian practice and thought wherein existed a confluence of religious ideology and cultural perceptions. Therefore, a similar confluence of religious ideology (the religion of Yahweh) and cultural perceptions (the significance of the body within society) may have obtained also in ancient Israel. Consequently, the ritual laws of Leviticus 12-15

---

57. In the Ancient Near East, those who were disabled or infirmed were not to be abused (the blind, "the dwarf…the lame…") and were seen as an integral part of society, yet they were not seen as proper officiants in the divine sphere. See Neal H. Walls, "The Origins of the Disabled Body: Disability in Ancient Mesopotamia," in *This Abled Body*, (Avalos, Melcher, Schipper), 14, 29-30. For a discussion on the complexity of social status and disfigurement, see T. M. Lemos, "'Like the Eunuch Who Does Not Beget': Gender, Mutilation, and Negotiated Status in the Ancient Near East," in *Disability Studies and Biblical Literature*, eds. Candida R. Moss and Jeremy Schipper (New York: Palgrave Macmillan, 2011), 47-66.

58. For an alternate view on the rationale behind ritual purity laws see Thomas Kazen, "Dirt and Disgust: Body and Morality in Biblical Purity Laws," in *Perspectives on Purity and Purification in the Bible*, eds. Baruch J. Schwartz et al. (New York: T&T Clark, 2008).

may be better understood through the lens of religious and cultural perceptions within ancient society.[59]

This study may also help us understand the nature of Biblical ritual law, especially within its ancient context. It points to the idea that Biblical ritual law was not isolated from the cultural practices of its time, but it may have been influenced by persistent ideologies and perceptions that were common across national, geographic, and ethnic boundaries.

---

59. The cultural perceptions of Ancient Israelite and Mesopotamian societies were based on a patriarchal paradigm and one cannot completely divorce these societies from this fact. Thus, it certainly would be possible to suggest that these ancient societies had a culture that engendered gender disparity. It would be difficult to do a comprehensive study on the status of women in each of these societies; however, some studies have approached this question. See Marsman, *Women in Ugarit and Israel*; Mark Chavalas, ed., *Women in the Ancient Near East: A Source Book* (London: Routledge, 2014). Bahrani, Zainab, *Women of Babylon: Gender and Representation in Mesopotamia* (London: Routledge, 2001). Gerda Lerner, *The Creation of Patriarchy* (New York: Oxford University Press, 1986).

The Biblical Law of *Niddah* and Its Muslim Parallels

Jan A. Sigvartsen

This chapter will look at the biblical law of *niddah* and its Muslim parallels. First, it will examine the laws of *niddah* in the Bible and their later developments within Judaism from the Second Temple Period until the present time. Second, it will explore the Muslim parallels, noting the similarities and differences with the Jewish regulations. Last, it will consider the role these laws have held in the Christian church and of whether these laws are relevant for Christians today.

It should be emphasized that this chapter will not address every sect's views or the minute details of the laws of *niddah* within each of these monotheistic religions. It will, however, look at the broader contextual picture and discuss some pertinent details of interest.

The Biblical Law of *Niddah* and Judaism

Jacob Milgrom argued the noun "*niddah*" has the general meaning of "expulsion" and "elimination."[1] A word study reveals this word occurs 29 times in the Hebrew Scripture and falls into three main categories (see Table 1): the first describes the water for purification; the second, general impurity or abominations;

Table 1. Meaning and frequency of *niddâ* in the Hebrew Scripture

Meaning/Theme	Frequency	Percentage	Passage
Menstrual Flow	15	51.7%	Lev 12:2, 5; 15:19, 20, 24, 25x3, 26x2, 33; 18:19; Ezek 18:6; 22:10; 36:17.
General Impurity/ Abomination	9	31%	Lev 20:21; Ezek 7:19-20; 16:33; Zech 13:1; Lam 1:17; Ezra 9:11x2; 2 Chr 29:5.
Purification (water)	5	17.3%	Num 19:9, 13, 20-21; 31:23.
Total Occurrences	29	100%	

the third, and the most common, menstrual flow or expulsion of blood. This noun developed from describing the expulsion of blood represents the state of menstrual impurity itself, and refers to general impurity and abomination. Milgrom observed:

---

1. Jacob Milgrom, *Leviticus* 1-16, AB 3 (New York: Doubleday, 1991), 744-745.

In addition, *niddâ* came to refer not just to the menstrual discharge but to the menstruant herself, for she too was "discharged" and "excluded" from her society not by being kept at arm's length from others but, in many communities, by being banished to and quarantined in separate quarters.[2]

There are three additional terms related to menstruation: the word "*dāwâ*" describes menstrual sickness; the word "*zûb/zôb*" has the basic meaning of "flow, gush, issue, discharge" and has the idea of flowing liquid, like the normal and abnormal genital discharges; and the noun "*māqôr*," which is in most cases figurative, although the literal meaning is fountain. It is used twice in the phrase "fountain of blood," referring to menstruation. Tables 2-4 give the usage and frequency of each of these three words.

Table 2. Meaning and frequency of *dāwâ* in the Hebrew Scripture

Meaning	Frequency	Percentage	Passage
Mental Feeling	7	53.8%	Is 1:5; Jer 8:18; Ps 41:3; Job 6:7; Lam 1:13, 22; 5:17.
Menstrual Sickness	4	30.8%	Lev 12:2; 15:33; 20:18; Is 30:22.
Diseases (of Egypt)	2	15.4%	Deut 7:15; 28:60.
Total Occurrences	13	100%	

Table 3. Meaning and frequency of *zûb/zôb* in the Hebrew Scripture

Meaning/Theme	Frequency	Percentage	Passage
Genital discharge (normal and abnormal)	31 [16x man, 12x woman, and 3x both]	56.4% [29.1%, 21.8%, 5.5%]	Lev 15:2x2, 3x3, 4, 6, 7, 8, 9, 11, 12, 13x2, 15, 19x2, 25x4, 26, 28, 30, 32, 33x2; 22:4; Num 5:2; 2 Sam 3:29.
Description of the Promised Land: "*flowing with milk and honey.*"	19	34.5%	Exod 3:8, 17; 13:5; 33:3; Lev 20:24; Num 13:27; 14:8; 16:13, 14; Deut 6:3; 11:9; 26:9, 15; 27:3; 31:20; Josh 5:6; Jer 32:22; Ezek 20:6, 15.
Movement of water in a stream	5	9.1%	Is 48:21; Jer 49:4 (blood); Ps 78:20; 105:41; Lam 4:9 (blood).
Total Occurrences	55	100%	

Table 4. Meaning and Frequency of *māqôr* in the Hebrew Scripture

Meaning	Frequency	Percentage	Passage
Poetic - Source (of life): goal of prudent action	8	44.4%	Zech 13:1; Prov 5:18; 10:11; 13:14; 14:27; 16:22; 18:4; 25:26 (negative).
Poetic: God the Source of Life	4	22.2%	Jer 2:13; 17:13; Ps 36:9; 68:27.
Fountain (of blood): Menstruation	2	11.1%	Lev 12:7; 20:18.
Poetic: Dry fountain (Judgment)	2	11.1%	Jer 51:36; Hos 13:15.
Figuratively - Fountain: Reproduction organ	1	5.6%	Lev 20:18.
Poetic - Figuratively: Fountain of tears (eyes)	1	5.6%	Jer 8:23.
Total Occurrences	18	100%	

2. Jacob Milgrom, *Leviticus* 17-22, AB 3A (New York: Doubleday, 2000), 745.

The Biblical Laws of *Niddah*

The biblical laws of *niddah* are a part of the Purity Laws described in Leviticus. Jiří Moskala observed in his doctoral dissertation[3] that there are seven thematic sections of Leviticus 11-15 which all deal with various forms of impurity. These seven sections fall into four categories: dietary laws, childbirth, skin diseases and mildew, and genital discharges (see Table 5). Milgrom believed these sections have been ordered according to the seriousness of the impurity and the decreasing length of their purification.

Table 5. The seven thematic sections of Leviticus 11-15

Category	Thematic Section	Biblical Reference	Length of the Purification
1	1. Dietary Laws	Lev 11:1-47	The unclean animal is permanent unclean
2	**2. Childbirth**	**Lev 12:1-8**	40 or 80 days
3	3. Skin Diseases	Lev 13:1-46	x+8 days
	5. Purification Sacrifices	Lev 14:1-32	
	4. Mildew and Mold	Lev 13:47-59	7days: if unclean => destroyed if inactive => wash + 7 days if healed => wash => clean
	6. Purity Rules: House	Lev 14:33-57	7 days: if active => remove infection + 7 days if active => destroy if inactive => clean
4	**7. Genital Discharges**	**Lev 15:1-33**	**Man:** Long-term, x+8 days / Short-term, 1 day
			Woman: Short-term, 7 days / Long-term, x+8 days

- Each section elaborates on the laws of clean and unclean introduced by Lev 10:10.
- Each section is introduced by the formula: "The Lord said to Moses (and Aaron)" (Lev 11:1; 12:1; 13:1; 14:1; 14:33; 15:1).[4]
- Each section ends with the concluding formula: "These are the regulations concerning/for" (Lev 11:46; 12:7; 13:59; 14:32; 14:57; 15:32).[5]
- The sections are ordered according to the decreasing length and seriousness of their purification

It is important to emphasize that Table 5 shows that there are several sources for impurity and that none of them is the result of human activities. An unclean animal cannot be blamed for being unclean in the same way as a woman cannot prevent her monthly menstruation. This suggests there is nothing inherently wrong with being ritually unclean. A person is not bad or immoral for being impure. In fact, every human, ranging from the High Priest to the next door neighbor, goes through the cycle of cleanness and impurity. It might come as a surprise for most Christians to know that Jesus, by this definition, was probably impure at least several times in his lifetime.[6] It should also be clear from this list that

3. See Jiří Moskala, *The Laws of Clean and Unclean Animals in Leviticus 11: Their Nature, Theology, and Rationale (an Intertextual Study)*, ATSDS 4 (Berrien Springs, MI: Adventist Theological Society, 2000), 167-168.

4. Moskala pointed out that the introduction formula is missing in the fourth section (Lev 13:47), but the delimitation is based on the clear change of topic: uncleanness related to mildew and mold. See Moskala, *Laws*, 168, n. 1.

5. Moskala observed that this concluding formula is used as the introduction formula in the fifth section (Lev 14:2). See Moskala, *Laws*, 168 n. 2.

6. Jesus would have become impure when burying his father, Joseph, and when touching lepers and dead people. He might even have had a natural genital discharge.

greater defilement is not necessarily an indication of less social worth. Making a distinction between holy and unholy, between clean and unclean, is all bound up with the Temple (Lev 10:10). A person would sin if he mixed the unclean or the unholy with the holy. It was not a sin to be ritually unclean, but it would become a sin if that person intentionally came in contact with the holy, such as the Temple or items belonging to the Temple. It is also important to acknowledge that the Israelite religion severed the link between impurity and the concept of demonic forces, a belief which was commonplace in the ancient world. From a struggle between the gods and demonic deities, the issue became a question of obedience or defiance of God's commandments.[7]

Leviticus 15:19-24

The appendix of this chapter shows Milgrom's structure of Leviticus 15. This outline of the chapter shows the different types of genital discharges that cause ritual impurity. It is important to note the chiastic structure which is centered around the union between man and woman, with male discharges covered in the first half of the chapter and the female equivalents in the second half. Leviticus 15:19-24 contains the following instructions about menstruation:

• *"If a woman has a discharge, and the discharge from her body is blood, she shall be set apart seven days."*

• *"Whoever touches her shall be unclean until evening."* Interestingly, the text does not mention what happens if she touches someone else. This suggests that she does not transmit impurity by her touch. Further support for this view can be made by referring to the case of abnormal male discharge. If such a person has rinsed his hands, he does not transfer his impurity to another individual. Since a man's case is considered more serious than that of a menstruating woman, it could be assumed that this rule would also hold true for the woman.

• *"Everything that she lies on [bed] during her impurity shall be unclean; also everything that she sits on [chair] shall be unclean. Whoever touches her bed shall wash his clothes and bathe in water, and be unclean until evening. And whoever touches anything that she sat on shall wash his clothes and bathe in water, and be unclean until evening."* It is interesting that only the bed and her chair are singled out since they are the only two items which would have had prolonged potential contact with the women's discharge. This is a further indication that things she touches for a limited time with her hands would not be rendered unclean.

• *"If anything is on her bed or on anything on which she sits, when he touches it, he shall be unclean until evening."* This indicates that for an object to function as a carrier of impurity, it has to be on the bed or the seat she is sitting on. It implies that as soon as the women leaves the seat or the bed, the object will no longer be a carrier.

---

7. Jacob Milgrom, *Numbers*, JPS Torah Commentary (Philadelphia: Jewish Publication Society of America, 1990), 344-346.

•*"If any man lies with her at all, so that her impurity is on him, he shall be unclean seven days; and every bed on which he lies shall be unclean."* This case is most likely referring to an unintentional act where both people are surprised by an early discharge. This view would harmonize with the prohibition given in Lev 18:19 and Lev 20:18 which forbids intercourse with a menstruating woman. Regardless of the reading, the man would become unclean and would be prohibited from touching sacred objects and entering sacred space.

Although changing clothes and bathing in water is not specifically mentioned among the instructions regarding menstruation, it can be assumed. In all other cases of temporary impurity, the person goes through a purification process which includes washing clothes or changing clothes followed by a purifying bath in order to become clean. This assumption fits with the later Jewish tradition of the Mikvah and the indication that Bathsheba's famous bath was at the conclusion of her menstrual period (2 Sam 11:2, 4).

It is also implied from this passage that a menstruating woman remained in her home, but was not isolated from her family, as was common in some of the neighboring cultures.[8] If she had been isolated, there would be no need for giving laws concerning the transfer of impurity to the people sharing her living space. This passage does not leave any indications that she lived anywhere else than in her home. This point is once more supported by the Bathsheba story. She was having her purification bath in her home inside the city since David was able to observe her from the roof of his palace.

The two other cases involving female discharge of blood are abnormal female discharge (Lev 15:25-30) and childbirth (Lev 12). Both of these cases build on the normal female discharge with added length of impurity and added sacrifice to complete the purification. Table 6 gives the length of separation and the purification rites for each case of female impurity, listed according to the seriousness/length of the impurity.

Table 6. *Niddah* – Length of separation and purification rites

Case	*Niddah*	Key Biblical References	Length of Uncleanness	Purification Rites	Sacrifice[9]	Categories of Uncleanness
1	Uncleanness after Childbirth	Lev 12:1-8	Boy: 7+33 days Girl: 14+66 days	Bathing Laundering Evening	1 bird 1 bird/lamb	Temporary (Acquired)
2	Abnormal Female Discharge	Lev 15:25-30	x+ 7 pure days	Bathing Laundering Evening	1 bird 1 bird	Temporary (Acquired)
3	Normal Female Discharge	Lev 15:19-24	7 days	Bathing Laundering Evening	—	Temporary (Acquired)
4	Marital Intercourse	Normal Lev 15:18	Until evening	Bathing Laundering Evening	—	Temporary (Acquired)
		Menstruating Lev 15:24	Man = Woman 7 days	Bathing Laundering Evening	—	Temporary (Acquired)

---

8. See, e.g., Kathleen O'Grady, "Menstruation," *Encyclopedia of Women an World Religion* 2:649-652; Emily E. Culpepper, "Zoroastrian Menstruation Taboos: A Women's Studies Perspective," in *Women and Religion: Papers of the Working Groups in Women and Religion 1972-73*, ed. Judith Plaskow and Joan Arnold Romero (Missoula, MT: Scholar's Press, 1974), 204; William Robertson Smith, *Lectures on the Religion of the Semites*, Elibron Classics Series (1894; repr., Chestnut Hill, MA: Adamant Media Corporation, 2005), 446-448; Milgrom, *Leviticus 1-16*, 763-765, 949-952.

Leviticus 12 - Childbirth[10]

Leviticus 12, which deals with the regulations concerning impurity after child-birth, spells out two additional regulations relating to normal female discharge. This is inferred from the blood connection between the two passages:
- "She shall not touch any hallowed thing," (v. 4b)
- "nor come into the sanctuary until the days of her purification are fulfilled." (v. 4c)

It is important to note that there are no indications in the text that the child became impure through the birth process or the touch from the mother during her period of impurity. The mentioned purification activities are related only to the woman. This is one more break from the neighboring cultures, Greek, Anatolian, Hittite, Babylonian, and Egyptian,[11] which all considered both the mother and child impure and in need of purification.

A close reading of this passage gives an indication that the mother could proceed with normal sexual contact with her husband and was considered pure after the first stage of her purification process. The only remaining prohibition during the second phase of the purification process was to avoid contact with the holy: the Sanctuary and objects related to that sphere. This issue, however, was hotly debated by later Jewish sects.[12]

Leviticus 18:19 and Leviticus 20:18

The last prohibition given concerning the menstrual period, with its analogs, is found in Leviticus 18:19 and is repeated in Leviticus 20:18. It is a prohibition against sexual relations with a menstruating woman. These two verses are unique since they appear in a list of moral prohibitions and not in a list of purity regulations as in the previous cases. It is important to note that this ban is only connected with sexual relations and not with the Temple. Hyam Maccoby observed that "intercourse with a menstruant is the only way of incurring impurity that is also a forbidden act. Every other way of incurring impurity is free from sin, since impurity in itself is not sinful."[13] Maccoby pointed out that the ritual laws intersect with the moral laws in the law of *niddah*. Therefore, the law of *niddah* is both a purity law and a moral law.

Leviticus 18 deals with laws concerning illicit sexual practices, and these prohibitions hold the central stage of the chapter (see Milgrom's outline of Leviticus 18 in the appendix).[14] The prohibitions against forbidden sexual relations are divided into two sections: the first section defines the relationships which would be considered as incestuous; the second section lists an additional five

---

9. The first bird for sin offering and the second bird/lamb for burnt offering.

10. See Appendix for a structure of this chapter.

11. Milgrom, *Leviticus 1-16*, 762-764.

12. The Karaites, Samaritans, and Falashas were all of the opinion that sexual contact could not take place before the second stage of the purification was completed. See Milgrom, *Leviticus 1-16*, 748.

13. Hyam Maccoby, *Ritual and Morality: The Ritual Purity System and Its Place in Judaism* (New York: Cambridge University Press, 1999), 38.

14. Milgrom, *Leviticus 17-22*, 1516-1517.

sexual practices. They are sexual relations with a menstruating woman (probably the wife, an accepted sexual partner), the neighbor's wife, male homosexuality, and bestiality. The list also includes a prohibition against offering up children to Molek.[15]

Leviticus 20 gives a list of serious offenses that the people of Israel should avoid. According to Milgrom's outline of the chapter (see appendix),[16] the list of penalties for sexual violations is the central section in this chapter. These penalties are listed according to the severity of the punishment of the crimes. The first set of violations carries the death penalty; the second group, the penalty of kārat; and the last section, the penalty of childlessness.

The penalty for violating the prohibition against intercourse during the menstrual period is the penalty of kārat (v. 18e). This case law repeats the activity causing this penalty thrice as if to underscore the seriousness of the act which brought this penalty. The penalty of kārat is the same penalty prescribed for breaking the prohibitions in Leviticus 18 (v. 27-29). This is a divine penalty different from the death penalty executed by man (Lev 20:2-3). This divine penalty befalls either the guilty person or his descendants (Num 16:33 [‖ ’ābad]; Mal 2:12; Ps. 103:13), since it is a removal of the entire family line so his name will disappear among the people. Milgrom made the case that this penalty could also relate to the afterlife, which would be in line with the personal usage of the verb. This would mean that the penalty would remove his name both in this world and the world to come.[17]

The ultimate result from breaking the prohibitions in Leviticus 18 and Leviticus 20 is expulsion from the land. If they follow these regulations, they will continue to be a separate people who behave differently (have their unique culture) from that of the neighboring cultures. God's argument is that if you behave like my people, I will treat you as My people and you will stay in My holy land, but if you behave like the people of Canaan you will also meet their destiny (Lev 18:3-5, 24-30; 20:22-26). This point is driven home by Ezekiel, who lists intercourse with a menstruating woman as one of the causes for the Babylonian exile (Ezek 18:6; 22:10).

Tables 7-9 summarize the regulations given in the Hebrew Scripture concerning the state of niddah. Table 7 lists the prohibitions, Table 8 gives the activities which transmit impurity, and Table 9 indicates the activities which the menstruant is not barred from.

Table 7. Prohibitions during the menstrual period as outlined in Leviticus

Case	Prohibition	Reference
1	Go to the Sanctuary	Lev 12:4b
2	Touch anything Holy – Any object that belongs to the Devine Sphere[18]	Lev 12:4c
3	Intercourse	Lev 18:19; 20:18

15. It could be argued that sexual relations belonging to this section are forbidden since they will not produce any offspring and would, therefore, break God's command to fill the earth. This argument is problematic since there are no biblical prohibitions against intercourse after menopause or with a barren woman (Sarah, Rebekah, Rachel, Manoah's wife, and Hannah).
16. Milgrom, Leviticus 17-22, 1728, 1743.
17. Milgrom, Numbers, 405-408.

62

Table 8. Activities which transmit impurity

Case	Activity	Reference
1	Intercourse: -The man obtains the impurity of that of a menstruating woman	Lev 15: 24, 33
2	Her bed / Lying in her bed	Lev 15: 20a, 21, 26a, 27
3	Her chair / Sitting in her chair	Lev 15: 20b, 22, 26b, 27
4	Touching her: contact with her body, **not** with her clothes	Lev 15:19c
5	Only if an object is on the bedding on which the menstruating woman **is reclining** or on the chair on which she **is sitting** can the object function as a carrier of impurity	Lev 15: 23

Table 9. Activities not barred from the menstruant

Case	Activity	Reference
1	Touching anyone and anything -Her hands **do not** transmit impurity, only the items she sits and lies on =>She can prepare her family's meals and perform the necessary household chores	Lev 15: 19c, 20, 26
2	Remain in her home => not isolated from her family	Lev 15:20-22, 26-27 (implied)

Concluding Remarks Concerning the Biblical Laws

The above regulations concerning the laws of forbidden sexual practices and the concept of *niddah* should not be surprising. Forbidden sexual relations and periods when intercourse with an accepted partner is off limits fit very well within the "freedom-with-limitations" culture God established for His Holy people. Before the fall, humans could eat from every tree in the garden except from one. After the fall, "the plants of the fields" were added to their food menu, but animals were off limits. After the flood, humans were permitted to eat meat, but only that of clean animals. They also had to remove all the blood from the meat before eating it. God also enforced limitations on work and the produce of humans' work. Humans can work every day but one, which belongs to God (Exod 20:8-11; Deut 12-15), and all the produce belongs to them, except for 10% which belongs to God. All aspects of humans are regulated by God: food, work/income, and procreation, reminding humans of God's sovereignty and humans' own limitations.

Table 10 shows all the narrative passages in the Bible where *niddah* plays a role. The first case is in Genesis, which recounts the story of Rachel who has stolen her brother's household idols. The second is the well-known bath of Bathsheba and the following affair with David in 2 Samuel. The third records Mary's purification after the birth of Jesus. The last is the narrative about the woman who had been bleeding for 12 years and was healed by Jesus. There is also one passage which alludes to a man's impurity. In 1 Samuel 20:26, King Saul assumed that David was unclean since he was not present at the feast.

18. A person has to be in the state of ritual purity in order to touch anything belonging to the Divine sphere: see Gen 31:34-35 (Rachel and Laban's household idols); Lev 7:19-20 (Well-being offering); Num 9:6 (Paschal offering); Lev 22:3-9 and Num 18:11, 13 (Priestly prebends); Deut 26:14 (Tithes); 1 Sam 21:5-6 (David and the holy bread).

Table 10. *Niddah* and biblical narrative

Case	Reference	Character	Narrative
1	Genesis 31:33-35	Rachel	Rachel and Laban's household idols
2	2 Samuel 11:2, 4	Bathsheba	David commits adultery with Bathsheba
3	Luke 2:22-39	Mary	Purification right after childbirth, 40 days after giving birth to Jesus
4	Mk 5:25-34 Luke 8:43-48	Woman with abnormal female discharge	Sick for 12 years and was healed when touching the hem of Jesus' garment

Second Temple Period/Rabbinic Judaism

In the period following the recording of the *niddâ* laws in Leviticus, the term evolved from a narrow definition of the menstrual discharge to include the menstruant herself. This term was also used by Ezekiel (36:17) and Ezra (9:10-11) as a metaphor for moral impurity and degradation. These two changes were possibly triggered by the destruction of the First Temple. This greatly impacted the woman's daily life and her status in society. She regularly became the "discharged," the one that should be avoided during her menstrual period. This led many sects of the Second Temple period to quarantine the woman during her period in separate quarters to protect the larger community from the impurity.[19]

Not much is known about the purification bath following the menstrual period before the Second Temple and Rabbinical periods apart from the case mentioned above. It was during this period that many of the laws and regulations concerning the construction of the *mikva'ot* and its water were formed and later written down in a separate tractate of the Mishnah.[20] It also became necessary for the woman to perform the ritual of the Mikvah in order to be considered pure (b. Šabb. 64b). Over time, the ritual nature of the bath was emphasized. Today, a woman has to be completely clean before she enters the pool. She has to immerse herself, fully, three times and each immersion has to be accepted as completed by a witness. She would also recite a blessing of intention between the first and the second immersion.[21] The importance of the mikvah is seen in Jewish law, which states that building a mikvah takes precedence above the building of a Synagogue.[22]

Complex laws concerning *niddah* developed during the Second Temple period and the following Rabbinical period. In fact, a whole tractate of the Mishnah was devoted to this topic. One complicated issue dealt with in this tractate was the fact

---

19. It is known that the following Jewish communities imposed quarantine on the woman during her menstrual period and after childbirth: Arabians, Samaritans, Karites, Falashas, Sectarians of Qumran, and within certain Rabbinic communities. See, Milgrom, *Leviticus 1-16*, 765 and 11QTemple 48:14-17.

20. Although the Mishnah was not completed before the end of the second century C.E., it reflects early traditions. This is supported by archaeological excavations at Qumran, Masada, and Jerusalem in which several Mikva'oth following the laws recorded in the Mishnah have been discovered. For a summary of the mikveh in Judaism, see David Kotlar, "Mikveh," *Encyclopaedia Judaica* (2007), http://www.encyclopedia.com/article-1G2-2587513881/mikveh.html.

21. For information about ritual immersion in the mikveh during *niddah*, see Blu Greenberg, *On Women and Judaism: A View from Tradition* (Philadelphia: Jewish Publication Society of America, 1981), 109-111.

22. Michael Kaugman, *Love, Marriage, and Family in Jewish Law and Tradition* (Northvale, NJ: Jason Aronson, 1992), 212.

that not every female discharge was considered unclean. Therefore, detailed laws developed to help a person to determine which discharge was clean and which was impure (b. Nid. 19a-20b). Unfortunately, these laws became so complex that women had to rely on expert examination. In order to simplify the regulations and leave the decision in the hands of the woman, women themselves, with the support of the Rabbis, created the idea of 7 white days, by combining the laws of *niddah* with that of the *zavah*. This meant that the seven-day total period of her impurity was increased to seven clean days in addition to the days of menstruation.[23]

The Second Temple period saw the appearance of several new Jewish sects, which gave a new plurality to Judaism. The different sects tended to differ in their interpretations and practices of Jewish laws, which became a source of tension. To generalize, the Qumran community was probably the strictest sect while the Rabbis were on the liberal side, especially the school of Hillel. Hannah Harrington observed that one reason for this was the Essene's classification of Jerusalem as a Temple city, while the Pharisees tried to make the laws operable within a Gentile society.[24] It is important to note that the Rabbis living in Israel were much more conservative than the Rabbis from Babylon on this issue. Commenting on Gen 31:35, Nachmanides wrote about a view on the menstruating woman which makes a drastic break from the Priestly laws and Rabbinic Judaism.[25] It is speculated that it reflects the view of the Karaites or an unknown Jewish sect of this time period:

> In ancient days menstruants kept very isolated for they were ever referred to as *niddoth* [literally, excluded ones] on account of their isolation since they did not approach people and did not speak with them. For the ancients in their wisdom knew that their breath is harmful, their gaze is detrimental and makes a bad impression. . . . And the menstruants dwelled isolated in tents where no one entered, just as our Rabbis have mentioned in the *Baraita* of Tractate Niddah: "A learned man is forbidden to greet a menstruant. Rabbi Nechemyah says, 'Even the utterance of her mouth is unclean.' Said Rabbi Yochanan: 'One is forbidden to walk after a menstruant and tread upon her footsteps, which are as unclean as a corpse; so is the dust upon which the menstruant stepped unclean, and it is forbidden to derive any benefit from her work.'"[26]

The destruction of the Second Temple had a seismic effect on Judaism and the law of *niddah*. Without the Temple, all the purity laws of the Hebrew Scripture

---

23. Rachel Biale, *Women and Jewish Law: The Essential Texts, Their History, and Their Relevance for Today* (New York: Schocken Books, 1995), 152-153.

24. Hannah Harrington concluded: "In comparing the rabbinic understanding of impurity of discharges with that of the sectarians at Qumran, I find a much less stringent interpretations of Scripture among the Rabbis. . . the sectarians of Qumran excluded all women (not just menstruating women) from Jerusalem, regard even excrements as defiling, and declare a three-day impurity period for those with seminal emissions. Hence, the Rabbis, viewed in contrast to their own contemporaries, were not seeking to intensify the Bible's purity rules but were trying to make them operable within a Gentile society. The sectarians, by contrast, are found, partly due to their strict, unbendable interpretation of Scripture, in the Judean desert, isolated from the world." See Hannah K. Harrington, *The Impurity Systems of Qumran and the Rabbis: Biblical Foundations* (Atlanta: Scholars Press, 1993), 260.

25. See Michael Goldman, "Baraita De-Niddad," in *Encyclopaedia Judaica*, CD-ROM edition, ed. Judaica Multimedia (Shaker Heights, OH: Judaica Multimedia, 1997) and Biale, *Women and Jewish Law*, 169-172.

26. Ramban (Nachmanides) and Charles B. Chavel, *Commentary on the Torah: Genesis*, trans. Charles B. Chavel (New York: Shilo Publishing House, 1971), 387-388.

previously tied to the Temple became obsolete or were reapplied.[27] The general understanding was that the law of *niddah* was no longer a part of the public life;[28] only the prohibition against intercourse during the menstrual period was still applicable since it was a moral law. This is the reason why all biblical laws referring to male discharges disappeared and are no longer observed in Judaism. The laws concerning *niddah* recorded in Leviticus 12 and 15 were only applicable within the marriage, and the laws which developed after the destruction of the Temple had the purpose of lessening the temptation for intercourse between husband and wife during her menstrual period. This is why a couple should sleep in separate beds, avoid physical contact, and perform activities associated with the intimate relations[29] between husband and wife.[30] The woman was only untouchable by her husband, not by other people. This also explains why a woman goes to the Mikva for her first time when she prepares for her wedding; this assumes that pre-marital sex is out of the picture.

The common Halakhic view was that a menstruating woman could enter and take part in the Synagogue service since it was of no consequence if people came in contact with her.[31] An impure person could even touch the Torah scroll, the most sacred item, since it is immune to impurity. The legal reasoning goes that since everyone is in a state of impurity due to the lack of the ashes of the *red heifer*, touching something impure does not make a difference. If you are impure, you are impure. The strongest argument for this view was that the Synagogue should not be equated with the Temple, and the laws related to it should not be carried over to the Synagogue. This is the argument found in the *Sefer HaPardes*, legal rulings which grew out from the school of Rashi:

> And there are women who avoid entering the synagogue while they are menstruating, and also avoid touching a Torah Scroll and this is a needless stringency, which they need not observe. For why should they act this way? If it is because they think that the sanctity of the synagogue is the same as that of the Holy Temple, then even after immersion why may she enter? . . . And if it [the Synagogue] is not the same as the Holy Temple, let them enter! What is more, we are all impure and nevertheless enter it. From this we may derive that the synagogue is not the same as the Holy Temple and the menstruant may enter it. However, the synagogue is still perceived as a place of purity for them, and therefore they act in a proper and praiseworthy manner.[32]

---

27. The process of reapplying and broadening the scope of the biblical purity laws had already started in the Second Temple Period (inferred from archaeological findings) and were the cause for much debate between the many religious groups (reflected in the multiple religious/historical sources). See Eyal Regev, "Non-Priestly Purity and Its Religious Aspects According to Historical Sources and Archaeological Findings," in *Purity and Holiness: The Heritage of Leviticus*, ed. Marcel Poorthuis and Joshua Schwartz (Boston: Brill, 2000), 223-244.

28. Jeffrey Robert Woolf, "Medieval Models of Purity and Sanctity: Ashkenazic Women in the Synagogue," in *Purity and Holiness: The Heritage of Leviticus*, ed. Marcel Poorthuis and Joshua Schwartz (Boston: Brill, 2000), 267.

29. There are three activities the *niddah* could not perform of all the domestic activities: (1) filling his wine cup, (2) washing his face, hands, and feet, and (3) preparing his bed. These three activities were considered by the Rabbis to characterize the special relation in a marriage (b. Ketub. 61a). See also Rashi, Responsa, No. 336.

30. Biale, *Women and Jewish Law*, 158-160.

31. The legal code compiled by Rabbi Joseph Caro (1488-1575 C.E.), records the following custom: "All persons who are impure read the Torah, and recite the Shema, and pray [in the synagoue]." Joseph Caro, *Shulhan Arukh, Orah Hayyim* 84:1. Translated and Quoted in Biale, *Women and Jewish Law*, 168.

32. Rashi and C. L. Ehrenreich, eds., *Sefer Ha-Pardes:Liturgical and Ritual Work Attributed to Rashi* (Budapest: Bi-Defus ha-Ahim Kattsburg, 1923), 3. Translated and quoted in Woolf, "Medieval Models of Purity and Sanctity," 268.

It is interesting to note that although Rashi argued from a legal position that a menstruating woman should not be excluded from the synagogue, he, nevertheless, admired women who voluntarily avoid the synagogue, thereby showing their high regard for the Holy sphere. He considered the custom noteworthy, as long as it is a voluntarily decision made by each individual woman.[33]

The Ashkenazic Jews, however, saw a strong link between the synagogue and the Temple, even going as far as equating the two. This view influenced the halakhic tradition relating to the laws of *niddah*. Since the Synagogue was still considered a place of purity, and they believed that the Synagogue had replaced and taken the place of the Temple, they would argue the purity laws were still applicable, at least for the woman. In the same way as an impure woman was prohibited from entering the Temple, it became a common practice for the woman to stay away from the Synagogue during her menstrual period.[34] The Ashkenazic view is succinctly summarized by Rabbi Moses Isserles (1525-1572 CE) from Cracow, Poland:

> Now there are those who have written that a *niddah*, during the days that she sees [blood] ought not to enter the synagogue, nor pray or mention the Holy Name or touch a [Torah] book (Hagahot Maimoniyot) and there are those who say that she is permitted [to do] all those things; and that is the [correct] essence [of Halakhah] (Rashi, on Hilkot Niddah). But the custom in these countries is according to the first view. And during the 'white days' it is the custom to permit even in the places where they are accustomed to rule more strictly. On the High Holidays and Yom Kippur, she can enter the synagogue like other women for otherwise it would cause her great sorrow to remain outside while everyone congregates [in the synagogue].[35]

The halakhic tradition concerning the concept of *niddah* was also highly nuanced in the period after the destruction of the Second Temple. This period saw the light of two main halakhic traditions, the Ashkenazic and the Sephardic.[36] The Ashkenazic tradition was generally stricter than that of the Sephardic, which is also reflected in their differing attitudes towards the case of *niddah*. The Ashkenazic attitude changed, however, towards the end of the eleventh century when the Babylonian Talmud became the exclusive authority of halakhic law. This caused the need for harmonization between the Talmudic law and the Ashkenazic tradition, which was seen in Rashi's comment above.[37]

---

33. It could be argued that his high regard for this tradition may be due to his Ashkenazic background and his need to harmonize the legal rulings regarding *niddah* found in the Talmudic and the Ashkenazic legal traditions. By saying this, he potentially harmonized the law and his tradition. He may also have been a supporter of women themselves having a conclusive voice in determining practices that concerned them.

34. Biale, *Women and Jewish Law*, 167.

35. This comment by Moses Isserles is recorded as a gloss to Rabbi Joseph Caro's ruling in *Shulkhan Arukh, Orah Hayyim* 84:1. Translated and quoted in Biale, *Women and Jewish Law*, 168.

36. Abraham Heschel suggested that the Sephardic culture and religious attitudes are very different from the Ashkenazic. The Sephardic Jews were extraverted and were in dialogue with the larger world, while the Ashkenazic Jews were introverted and kept to themselves. The Sephardim aspired to personal and rationally defined perfection and tried to take a middle course, avoiding extremes. The Ashkenazim were ever striving for the undefinable perfection, always seeking higher [see Abraham Joshua Heschel, *The Earth Is the Lord's: The Inner World of the Jew in East Europe* (Woodstock, VT: Jewish Lights, 1995)]. It could be argued that these two opposing mind sets are also reflected in the attitude towards the menstruant. The Sephardic rationale led them to conclude that the laws of *niddah* did not apply to the Synagogue, while the Ashkenazic ever-striving quest for heightened spirituality in their daily life led them to equate the Synagogue with the Temple and thereby reapply the laws of *niddah* to the Synagogue.

37. For further reading about the law of *niddah* in the Ashkenazic tradition, see Woolf, "Medieval Models of Purity and Sanctity."

Niddah and the Muslim Parallel

In Islam, there is only one primary text dealing specifically with the case of a menstruant. The rest of the picture must be pieced together by the many hadiths, oral traditions attributed to Muhammad concerning this topic. The key text in the Koran is recorded in the second chapter, which was the first surah revealed at Medinah:

> They will question thee concerning the monthly course. Say: 'It is hurt; so go apart from women during the monthly course, and do not approach them till they are clean. When they have cleansed themselves, then come unto them as God has commanded you.' (Koran, 2:222)

The following regulations are extrapolated from this verse:
• Sexual intercourse is prohibited during the menstrual period.

• The menstrual period is completed by a (ritual) bath. A bath could be taken as soon as her bleeding had stopped since there is no stated minimum of maximum length of time for her menses.

• The woman should be in a state of purity for sexual intercourse.

• The regulation seems to have a moral aspect since God is taken into the picture, stating that when the wife is pure, the husband can have sexual contact with her as God has commanded.

• The regulation seems to be connected to her pain, so this might be the reason her husband should not have intercourse with her.

These regulations are very similar to the laws given about *niddah* in the Hebrew Scripture. In the same way as the biblical law of *niddah* was both a purity law and a moral law, so is the regulation given in the Koran. There is, however, one major difference. In the Hebrew Scripture, the sexual impurities were contagious, and even after the removal of the ritual aspect of these laws, following the destruction of the Temple, the husband was still required to abstain from physical contact with his wife during her monthly menstruation. Islam, on the other hand, did not have any regulations preventing physical contact. Although the above passage seems to indicate a husband should not have any contact with his wife during her menstrual period, the text implies that the issue is sexual contact. This point is driven home by hadiths going back to two of Muhammad wives, Aisha and Maymuna:

> Aisha said, "The Prophet and I used to wash from one vessel when we were both ritually unclean from sex. . . . I would drink when I was menstruating, then hand it to the Prophet and he would put his mouth where mine had been and drink; and I would eat flesh from a bone when I was menstruating, then hand it to the Prophet, and he would put his mouth where mine had been. . . ." She also said: "The Prophet would recline in my lap when I was menstruating, then recite the Quran." She also said: "The Prophet said to me, 'Get me the mat from the mosque,' and when I said I was menstruating, he said, 'Your menstruation is not in your hand.'" Maymuna said: "God's Messenger used to pray in a woolen garment which was partly over him and partly over me while I was menstruating." (Baghawi, Mishkat al-Masabih 3.13)[38]

---

38. Francis E. Peters, *Judaism, Christianity, and Islam: The Classical Texts and Their Interpretation*, 3 vols. (Princeton, NJ: Princeton University Press, 1990), 2:325-326.

These hadiths indicate that normal physical contact with a menstruating woman does not transfer impurity. A hadith going back to a third wife of Muhammad, Umm Salama, goes a step further; she reported:

> Umm Salama reported: While I was lying with the Messenger of Allah (may peace be upon him) in a bed cover I menstruated, so I slipped away and I took up the clothes (which I wore) in menses. Upon this the Messenger of Allah (may peace be upon him) said: Have you menstruated? I said: Yes. He called me and I lay down.[39]

Furthermore, the only part of a woman's body which should not be touched during her period was her genitalia. This is an important difference since the Rabbinic Sages required the couple to sleep in separate beds. This underlines the effort among the sages to limit sexual temptation by building "fences" around the main prohibition: intercourse during the menstrual period. In Islam, they believed men would be able to control their desire and the only way an impure person could transfer his impurity is through sexual contact.

There were grave consequences, however, if a Muslim man was not able to control himself during this period. An-Nawawi states:

> If a Muslim believes it is permissible to have intercourse with his menstruating wife, he becomes an unbelieving apostate. If he does it, not thinking that it is permissible, but out of forgetfulness or not knowing that it is forbidden or not knowing that his wife was menstruating, then there is no sin or expiation upon him. If he does it on purpose, knowing that it is forbidden, he has committed a grave sin and must repent.[40]

This is a close parallel to the Leviticus law code, which gave the penalty of *kārat* to a couple who broke the regulation on purpose, while if it happened unintentionally, the husband should also be unclean for seven days.

There are also regulations concerning post-childbirth bleeding and women with prolonged flows of blood in the Muslim legal code. The period of impurity lasted until she had stopped bleeding or a maximum duration of forty days.[41] This is similar to the forty days in Judaism, although the biblical period could not be shortened. There are no indications within the Muslim traditions that the period of impurity was lengthened if the woman gave birth to a girl. In this sense, the Rabbinic Jewish regulations are in one way closer to the Muslim regulation. When changing the regulations for normal menstruation, a change was also made to the case of childbirth. The new regulations had the woman start counting her 7 or 14 days following her 7 white days.

---

39. Imam Abul-Husain Muslim, "The Book of Menstruation (Kitab Al-Haid)," in *Sahih Muslim*, trans. Abdul Hamid Siddiqui (Book 3, no. 581). Online: http://theonlyquran.com/hadith/Sahih -Muslim/?volume=3&chapter=1

40. Sayyid Sābiq, *Fiqh-Us-Sunnah*, 1:71b. Online: http://hadithcollection.com/fiqh-ussunnah/ 328-Fiqh-us%20Sunnah%20Section%2005.%20Menstruation/20782-fiqh-us-sunnah-volume -001-purification-and-prayer-fiqh-1071b.html

In the Shia tradition, the man has to pay a penalty in order to be forgiven for such a deed. The amount the man would pay in the weight of gold coins in grams when asking for forgiveness from God is as following: (1) if he has intercourse with her during the early days of her menstruation he pays 3.457g, (2) if he has intercourse during the middle of the days of her menstruation he pays 1.729g, and (3) if he has intercourse during the last days of her menstruation he pays 0.865g. See http://www .al-shia.org/html/eng/books/beliefs/islam-says/islam-says.htm.

41. Sayyid Sābiq, *Fiqh-Us-Sunnah*, 1:70a.

In the case of prolonged flows of blood, Islam teaches that she should act according to her customary period and count the remaining as days of prolonged blood flow. She should wait her customary days and then perform her ritual bath and be counted clean although her bleeding has not stopped. She is then free to do all the activities, including intercourse, which a ritually pure person can perform.[42] Table 11 shows a comparison between the length of uncleanness for the different cases of impurity in Judaism and Islam.

Table 11. Length of uncleanness in Judaism and Islam

Case of *Niddah*	Hebrew Scripture	Rabbinic Judaism	Islam
After Childbirth	Boy: 7+33 days	Boy: 7 white days +7	$x \leq 40$ days
	Girl: 14+66 days	Girl: 7 white days +14	
Abnormal Female Discharge	$x + 7$ days	$x+7$white days	Same as normal female discharge
Normal Female Discharge	7 days	$1+(5 \leq x)+7$ white days	x days
Marital Intercourse	Until evening	—	Tartibi Ghusl - Sequential wash Ertimasi Ghusl - Full immersion

Two more passages in the Koran have relevancy for a menstruating woman and they deal with different forms of impurity and the relation with the spiritual realm:

O believers, draw not near to prayer when you are drunken until you know what you are saying, or *defiled* – unless you are traversing a way – until you have washed yourselves (Koran, 4:43)

O believers, when you stand up to pray wash your face, and your hands up to the elbows, and wipe your heads, and your feet up to the ankles. *If you are defiled, purify yourselves*; but if you are sick or on a journey, or if any of you comes from the privy, or *you have touched woman*, and you can find no water, then have recourse to wholesome dust and wipe you faces and your hands with it. (Koran, 5:6)

The following regulations are extrapolated from this verse:

• During the menstrual period a woman should cease to carry out her prayers, both obligatory and voluntary.[43]

• If in a state of defilement, a full purification bath is required before prayers.

It could be argued that abstaining from prayers when in a state of ritual impurity refers to the prayer services in the Mosque. If this is the case, it parallels the biblical law that an impure person cannot enter the holy sphere before the days of purification are fulfilled. There are, however, no indications in the Hebrew Scripture that prevent a person from praying when in the state of ritual impurity.

---

42. Sayyid Sābiq, *Fiqh-Us-Sunnah*, 1:72-74d.
43. See also Shaih Al-Bukhari, *Shaih Al-Bukhari*, trans. M. Muhsin Khan (vol. 1, Book 6, no. 327, 329), http://sahih-bukhari.com/Pages/Bukhari_1_06.php

Table 12 shows ten Muslim prohibitions during the menstrual period. In addition to the restrictions already mentioned, she was not allowed to fast, perform the circumambulation of the Ka'ba, read and recite the Koran, touch a copy of the Koran, remain in a Mosque, or be reckoned in a period of voluntary continence. In addition, her husband could not divorce her during her menstrual period. These prohibitions do not have any counterpart in Rabbinic Judaism.

Table 12. Ten Muslim prohibitions during the menstrual periods

	Prohibition	Reference
1	Performance of prayer	Kur'ān, IV, 46; V,6
2	Obligatory prayer [not valid]. She does not need to make up missed prayers when her menstrual period has ended	Sahih Al-Bukhari, vol. 1, p. 196, no. 327
3	Fasting: The obligatory fast (fast during the month of Ramadan) will have to be complete when her menstrual period has ended	Sahih Muslim, vol. 1, pp. 47-48, no.142
4	Circumambulation of the Ka'ba	Sahih Al-Bukhari, vol. 1, pp. 177-178, no. 293; Sahih Muslim, vol. 2, p. 607, no. 2791
5	Reading/Reciting the Quran [If needed she is permitted to recite 1-2 verses to ward off evil]. However, the prohibition does not apply to other books which contain Quranic passages such as commentaries of the Holy Quran or works of Islamic jurisprudence	Fiqh-us-Sunnah, vol. 1, pp. 52d-53
6	Touching a copy of the Quran	Kur'ān, LVI, 77-9
7	Remaining in a Mosque [or even walking through it unless of necessity]	Fiqh-us-Sunnah, vol. 1, pp. 54
8	Sexual contacts [intercourse]	Kur'ān, II, 222
9	Formal repudiation of a wife [the divorce would be invalidated]	Sahih Al-Bukhari, vol. 7, p. 129, no. 178; Sahih Muslim, vol. 2, p. 756, no. 3457.
10	Being reckoned in a period of voluntary continence	

There are four major ritual impurities which require a full bath in order to become ritually clean in Islam. These are (1) after sexual intercourse, whether it is actual or imaginary; (2) after a woman's monthly menstruation; (3) once bleeding stops following childbirth; and (4) after death, before the funeral service.[45] A ritual bath was also required for each of these cases in Ancient Judaism, but due to the destruction of the Temple and the resulting irrelevancy of the impurity laws associated with the Temple, only cases 2 and 3 are still valid. There are two ways of performing the obligatory bath (Ghusl) required by a major ritual impurity; the first method is sequential and the second, a full submersion in water. In order for the obligatory bath to be valid, two essential requirements need to be met. First, it is required that a statement of intent to perform Ghusl is given since it is a ritual fulfilling God's command. Second, the water should reach every part of the body. These two requirements are the same in Judaism for the Mikvah ritual to be accepted. Although there is no parallel to the sequential Ghusl in Judaism, it should be noted the number three is a part of both rituals. To perform the Mikvah ritual, the

44. The ten prohibitions are outlined by the jurist Ibn Qudama (d. 1223 CE). See Peters, *Judaism, Christianity, and Islam*, 2:326.

45. Kamil Y. Avdich, Survey of Islamic Doctrine (Cedar Rapids, IA: Unity Publishing, 1979), 32.

woman has to immerse three times in the pool. A person performing the sequential bath must wash his hands three times and pour water on his head three times.

Conclusion

Comparing the two monotheistic religions, it becomes apparent that they have many similarities. The prohibition against intercourse during the menstrual period is shared by both of them, and intentionally breaking this restriction has grave consequences. The essential requirements for the obligatory bath by full submersion are almost identical to the Mikvah ritual. There are, however, three fundamental differences between Judaism and Islam. First, the impurity rules are still valid in Islam, but not in Judaism. Second, the length of impurity is much shorter in Islam for the same case of impurity. Third, Muslims do not consider impurity contagious, and physical contact between husband and wife is therefore not avoided during the menstrual period. It is interesting to note that although the impurity laws are no longer relevant in Judaism, the laws regulating the menstrual period are more stringent than in Islam.

The Biblical Law of *Niddah* and Christianity

The case of a menstruating woman was also a debated issue in the Christian Church. A careful reading of Luke-Acts depicts Jesus and other important figures in the Early Church as law-abiding and conscious of purity laws,[46] but not much interest was shown in the purity laws recorded in Leviticus 12-15 by the earliest Christian commentaries and none of these chapters were included in the liturgical cycle.[47] Over the course of time, however, the interest in these chapters increased, and commentaries elaborated and dealt with them in more detail. Peter Tomson observed that "since the days of the Church Fathers, Christian exegetes have maintained that with the coming of Jesus, purity laws were abolished along with all Jewish rituals."[48] This view could be due to the Christian tendency to define themselves as non-Jews. When reading the Early Church Fathers, it becomes apparent that the Church leaders felt a need to restrict the appeal of Judaism and even to discredit the religion. It could be argued that this was a reaction against the Church members' attraction to Judaism and that many were following Jewish practices. Peter Tomson argued that Origen's (184-254 CE) and Chrysostom's

---

46. Bart J. Koet, "Purity and Impurity of the Body in Luke-Acts," in *Purity and Holiness: The Heritage of Leviticus*, ed. Marcel Poorthuis and Joshua Schwartz (Boston: Brill, 2000), 98-105.

47. Gerard Rouwhorst, "Leviticus 12-15 in Early Christianity," in *Purity and Holiness: The Heritage of Leviticus*, ed. Marcel Poorthuis and Joshua Schwartz (Boston: Brill, 2000), 181-182.

48. Peter J. Tomson, "Jewish Purity Laws as Viewed by the Church Fathers and by the Early Followers of Jesus," in *Purity and Holiness: The Heritage of Leviticus*, ed. Marcel Poorthuis and Joshua Schwartz (Boston: Brill, 2000), 74. This is the basis for the opinion voiced in the Didascalia Apostolorum (c. 200-250 CE). This is a collection of pseudo-apostolic church laws originating from Syria presented as having been written by the Apostles at the time of the Council of Jerusalem (Acts 15). In chapter 26 [vi, 22], it is argued that normal fluids of sex and intercourse in marriage are clean, and that men should not reject women during their menstrual periods:
Do not load yourselves again with that our Lord and Saviour has lifted from you. And do not observe these things, nor think them uncleanness; and do not refrain yourselves on their account, nor seek after sprinklings, or baptisms, or purification for these things. . . . And when (your wives) suffer those issues which are according to nature, have a care that, in a manner that is right, you cleave to them. (R. Hugh Connolly, *The Didascalia Apostolorum* [Oxford: Clarendon, 1929], Online: http://www.bombaxo.com/didascalia.html)

(347-407 CE) strong attack on the purity laws indicates the popularity of purity observance in the third century Church.[49] Gerard Rouwhorst suggested: "From the third and the fourth century onwards, the celebration of the Eucharist by the priest as well as the reception of the Holy Communion by monks and laymen became bound by certain purity rules which in a considerable degree are based upon some passages of Leviticus."[50] One example of this view is found in the second Canon of Dionysius, the Archbishop of Alexandria (247 CE). This letter gives the following answer to an inquiry made by the Bishop Basilides: "Menstruous woman ought not to come to the Holy Table, or touch the Holy of Holies [the body and blood of Christ], nor to churches, but pray elsewhere."[51]

Two competing views on ritual purity, issued in the sixth and the seventh century, became authoritative for Church leaders in the following centuries. The seemingly lenient view was held by Pope Gregory the Great (540-604 CE). He argued that the biblical purity laws should be read on a spiritual level rather than in a literal way. From this, he held that each person was free to make up his/her own mind on these laws. Rob Meens summarized:

> For Gregory it was inward convictions that counted, not outward behavior. Women should make up their own mind: when they decided not to approach the body and blood of the Lord when menstruating, they were to be praised, but when they got carried away by the love of the sacred mystery they were not to be prevented from going to church or from receiving communion.[52]

While women were not prevented from attending church or communion during menstruration, they were certainly not given a neutral option. If she decided to abstain, she was praised, but if she chose to participate, she was not—a rather loaded choice. The view held by Pope Gregory I is a good example of *benevolent sexism* which is discussed in the chapter "The Dawn of the Battle of Sexes – Genesis 3:16."

Meens also observed that regarding the case of entering church after sexual intercourse, Gregory thought that one should always wash and keep out of church for a short time. This was based on the idea that sexual intercourse was caused by man's desire and that there is no desire without sin.[53] A person in such a mindset should not be in the church, since a person should be in the "right state of mind" when he is in God's presence.[54]

The strict ruling was given by Archbishop Theodore of Canterbury (668 CE). Meens wrote:

> [Theodore] ruled in his collection of penitential decisions that a woman who entered a church during forty days after giving birth, should do penance for three weeks. The

---

49. Tomson, "Jewish Purity Laws," 75-78.

50. Rouwhorst, "Leviticus 12-15 in Early Christianity," 184.

51. Dionysius of Alexandria, *The Letter of the Blessed Dionysius, the Archbishop of Alexandria to Basilides the Bishop* (*NPNF2* 14:600).

52. Rob Meens, "'A Relic of Superstition': Bodily Impurity and the Church from Gregory the Great to the Twelfth Century Decretists," in *Purity and Holiness: The Heritage of Leviticus*, ed. Marcel Poorthuis and Joshua Schwartz (Boston: Brill, 2000), 284-285.

53. Meens, "A Relic of Superstition," 285.

54. Gregory classified ejaculation during sleep into three categories: natural superfluity or illness, gluttony, and evil thoughts. The third case is the most severe and a priest in this situation should abstain from saying Mass and receiving communion. It is not clear if this opinion also relates to non-priests. If it does, it is a very similar attitude as that of the Muslim tradition.

archbishop also forbade menstruating women from entering the church or from receiving Holy Communion, a provision applying to laywomen and nuns alike. If women nevertheless contravened this, they had to do penance by three weeks of fasting.[55]

It is important to note that Theodore was not only prohibiting a woman from taking part in the Communion service in the period of her menstruation, but he considered it a sin in need of penance if broken. It should also be noted that Theodore followed the laws of Leviticus 12 prohibiting a woman to enter the church the first forty days after childbirth. However, he made no differentiation between the birth of a boy or a girl.

Bishop Timothy of Alexandria gave the following answers to the questions proposed to him concerning Bishops and Clerics at the Third Council of Constantinople in 680-681 CE. He followed the strict ruling of Theodore:

Question V. Can a man or woman communicate after performing the conjugal act over night?
Answer. *No. 1 Cor Vii. 5.*
Question VI. The day appointed for the baptism of a woman; on that day it happened that the custom of women was upon her; ought she then to be baptized?
Answer. *No, not till she be clean.*
Question VII. Can a menstruous woman communicate?
Answer. *Not until she be clean.*
Question VIII. Ought a woman in child-bed to keep the Paschal fast?
Answer. *No.*
Question XII. If a layman asked a clergyman whether he may communicate after a nocturnal pollution?
Answer. *If it proceeds from the desire of a woman, he ought not: but if it be a temptation from Satan, he ought; for the tempter will ply him when he is to communicate.*
Question XIII. When are man and wife to forbear the conjugal act?
Answer. *On Saturday, and the Lord's day; for on those days the spiritual sacrifice is offered.*[56]

From this, it becomes apparent that the strict ruling, represented by Theodore and Timothy, follows closely the purity regulations of Leviticus relating to the Temple. A woman cannot take part in public religious life as long as she is menstruating or during the forty days following childbirth. It was not acceptable to have intercourse over the weekend or the night before taking part in the communion service. It could be assumed that the religious leaders considered the Church, especially the communion service, to have the same sanctity as the Jewish Temple. The custom of purification and churching is a further support of this view. This custom was rooted in the Jewish purity laws and followed the example of Mary, Jesus' mother, when she visited the Temple as the fulfillment of the stipulations of Leviticus 12. The celebration of the first visit that the mother made to the parish church after childbirth, after she had completed her required "religious quarantine," became a very popular ritual. The popularity only started to fade at the onset of the Reformation when the Protestants denounced it as Judaizing. The ritual ceased to exist in the Catholic Church in the 20th century.[57]

55. Meens, "A Relic of Superstition," 286.
56. Timothy of Alexandria, *The Canonical Answers of Timothy* (NPNF[2] 14:612-613).
57. Charles Caspers, "Leviticus 12, Mary and Wax: Purification and Churching in Late Medieval Christianity," in *Purity and Holiness: The Heritage of Leviticus*, ed. Marcel Poorthuis and Joshua Schwartz (Boston: Brill, 2000), 295-309.

The tension in the Church caused by the Jewish purity laws started when the Jesus movement shifted from a purely Jewish sect to become a mainly Gentile church. The center of the issue was the Church's relationship with Judaism and the role of the Jewish laws in the Messianic era. Gregory the Great's supposedly more lenient views on ritual purity provided little competition with those of Theodore. Ultimately, it was Theodore's stricter ruling that gained the upper hand and had the most influence on the Church and its doctrines. The Reformation stirred the debate about the role of the Jewish purity laws and most of the reformers made a sharp distinction between the old and the new covenant, living under the purity laws of the Hebrew Scripture and being free under the law of grace in the Christian era.

Conclusion

This study demonstrates that the biblical law of *niddah*, and its Muslim parallels, played and still play an important role in Judaism, Islam, and during periods of Christian history. This leads to the question: Do Christians today need to adhere to these laws?

The following statement by William J. Webb represents the common attitude among modern Christian toward the concept of *niddah*:

> One has to admit that we no longer apply the menstrual-intercourse prohibition today. We might generally comply with the text simply out of personal preference and comfort levels (This kind of compliance may be considered the same as taking a shower after intercourse and semen emission. While we may still do the text, we would not feel under any covenant obligation to do so). However, if by mutual consent, a husband and wife have intercourse during menstruation, would they be sinning today? Likely not. The New Testament has repealed the cultic impurity laws.[58]

Webb was, in a sense, both accurate and inaccurate. It is accurate that the cultic impurity laws are no longer applicable, especially after the destruction of the Jewish Temple.[59] However, the conclusion that a couple is therefore free to have intercourse during menstruation is problematic. As noted earlier in this chapter, the issue of *niddah* also appears in lists of moral prohibitions. In other words, the regulations of *niddah* belong both to the set of moral laws and the set of impurity laws. The cultic impurity aspects have been canceled, but the moral aspect could still be in effect. If one aspect is no longer relevant, it does not automatically nullify the other.

This chapter also shows that a violation of the prohibition against intercourse during the menstrual period gave the penalty of *kārat*, a penalty that God himself would execute. It would not only affect the person and his family in this life, but it might also have consequences for the afterlife. It also noted that these prohibitions were not exclusively given to the Jews, but the context of Leviticus 18 and 20 deals with the sins the people committed who lived in the land before them. God told them that if his people behaved in the way of the Canaanites, they would suffer the same consequence: expulsion from the land. This point was driven home by Ezekiel, who listed intercourse with a menstruating woman as one of the causes for the Babylonian exile (Ezek 18:6; 22:10). An important observation of this study is that non-Israelite people were also judged by their adherence to this issue. Since God cannot judge a people or a person by laws which do not apply to them, the law of *niddah* may need to be considered a universal law.

---

58. William J. Webb, *Slaves, Women & Homosexuals: Exploring the Hermeneutics of Cultural Analysis* (Downers Grove, IL: InterVarsity Press, 2001), 169.

59. It is important to note that the Rabbis also considered the cultic purity laws obsolete since the Temple was destroyed, although some of the laws were reapplied.

The *niddah* prohibitions were important to the Jews both before and after the destruction of the Temple and they were adhered to by Muslims. They played an important role in the Christian Church, but, again, what of modern Christians? How should they regard *niddah* prohibitions? There is certainly room for further discussion regarding this issue, both by religious organizations and by individual couples. This is outside the scope of this study, which is to explore the broader contextual picture and discuss some pertinent criteria that should be included in both those discussions.

Crucially, women need to have a very strong voice in these discussions, both within religious organizations and in their own homes. Women should not be forced into decisions that will contribute to their physical and moral discomfort, nor should they be given loaded choices as in the case of Pope Gregory I.

As the cultic aspect of this prohibition no longer applies and many modern Christian faiths do not regard their church as a replacement for the Jewish temple, the laws of *niddah* may no longer belong in the public square either—in the Church or in society at large. Instead, it could well be that the application of this prohibition is merely a personal issue that is best left to be negotiated by individual couples, and renegotiated in the future if their needs change with great sensitivity shown by both parties so neither feel pressured or forced to do something he or she is uncomfortable with. Whatever is decided, menstruation should not affect or limit how women or their husbands are treated or the roles they can perform within their churches or within their greater cultural context.

APPENDIX

Leviticus 12 - Childbirth

The following structure of Leviticus 12 is based on John Hartley's outline of the chapter.[1]

Introduction (v. 1)
    A. Regulations concerning separation following childbirth (vv. 2-5)
        1. Birth to a boy (vv. 2-4)
            a. Time of impurity (v. 2) = Status as for normal female discharge
            b. Instruction about circumcision (v. 3)
            c. Additional time of impurity and her new status (v. 4)
        2. Birth to a girl (v. 5)
            a. Time of impurity (v. 5a) = Status as for normal female discharge
            b. Additional time of impurity and her new status (v. 5b)
    B. Sacrifices for purification (vv. 6-7a)
    C. Summary Statement (v. 7b)
    D. Appendix: Alternative sacrifices for a poor woman (v. 8)

Leviticus 15 - Genital Discharges

Milgrom gave two different structures for Leviticus 15.[2] The first structure presents the four main cases of genital discharges framed by an introduction and a conclusion. Each of these cases are introduced by the Hebrew particle *kî* (Lev 15:2, 16, 19, 25). The second structure recognizes that v. 18, which deals with marital intercourse, is the central focus of the chiastic structure (ABC - X - C'B'A'). The key sections for this chapter have been highlighted in each of the structures.

Structure 1

    A. Introduction (vv 1-2a)
        B. Male discharges, long-term (vv 2b-15)
        1. Definition (vv 2b-3)
        2. Consequences (vv 4-12)
        3. Purification by sacrifice (vv 13-15)
        C. Male discharge, short-term (vv 16-18)
        1. Semen emission (vv 16-17)
        2. Intercourse (v 18)
            C'. Female discharge, short-term (vv 19-24)
            1. Menstruation (vv 19-23)
            2. Intercourse (v 24)
        B'. Female discharges, long-term (vv 25-30)
        1. Definition (v 25)
        2. Consequences (vv 26-27)
        3. Purification by sacrifice (vv 28-30)
        [Consequences for the Sanctuary and for Israel (v 31)]
    A'. Summary (vv 32-33)

---

1. See John E. Hartley, *Leviticus*, WBC 4 (Dallas: Word, 1992), 166.
2. Milgrom, *Leviticus 1-16*, 904-905.

Structure 2

A. Introduction (vv 1-2a)
  B. Abnormal male discharges (vv 2b-15)
    C. Normal male discharge (vv 16-17)
      X. Marital intercourse (v 18)
    C'. Normal female discharge (vv 19-24)
  B'. Abnormal female discharge (vv 25-30)
   [motive 9v 31)]
A'. Summary (vv 32-33)

Leviticus 18 - Illicit Sexual Practices

The first structure gives an outline of Leviticus 18, observing that the prohibitions concerning forbidden sexual relations are the center of the chiastic structure. The second outline shows the location of the prohibition against sexual relations with a menstruating woman in the list of prohibitions. The third structure, dealing with forbidden acts, shows that the prohibitions falls into two major sections. The first, is ordered by family relationships. The second, focuses on forbidden acts. The case of intercourse with a menstruating woman falls into the second group. The key sections for this chapter have been highlighted in each of the structures.

Structure 1[3]

Introduction (vv. 1-2a)
A. Opening exhortation (vv. 2b-5)
  1. YHWH's self-introduction (v. 2b)
  2. Two prohibitions against following foreign practices (v. 3)
  3. Two exhortations to keep God's laws (vv. 4-5)
   X. The prohibitions (vv. 6-23)
A'. Closing exhortations (vv. 24-30)
  1. Admonition with historical substantiation (vv. 24-25)
  2. Threat of expulsion and excision (vv. 26-29)
  3. Exhortation to heed these prohibitions (v. 30a)
  4. YHWH's self-introduction (v. 30b)

Structure 2[4]

The Prohibitions - Forbidden Sexual Relations (vv. 6-23)
I. Prohibitions against incests (vv. 6-18)
 A. Primary relationships (vv. 6-17a)
   1. General law (v. 6)
   2. With a mother (v. 7)
   3. With a father's wife (v. 8)
   4. With a half-sister (v. 9)
   5. With a granddaughter (v. 10)
   6. With a stepsister (v. 11)
   7. With a paternal aunt (v. 12)
   8. With a maternal aunt (v. 13)
   9. With an aunt, wife of father's brother (v. 14)

---

3. Milgrom, *Leviticus 17-22*, 1516-1517.
4. Milgrom, *Leviticus 17-22*, 1523-1524.

10. With a daughter-in-law (v. 15)
11. With a brother's wife (v. 16)
12. With a mother and daughter (vv. 17a)
B. Additional prohibitions (vv. 17b-18)
    1. Against sexual relations with a woman and her granddaughter (v. 17b)
    2. Against marriage to a wife's sister (v. 18)
II. Prohibitions against certain sexual practices and sacrifice to Molek (vv. 19-23)
    A. Against sexual relations with a menstruating woman (v. 19)
    B. Against sexual relations with a neighbor's wife (v. 20)
    C. Against offering up children to Molek (v. 21)
    D. Against male homosexuality (v. 22)
    E. Against bestiality, male and female (v. 23)

Structure 3[5]

The Prohibitions - ordered by family relationship:
Relatives: the closest relatives (vv. 7-11) => parents' closest relatives (vv. 12-14) => relatives by marriage (vv. 15-16) => wife's closest relatives (vv. 17-18)

Non-relative: **intercourse with a menstruating woman (v. 19)** | intercourse with a married woman (v. 20) | Molek worship (v. 21) | Sodomy (v. 22) | Bestiality (v. 23)

Leviticus 20 - Serious Offenses

The first structure gives an outline of Leviticus 20, observing that the penalties for violating the sexual prohibitions are located at the center of the chiastic structure. The second outline shows that the penalties are grouped into prohibitions carrying the death penalty, the excision penalty, and the childlessness penalty. Intercourse during menstruation falls into the second group of penalties. The third structure gives the elements of this case law. The last structure notes that the penalties are ordered by punishment based on the severity of the crime. Intercourse during menstruation falls into the middle category. The key sections for this chapter have been highlighted in each structure, except for Structure 3, which is the key case-law for this study.

Structure 1[6]

A. Worship of chthonic gods (Molek and necromancy, vv. 1-6)
  B. Sanctification (v. 7)
    C. Exhortation for obedience (v. 8)
      X. Penalties for violation (vv. 9-21)
    C'. Exhortation for obedience (vv. 22-25)
  B'. Sanctification (v. 26)
A'. Worship of chthonic gods (necromancy, v. 27)

5. Milgrom, *Leviticus 17-22*, 1526.
6. Milgrom, *Leviticus 17-22*, 1728.

Structure 2[7]

Penalties for sexual violations (vv. 9-21)

The Fundamental Cause: Dishonoring Parents (v. 9)
A. Prohibitions carrying the *death penalty* (vv. 10-21)
    1. Adultery (v. 10)
    2. Incest (vv. 11-12)
        a. Sex with father's wife (v. 11)
        b. Sex with daughter-in-law (v. 12)
    3. Male homosexuality (v. 13)
    4. Marriage of a man to a woman and the woman's mother (v. 14)
    5. Bestiality (vv. 15-16)
        a. By a male (v. 15)
        b. By a female (v. 16)
B. Prohibitions carrying the *excision penalty* (vv. 17-19)
    1. Marriage to sister (v. 17)
    2. Sex during menses (v. 18)
    3. Sex with paternal or maternal aunt (v. 19)
C. Prohibition carrying the *childlessness penalty* (vv. 20-21)
    1. Sex with uncle's wife (v. 20)
    2. Marriage to a sister-in-law (v. 21)

Structure 3[8]

V. 18
    Case: If a man lies with a woman during her sickness
    Reason: 1. and uncover her nakedness
               2. he has exposed her flow
               3. and she has uncovered the flow of her blood
    Penalty: Both of them shall be cut off from their people

Structure 4

The Penalties - ordered by Punishment, based on the severity of the crime:
    Death (vv. 10-21) => **Excision (vv. 17-19)** => Childlessness (vv. 20-21)

---

7. Milgrom, *Leviticus 17-22*, 1743.
8. The structure of the key verse for this study is based on John E. Hartley's observation that each case law is composed out of the following four elements: case, penalty, reason, and declaratory formula. The combination of these elements varies from case to case, and not every decree contains all these elements. See Hartley, *Leviticus*, 330.

The Rationale Behind the Homicide Law
in Numbers 35:30–34

Slaviša Janković

This study will analyze the texts on the homicide law that is embedded in the law of the cities of refuge found in Numbers 35:6-34. Based on this law, a murderer[1] is to be put to death by the hand of the blood avenger after proven liable for the crime through the testimony of at least two witnesses in a legal process (35:16-21, 30-31). If proven in the legal process that the killing took place inadvertently, the manslayer[2] is to stay in a city of refuge until the high priest's death (35:9-15, 22-28, 32).

This study proposes that the concluding remarks of the homicide law in Numbers 35:30-34 augment the rationale behind the law against homicide by stating that the murderer, through the shedding of blood, pollutes the land due to its misuse. In addition, it explains how the death of the high priest is a substitutionary redemption of a manslayer's life.[3]

Even though this law was essential for dealing with very complex and complicated cases of murder in Ancient Israel, it has not received much attention in

---

1. "This term will stand for a human being who deliberately kills another human being. This is not the only case of capital punishment since there are at least sixteen crimes that called for the death penalty in the Old Testament: kidnapping, adultery, homosexuality, incest, bestiality, incorrigible delinquency in a child, striking or cursing parents, offering a human sacrifice, false prophecy, blasphemy, profaning the Sabbath, sacrificing to false gods, magic and divination, unchastity, the rape of a betrothed virgin, and premeditated murder. In each case, where the evidence was clear and beyond a reasonable doubt, the death penalty was demanded." Raymond Westbrook, "Punishments and Crimes (OT and NT)," *ABD* 5:546-556; "*Numbers: 35:21 No Ransom for a Murderer?*," in *Hard Sayings of the Bible*, eds. Walter C. Kaiser Jr., et al., (Downers Grove, IL: InterVarsity Press, 1996), 170. Hobson, however, suggested an even longer list of twenty crimes punishable by capital punishment. G. Thomas Hobson, "Cut off (One's) People: Punitive Expulsion in the Torah and in the Ancient Near East" (paper presented at the Annual Meeting of the Biblical Law of the SBL. San Francisco, CA, 24 November 2011).

2. This term will stand for a human being who unintentionally kills another human being.

3. Jacob Milgrom, *Leviticus 1-16*, 3 vols., AB 3-3B (New York: Doubleday, 1991), 1:1082; Roy Gane, *Leviticus, Numbers*, NIVAC 3 (Grand Rapids, MI: Zondervan, 2004), 798-799.

scholarly circles. Scholars have studied it mainly within the context of and in relation to other laws and the binary concept of purity/impurity.[4]

This study will not address questions concerning the textual variations of Numbers 35:32, where the BHS uses the noun *kohēn* to refer to an ordinary priest, instead of the nominal phrase הכהן הגדל, which is used three times in the same chapter to designate the high priest (vv. 25. 28).[5]

In order to grasp the meaning of this law properly, one needs to have an understanding of certain concepts and theological and literal elements embedded in it, since these form the working context for this study. The following theological concepts/elements will be discussed throughout the three parts of this study: (1) the structure of the passage and identification of the main elements of the law, (2) reasons for the death penalty of a murderer, (3) the nature and function of blood in the Old Testament, (4) the definition of *kop̲er* and its prohibition, (5) pollution of the land by a murderer or a run-away manslayer, and (6) the function of the priesthood/high priesthood in the Pentateuch and the law of homicide.

The Structure of the Passage and Identification of the Main Elements of the Law

Numbers 35:9-34 contains stipulations on who can and cannot stay inside the cities of refuge after killing a human being. This passage is rooted in the previous homicide Pentateuchal texts, which also demand the death penalty for a murderer.[6] However, Numbers 35:26-28 broadens this law with additional regulations for manslaughter[7] and provides the rationale for it, which is found in the concluding verses 30-34.[8]

The structure of the passage clearly delineates its main components. Scholars have suggested several structures for this passage,[9] but the most detailed and defensible one has been suggested by Rolf P. Knierim and George W. Coats, which is as follows:

(4) Additional qualifications	30-34
(a) Ordinance for death sentences	30
a. Witnesses required	30a
b. Number	30b

---

4. Jacob Milgrom, *Numbers*, JPS (Philadelphia: Jewish Publication Society, 1990); Timothy R. Ashley, *The Book of Numbers*, NICOT 4 (Grand Rapids, MI: Eerdmans, 1993); R. Dennis Cole, *Numbers*, NAC 3B (Nashville, TN: Broadman & Holman, 2000); R. K. Harrison, *Numbers*, WEC (Grand Rapids, MI: Baker, 1992); Baruch A. Levine, Numbers 21-36, AB 4A (New York: Doubleday, 2000); Jonathan Klawans, *Purity, Sacrifice, and the Temple: Symbolism and Supersessionism in the Study of Ancient Judaism* (Oxford: Oxford University Press, 2006); Jay Sklar, *Sin, Impurity, Sacrifice, Atonement: the Priestly Conceptions*, HBM 2 (Sheffield: Sheffield Phoenix Press, 2005).

5. For further research on the variants, see Milgrom, *Numbers*, 295, 331.

6. The references are Exod 21:12-13 and Deut 19:1-13. Levine, *Numbers*, 599.

7. An unintentional killer must remain in the city of refuge until the high priest's death or the redeemer has the right to kill him/her in case he finds him/her out of the cities of refuge. Sklar, *Sin, Impurity, Sacrifice, Atonement*, 54.

8. Levine, *Numbers*, 548; Ashley, *Numbers*, 655; Rolf P. Knierim and George W. Coats, *Numbers*, FOTL 4 (Grand Rapids, MI: Eerdmans, 2005), 327; W. H. Bellinger, *Leviticus* and *Numbers*, NIB-COTS 3 (Peabody, MA: Hendrickson, 2001), 316.

9. Sklar, *Sin, Impurity, Sacrifice, Atonement*, 54; Gane, *Leviticus, Numbers*, 797-798; Levine, *Numbers*, 548; Cole, *Numbers*, 36-43; Ashley, *Numbers*, 2-3.

(b) Prohibition against ransom	31-34
a. Against ransom for murderer	31
b. Against ransom for manslayer	32-34
aa. Prohibition	32
bb. Reason	33-34
a. Prohibition against pollution	33-34a
b. Reason	34b[10]

The structure properly reflects the main postulates of the law, which are (1) death penalty for a murderer based on the testimony of at least two witnesses (v. 30), (2) ransom prohibited for both murderer's life (v. 31) and manslayer who leaves the city of refuge before the high priest's death (v. 32), and (3) breach of these laws will result in the pollution of the land (vs. 33-34). The ways to expiate (*kāp_ar*) the land include shedding the blood of a murderer/run-away manslayer or the natural death of the high priest in the case of manslaughter.

The manslayer is safe in the city of refuge and even though alive, he does not pollute the land.[11] However, if the manslayer leaves the place of refuge, this regulation will be abrogated and the pollution of the land will take place. This state of affairs would be unacceptable because the land of Israel is the dwelling place of God. Thus, its inhabitants must preserve its holiness and refrain from allowing the land to be polluted.[12]

Reasons for the Death Penalty as Punishment for A Murderer (v.30)

The premeditated killing of a human being is prohibited in the Decalogue and variations of the same prohibition are repeatedly found throughout the OT legal corpus (Exod 20:13, 21:12-13; Lev 24:17; and Deut 19:11-13). Based on Num 35:30-34 and Exod 21:14, a murderer was even deprived of the chance to seek protection by grasping the horns of the sacrificial altar or by escaping to the cities of refuge after the trial proved that they were liable for the act of murder.[13] This confirms that blood is equal to life in biblical texts. First, the repetition of the prohibition itself speaks for its importance based on the scholarly consensus that in biblical literature, repetition is used to emphasize important ideas.[14] Murder puts one in opposition to God's standards of living. Second, scholars have correctly

10. Knierim and Coats, *Numbers*, 324-327.

11. In the case of the manslayer, once he leaves the city of refuge his blood will expiate the land. He is safe and even though alive, he does not pollute the land if he is in the city of refuge.

12. Sklar, *Sin, Impurity, Sacrifice, Atonement*, 54; Gane, *Leviticus, Numbers*, 795-796.

13. Dónal P. O'Mathúna, "Bodily Injuries, Murder, Manslaughter," DOTP 90; Westbrook, "Punishments and Crimes (OT and NT)," 5:550-556.

14. Repetition is a structural element in historical narratives. John Sailhamer, *The Pentateuch as Narrative: A Biblical-Theological Commentary* (Grand Rapids, MI: Zondervan, 1992), 25. It is considered to be the most powerful means in biblical texts. J. P. Fokkelman, *"Genesis," in The Literary Guide to the Bible*, eds. Robert Alter and Frank Kermode, (Cambridge, MA: Belknap Press, 1987), 46. Its task is to emphasize what is important, remind the listener of the previous steps or actions, or sometimes, simply to impress. Laurence A. Turner, *Genesis*, RNBC (Sheffield: Sheffield Academic Press, 2000), 16.

postulated that, based on the Creation account in Gen 1:26-27, the importance of this prohibition emanates from the fact that humans are created in the image of God. This idea is also stated in another prohibition against killing found in Gen 9:6.[15] The number of witnesses necessary to warrant the legitimacy of a legal decision is also discussed in Deut 17:6.[16] Besides these two significant reasons for capital punishment for the murderer, there is another key insight presented in this law. In order to grasp why a murderer must be put to death, one must understand the concept of blood[17] in the Pentateuch because the shedding of blood seems inseparable from the act of murder.

The conceptual link between blood and v. 30 is also confirmed by the fact that the phrase הכה־נפש "one who strikes fatally,"[18] also used in this verse, is synonymous with the phrase לא נכּנּ נפש "shed no blood," used elsewhere in the OT to describe death (Gen 9:4-6).[19] Also, Jacob Milgrom also noted that the same syntactical construction, the verb *šāp_ak* accompanied with the noun *dām*, refers to the act of killing a person elsewhere in the OT.[20]

These synonymous terms occur in Gen 37:21-22[21] and depict the account of Joseph's brothers' attempt to kill him, or at least get rid of him. When Reuben understood that his brothers planned to kill Joseph, he said to them: "לא נכּנּ נפש" - "Let us not take his life." He further appealed to them and said: "אל־תשפכו־דם" - "Shed no blood."

Even inappropriately shedding an animal's blood brings guilt upon the perpetrator, as stated in Lev 17:4.[22] It seems that OT writers considered these two syntactical combinations as synonyms and both of them refer to the act of murder since the act of murder inevitably involved the shedding of blood. Thus, the death penalty for the murderer may be justified by the two points presented above, but it seems this conclusion regarding the homicide law points to an additional reason, namely that the land is polluted by blood (vs. 33-34). Therefore, the next step of the present study will address this idea.

15. O'Mathúna, "Bodily Injuries, Murder, Manslaughter," 90.

16. Levine, *Numbers*, 559. All of the laws of the ancient Near East require more than one witness in order to sentence one to death. James B. Pritchard, *Ancient Near Eastern Texts Relating to the Old Testament* (Princeton, NJ: Princeton University Press, 1955), 16; Ashley, *Numbers*, 655.

17. "This important word appears 360 times in the OT, most often in Lev (88 times) and Ezek (55 times), followed by Exo (29 times), Deut (23 times), and Psa (21 times)." S. David Sperling, "Blood," ABD 1:761-763; Paul Trebilco, "דם," *NIDOTTE* 1:963-966.

18. The idiomatic expression is a general term that refers to homicide, whether it is intentional or unintentional. This results from the fact that the same term is used in Num 35:15.30; these are the texts for both kinds of homicide. Levine, *Numbers*, 554.

19. Sperling, "Blood," 1:761-763.

20. 1 Sam 25:31; 1 King 2:31; 2 King 21:16, 24:4; Deut 19:10, 21:7; Prov 1:16, 6:17; Isa 59:7; Jer 22:3.17; Ezek 16:38; 18:10; 22:3. 4. 6. 9. 12. Milgrom, *Leviticus 1-16*, 1:710.

21. Sperling, "Blood," 1:761-763.

22. Jacob Milgrom, *Leviticus 17-22*, 3 vols., AB 3-3B (New York: Doubleday, 2000), 2:1456-1457.

The Nature and Function of Blood in the Old Testament[23]

Blood is related to both life and death in the OT; therefore, its meaning can be equivocal.[24] Shedding or spilling blood results in bloodguilt in the OT (Gen 4:10-11, 1 King 2:31, Hos 4:2).[25]

The intensity of the association between blood and life is prominent not just in the Hebrew Bible, but also in other Ancient Near Eastern texts, such as Ugaritic and Akkadian. This is especially true in poetic works where they are lexical pairs.[26] In the OT, Gen 9:4-6 validates this observation because in his conversation with Noah after the flood, God equated blood and life by prohibiting the eating of flesh with blood in it because the life of the flesh is in its blood. The Hebrew adverbial particle *'ak* emphasizes and intensifies this prohibition.[27] It should be rendered, "Indeed, you shall not eat flesh with its blood."

The same prohibition is repeated in Deut 12:23 with an even stronger emphatic construction. The Hebrew adverbial particle *raq* implies an emphatic meaning - "only,"[28] and should be translated as "only be sure that you do not eat blood." The reason for the prohibition is the same as in the previous text: blood is equal to life.[29] The purpose of repetitions in the Bible mentioned above is also valid in this case. These multiple repetitions of this prohibition also point to its importance within biblical material. The significance of blood, which embodies life, is the reason why it has been allotted to God by biblical legislation.[30] In addition, this fact is demonstrated by the use of emphatic and intensive lexical particles to forbid its consumption by humans.

Baruch Levine's definition of blood as a "vital fluid that empowers life" is well supported in the OT.[31] As long as it flows inside of living beings, they are

---

23. Only those features concerning blood in the Pentateuch relevant to the present study are analyzed under this subheading.

24. Gerhard Hasel, "Studies in Biblical Atonement-I: Continual Sacrifice, Defilement//Cleansing, and Sanctuary," in *The Sanctuary and the Atonement*, ed. Frank B. Holbrook (Silver Springs, MD: Biblical Research Institute, 1989), 90-92, 99; Sklar, *Sin, Impurity, Sacrifice, Atonement*, 103.

25. Trebilco, *NIDOTTE* 1:963-966. "The shedding of animal blood is allowed in OT law, but only through ritual slaughter. This blood is treated with great respect. It may not be consumed (Lev 17:10), and it plays an essential element in the sacrificial cult. The blood of the animal is not only shed, but it is also brought into contact with the holy that is symbolized, for example, by the altar or the mercy seat in the Holy of Holies." "Blood," *DBI* 99-101. An animal would be brought to the tent of meeting for slaughter and as a well-being offering, after the blood was dashed against the altar, the fat was burned, thus turning into smoke, the priest and the owner would take their part and they were permitted to eat the meat of the animal. Profane slaughtering was permitted only for clean wild animals (deer, clean wild birds), but in such cases, their blood was to be covered with earth (Lev 17:13). On the other hand, Deuteronomy 12 permits the profane slaughter of clean animals, wild and domestic, but requires that the animal's blood should be poured on to the ground like water. The background for this procedure regarding wild animals was that what offends God should be hidden from His sight. Gen 37:26; Deut 23:14; 1 Sam 26:20; Isa 26:21; Ezek 24:7-8; Job 16:18). Sperling, "Blood," 1:761-763.

26. Sperling, "Blood," 1:761-763.

27. "אַךְ," *HALOT* 2:45; "אַךְ," *BDB* 36.

28. "רַק," *HALOT* 2:1286; "רַק," *BDB* 956.

29. For more reasons for this conclusion see Milgrom, *Leviticus 1-16*, 1:706-707.

30. (Lev 3:2–4, 8–10, 13–15). Along with the blood, the fat also is considered an element that embodied life, but blood had primacy over fat because any nonfood use of the fat of dead and torn animals was permissible (Lev 7:24) while, in contrast, the blood of a slaughtered animal that had not been sacrificed had to be discarded (Deut 12:24). Sperling, "Blood," 1:761-763.

31. Levine, *Numbers*, 561-562.

alive, but as soon as they lose it, death immediately takes place.[32] These claims are confirmed even more so by the research of Charles Owiredu, whose doctoral dissertation centers around the idea that blood is strongly associated with both life and death.[33]

The preceding discussion is indicative of the multifaceted and complex character of blood in the biblical text. Blood is apparently related to two very opposite experiences, namely life and death. This paradoxical aspect of blood found in the OT will be addressed later in a subsequent part of the present study.

The Role of Blood in the Cultic Sphere

Blood is one of the essential elements in the OT sacrificial system. Its use is fundamental in many sacrifices. Thus, the person healed from a skin disease was anointed with blood and oil in order to be ritually clean (Lev 14:6-20). The consecration of the priest and altar was performed with blood (Lev 8:14-15, 23-30). In the process of the covenant-making ritual between Yahweh and the Israelites, the people were sprinkled with the "blood of the covenant (Exod 24:6-8; Zech 9:11).[34]

Blood was used to cleanse both the sacrificial altar (Lev 8:15, 16:18, Ezek 43:20) and the incense altar (Exod 30:10). It was also used during the ritual of the Day of Atonement. The blood of the sin offering purged sin from the Tent of Meeting, later from the temple (Ezek 45:18–20), and consecrated the sacrificial altar from the uncleanness of the people of Israel (Lev 16:18).[35]

It is difficult to say which of the above-mentioned functions of blood is the most important, but atonement for sin is certainly significant and probably the most prominent one. The importance and prominence of blood in the OT sacrificial system has consequently caused many researchers to extensively study this multifaceted element in the biblical text. Most notable is Baruch J. Schwartz' well-researched essay "The Prohibitions Concerning the 'Eating' of the Blood in Leviticus 17,"[36] in which he proposes that blood is assigned and designated by God for sin atonement and as such, is forbidden for human consumption. He even limited the rationale for this prohibition only to this reason.[37]

In addition, helpful research in the field of defilement/purification/atonement has been done by Roy E. Gane in his book *Cult and Character Purification Offering: Day of Atonement and Theodicy.*[38] An especially relevant chapter for the present study is "Blood or Ash Water: Detergent, Metaphorical Carrier Agent, or

---

32. Levine, *Numbers*, 561; V. P. Hamilton, "דם," *TWOT* 1:190-191.
33. Charles Owiredu, "Blood and Life in the Old Testament" (PhD diss., Durham University, 2004).
34. Trebilco, *NIDOTTE* 1:963-966.
35. Sperling, "Blood," 1:761-763; Trebilco, *NIDOTTE* 1:963-966.
36. Baruch J. Schwartz, "*The Prohibitions Concerning the "Eating" of the Blood in Leviticus 17*," in *Priesthood and Cult in Ancient Israel*, eds. Gary A. Anderson and Saul M. Olyan, JSOTSup 125 (Sheffield: JSOT Press, 1991), 34-66.
37. Schwartz, *The Prohibitions Concerning the "Eating" of the Blood in Leviticus 17*, 47-48. The same position with more a comprehensive survey on the use in Lev 17:11 might be found in Sklar, *Sin, Impurity, Sacrifice, Atonement*, 166-174; Sperling, "Blood," 1:761-763.
38. Roy Gane, *Cult and Character: Purification Offerings, Day of Atonement, and Theodicy* (Winona Lake, IN: Eisenbrauns, 2005).

Means of Passage?"[39] Gane answered this question by comparing the positions of Milgrom and Noam Zohar and examined the possibility of whether blood can be defiled by absorbing impurity from the sanctuary. One of his conclusions is that Lev 17:11 is not just a prohibition against eating the blood of the well-being offering, but is also a prohibition against eating blood in general.[40] These two studies confirm that ingesting blood is forbidden in the biblical texts in both cultic and non-cultic settings. An exclusive reason for the prohibition is the fact that God has strictly prescribed blood for the atonement of sin. In conclusion, textual references to blood in the cultic texts emphasize its cleansing or purifying feature. This feature of blood was used to change the status of various impure human conditions into pure ones, and mundane, common inanimate objects into holy, sacred ones.

Blood—The Cause of Pollution

Even though blood can save an individual from his/her sins through various expiating rituals and reverse the impure state of an individual into a pure one by various cleansing procedures, as proposed above, blood can also pollute or "make an individual" ritually unclean. The following is stated in Num 35:33: "You shall not pollute the land in which you are, for bloodshed pollutes the land, and the land cannot be atoned for on which blood has been shed, except by shedding the blood of the one who shed it." Actually, Milgrom claimed that this is the only way blood defiles, specifically, when it is spilled illicitly.[41] The same idea is found in Ps 106:38 and Lam 4:13-14. Besides these examples, which are related to moral impurity,[42] blood can also cause ritual defilement, as many examples in the biblical text show.

A woman is unclean after she gives birth to a child because of the flow of her blood (Lev 12:4-7) and she is also unclean during her menstrual period (Lev 15:19-24). Therefore, blood can also pollute in some cases, especially human blood (Ps 106:38; Isa 59:3; Lam 4:14).[43] The following quotation seems to be very accurate: "blood, whether due to violence or other ills, destroyed the cleanness of creation."[44]

In summary, there are various aspects of blood in the biblical text. As a result of the previous discussion, the following facts can be ascertained: (1) blood is a life-bearer, (2) blood is assigned by God to be used for crucial cultic reasons (cleansing from sin, consecration and atonement for sin), and (3) blood can pollute in some cases.

The first and the second features articulate the vital importance of blood, not only at the existential and biological level, but also at the religious level. The third feature expresses at first glance a negative connotation of blood. However, if one looks closer, especially in the context of Num 35:30-34, it becomes obvious

39. Gane, *Cult and Character*, 163-197.
40. For the method of reaching this conclusion see William K. Gilders, *Blood Ritual in the Hebrew Bible: Meanng and Power* (Baltimore, MD: Johns Hopkins University Press, 2004), 21-22. 168.
41. Milgrom, *Leviticus 1-16*, 1:749.
42. Moral and ritual impurity will be discussed later in this chapter.
43. Sperling, "Blood," 1:761-763; Trebilco, *NIDOTTE* 1:963-966.
44. "Blood," 100.

that the third feature confirms the previous two. Thus, besides the two reasons behind the homicide prohibition known from previous biblical texts, namely that blood is equated with life and the prohibition of shedding blood is included in the Decalogue, this law highlights the fact that blood, if unlawfully shed, pollutes the land. In the homicide law, it is the illicit use of blood that causes the defilement of the land.

The Definition of the *Koper* and Its Prohibition (vs. 31-32)

This section will address the questions of why *koper* is forbidden for the murderer and the run-away manslayer and what the definition of *koper* is in this text?

Theologians propose several definitions for this term. Jay Sklar has done the most recent and up to date study on this topic. He collected the opinions of important theologians, compared them, addressed their weak and strong points, and suggested his own understanding of this concept. Therefore, his work will be heavily consulted here.

The verb *kāpar* has been traditionally translated as "atone/expiate," but scholars have understood the nature of the act of atonement/expiation differently. Actually, there are four major positions on how the verb should be understood.

The first group of scholars appeal to the Arabic term *kafara*, which led them to understand atonement/expiation as a covering, i.e., the priest covers the sin or the sinner in order to save him from God's wrath. The second group suggests that the emphasis of the atonement/expiation is on the act of the worshiper's symbolic dedication of his life to holy things through the atonement process. The third group sees atonement as cleansing in at least some sin contexts (Lev 4, 5). The fourth group states that atonement should be understood as "ransom." The fourth view is the most accepted understanding. It is accepted by prominent scholars such as Johannes Herrmann, Herbert Brichto, Levine,[45] Adrian Schenker, Bernd Janowski, and Milgrom. All of these theologians claim that *kāpar* occurs as the denominative of *koper* in at least some passages. Milgrom illustrates the clearest example of this:[46]

> There are other cases in which the ransom (כֹּפֶר) principle is clearly operative. (1.) The function of the census money (Exod. 30:12-16) is *lekapper alnapšotekem* "to ransom your lives" (Exod. 30:16; cf Num. 31:50): here the verb *kipper* must be related to the expression found in the same periscope *koper napšo* "ransom for his life" (Exod. 30:12). (2.) The same combination of the idiom *koper nepeš* and the verb *kipper* is found in the law of homicide (Num. 35:31-33). Thus in these two cases, *kipper* is a denominative from *koper*, whose meaning is undisputed: "ransom" (cf. Exod. 21:30). Therefore, there exists a strong possibility that all texts than assign to *kipper* the function of averting God's wrath have *koper* in mind: guilty life spared by substituting for it the innocent parties or their ransom.[47]

45. Baruch A. Levine, *In the Presence of the Lord: a Study of Cult and Some Cultic Terms in Ancient Israel* (Leiden: Brill, 1974), 61. 67.

46. Sklar, *Sin, Impurity, Sacrifice, Atonement*, 47.

47. Milgrom, *Leviticus 1-16*, 1:1082; Ibid., *Studies in Cultic Theology and Terminology* (Leiden: E.J. Brill, 1983), 29-30.

Sklar used two steps to define *koper*. The first step is to search for the meaning by an exegetical analysis of the texts where *koper* is found[48] and the second is to compare *koper* with other terms in its semantic field.[49]

Concept-Oriented Approach. In the first step, Sklar exegeted eight passages (Exod 21:28-32; 30:11-16; Num 35:30-34; Ps 49:8-9; Prov 6:20-35; 1 Sam 12:1-5 and Amos 5:12; Isa 43:3-4; Job 33:24). Through this step, Sklar was able to develop criteria to formulate the definition of the *koper*.

Sklar's exegesis[50] disclosed the following pattern in the *koper* texts: (1) There is a guilty party, (2) There is an injured party, (3) The guilty party is being rescued, (4) Peace is being established to the damaged relationship between the guilty and injured party, and (5) The guilty party is totally dependent on the reaction of the injured party and on the acceptance or rejection of the *koper*.[51]

Exod 21:28 clearly follows the above-mentioned pattern. The regulation given in the main case[52] of the law does not obligate the owner of a goring ox to do anything, but the variation[53] does. The variation of this law states that the owner of the ox is responsible for the death of the person whom his ox gored and he along with his ox are sentenced to death unless someone provides a *koper* on the owner's behalf.[54] All elements of Sklar's exegesis are present in this case.[55] The injured party accepts *koper*, which would imply a lesser punishment and would prevent the owner from receiving the death penalty.

In Exod 30:11-16, the guilty party is any person who does not pay a ransom for his life. The injured party is God himself. The *koper* rescues the people of Israel (a life) from certain plague and also brings peace between God and the Israelites.[56] It is guaranteed that the *koper* will be accepted in this case and will presumably lessen the punishment.

Num 35:30-34 contains all these elements and an additional rule is added in this case, namely, the prohibition or non-acceptance of *koper*. The guilty party has to be put to death.[57]

In the case of Ps 49:8-9, there is no specific sin that results in death, but death simply comes to all people. However, the way the wicked face death (vs. 14) is

---

48. He called this the concept-oriented approach, which means that a particular term is studied within its own context. He himself was aware of the fact that this approach had major weaknesses: distinguishing the actual lexical sense of the word from concepts that are present in any given context in which a word is used. Sklar, *Sin, Impurity, Sacrifice, Atonement*, 48.

49. Sklar called this the field-oriented approach, which refers to searching two other nominal forms of two verbs, *padah* and *ga'al*. He was aware that many other forms could be considered in doing this, but these two occur in contexts that are the most similar to *koper*. Sklar, *Sin, Impurity, Sacrifice, Atonement*, 61.

50. For some insignificant exceptions to this pattern in some texts which Sklar detected, see Sklar, *Sin, Impurity, Sacrifice, Atonement*, 48-64.

51. Sklar, *Sin, Impurity, Sacrifice, Atonement*, 48-61.

52. Introduced by the particle *'im*. Roy Gane (class notes for OTST 625 Biblical Hebrew III, Andrews University, SDA Theological Seminary, Berrien Springs, USA, September 2009).

53. Introduced by the particle k^e. Gane, (class notes, OTST 625 Biblical Hebrew III).

54. Also for this case see the useful study by Bernard S. Jackson, *Wisdom-Laws: A Study of the Mishpatim of Exodus 21:1-22:16* (Oxford: Oxford University Press, 2006), 255-290.

55. Sklar, Sin, *Impurity, Sacrifice, Atonement*, 50-51.

56. Sklar, *Sin, Impurity, Sacrifice, Atonement*, 52-53

57. Sklar, *Sin, Impurity, Sacrifice, Atonement*, 54-55

contrasted with the way the righteous face it (vs. 15). Therefore, the *koper* operates in the same pattern: there is a guilty party, the wicked one who faces death.
The only thing that could save him would be *koper*, which a rich person could
easily secure. However, only God himself can decide whether the *koper* will be
accepted or not. In this case, no *koper* would suffice (vs.7).[58]

The passage in Prov 6:20-35 addresses a father's instructions to his son against
adultery because the woman's husband will not accept any *koper*.[59] All elements
of Sklar's pattern are present in this case, along with the fact that, in this case,
koper is refused.[60]

The passages in 1 Sam 12:1-5 and Amos 5:12 are unique since the *koper* is
used in the sense of the "death penalty of a murderer." Even though these passages offer much less information about the context, they are patterned like the
previous and following ones. Samuel mentions a situation that has never actually
happened, namely, there is nobody from whom Samuel has received the *koper* in
order to judge favorably for him. In addition, in Amos a person tries to find a way
to avoid the normal procedures of law in order to avoid punishment by giving
koper.[61]

The cases found in Isa 43:3-4 and Job 33:24 are similar because in both of
them, the provider of the *koper* is not the guilty party, but the injured or third party. In Isa 43:3-4, God is the injured party, but also the party which provides *koper*
for Israel who is, on the contrary, the guilty party. As a result of the *koper*, there
was no material loss or penalty for the guilty party who was in exile and hopeless.
Instead, God re-established his relationship with his people. Exile was the ultimate sign of the broken relationship between God and Israel. Therefore, the *koper*
provided by God and the subsequent return of the people confirms the fact that
koper re-establishes peace between two parties and appeases the injured party.[62]

In the case of the passage in Job, *koper* functions as a deliverer saving an individual from "going down to the pit" (v. 24). This threat is the result of the sin of
the one sentenced to death (vs. 27) and, in this case, the *koper* is accepted (vs. 28).
Here again, it is not the guilty party who provides the *koper*, but someone else, in
this case, an angel (vs. 23).[63]

By using the concept-oriented approach, Sklar identified four facts[64] related
to *koper*, which helped him to define it in both positive and negative terms. His
positive definition also encompasses all the aspects of *koper* in the previous texts.
The definition is as follows:

---

58. Sklar, *Sin, Impurity, Sacrifice, Atonement*, 56.
59. In this chapter, Sklar's debate with Bernard S. Jackson, Anthony Philips, and Henry
McKeating will not be included because it is not relevant to the scope of this research, even though it
is very relevant for a topic that would treat the methodology of reading the biblical laws.
60. Sklar, *Sin, Impurity, Sacrifice, Atonement*, 57-58.
61. Sklar, *Sin, Impurity, Sacrifice, Atonement*, 58.
62. Sklar, *Sin, Impurity, Sacrifice, Atonement*, 59.
63. Sklar, *Sin, Impurity, Sacrifice, Atonement*, 59.
64. First, *koper* delivers the guilty party from punishment. Second, the offended party decides
whether koper will be accepted or not. Third, *koper* mitigates the punishment, which is still in force,
but mitigated. Fourth, *koper* functions in the sense that it mollifies the offended party and restores
peace to the relationship. Sklar, *Sin, Impurity, Sacrifice, Atonement*, 40.

A כֹּפֶר is a legally or ethically legitimate payment that delivers a guilty from a just punishment that is the right of the offended party to execute or to have executed. The acceptance of this payment is entirely dependent upon the choice of the offended party is a lesser punishment than was originally expected, and its acceptance serves both to rescue the life of the guilty and to appease the offended party, thus restoring peace to the relationship.[65]

This conclusion reflects the meaning of the above-mentioned biblical texts. In his negative definition of *koper*,[66] which is based on some contexts where the term *koper* is found, Sklar suggested the English word "bribe," since its illegal and unethical implications[67] justly represents what *koper* represents in these negative contexts.[68] The present study focuses on the positive aspect of this concept so it will proceed with Sklar's second approach.

Field-Oriented Approach. In his second step, Sklar identified two more roots that, along with their derivatives, share the same meaning and contexts with the term *koper*. The first root is *pādāh*, along with its four derivatives (*pᵉduyim*, *pᵉdut*, *pidyom*, and *pidyon*). Through the study of these terms, Sklar identified three distinct usages. The second root is *gā'al* and its derivatives *gᵉ'ullāh* and *go'el*. Regardless of the overlap in meaning in some contexts, there are cases in which the meaning of *koper* differs from the meaning of the terms that will be discussed below.

The first usage of the four derivatives of the first root *pādāh—pᵉduyim, pᵉdut, pidyom, and pidyon*—shows that, contrary to the *koper* contexts, a person being saved by *pᵉdut* has not necessarily done any wrong, nor is the decision to save or redeem in the power of the party from whom they are being redeemed.[69] The second use reveals that *pidyon* can share similar contexts with *koper* when wrong is done, while *koper* cannot share context with *pidyon*, for in some instances, it excludes any wrong (the ransom for the first-born).[70] In the third use, it is hard to

---

65. Sklar, *Sin, Impurity, Sacrifice, Atonement*, 60.

66. "... legally or ethically questionable payment which delivers a guilty party from a just punishment by the offended party or the forces of law, or which otherwise subverts the normal course of justice. ... acceptance of this payment is dependent upon the one to whom it is given (e.g. judges, elders in the city gate)" Sklar, *Sin, Impurity, Sacrifice, Atonement*, 60-61.

67. This assessment applies to both nominal and verbal forms of the word. See the following English dictionaries for the definition of the word "bribe," http://www.oxfordlearnersdictionaries.com/us/definition/american_english/bribe_1; Oxford Advanced Learner's Dictionary of Current English, 2nd ed. (Oxford: Oxford University Press, 1992), s.v. "bribe"; The Oxford Dictionary and Thesaurus, 1st ed. (New York: Oxford University Press, 1996), s.v. "bribe"; Webster's New World Large Print Dictionary, 1st ed. (New York: Macmillan, 1989), s.v. "bribe"

68. There are at least 2 negative contexts in 1 Sam 12:1-5; Ps 49:8-9.

69. In the first usage is *pᵉdut*, which is the most general among all the others; it occurs in Ps 111:9 and 130:7 with the broad meaning of rescue or redemption from some type of negative situation. While *koper* refers to a type of payment, *pᵉdut* is used to refer to the act of redeeming or rescuing someone from trouble (Ps 25:22), enemies (Ps 55:28), or some negative situation (2 Sam 4:9; Job 5:20; 6:23; Pss 26:11; 31:5; Isa 51:11; Jer 15:21). Sklar, *Sin, Impurity, Sacrifice, Atonement*, 62.

70. It includes the nouns *pᵉduyim* and *andpidyom*. They are found in Num 3:40-51, which talks about ransoming of the first-born. Both terms are very close to כפר because they refer to a payment. Actually, the first-born belonged to the Lord and he himself stipulates the ransom (is to be a Levite or five shekels ransom). In this context, the first-born (man or animal) being ransomed belongs to the Lord and the Lord, as controlling party, stipulates what the ransom will be. Sklar, *Sin, Impurity, Sacrifice, Atonement*, 62-63.

differentiate between the meaning of *pidyon* and the meaning of *koper* since their meanings may overlap.[71]

There are two derivatives from the root *gā'al*: the nominal form *g^e'ullāh*, as well as a nominal use of the participle *go'el*. The first term refers either to the legal right of redemption (Lev 25:29, 32; 24:31, 48; Ruth 4:6; Jer 32:7-8), the action thereof (Ruth 4:7), or the redemption price (Lev 25:26, 51, 52).[72] Similarities between *g^e'ullāh* and *koper* contexts are the following: (1) the release of one party or object from the authority of another and (2) the process of the release by means of payment of some item of value. Differences with *g^e'ullāh* and *koper* contexts are the following: (1) the person who is under the authority of another party has not done anything wrong and (2) the permission of the person in charge is not necessary in order for the act of redemption to proceed, since the one who does the redeeming has the right to do so.[73]

The participle form *go'el* first occurs in a legal context and refers to a near relative of the person who was able to exercise the right of redemption on that person's behalf (Lev 25:25-26; Ruth 2:20; 3:9, 12). In the second usage, also in legal context, it refers to the "avenger of blood," who is usually a near relative (Num 35:19, 21, 24, 25; Deut 19:6,12; Josh 20:3, 5, 9; 2 Sam 14:11). In the third usage, *go'el* is used more broadly to refer to the Lord as the one who rescues someone from a harmful situation (Isa 49:26; Pss 19:14; 78:35; Isa 41:14; 43:14; 44:6, 24; 60:16; Jer 50:34). The first sense of *go'el* is evidently the same as g^e'ullāh in terms of comparison with *koper*. The second sense involves an unrelated context with *koper*. As in the third sense, *go'el* refers to a context in which one party is being rescued from another.[74]

Thus, *koper* shares some contexts and meanings with certain related terms, i.e. the root *pādāh* and its derivatives, *p^{e}duyim*, *p^{e}dut*, *pidyom*, and *pidyon*, and the root *gā'al* and its derivatives, *g^e'ullāh* and *go'el*, while in some cases, *koper* differs from the other contexts.[75]

The final step in understanding the meaning of *koper* is finding the most appropriate English word to reflect its meaning. Three of the most used options—ransom, appeasement, and composition—are presented below.

Ransom. This is the most frequent translation of *koper* and it is accepted by major Hebrew lexicons,[76] as well as by prominent scholars such as Herrmann, Levine, Milgrom, B. Lang and Janowski. Herman's and Lang's definitions are

71. The third usage includes *pidyon*, which occurs only twice, both times with a close conjunction with *koper*, Exod 21:30. It is hard to distinguish any difference between *koper* and *pidyon* besides the fact that both words are passive subjects of the verb *yushat*, but the phrase ונתן פדין נפשׁו is parallel with Exod 30:12, ונתנו אישׁ כפר נפשׁו. These facts suggest that the terms are basically equivalent and the choice of *pidyon* over *koper* is a matter of stylistic considerations. The second passage is Ps 49:7-8; within the text it will be clear that the terms have overlapping with meanings. "No man can by any means ransom (לא־פדה) his brother, or give God a ransom (*koper*) for him; for the ransom (*pidyon*) of their life is costly, and he should cease forever." Ibid., *Sin, Impurity, Sacrifice, Atonement*, 63.

72. Sklar, *Sin, Impurity, Sacrifice, Atonement*, 64.

73. Sklar, *Sin, Impurity, Sacrifice, Atonement*, 64-65.

74. Payment of an item of value is not involved and the party has not necessarily done anything wrong, nor is it up to the party who controls the item/person being redeemed as to whether or not redemption may take place. Sklar, *Sin, Impurity, Sacrifice, Atonement*, 65-66.

75. Sklar, *Sin, Impurity, Sacrifice, Atonement*, 66-67.

76. "כפר," *HALOT* 1:495; "כפר," *BDB* 497; Hamilton, *TWOT* 1:452-453. *HALOT* also includes "bribe."

quite similar.[77] These definitions state that (1) there is a guilty party and an injured party, (2) the guilty party is under obligation to the injured party, and (3) the *koper* functions to reconcile the two parties. Sklar's work also involves a brief analysis of the English word ransom, in which he claims that the ransom fits some aspects of *koper*, such as the establishment of freedom for the guilty party, appeasement, and reconciliation. These aspects of *koper* result from the fact that the *koper* is given by the offended party to the injured one.[78] However, Sklar also claimed that some elements of *koper* are not contained in the English word ransom, such as the fact that ransom does not signify that the party receiving *koper* has been wronged by the party who gives it, "as when ransom is paid to a kidnapper who has in no way been wronged by their captive. Indeed, in this example it is not the injured party who receives the ransom but the party who is doing wrong."[79] It should be noted that for this difference, Sklar gave only one example, which weakens his argument. In addition, ransom does not include the most prominent idea, namely appeasement of the injured party.[80]

Appeasement. Schenker claimed that *koper* should be translated as appeasement. His argument is based on Exod 21:28-32, where *koper* occurs in relation to the law of the goring ox and later adds two more passages that are contextually comparable to this one. His criteria are (1) a settlement takes place that negotiates a peaceful solution instead of a violent one and (2) the verb *kāpar* is used in a profane sense, i.e. conflict between men. Passages which fit these criteria are Gen 32:20 and Prov 16:14 and both of them present a rupture in a relationship between the parties, such that the injured party is ready to execute the offending party. In order to achieve peace, the guilty party must *kāpar* the injured party, which led Schenker to conclude that the verb *kāpar* in these contexts is best understood as "mollifying" or "appeasing."[81] Furthermore, he transfers the meaning of the verb *kāpar* into a noun *koper*, claiming that *koper* is appeasement or mollification. Thus, Schenker concluded that the emphasis of *koper* is to restore peace between the guilty and injured party, i.e., appeasement, while it is only indirectly a reference to buying back or ransoming one's life from another.[82]

Comparing his exegesis with Schenker's work, Sklar concluded that (1) *koper* occurs in some contexts where some wrong has been done, which makes the offending party liable. Therefore, *koper* is never appeasement alone, but appeasement for the sake of avoiding the penalty; thus, (2) the ransoming or rescuing of the guilty party is not simply an indirect objective of *koper*, but is the central

---

77. Herman: "It denotes a material expiation by which injury is made good and the injured party is reconciled, i.e. by which the hurt is covered and the guilty party is released from obligation." Lang: "The noun *koper* is a legal term. It denotes the material gift that establishes an amicable settlement between an injured party and the offending party." Sklar, *Sin, Impurity, Sacrifice, Atonement*, 68.

78. Sklar, *Sin, Impurity, Sacrifice, Atonement*, 68.

79. Sklar, *Sin, Impurity, Sacrifice, Atonement*, 68.

80. Sklar, *Sin, Impurity, Sacrifice, Atonement*, 68. For the variations on translation for *koper*, see analysis by Jay Sklar on positions of Janowski, Herrmann, Land and Maas on this. Ibid., *Sin, Impurity, Sacrifice, Atonement*, 69-72.

81. Adrian Schenker, "*kōper* et Expiation," Bib 63 (1982), 37.

82. Sklar, *Sin, Impurity, Sacrifice, Atonement*, 72-72.

part of what *koper* accomplishes.[83] Appeasement does not necessarily appease, as when one person appeases another who is angry with him/her and yet has no power or authority to punish them. It is up to the injured party whether or not he/she accepts appeasement, just as it is up to the injured party to allow or reject *koper*. The difference is that a refusal of appeasement does not mean that the penalty will follow in its stead, whereas the refusal to grant *koper* does imply that penalty will therefore follow.[84]

Composition. Brichto used this term to translate *koper* and his definition follows:

> The biblical context of *koper* is most closely approximated by the term "composition" in its legal sense, the settling of differences. An imbalance between two parties (individuals, families, clans or larger social groupings) results from a damage or deprivation inflicted upon one by the other. Equilibrium is restored by a process which consists of a transfer of something of values (a person, an animal, or a commutation of such in the form of commodity or currency) from the injuring party to the injured. The acceptance of this value-item by the lather, itself termed "the composition" (as is the process itself also), serves to "compose" or settle the difference.[85]

Thus, Brichto included both of the main elements of *koper*, ransom and appeasement. Ransom is expressed by the fact that one party is subject to another. The "composition" works in terms of releasing the party for whom it is paid from the party that receives it. Appeasement is included by the fact that one party has wronged another and that the paying of the "composition" is acceptable to the injured party for settling the dispute.

There are two weaknesses with this definition: (1) The term "composition" is used primarily in the context of financial offenses, which means that *koper*, in this context, is a reference to either the breach of criminal law or some offense against the Lord Himself. However, this problem does not completely disqualify this definition since the context of *koper* reveals the type of committed offence. (2) A more serious weakness is that composition is infrequently used in spoken English today and it is difficult to know its precise meaning. Therefore, the best choices for *koper* are "ransom" and "appeasement." However, neither of these terms covers in its entirety what *koper* embodies as the following quotation states:

> In particular, the term 'ransom' conveys that one party is under the authority of the another (and most likely with severe consequences imminent) and that the כֹּפֶר releases them, but does not necessarily imply that any wrong has been committed by the captive party. The term 'appeasement' does not convey that some wrong has been committed and that the כֹּפֶר mollifies the injured party, but does not necessarily imply that the guilty party is under the authority of the injured party or that the guilty party will be punished.

---

83. כפר נפשׁו in Exod 30:12 and the frequently used phrase *koper* + '*al* + personal object (Exod 30:15-16; Lev 1:4, 4:20...), which means that rescuing and ransoming is for them, for their lives not in order to mitigate appeasement but to underscore the element of rescuing or ransoming. Sklar, *Sin, Impurity, Sacrifice, Atonement*, 75.

84. Sklar, *Sin, Impurity, Sacrifice, Atonement*, 74-75.

85. H. C. Brichto, "On Slaughter and Sacrifice, Blood and Atonement," *HUCA* 47 (1976): 27-28.

Therefore, one should decide between the words ransom and appeasement, depending on the context.

Sklar's definition of *koper*, which is cited in this study, reflects his understanding of what the concept means in its relationships to the root *pāḏāh*, and its derivatives *peḏuyim* , *peḏuṯ*, *piḏyom*, and *piḏyon*, and also to the root *gā'al* and its derivatives *ge'ullāh* and *go'el*.[86] Regarding the Num 35:31-34 context, *kāpar* is best understood in relationship with *koper*. The verb *kāpar* not only means the purging of sin and impurity, but it does so by the means of a *koper* (blood sacrifice), which rescues the impure person or sinner from the judgment of the Lord. Even though Milgrom and Sklar chose different English words to translate *koper*, they agreed that in Num 35:31-32, it must be considered as the means through which the expiation is achieved.[87]

Following Sklar's in-depth analysis, the present study accepts the word ransom as the most accurate translation for *koper*, since it encompasses all of the main elements of the concept *koper*, such as (1) there is a guilty and injured party, (2) the guilty party is under the obligation of the injured one, and (3) *koper* functions to reconcile the two parties. However, it also accepts the word *appeasement* for the contexts for which *ransom* alone would be inadequate.

The law states in v. 31 that no form of *koper*, whether a legal payment in a positive sense or a bribe in a negative sense, is allowed for the murderer. God, as the ultimate offended party, not the family of the murdered person, does not allow for it. The murderer has to receive capital punishment.

Based on vss. 25, 28, and 32, no sort of *koper* is allowed for the manslayer, who has fled from the city of refuge. The only way the manslayer could leave the city of refuge and not be in danger of the blood avenger or of causing land pollution is after the death of the high priest. By leaving the limits of the city of refuge, he is causing the pollution of the whole land.

It seems that in both cases, the one involved in the murder is not allowed to walk/live in the land. The murderer is executed while the manslayer is limited to living in the city of refuge until the death of the high priest, whose death is accepted before God instead of that of the manslayer.

There is no opportunity for rescue for the murderer, while the manslayer does have such an opportunity under certain conditions. God is also appeased by the death of the murderer or the treatment of the manslayer outlined in this law. Such a treatment of the murderer and manslayer would restore the relationship between the murderer's family and the offended family, as well as the relationship between the manslayer and his family and the offended family. As for God, as the one who prescribed this law, there would be no barriers to relate to both the murderer's family and the manslayer's family.

There is one more piece in this law that remains unanswered and that is the role of the high priest in the case of the manslayer. Therefore, this study will examine the function and role of the high priest in the Pentateuch as well as in this law.

---

86. Sklar, *Sin, Impurity, Sacrifice, Atonement*, 76-77. 99.

87. Both of them have payment of silver in mind. Milgrom labeled it as ransom or substitution. Milgrom, *Leviticus* 1-16, 1:1082. Sklar labeled it as purgation. Sklar, *Sin, Impurity, Sacrifice, Atonement*, 155-156.

Pollution of the Land by a Murderer or a Run-away Manslayer
(vs. 33-34)

The main aspect of the law regarding the prohibition against the annihilation of human life is found in vss. 33-34. Before the concept of the pollution of the land is explored, there is another issue—function of the priesthood/high priesthood in Israel—that this study needs to address. There is no way of redemption for the murderer as vss. 30-31 state. However, based on the last part of v. 32, the manslayer can freely leave the city with no liability of polluting the land. Thus, the present study proceeds with the analysis of the priestly office and the pollution of the land, respectively.

Function of the Priesthood/High Priesthood
in the Pentateuch and the Law of Homicide

The priesthood, including the high priesthood, was an honorable and hereditary office in ancient Israel. God himself reserved it for the tribe of Levi. Individuals eligible for this office were anointed for cultic service (Exod 28; 39:1-31).[88] Aaron was further set apart by God to occupy the office of high priest, and the privilege of being high priest was hereditary since it devolved upon every high priest's firstborn.[89] They could perform all cultic activities that regular priests could and, in addition, they, and only they, could perform some cultic activities which regular priests were not fit for, such as ministration of the lampstand (light), table (bread), altar (incense), and the special ritual on the Day of Atonement (Exod 28; 30:6-10; Lev 16; 24:1-9). This group of people occupied the most exalted cultic position in Israel.[90] Other sons of Aaron were chosen to be priests and they could perform all priestly duties except for those reserved for the high priest's office (Num 3:5-39; 8:6-22). Other members of Levi's descendants were assistants to the priests.[91] This hierarchal order between high priest, priests, and priests' helpers was assigned by God himself and was very strict.[92]

The priestly office in ancient Israel cannot be fully appreciated unless it is compared with its counterpart in the ancient Near East. The list of functionaries in the Assyrian temple included the high priest, lamentation priest, male/female musicians, exorcist, and four kinds of diviners (extispicist, necromancer/dream interpreter, ecstatic, and observer of birds). The organization of the Babylonian temple was even more complex and included even more priestly sub-groups.[93] In contrast, in ancient Israel, there was only one caste of priests. Their functions, based on Deut 33:10 and 1 Sam 2:28, were significantly more limited and simpler.

88. John M. Scholer, *Proleptic Priests: Priesthood in the Epistle of the Hebrews*, JSNTSup 49 (Sheffield: JSOT Press, 1991), 14; Milgrom, *Leviticus 1-16*, 1:53; Wallace B. Nicholson, *The Hebrew Sanctuary: A Study in Typology* (Grand Rapids, MI: Baker Book House, 1951), 48.

89. Nicholson, *The Hebrew Sanctuary*, 47.

90. Menahem Haran, *Temples and Temple-Service in Ancient Israel: An Inquiry into the Character of Cult Phenomena and the Historical Setting of the Priestly School* (Oxford: Clarendon Press, 1978), 59.

91. Sanford Lyle Crossley, "The Levite as a Royal Servants during the Israelite Monarchy" (PhD diss., Southwestern Baptist Theological Seminary, 1989), 68-71.

92. Nicholson, *The Hebrew Sanctuary*, 47; Haran, *Temples and Temple-Service in Ancient Israel*, 59.

93. Milgrom, *Leviticus 1-16*, 1:52.

The priests' duties were to offer sacrifices and incense, declare oracles, and teach God's law (Deut 24:8). Any priest could have performed these roles, while the high priest exclusively performed some of them at particular times. The work of the regular priest will be presented first.

The priests were in charge of offering sacrifices.[94] This is the main and the most predominant priestly duty that laid the foundation for many other priestly functions. Thus, through offering sacrifices, the priest achieved mediation between a holy God and a sinful people.[95] A commoner could bring his sacrifice, lay his hand on an animal's head, and slay it, but from that moment on, the priest began the blood ritual and completed the ritual without any further involvement of the offerer. Since only the priests were allowed to perform this ritual, the ancient Israelite could have communion with God only through priestly ministry.[96] In addition to mediation, reconciliation between a holy God and sinful people in case of sin was also achieved through the blood ritual performed by the priest.[97] Lev 4, 5, and Num 5:22-29 contain the regulations which, if performed properly, would free an ancient Israelite of his/her sin granting him/her reconciliation with God.

Second, the priests were teachers of God's law (Deut 33:8-10).[98] This was especially true when the Aaronic priests grew in number and had to be divided into twenty-four courses, each to serve in the sanctuary only twice a year. The rest of the time, they spent teaching the people God's law in their home districts.[99]

Third, the priests were involved in judicial activities as stated in Deut 17:8-13, 21:5.[100] Their advanced knowledge of God's law enabled them to judge difficult cases ancient Israelites were involved in. This ministry was intended to establish God's law as an ethical standard for any given life situation and show what God's will was for any given situation.

There were two additional priestly functions, namely the representation and giving of divine oracles, but these were reserved for the high priest. Both of them will be discussed in the next section, which will focus on the office of the high priest.

As mentioned above in relation to the priestly office, God himself also chose the high priest for the office, with Aaron as the first high priest.[101] The clothes for the high priest numbered eight pieces (the coat, the girdle, the turban, the breeches, the ephod, the breastplate which contained the 12 precious stones inscribed with the names of the 12 tribes, a robe made of blue wool, and a gold-plated headband on which were inscribed the words "Holy to the Lord"), in contrast to the clothes for a regular priest, which consisted of four pieces (coat, girdle, turban, breeches). The office of the high priest embodied all of the functions of the priesthood, as if

---

94. P. Ellingwroth, "Priests," *NDBT* 697.

95. Roland de Vaux, *Ancient Israel: its Life and Institutions* (Grand Rapids, MI: Eerdmans, 1997), 349; Scholer, *Proleptic Priests*, 22.

96. M. L. Andreasen, *The Sanctuary Service* (Washington, DC: Review & Herald, 1947), 45-46; Milgrom, *Leviticus 1-16*, 1:52; Nicholson, *The Hebrew Sanctuary*, 48; Ellingwroth, *NDBT* 698.

97. Andreasen, *The Sanctuary Service*, 47-48.

98. Ellingwroth, *NDBT* 698.

99. Andreasen, *The Sanctuary Service*, 40.

100. Milgrom, *Leviticus 1-16*, 1:54; Andreasen, *The Sanctuary Service*, 41; Ellingwroth, *NDBT* 698.

101. Nicholson, *The Hebrew Sanctuary*, 48; Andreasen, *The Sanctuary Service*, 39.

the high priest were standing for the entire office of priesthood.[102] Milgrom went even further to note correctly that "the high-priest assumes responsibility for all Israel. The twelve tribes are inscribed on the two lazuli stones worn on his shoulders and on the twelve stones 'before the Lord at all times' (Exod 28:29)."[103] Thus, the representative function of the high priest envisioned the entire nation along with the priestly office. Even more, the representational role had another side to it. The high priest was also God's representative to the people[104] performing all those roles assigned to them specifically.

Thus, in addition to the twelve stones inscribed with the names of the twelve tribes of Israel, the high priest was to carry the Urim and Thummim (instruments of decision-making) over his heart at all times (Exod 28:30),[105] which were also called "sacred lots." These items were intended to be instruments through which God would reveal his will in regards to various issues Israelites would bring before him. It functioned on the principle of elimination with "yes" or "no" answers as contemporary "heads and tails" on the coin.[106]

One more item of the high priest's clothes is worthy of mention, since it was critically important and significant for the welfare of Israelites, namely the ṣiyṣ. The ṣiyṣ was a prophylactic since it was intended to expiate imperfections inadvertently offered by the people. The rabbis went one step further to claim that the ṣiyṣ had power to expiate all sacrifices (public and private) and all sacrificial blood and bodily impurity.[107]

The materials from which the pieces of the high priest's clothes were made were enormously valuable. The use of gold, blue, and purple, the gold plate worn on his head, and the oil for anointing made the High Priest resemble royalty by sharing these features with the Jewish monarch. Thus, even though distinguished and exalted above the people of Israel, the high priest also stood in a peculiarly close relationship with them. He was chosen from among them, had the same nature as they had, and identified with them in their guilt.

God himself was the initiator of the priestly/high priestly office in Israel, and this office, through the offering of sacrifices, was supposed to achieve mediation between a holy God and a sinful people. A commoner could participate in the ritual of sacrifice offering, but not after the point when blood application began to take place. From that point on, it was only the priest who was allowed to perform the blood-related activities. The members of the priest/high priest office were to teach God's law, which also enabled them to be involved in judicial processes. In this way, they were to spread the knowledge about God's law and help establish God's life standards within the Israelite nation.

Two additional functions of giving oracles and representation were reserved for the high priest. Several facts lead many scholars to claim rightly that the high priest was a representative of the entire priestly office and of the nation as a whole. First, the high priests could perform all priestly functions and also per-

---

102. Andreasen, *The Sanctuary Service*, 50.
103. Andreasen, *The Sanctuary Service*, 53; Milgrom, *Leviticus 1-16*, 1:54.
104. "Priests," *DBI* 663; Rodney K. Duke, "Priests, Priesthood," *DOTP* 653.
105. Andreasen, *The Sanctuary Service*, 53.
106. Vaux, *Ancient Israel: its Life and Institutions*, 352.
107. Milgrom, *Leviticus 1-16*, 1:512.

formed some reserved for them only. Next, the high priest's clothing was more elaborate than that of the regular priests. For example, the high priest's clothing included the breastplate with 12 precious stones inscribed with the names of the 12 tribes, the gold-plated headband on which were inscribed the words "Holy to the Lord," and the ṣiyṣ intended to expiate imperfections inadvertently offered by the people. Finally, they also wore the Urim and Thummim, which allowed them to communicate with God. Thus, scholars perceive the high priest as being the central figure in all of ancient Israel.

Keeping in mind all these duties related to the priest, and even more so, the additional ones closely associated to the high priestly office, it is obvious that God initiated the priestly/high priestly office to represent him and to act on his behalf in favor of the people of Israel. Thus, there are two potential answers that explain why it was acceptable for the manslayer to leave the city of refuge only after the high priest's death without any potential pollution of the land.

Those who see the two testaments as organically connected think that the high priest's natural death in the case of the manslayer represents his substitutionary atonement for the manslayer's sin because this resembles the work of Christ in the New Testament (Heb 7-10, 7:27; 9:12, 14-15, 26, 28; 10:5-14).[108] Christ, as an innocent priest, died instead of sinful humanity. The sin of the slayer could not be borne by a regular priest. Even the high priest could not bear it. However, it appears that God accepted his natural death to atone for this unintentional sin by which a human life was annihilated. The priests/high priests were assigned by God to bear other sins of the people (Lev 10:17), but the killing of a human being, due to God's respect for human life, was dealt with in different way.

Those who do not see a connection between the two testaments do not offer a rationale for the question of why this law allows such a substitutionary ransom in the case of a manslayer, but they do recognize it.[109] However, there is one more concept that should be explored in order to grasp the entirety of the rationale behind this law, and that is pollution of the land.

Pollution of the Land

Pollution of the land caused by human sin is a common notion in the OT.[110] The question raised in the introduction focuses on the reason why and how murder pollutes the land.

It is important to notice that 'ereṣ is used instead of 'aḏāmāh [111] in this law

---

108. Gane, *Leviticus, Numbers*, 798-799.

109. Milgrom, *Leviticus 1-16*, 1:1082.

110. Gen 4:2, 8:21; Lev 26:34-35.43; Num 35;33-34; Deut 2:23, 24:4; Isa 24:4-6; Jer 3:2; Ezek 36:17; Ezra 9:11. Milgrom, *Leviticus 1-16*, 512.

111. This term is used in a cosmological sense and also as a specific territorial destination. It is basically a nonpolitical term designating agricultural land owned by individuals or groups. Jong Keun Lee, "The Theological Concept of Divine Ownership of the Land in the Hebrew Bible" (ThD diss., Boston University, 1993), 16.

because it strongly alludes to God as Creator,[112] pointing out the fact that God himself is the ultimate owner of the land.[113] Therefore, "the fulfillment of the land 'promise' is the crux of the biblical narratives concerning early Israel. The conquest of Canaan and the allotment of the land are regarded as the fulfillment of Yahweh's promise. Yahweh thus gives the land to the descendants of Israel."[114]

Since God owns the land, it is in a special relationship with him[115] and it is holy, due to his presence in it as the true source of holiness. Even though the land was regarded as inherently holy in the ancient Near East, the holiness of the land is always derivative in the Bible without any mythological component to it.[116]

Many texts in the OT state that the land has to keep its holiness and cannot tolerate severe impurity (Lev 18:25-30; Num 5:1-4, 31:19; Deut 23:10-15).[117] A review of the current research, in order to rank different kinds of sins in the OT, will help to explain why the sin of murder pollutes the land. Theologians basically recognize two basic groups of sins, even though they label them differently.

David Hoffmann. Hoffman mentioned two types of impurities. The first is in opposition to holiness and contains all the sins that stand in opposition to holy living and comes through sinful behavior. Some scholars[118] call this *moral impurity.* This type has power to separate the sinner from God and, in Hoffmann's view, there is no means of purification for it. The second one is in opposition to purity, as opposed to holiness, and is found in the regulations of Lev 11-15. This type does not come from sinful actions, but originates from dead people, animals, and various emmissions. It can be cleansed by the means of purification. While Hoffmann correctly distinguished between impurities that come from moral wrongdoing and those that come from amoral circumstances, he did not differentiate between impurities that come from intentional or unintentional sin. [119]

Adolph Büchler. Büchler's understanding of the two types of sin is more detailed, but similar to Hoffmann's. He distinguished between levitical and moral impurity and he contrasted them in four ways: (1) moral impurities are a result of some moral lapse, while levitical impurities are not, (2) moral impurities are cleansed by punishment while levitical impurities are cleansed ritually, (3) moral impurities are not contagious while levitical impurities can be, and (4) biblical use of impurity language to discuss moral impurity is symbolic and figurative while this is not the case with levitical impurities. Defining sin as either moral wrongdoing or that which arises from amoral conditions is very similar to Hoffmann's definition, even though the two theologians used different

112. Transcendental reality. Lee, 69-79; Milgrom, *Leviticus 17-22,* 2:1572.

113. Historical, political reality. Lee, 20.

114. Lee, 21.

115. The ancient Israelite idea known as "triple relationship" is the very dynamic and holistic concept that put God, Israel, and people in a strong relationship. Daniel Block pointed out that this was a very common phenomenon in the ancient Near East and called it a triangle relationship. Graphically God, Israel, and the people are on each point of the triangle. Lee, 63.

116. Daniel Isaac Block, *The Gods of the Nations: Studies in Ancient Near Eastern National Theology* (Grand Rapids, MI: Baker Academic, 1988), 4-5.

117. Lee, "The Theological Concept of Divine Ownership of the Land in the Hebrew Bible," 66-70.

118. Milgrom, *Leviticus 1-16,* 1:724. For a more detailed list of scholars see Klawans, *Purity, Sacrifice, and the Temple,* 53.

119. Sklar, *Sin, Impurity, Sacrifice, Atonement,* 141-142.

terminology. The weakness of Büchler's work is that he also did not distinguish between impurity and intentional and unintentional sin.[120]

Jonathan Klawans. Klawans also identified two basic types of impurity: ritual and moral. Ritual impurity results from direct or indirect contact with a number of natural sources[121] and its characteristics are that (1) the source of ritual impurity is natural and more or less unavoidable, (2) it is not a sin to contact these ritual impurities, and (3) ritual impurity can convey an impermanent contagion to people and things.[122]

On the other hand, moral impurity results from committing certain acts so heinous that they are considered defiling. Such acts are sexual sins (Lev 18:24-30), idolatry (Lev 19:31; 20:1-3) and bloodshed (Num 35:33-34). These impurities defile a sinner (Lev 18:24), the land of Israel (Lev 18:25; Ezek 36:17), and the sanctuary (Lev 20:3; Ezek 5:11) not ritually, but morally. This defilement leads to the expulsion of the people from the land of Israel (Lev 18:28; Ezek 36:16). The basis for these conclusions is found in the priestly tradition, especially in the Holiness Code.[123]

Klawans's division fails to address the difference between minor and major ritual impurity. In addition, there is no difference between intentional and unintentional sins.[124]

David P. Wright. Wright also saw two types of impurity, but defined them as tolerated and prohibited ones. Tolerated impurity includes those that the above-mentioned theologians called ritual impurities and the laws that regulate them are mostly in Leviticus 11-16 and Numbers 19. They arise from normal events of everyday life, such as having a baby (Lev 12) or coming into contact with the dead (Num 19), and originate from amoral sources. Wright formed three subcategories of these graded situations according to three factors: (1) the means required for cleansing them (sacrifice is not obligatory for lesser impurity but it is for the higher ones); (2) the extent of pollution, i.e., lesser grade if the pollution did not defile the sanctuary or higher grade if it did extend to the sanctuary; and (3) the communicability of the pollution, i.e., in case it was non-communicable to the profane sphere, it would be allowed within the camp (but not the sanctuary), or in case it was communicable to the profane, it would be prohibited from both the sanctuary and, in some instances, the camp as well.[125]

Prohibited impurities arise from sinful situations and are parallel to what theologians called moral impurities. For this type, Wright also had subcategories formed according to whether the sin was unintentional (column 3) or intentional

120. Sklar, *Sin, Impurity, Sacrifice, Atonement*, 142-144.
121. Childbirth (12:1-8), certain skin diseases (13:1-46; 14:1-32), fungi in clothes (13:47-59) and houses (14:33-53), genital discharges (15:1-33), the carcasses of certain animals (11:1-47), and human corpses (Num 19:10-22). The specific subcategory is ritual impurity that comes as a by-product of some sacrificial procedures (Lev 16:28, Num 19:7-8). Sklar, *Sin, Impurity, Sacrifice, Atonement*, 144-145.
122. Klawans, *Purity, Sacrifice, and the Temple*, 53.
123. Klawans, *Purity, Sacrifice, and the Temple*, 54.
124. Klawans, *Purity, Sacrifice, and the Temple*, 55.
125. Sklar, *Sin, Impurity, Sacrifice, Atonement*, 150.

(column 4). The following table[126] graphically presents Wright's division and after it follows a brief explanation of prohibited impurities.

Tolerated		Prohibited	
(no distinction between unintentional and intentional)		Unintentional	Intentional
No sacrifice	Individual ad hoc sacrifice	Individual, sometimes communal, ad hoc sacrifice	Day of Atonement sacrifice[127]
Pollution of person	Pollution of sanctuary (outer altar) and person	Pollution of sanctuary (outer altar or shrine); ritual personal pollution if deriving from tolerated impurity	**Pollution of sanctuary (adytum, shrine, outer altar), sometimes land; moral pollution of persons; ritual personal pollution if from tolerated impurity**
Non-communicable to profane; hence, restriction only from sanctuary as sacred	Communicable to profane; hence, restriction from the sanctuary and other sacred matters and restriction from or within the (profane) habitation	Potential removal from life; restriction from sanctuary and sacred, and sometimes from habitation (if communicable to profane) if the sin derives from a tolerated impurity	Removal from life; *karet* or capital penalty; in some cases, exile; restriction from sanctuary and sacred, and sometimes habitation if sin derives from a permitted impurity (unlike the penalty takes effect)

An example of an unintentional prohibited sin that causes impurity is inadvertent delay of purification ritual from tolerated impurity, which causes defilement of the sanctuary (Lev 5:2-3). General inadvertent sins of Lev 4 also pollute the sanctuary. In both cases, the sanctuary is polluted and is cleansed by means of a purification offering. Examples of intentional sin that cause impurities are child-sacrificing to Moloch (Lev 20:2-5); purposely polluting sacred items, such as touching or eating sacred items while impure (7:19-21; 22:3-7); and sexual sins (18:6-23). The consequence of these sins is more severe with respect to a guilty party; he is *karet* (the premature death of the sinner) and no personal sacrifice is allowed because of the sinner's intention to sin. In addition, in regard to the sanctuary, the Most Holy Place is defiled. Milgrom suggested that these rebellious deeds, as well as the unrepentant sins of the Israelites, are stored in the Most Holy Place.[128]

Thus, Wright went one step further by identifying a difference between types of ritual (tolerated) impurity and types of moral (prohibited) impurity, allowing similarities between them to become more evident.[129] In other words, he made distinctions within each type. Ritual impurities can be of a lesser and higher value and moral offenses can be unintentional and intentional, which makes his

---

126. David P. Wright, "*The Spectrum of Priesly Impuritiy*," in *Priesthood and Cult in Ancient Israel*, eds. Gary A. Anderson and Saul M. Olyan, JSOTSup 125 (Sheffield: JSOT Press, 1991), 153; Sklar, *Sin, Impurity, Sacrifice, Atonement*, 150-152.

127. Wright's position when sins of this category are cleansed is not accepted in this study, but since it is not crucially relevant to this paper, it is not analyzed here.

128. Sklar, *Sin, Impurity, Sacrifice, Atonement*, 151.

129. Sklar, *Sin, Impurity, Sacrifice, Atonement*, 152-153.

division the most complete and accurate among other divisions mentioned in the present study.

The sin of Num 35:30-34 falls into the category located in the fourth column. These sins are of the highest level and most severe. They pollute the sanctuary and, in some cases, the land, which is the case in Num 35:30-34 if it happens that the murderer is not killed or the manslayer leaves the city of refuge. A person who commits these sins is morally polluted with the potential to spread pollution.

In conclusion, the research presented in this chapter forms a satisfactory basis for deriving answers to the questions raised in the introduction. Biblical texts present the blood as life-bearer and God himself has set it apart for unique purposes such as cleansing from ritual impurities, consecration, and sin expiation/atonement. The prohibition against one human killing another human is found throughout the biblical legal corpus and emphasizes the importance of this prohibition (Gen 9:5-6; Exod 20:13; 21:12; Lev 24:17; Deut 19:11-13). The murderer thus transgresses one of the essential aspects of God's commandments. A person involved in any kind of killing misuses blood because it was not meant to be shed prematurely. Therefore, he/she must be put to death[130] because of terminating the life of another human being. In light of these claims, the prohibition of *koper* in the case of the murderer and manslayer seems to be very logical and right. God protects the sanctity and value of human life.

Accordingly, vss. 32-33 state that *koper* is not acceptable in the event of murder/manslaughter. The meaning of *koper* in this text automatically covers the reasons why the ransom for the murderer and manslayer is not acceptable. As it was pointed out, *koper* refers to legal payment, and human life cannot be subject to any monetary compensation even though the majority of other ancient Near Eastern law collections allowed for such compensation.[131] That is the case even for the manslayer, whose guilt is eliminated by the substitutionary death of the high priest, due to the significance of life. Thus, the life of all humans has the same worth[132] and no other human being has the right to terminate it.

The last two verses, 33-34, give the theological explanation for previous prohibitions, augmenting the rationale behind this law. As can be seen from Wright's division of sin types, the sin of murder pollutes the land and is in the group of the highest ranked sins. In addition, as it was pointed out, the land is the place of God's presence,[133] who is the source of its holiness, and that requires holy living by the people.[134] If a murderer were allowed to walk unpunished, then the land would be polluted by his presence there.[135] The prophet Jeremiah also uses this

---

130. The elliptical phrase used in this verse should be understood as passive cognate-accusative, to murder the murderer, רצח את־הרצח. It is unique in OT. Levine, *Numbers*, 559; Milgrom, *Leviticus 1-16*, 1:295.

131. David L. Lieber et al., *Etz Hayim: Torah and Commentary* (Philadelphia: Jewish Publication Society, 2001), 965.

132. A. Noordtzij, *Numbers*, BTC (Grand Rapids, MI: Zondervan, 1983), 301-302.

133. Lieber et al., *Etz Hayim: Torah and Commentary*, 965.

134. Bellinger, *Leviticus and Numbers*, 317.

135. Richard Elliott Friedman, *Commentary on the Torah: with a New English Translation* (San Francisco: HarperSanFrancisco, 2001), 544.

concept of *koper* prohibition in reference to adultery (Jer. 3:1), which is also a sin of the same group as murder.[136]

Thus, the purpose of this law, as it builds on the previously mentioned laws against the murderer, seems to be adding guidelines for another probability in the murder event in the context of cities of refuge, namely unintentional killing-manslaughter. In addition, it states that besides the violation of the explicitly mentioned prohibition in the Decalogue and illicit shedding/misuse of blood as a life-carrier, the act of murder brings double pollution of the land through contact between the shed blood by the murderer or run-away manslayer and their own existence in the land. Finally, this law confirms the notion of substitutionary redemption in the Pentateuch.

---

136. W. Gunther Plaut et al., *The Torah: a Modern Commentary* (New York: Union of American Hebrew Congregations, 1981), 565.

Judgment for the Saints:
The Justice of God in Psalms 3–14

Jerome Skinner

God's Justice and Psalm Interpretation

In his timely *Letter from Birmingham Jail* (1963), Martin Luther King stated, "Injustice anywhere is a threat to justice everywhere. We are caught in an inescapable network of mutuality, tied in a single garment of destiny."[1] Another voice, Abraham Heschel, well known for his philosophical thought and social activism, is known to have said that "the opposite of good is not evil, it is indifference." These notions of justice, their universality and timeless ethical dimensions, hold true not only in a civic sense, but are also vital regarding the moral life of God's people because they are ingrained in the Bible's eschatological context.[2] In the Book of Psalms, the petitioner's pleas are driven by his notion of justice: whom it comes from, what it is, why it is needed, and its implications. A brief investigation of Pss 3–14 reveals the theological perspective and practical implications of the links between God's justice and the ethical life of his people as central to understanding eschatological justice. For the Psalmist, like the prophets, *moral life is tied to God's role in human destiny.*

The ways in which the Bible addresses the subject of justice at times has had unsettling effects, especially when it comes to the Psalter. Proclamations of judgment, protestations of innocence, and curses of the so-called imprecatory psalms have drawn out various responses regarding their application for the Christian

---

1. Reprinted in David Howard-Pitney, *Martin Luther King Jr., Malcolm X, and the Civil Rights Struggle of the 1950s and 1960s: A Brief History with Documents* (Boston: Bedford, 2004), 74–90.

2. Biblical justice was part and parcel of covenant living. The prophets utilize two key and enduring themes throughout their writings, "justice and righteousness," as central in the establishment of the kingdom of God. Cf. Isa 1:21, 27; 5:7, 16; 9:7; 32:16; 33:5; Jer 4:2; 9:24; 22:3; 33:15; Ezek 45:9; Hos 2:19; Amos 5:24; Zeph 3:5.

life.[3] In a world where secular, relativistic, and skeptical notions about justice confine and contort the biblical message, one must answer critical objections a cohesive ethic and at the same time, present a clear understanding of the objective nature of divine justice. The issue of biblical justice is of particular importance to biblical theology and needs to be addressed from the whole canon. The overarching backdrop of justice is expressed in the revelation of God's character and covenantal Lordship regarding righteousness and unrighteousness. Whether in its immanent or eschatological perspective, God's justice rests on the very nature of his sovereignty and character. God's role as the Supreme Judge is recognized in theological circles. In light of this, it behooves readers to ask how God's sovereignty relates to justice and its implications for the individual, the church, and the world's destiny.

The Psalter vividly portrays aspects of God's justice that correspond to and elucidate the prophetic and personal focus on judgment. Several significant studies have been done on the books of Daniel and Revelation, but to my knowledge, none has yet focused specifically on the Psalter's voice in the discussion.[4] This lack can be attributed to, among other things, understandings of what "eschatological" means in Psalm analysis.[5] Recent gains in Psalm studies make it necessary to revisit current assumptions.[6] The recent focus on the structure of the Psalter has added another element to the discussion of the canonical voice of the Psalter. As David Howard Jr. notes, "a shift has taken place, and the prevailing interest in Psalms studies has to do with the question of the composition, editorial unity and overall message of the Psalter as a book, a literary and canonical entity that coheres with respect to its structure and message."[7] The literary or canonical context has encouraged many in the field of Psalm studies to see the narrative-like quality of the Psalter.[8]

---

3. For several different views, consult J. C. Laney, "A Fresh look at the Imprecatory Psalms," *BibSac* 138 (1981): 35–45; John N. Day, "The Imprecatory Psalms and Christian Ethics," *BibSac* 159 (April-June 2002): 166–86; J. G. Vos, "The Ethical Problem of the Imprecatory Psalms," *WTJ* 4 (May 1942): 123–138; Roy B. Zuck, "The Problem of the Imprecatory Psalms" (ThM thesis, Dallas Theological Seminary, 1957), 45–58.

4. Hans LaRondelle's book is the only book-length treatment of the Psalms to date from an Adventist author. Aside from the DARCOM series, more recent works include Richard M. Davidson, "The Divine Covenant Lawsuit Motif in Canonical Perspective," *JATS* 21/1-2 (2010): 45–84; Jiří Moskala, "The Gospel According to God's Judgment: Judgment as Salvation," *JATS* 22/1 (2011): 28–49; Idem, "Toward a Biblical Theology of God's Judgment: A Celebration of the Cross in Seven Phases of Divine Universal Judgment (An Overview of a Theocentric-Christocentric Approach)," *JATS* 15/1 (Spring 2004): 138–165; Zdravko Plantak, "For The Healing Of The Nations: Repairers of Broken Walls and Restorers of God's Justice," *AUSS* 48/1 (2010): 17–27.

5. Typically, the focus in the Psalms is Messianic.

6. For instance, see David C. Mitchell, *The Message of the Psalter: An Eschatological Programme in the Books of Psalms*, JSOTSup Series 252 (Sheffield: Sheffield Academic Press, 1997).

7. David Howard, "The Psalms and Current Study," in *Interpreting the Psalms: Issues and Approaches*, eds. David Firth and Philip S. Johnston (Downers Grove, IL: IVP Academic, 2005), 24.

8. Gordon Wenham, "Toward a Canonical Reading of the Psalms," in *Canon and Biblical Interpretation*, eds. Craig Bartholomew et al., SAHS 7 (Grand Rapids, MI: Zondervan, 2006); Idem, *Psalms as Torah: Reading Biblical Songs Ethically* (Grand Rapids, MI: Baker Academic, 2012); R. E. Wallace, "The Narrative Effect of Psalms 84–89," *JHS* 11 (2011): 2–15; Nancy deClaissé-Walford, *Reading from the Beginning* (Macon, GA: Mercer University Press, 1997); Norman Whybray, *Reading the Psalms as a Book*, JSOTSup Series 222 (Sheffield: Sheffield Academic Press, 1996); David M. Howard, Jr. "Review of Reading the Psalms as a Book by Whybray, Norman," *Review of Biblical Literature* (1998).

This study will follow the strategy of a narrative reading by tracing the storyline of God's justice in a small grouping in the Psalter. This narrative reading concentrates on the final form's structure. A structural view allows a broader articulation of a point, an example, and a worldview for thought, prayer, attitudes, and actions. To trace this throughout the whole book is not feasible here. A small sampling here serves as a springboard for a richer corpus of future works.

The question of style and structure is fitting to discuss here because the Psalmist uses them to instruct us to look at God's justice through its rich poetic tapestry for our personal growth in thinking and practical life of application. The ethical is draped in the emotive. The overtones of supplication, the verbose imperatival pleas, and the direct designations of moral qualities are seen in rhythmic cadence, pithy proclamations, and the metaphorical nuances of everyday life.[9] These literary aspects help us see patterns that express composite profiles of moral life. Structural analysis leads us to think about prayer, Christian life, and ethics in dialectical terms. The art of dialogue, the interfacing of semantics and syntax in comparing psalm with psalm followed by its theological application are now seen as a part of Psalm interpretation.[10] Broadening the analysis to the psalms as groups, we can perceive the thematic parallels that emerge from the individual psalm. This method, more recently and readily seen in the works of Karl Fredreich Keil and Franz Delitzsch, J. Clinton McCann, Gerald Wilson, Eric Zenger, Frank Hossfeld and others, is termed a "concatenation" reading (cf. Figure 1) by those who study the structure of the Psalter. It refers to the adjacent reading of psalms expanding to the level of groups, collections, and books.[11]

The dynamic interaction of psalms in groups, collections, and books help the reader to hear the 'socializing' effect of structure.[12] The cumulative effect of patterns grounded in linguistic and thematic parallels creates a heightened impact on

---

9. William Brown, *Seeing the Psalms: A Theology of Metaphor* (Louisville, KY: Westminster, 2002).

10. For an example of this approach see J. L. Mays, *Preaching and Teaching the Psalms* (Louisville, KY: Westminster John Knox, 2006), 27–29.

11. Gerald Wilson's approach in *The Editing of the Hebrew Psalter* is a significant paradigm shift in Psalm studies that utilizes a methodology from which conclusions are drawn that rest on the final form of the text and interrelationships of psalms within that final form. Hence, the structure of the final shape of the text is used as the hermeneutical foundation to derive the communicative significance through the concatenations of each collection and book division. A canonical reading of the Psalter allows the reader to observe the thematic development of linguistic content and theological emphases through reading the psalms in relationship to their surrounding neighbors. See Joseph P. Brennan, "Some Hidden Harmonies of the Fifth Book of Psalms," in *Essays in Honor of Joseph P. Brennan*, ed. R. F. McNamara (Rochester, NY: St. Bernard's Seminary, 1976), 126-58; idem., "Psalms 1–8: Some Hidden Harmonies," BTB 10 (1980): 25–29; Claus Westermann, *Praise and Lament in the Psalms*, trans. K. R. Crim and R. N. Soulen (Atlanta: John Knox, 1981), 250–258.

12. Branson Woodard Jr. and Michael Travers borrowed E. D. Hirsch's word that describes the process of generic affinities that "prepare a reader to respond appropriately to the text." Branson Woodard Jr. and Michael Travers, "Literary Forms and Interpretation," in *Cracking Old Testament Codes: A Guide to Interpreting the Literary of the Old Testament*, eds. D. Brent and Ronald Geise Jr. (Nashville, TN: Broadman and Holman, 1995), 37.

the reader.[13] Rather than a full exposition of each psalm, this study shows three different ways to approach a concatenated reading: structural, lexical, and thematic. First, this study justifies a case for a reading of justice based on introductory themes in the Psalter through the structure. Then Psalms 3–7 are commented on looking at the points of their lexical correspondences. Finally, a brief analysis of Psalms 9–14 articulates the broad thematic topics that emerge from the analysis of Psalms 3–7.

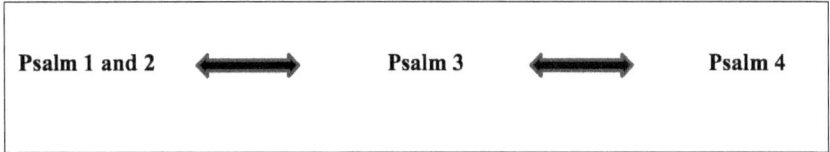

Psalm 1 and 2	⟵⟶	Psalm 3	⟵⟶	Psalm 4

Figure 1. Concatenated or duo-directionality reading of Psalms.

Literary Context of Psalms 1 and 2
as Introductory to Psalms 3–14

The table below (Table 1) illustrates how a concatenated reading emphasizes comparative frames of reference on the contextual level. The blessed man in Ps 1 is best seen in the Messianic figure of Ps 2. The Messianic figure is typified in the portrait of the Davidic king when Pss 2 and 3 are compared. The Davidic king is typified in the accused man when comparing Pss 3 and 4. The comparisons and contrasts work primarily at the lexical level and secondarily at the thematic level. Yet, the role of the thematic subject in the psalms broadens as the theological language emphasizes the experience of the Davidic king and its implications for the relationship of the Davidic king to history, Yahweh's covenant, and in its final form, the theology of the Psalter.

Table 1. Concatenated structural parallels of Psalm 3

	Psalm 1	Psalm 2	Psalm 3
Psalm Type	Untitled	Untitled	מזמר
Thematic subject	The Blessed Man	Messianic/Royal	Davidic King
Source of conflict	The Ungodly	Nations	Many . . . Enemies
Notation of authorship and collection	Untitled	Untitled	לדוד

---

13. This approach represents a reading strategy that, as Wilson states, is "another way to appreciate the ensemble that the ancient editors created and arranged in the Psalter." Gerald Wilson, *Psalms: Vol. 1*, NIVAC (Grand Rapids, MI: Zondervan, 2002), 237. Jon Paulien has seen this phenomenon in the book of Revelation which he calls 'duo-directionality.' Jon Paulien, "Looking Both Ways: A Study of the Duo-directionality of the Structural Seams in the Apocalypse" (paper presented at the Annual Meetings of the Hebrews, General and Pastoral Epistles, Apocalypse of the SBL. Chicago, 19 November 1988).

Table 2. Literary Parallels between Psalms 3–14

Psalm	Genre	Crisis	Authorship/Collection
3*[14]	Lament	Enemies-persecution	Davidic
4	Lament	Distress- men	Davidic
5	Lament	Enemies- deceit	Davidic
6	Lament	Enemies /Sickness-physical/spiritual	Davidic
7*	Lament	Enemies- falsely accused	Davidic
8	Hymn		Davidic
9/10	Thanksgiving/Lament	Enemies- nations	Davidic
11	Lament	Enemies- wicked	Davidic
12	Lament (communal)	Enemies- liars, boasters	Davidic
13	Lament	Enemies- the enemy, death	Davidic
14	Lament	Enemies- fools, evildoers	Davidic

By observing a larger corpus, the repetition of themes as special points of emphasis from the structural flow becomes evident. From this perspective, the nature of justice is understood in rhetorical modes where ethical predicates are based on the character and acts of God and man in relation to the two foci of the Psalter (Pss 1 and 2).[15] Followed by a collection of laments, these two realities give the reader a sense of the significance of the concept of justice that follows.

The relationship between these psalms is well documented and needs little comment.[16] What this shows is that what is given in general broad strokes in Pss 1 and 2 becomes specific and focused throughout 3–14 and the rest of the Psalter. More than just haphazard placement, there is a flow of thought regarding the impending end regarding the people of God. Here is where a broader reading of the Psalter sharpens one's understanding of the role of the Word of God in human destiny in Ps 1 and the function of the Messiah in God's plan for humanity in Ps 2.

14. * Indicates the presence of a Historical Superscription.

15. These two psalms are called the "doorways" to the Psalter and refer to the Word of God and the Messiah, respectively. Different designations for these two foci have been given, like *royal* and *wisdom*, or *kingship* and *Torah*. On the relationship between the two, see Gerald H. Wilson, "Shaping the Psalter: A Consideration of Editorial Linkage in the Book of Psalms," in *The Shape and the Shaping of the Psalter*, ed. J. Clinton McCann, JSOTSup 159 (Sheffield: Sheffield Academic, 1993), 81. On the methodological presuppositions that undergird a scholar's understanding of what constitutes a "Messianic" psalm, see Richard Belcher, *The Messiah and the Psalms: Preaching Christ from all the Psalms* (Fearn, UK: Mentor, 2006), 21–30. I agree in the main with Belcher's analysis and will follow his main thrust in this article.

16. The links between Psalm 1 and 2 are clear on the lexical level, as well as in its use of imagery and puns and plays on words. In several articles, Phil Botha has noted several parallels and links between Pss 1 and 2: the lexical connections as well as in its use of imagery and plays on words. Phil Botha, "The Junction of the Two Ways: The Structure and Theology of Psalm 1," *Old Testament Essays* 4 (1991): 381–96; Idem, "The Ideological Interface Between Psalm 1 and Psalm 2," *Old Testament Essays* 18.2 (2005): 189–203; Idem, "Intertextuality and the Interpretation of Psalm 1," *Old Testament Essays* 18.3 (2005): 503–520. McCann noted, "At the beginning of Book I, Psalms 1 and 2 provide a literary context for reading Psalms 3–41 as well as for the Psalter as a whole." J. Clinton McCann Jr., "Books I–III and the Editorial Purpose of the Hebrew Psalter," in *The Shape and Shaping of the Psalter*, 103. Mays also noted, "Psalms 1 and 2 together elevate the paired topics of Torah and kingship of the Lord." James L. Mays, "The Question of Context in Psalm Interpretation," in *The Shape and Shaping of the Psalter*, 16.

From one viewpoint, it is noted that "in the psalms that follow [1 and 2], the concern for the destiny of the righteous does not diminish. In fact, the vocabulary related to the righteous and their plight appears so frequently it draws constant attention to the subject."[17] As figure 2 points out, the types of crises are varied, yet there is a parallel pattern throughout where there is a residing tension between the temporal nature of the oppression of the people of God matched by calls for justice that are implored for the end of wickedness. Such a conviction in the Psalmist is built on a premise in which the trajectory of the character seen in actions is done and irritated by the wicked, the sinner, and the scornful, who are seen as the antithesis of covenant fidelity to God's reign outlined in the Torah.[18]

Furthermore, God's reign is expressly spoken of regarding his promise to David and his descendants. The Davidic dynasty, through the anointed figure, is God's means to mediate justice throughout the world (cf. Pss 2; 110). A canonical reading of the Psalter clarifies that the cries for justice spoken directly to God are to be fulfilled through his designated mediator; the Messiah. The ethical expressions found in these laments that deal with the crisis of injustice are designations on account of one's relation to the Messianic person, promise, and plan, and the Word of God. Jerome Creach noted that "when those within Israel do not act in accordance with God's intentions, they become like the nations (such as Babylon) that oppose the Lord and the Lord's anointed (Ps 2:1–3 MT) by undercutting the divine purpose that comes through Israel."[19] New Testament writers expressed a broad understanding of the work and roles of the Messianic figure of the Psalms. These included his suffering and royal dominion, as well as the roles he would serve as an anointed figure: prophet, priest, and king. These facets are brought out by the language used in the Psalms especially regarding atonement. These roles are spotlighted through a canonical reading of David's place in the Psalter as a representative of Israel, who intercedes for the righteous, proclaims God's will, as well as seeks the vindication of God's character.

A close reading of Psalms 3–14 uncovers a repetition of words, phrases, and concepts that express a connection between the role of David and justice. Indeed, this grouping is held together by authorial, lexical, thematic, structural, and generic linkages.[20] Taken as a smaller collection,[21] it becomes evident that there is a

---

17. Jerome Creach, *The Destiny of the Righteous in the Psalms* (St. Louis: Chalice, 2008), 1.

18. The focus on man in this collection keeps us connected to their ethical dimensions. Cf. Pss 1:1; 5:6; 7:12, 14; 8:4; 9:19; 10:18; 11:4; 12:1, 8; 14:2, where in most instances the commentary is negative.

19. Creach, *The Destiny of the Righteous in the Psalms*, 8. He also noted, "The righteous in the Psalms are those who have a right relationship with God and whose relationships with other people are governed by God's expectations for human community," 3. Clarification on how to understand the messianic role in the Psalms is needed. As Belcher has noted using Luke 24 as an approach to the Psalter, "The comprehensive nature of Jesus' reference to the Old Testament is meant to demonstrate that all the Old Testament speaks of Jesus in some way, not merely those texts commonly accepted as 'Messianic.'" Belcher, *The Messiah and the Psalms*, 32.

20. The present writer has tried to avoid commonalities of regular linguistic usage such as prepositions, conjunctions, and adjectives. Only those words which are semantically loaded and thematically relevant have been selected.

21. Pss 15–24 form a collection by the inclusion of entrance or processional liturgies. William Brown, "'Here Comes the Sun!' The Metaphorical Theology of Psalms 15–24," in *The Composition of the Book of Psalms*, ed. E. Zenger, BETL 238 (Leuven: Peeters, 2010), 259–277.

shift in the formal aspects of this collection between Psalms 3–7 and 9–14. Psalm 8 serves as a hinge psalm that brings the varied foci of each smaller unit together as shown below. Taking an all-inclusive view of the textual evidence, coincidence seems implausible. Editorial intentionality has been demonstrated from psalms to psalm and in groupings.[22]

The laments or psalms of disorientation in Psalms 3–7[23] demonstrate familial resemblances of evoking God, affirming a problem (complaint), proclaiming one's faith, pleas/petitions, and a promise, pledge, or oath in doxology or ethical living.[24] Ethical life for the Psalmist does not operate in the abstract. He is aware of the dilemma, cognizant of the ways in which the plan of God is frustrated, and sensitive to the subtle nuances of how God deals with the various aspects of the exchanges between the righteous and the wicked. Rather than seeking to correct the crisis himself, the Psalmist uses prayer and poetic rhetoric as recognition of how these interactions ought to be sorted out.[25] Also, regarding generic parallels, the historical superscriptions serve as another basis for seeing the structure as intentional within this smaller unit. As structural indicators, they form an inclusio

---

22. Klaus Seybold noted that "the seventy-three psalms associated with David are not distributed at random throughout the Psalter, but rather they are ordered in groups and cycles," Klaus Seybold, *Introducing the Psalms,* trans. R. Graeme Dunphy (London: T & T Clark, 1990), 18. Claus Westermann noted that the "superscriptions to the Psalms identify several specific groupings." Claus Westermann, *Praise and Lament* (Atlanta: John Knox, 1981), 257; David M. Howard, *The Structure of Psalms 93–100,* Biblical and Judaic Studies 5 (Winona Lake, IN: Eisenbrauns, 1997); Gordon Wenham, "Toward a Canonical Reading of the Psalms," in *Canon and Biblical Interpretation,* eds. Craig Bartholomew et al., SAHS 7 (Grand Rapids, MI: Zondervan, 2006). Brueggemann cautioned, "And we need not treat each separate psalm as an isolated entity to be interpreted as though it stood by itself. We may rather take up certain representative psalms that serve as characteristic and typical examples of certain patterns of speech, articulating certain typical gestures and themes of faith, and reflecting certain typical situations of faith and unfaith." Walter Brueggemann, *The Message of the Psalms: A Theological Commentary* (Minneapolis: Augsburg, 1984), 16.

23. On the patterns and pathos of laments, see Hermann Gunkel, *An Introduction to the Psalms: The Genres of the Religious Lyric of Israel,* trans. J. D. Nogalski (Macon, GA: Mercer University Press, 1998), 121–198; W. H. Bellinger, *Psalms: Reading and Studying the Book of Praises* (Peabody, MA: Hendrickson, 1990), 44–73; Brueggemann, *The Message of the Psalms,* 51–121; Claus Westermann, *The Psalms: Structure, Content and Message,* trans. Ralphe D. Gehrke (Minneapolis: Augsburg , 1980), 53–70.

24. See Bullock, *Encountering the Book of Psalms,* 144. He called these particular psalms 'Songs of the Persecuted and Accused.' Other looks at the individual strophic structure of each psalm instead of Bullock's thematic reading. Cf. Samuel Terrien, *The Psalms: Strophic Structure and Theological Commentary* (Grand Rapids, MI: Eerdmans, 2003), 94–102. Though there are reasons to take issue with Gunkel's worldview, his classification of psalm types is helpful in showing a phenomenon at work which may have influenced the editorial work of the book of Psalms.

25. The pattern of the Davidic king using intercession as a method to bring about God's plan as seen in 2 Chr 6 bears special importance on how NT writers understood one aspect of the Messianic/ Christological nature of the Psalms. See Richard Pratt, "Royal Prayer and the Chronicler's Program" (ThD diss., Harvard University, 1987).

of history and memory as individual laments focusing on the theme of persecution and the plea for justice.[26]

Noting a thematic flow, Geoffrey Grogan stated that "Psalms 3–7 all show the Psalmist seeking refuge from his foes in God."[27] Both historical superscriptions in this grouping focus on a crisis where David is seeking shelter and, as shown below, the intervening psalms deal with God as a refuge in varied circumstances focusing on the judgment *for* the righteous and *against* the wicked. Psalm 3 is a lament of David as the victim of the doubts of the faithless (cf. v. 3), whereas, in Ps 7, he seeks to know if he has perpetrated injustice in his acts (cf. vv. 4–5). These two, both taken as relating responses to Absalom's rebellion, frame responses that relate to the Davidic dynastic covenant and hence, the Messianic hope. Thematically, in this unit, the reader encounters both the awareness of the external forces that contribute to injustice and the introspective questionings of a sensitized conscience. The Psalmist was not seeking personal vengeance against someone as a sort of sordid reciprocity, but as a covenantal response to and refuge from the injustices of the antagonists within and without regarding the reign of God.[28]

Keywords and themes that tie Psalms 3–7 to 9–14 meet in Ps 8. By moving from the specific to the general, Psalms 3–14 reverse the focus of Psalms 1 and 2, which look at the general man and move to the specific Messiah figure. As shown below, Psalms 3–7 focus on the confrontation of the Davidic king with threats to the Davidic covenant expressed in Ps 2.[29] Psalms 9–14 focus more on the worldwide judgment and the destiny of the righteous and the wicked articulated in Ps 1.

---

26. Jerome Skinner, "The Historical Superscriptions of Davidic Psalms: An Exegetical, Intertextual and Methodological Analysis" (PhD diss., Andrews University, 2016), gives a more detailed analysis of lexical, structural, thematic, and formal links. See also Patrick Miller, "The Beginning of the Psalter," in *The Shape and Shaping of the Psalter*, 89–90; Idem, "Kingship, Torah Obedience and Prayer," in *Neue Wege der Psalmenforschung*, eds. Klaus Seybold and Erich Zenger (Freiburg: Herder, 1995), 127–42. In Pss 3–7, the Psalmist faces the attacks of his enemies with God in a lament form. Each psalm deals with threats to Davidic kingship, the theme of danger, and God as a refuge (cf. Pss 5:12; 7:2).

27. Geoffrey Grogan, *Psalms*, The Two Horizons Old Testament Commentary (Grand Rapids, MI: Eerdmans, 2008), 255. Wilson saw Pss 7–10 as a consecutive grouping which "provides new insights regarding psalm interpretation as a whole and regarding understanding of the specific message of the psalm," Wilson, *Psalms*, 239.

28. Indeed, Gunkel noted the juridical aspect explicit in the lament genre, saying that "sometimes one can recognize that a *trial* and its proceedings can cause the complaint." Gunkel, *An Introduction to the Psalms*, 139.

29. In Psalm 3, the main issue is brought to focus by the use of the appositional phrase בְּנוֹ "his son." This appositional phrase points to the dynastic expectation of sons following their fathers as kings, which is prevalent in the HB and ANE. So, the relationship between the psalm and the h/ss deals with kingship. The threat to kingship by acts of hostility or regicide is well attested in the HB and ANE literature. Cf. 2 Kgs 14:19; 2 Chr 22:5–12. ANE texts also exhibit this phenomenon. Cf. COS 1.76; COS 2.16; 2.37; *ANET* 287–288. Cf. Victor Matthews and Don Benjamin, *Old Testament Parallels: Laws and Stories from the Ancient Near East* (Mahwah, NJ: Paulist, 1991), 205. In Psalm 7, there is a reference in 2 Sam 18:30–32 that uses the same grammatical construction קוּם + עַל ("rising up against") that is addressed regarding a strong connection between Pss 3 and 7, pointing to a threat to David's kingship.

Justice here is not an abstract principle; it is acclaimed in association with God's sovereignty (Pss 9:7–8; 10:16–18).[30]

The analysis below shows that it is in Ps 8 where several foci are brought together. First, reflections on creation mark out true sovereignty regarding God and man. That relationship is described using mixed metaphors and diverse imagery, but the correlation of king and vice-regent is evident throughout. Second, man's role as outlined in Ps 8 describes the jurisdiction and subjects of dominion. For the Psalmist, it is in creation that the Word of God and Messianic connection converge and establish God's justice as a universal principle. Third, without creation ethics is relative, judgment is subjective, and eschatology loses its "restorative" focus. Psalm 8 stresses God's role as Sovereign,[31] so ethical life is grounded in a common origin and subjection to the governance of God. Justice is rooted in God's character and divine design as the objective basis for evaluation, and eschatology is built on protology.[32]

Structurally, it is significant that this hymn of creation (Ps 8) that sets forth humanity's proper role in God's creation design is surrounded by laments of how morally debased humankind has become.[33] The connection between creation and justice regarding God's sovereignty is the focus on his name/character. This notion can be seen in the nuances brought out in connection with God's name where Ps 8 brings the two smaller sections together.[34] His name is worthy of praise in relation to his power, but also in relation to his care. The Psalmist proclaims

---

30. Versification follows the Masoretic Text (MT) of the Hebrew Bible (HB) unless otherwise indicated by ET (English translation). The Psalter contains proclamations about God's nature in relation to justice (cf. Ps 119:149, 156 to see examples of God's relation to justice in terms of His acts). In the broader structure expressed here, examples can be utilized in a dialectic form as a model that articulates the nature of justice in relation to God. Through images, metaphors, and language in poetic style, examples elucidate an understanding that enables readers to find their way around the concept. Justice is exemplified by the activity of God because it is part and parcel of his being. God operates in ways consistent with who he is. Abstractions by themselves do not deal substantially with the ethical objective. From the Psalmist's perspective, the activity of the wicked is judged in relation to the Person, word, will, and activity of God and his directives as Sovereign. This point is further supported by the first usage of justice (מִשְׁפָּט) in Genesis 18:19 where it is used in a relational and ethical way dealing with God's election of Abraham to carry forward the work of the covenant mission.

31. Pss 3:5; 4:4, 9; 5:3, 13; 6:5, 9, 10; 7:2, 7–14; 8:2, 4, 7–9; 9:5, 6, 12, 17; 10:14, 16; 11:4; 12:6; 14:2.

32. Philosopher Daniel Robinson noted that the three fundamental issues of philosophy are the problems of knowledge (metaphysics, epistemology), of conduct (ethics), and of governance. Daniel Robinson, *The Great Ideas of Philosophy*, 2nd ed., The Great Courses Video Lecture series (Chantilly, VA: Teaching Co., 2004), http://www.thegreatcourses.com/courses/great-ideas-of-philosophy-2nd-edition.html. Through the series, he traced humankind's philosophical wrestling with these three notions. The Psalmist seems to have something to say that addresses the foundation of these three concerns. The Word of God addresses the issue of knowledge, and conduct, and the role of the Messiah figure addresses God's plan for His governance in the hearts of men.

33. This thought was original to me and I later found support for this in Belcher's work *The Messiah and the Psalms*.

34. Cf. Pss 5:12; 7:18; 8:2, 10; 9:3, 11. M. G. Easton noted that "justice is not an optional product of his will, but an unchangeable principle of his very nature." M. G. Easton, "Justice of God," *Easton's Bible Dictionary* (New York: Harper & Brothers, 1893). Cf. Pss 7:9, 12; 9:5, 9, 20; 10:18. See the lexical connections between Pss 7–9 below. It is no coincidence that the NT uses this psalm by and about Jesus to support the references to Him as the Son of David (Matt 21:16) and as having complete dominion over all creation (1 Cor 15:27; Heb 2:6–8).

that God denounces or passes sentence on injustice every day (7:12).[35] As the previous parallel line states, the perfect, righteous Judge detects the motives of man and holds them accountable for those motives and actions (cf. vv. 13–17) in light of His character and *hesed* he makes available. Considering man's failure to appropriate his given dominion according to God's original creation design, a new rule, a new type of dominion is needed to return man to the original creation design and that is found in the work of the Messiah figure outlined in Ps 2. Notice that humanity's destiny is associated from the beginning of the Psalter with their relation to God's anointed.[36]

The Semantics of Justice: Lexical Parallels in Psalms 3–7[37]

Table 3. Lexical parallels between Psalms 3–4 (MT)

Psalm 3	Lexical Links	Psalm 4
3:2	צר	4:2
3:2	רבב	4:8
3:3*	רבים אמרים	4:7
3:4	כבדי	4:3
3:5	קרא + ענה	4:2, 4
3:6	שכב + ישן	4:9
3:8- Hiph Impv/1cs	הושיעני	4:9 Hiph Impv/1cs

* In both chapters, the phrase "many are saying" is followed by a statement of distrust.

The main issues outlined in Ps 2 are grounded in a historical incident in Ps 3. Indeed, 2 Samuel 14–16 gives vivid expression to the antagonism against the Lord's anointed, David. When first encountering these laments, the reader is arrested by the variety of crises.[38] In Ps 3, the Psalmist moves from crisis (vv. 2–3) to trust (vv. 4–9), emphasizing the point of distress as the multitude of enemies and God's support as the source of protection. The historical superscriptions[39]

---

35. Cf. Ps 121:3. Wilson noted that "the psalmist's hope and claim are that Yahweh is constantly overseeing human affairs and declaring *mišpat*. His case will not slide by unnoticed but will receive the attention it deserves." Wilson, *Psalms*, 192. This notion of judgment need not be seen in a negative light. Jerome Creach outlined several reasons why this focus is healthy for the church and can establish what he called a "constructive understanding of divine judgment." Creach, *The Destiny of the Righteous in the Psalms*, 12.

36. This reference is understood as a Messianic psalm that points beyond any historical Davidic ruler in Israel's monarchy. The universal scope of the psalm in its content and placement make it clear the no king lived up to that divine-design. New Testament writers pointed to Christ as the Son of David who fulfilled the task of setting forth God's glory while restoring the divine design for humanity through his life.

37. The Tables list the verses where the lexical links occur according the versification of the MT because the historical superscriptions are taken as originally part of the text. Readers should reference the Tables to see parallels and to compare the verses.

38. The type of crisis can be summed up as the relationship of the Psalmist to God, to the "other," and to himself. The Psalmist can be the victim or the perpetrator. God can be (as seen through the eyes of the Psalmist) the Judge, Savior, or Perpetrator. The "other" is seen primarily as the enemy, though at times the Psalmist questions whether he has done wrong to the other. Those crises can be mental, spiritual, physical (material) seen through false accusations, illness, or physical attacks.

39. Peter Craigie noted that "in summary, the parallels indicate a close link between the psalm and David's flight from Absalom, but the significance to be attached to the parallels could be interpreted in a variety of ways." *Psalms 1–50*, 2nd ed., WBC 19 (Nashville, TN: Nelson Reference & Electronic, 2004), 73.

clarify that the anointed one's foes need not be those outside God's people.[40] The correspondence of the (צר) enemy/distress in both psalms points out that whether it is the perpetrator (in v. 3-noun) or the effect (in v. 4-adjective) the result is the same, the Psalmist feels confined by a historical entity.

The parallels with Ps 4 highlight the themes of the enemies' speech. In Ps 3, the probing is external, about the Psalmist, whether God is present within the corridors of hope (v. 5), whereas in Ps 4, it is internal to the enemies' perception of their situation (v. 7).[41] In both cases, the questions evince distress concerning the justice of God. In both instances, the pattern of call (i.e. plea) and response (קרא + ענה) elicits parallel statements of trust. In Ps 3, the trust is associated with God's locale, his holy hill, which could be a metonymy for sovereignty.[42] This connects the readers back to Ps 2, where God says he sets his anointed (v. 6). The Messianic overtones stand out here because the response of the nations is tied to a destiny which points beyond the scope of the reign of David or Solomon (vv. 1–2).[43] The Psalmist is assured of justice because of God's authority over all creation (v. 4). In Ps 4, the outcome of trust is associated with God's righteousness, the cause being God's vindication. These themes of God's throne and righteousness are continuously linked throughout the rest of this collection (Pss 7:8; 9:4, 8), and it is in Ps 2 where the connection between these two is first seen. The assurance of the triumph of the Davidic king in Ps 2 is expressed in the outcomes in subsequent psalms (Pss 3:9; 4:9; 5:13; 6:10, 11; 7:8; 9:20, 21; 10:17, 18; 12:8; 13:6; 14:7). Now the Psalmist is secure because of God's intervention; he can lie down and sleep (שכב + ישׁן).

In both psalms, the use of imagery that describes the reasoning behind his confidence is given. In Ps 3, the Psalmist envisages God's protection through the metaphor of a shield (v. 4) and in Ps 4, he reflects on the light of God's face by a citation to the Aaronic covenant blessing (v. 7).[44] Taken together, nascent in the complaints and pleas of these psalms is the question of justice surrounding the promises of God. The threat to dynastic fulfillment for David and the threat to God's people's future revolve around covenant promises to establish righteousness through the Davidic line and God's protection as seen in Deut 28:1–14 and 2 Sam 7:1–17. The inference here is that the plea is reasonable and legitimate because the people of God are faithful to the covenant Lord and his Torah. For the Davidic king and those faithful to the covenant, the answer to queries of God's justice regarding his promises is answered in the affirmative.

---

40. Wilson posited that "the conflict here is between different interpretations of the faith rather than between believer and unbeliever." Wilson, *Psalms*, 148. Craigie wrote that "the dubious help of doubters can sometimes be as dangerous as the arrogant words of enemies!" Craigie, *Psalms 1–50*, 81.

41. J. L. Mays proposed that in Ps 3, the "central theological issue of the prayer is what many are saying about the petitioner... It discloses the true significance of the hostility." J. L. Mays, *Psalms*, Interpretation (Louisville, KY: Westminster John Knox, 1994), 52. If this assessment is indeed correct, it may serve as a reasoning for the editors placing Ps 4 adjacent to it to highlight the statements of the enemies.

42. Goldingay, noting the connection with Ps 2, stated that "if the king utters this plea, the reference to Yhwh's holy mountain will take up the fact that Yhwh did install him there (2:6)." John Goldingay, *Psalms*, 3 vols., BCOTWP (Grand Rapids, MI: Baker Academic, 2006), 1:111–112.

43. For a canonical analysis on the subject, see Eugene H. Merrill, "Royal Priesthood: An Old Testament Messianic Motif," *BibSac* 150 (1993): 51–61.

44. This imagery is taken from the Aaronic benediction in Num 6:24–26 as another nod to the covenant notion of justice.

Table 4. Lexical parallels between Psalms 4–5 (MT)

Psalm 4	Lexical Links	Psalm 5
4:3	כזב	5:7
4:4 (adjective)	חסיד	5:8 (noun)
4:1, 6	צדק	5:9
4:8 (noun)	שמחה	5:12 (verb)

Where Ps 3 focused on the quantitative impact of disbelief, Ps 4 articulates the qualitative shades of wickedness. Psalm 3 focuses on the speech of the wicked (v. 3), and Ps 4 focuses on the nature of that speech (v. 3). Compared with Ps 5, which communicates God's response to false testimony, Ps 4 conveys the wicked person's relation to it and why God's response is what it is. In fact, they love it (v. 3). Instead of meditating on the Torah, they embrace a deceptive mindset and manner. As Wilson noted, taken in a more technical religious sense of imploring deity, "seeking lies" can be a "disparaging reference to false/foreign gods."[45] Here, then, injustice relates to operating out of a false system of belief which may not only be false, but also syncretistic.

Psalm 4 highlights the contrasts between the righteous and the wicked through covenant terms. The godly (חסיד) exemplify the qualitative aspect of loyalty to God and man and are characterized by fulfilling their obligations to their established covenant relationship as the response to God's justice.[46] The righteous are the objects of God's *hesed*. Psalm 5:8 focuses on the consequences of God's covenant love: access. Those who are "set apart," who live a life of doxology, are contrasted to those previously described who cannot stand in God's presence because they live lives of injustice.[47] Hans-Joachin Kraus, making the connection between 4:4 and 5:8, stated, "The benevolent favor of Yahweh reveals itself in a real act of grace and reception (in Ps. 4:3 [4] the real act is the turn to salvation taking place in the verdict of God)."[48]

In Ps 4:6, the Psalmist urges the unrighteous to right their wrongs by offering

45. Wilson, *Psalms*, 154. Others have noted this point. Cf. Craig Broyles, *Psalms*, NIB (Peabody, MA: Hendrickson, 1999), 52–53; Grogan, *Psalms*, 47.

46. A חסיד is one who does what is right in God's eyes and remains faithful to God (cf. Pss 12:1; 18:25; 31:23; 37:28; 86:2; 97:10). Willem A. VanGemeren noted that the Psalmist is "set apart by the Lord, who has bestowed on him his steadfast love, confirmed to him by covenant (v.3; cf. 2 Sa 7:15a)." VanGemeren, Psalms, EBC 5 (Grand Rapids, MI: Zondervan, 2008), 109. Cf. Robert Davidson, *The Vitality of Worship: a Commentary on the Book of Psalms*, ITC (Grand Rapids, MI: Eerdmans, 1998), 27. Rather than the common word for *set apart* (בדל), the Psalmist uses a term (פלה), that, coupled with the covenant designation, point to a distinction based on the presence and juridical activity of God. Comparing usage in other contexts, Keil and Delitzsch defined this word as "to make a separation, make a distinction Exod. 9:4; 11:7, then to distinguish in an extraordinary and remarkable way Exod. 8:18, and to show Ps. 17:7, cf. 31:22, so that consequently what is meant is not the mere *selection* (בָּחַר), but the remarkable selection to a remarkable position of honour." Carl Friedrich Keil and Franz Delitzsch, *Commentary on the Old Testament*, vol. 5 (Peabody, MA: Hendrickson, 1996), 68.

47. Wickedness is connected to injustice here for two reasons: 1) because people are the object of the evil deeds, which makes the action relational and 2) evil here is described as a way of life, which connotes the reality that deception and greed color their actions.

48. Hans~Joachin Kraus, *Psalms* 1–59, trans. Hilton C. Oswald, CC (Minneapolis, MN: Fortress, 1995), 155.

sacrifices of righteousness (צדק).[49] Wilson noted that "in view of the psalmist's earlier description of Yahweh as "God of my righteousness" (v. 1), the "right [*sedeq*, right/righteous] sacrifices required of the opponents are to be understood as acknowledgments of 'the justice proceeding from Yahweh' – the reaffirmation of covenant obligations to God."[50] Both psalms close on a high note of expectation and rejoicing for God's just dealings with humanity.

Table 5. Lexical parallels between Psalms 5–6 (MT)

Psalm 5	Lexical Links	Psalm 6
5:3 (verb)	פלל	6:10 (noun)
5:4	שמע + קל	6:9
5:6	פאלי און	6:9
5:8	חסד	6:5
5:9	שוררי	6:8

The psalms move from the life of the righteous to the life of the wicked. The connections between Ps 5 and Ps 6 focus mainly on prayer, the characteristics of the righteous and the wicked, and God's relation to both classes. In Ps 5, the Psalmist appeals for God's response as the true Sovereign of all creation through prayer (פלל) and sacrifice on account of his suffering where his faith is expressed in waiting. On the notion of prayer, Wilson noted that "He calls on God to hear not only the clearly articulated and verbalized pleas but also to attend even to the inarticulate murmuring of an agonized soul."[51] In Ps 6, the Psalmist has the assurance that God does indeed hear and acts on his behalf. That assurance is further supported by the assertion that moves from God will hear (שמע + קל) in Ps 5 to God has heard in Ps 6.

Inclusive of four descriptive terms of the wicked,[52] a case is mounted in Ps 5 for the need for God "to hear," to intervene against the workers of iniquity (פאלי און). Not simply occasional slights or misdeeds, their actions are character flaws where acts, words, and motivations are played out in human interactions with no repentance. In Ps 6, the Psalmist appeals to them to turn away from him (v. 8). Yahweh hears and gives the Psalmist confidence that the destiny of the wicked is in his arena, and the Psalmist need not infuriate the tension by continued association. This turning is not one of a proud condemnation, but the response of assurance because the Psalmist identifies his situation as the result of God's grace (חסד), and not any innate moral superiority. Beyond the implication of survival, the Psalmist prays for life (v. 4). The imperatives (v. 5) here suggest a complete renewal: grace, healing, returning, rescue, and salvation. The bestowal of God's grace is fully restorative in its eschatological sense when the presence of death no

---

49. The phrase used in Deut 33:19 seems to focus on the response of the people for blessings they receive.

50. Wilson, *Psalms*, 157–158.

51. Wilson, *Psalms*, 165. The root of הגיג found in Pss 1 and 2 (הגה) is used for meditation in the positive sense in Psalm 1, but in the negative sense of plotting in Psalm 2. In Ps 5, it is taken as positive as a meditative prayer which associates the Davidic king with Psalm 1.

52. Ps 5:5, 6 characterize the evil people as (1) the boastful, (2) evildoers, (3) those who speak lies, and (4) the bloodthirsty and deceitful man.

longer threatens.[53] In its depleting character of draining life, death is associated in a way with the work of his enemies (צוֹרְרִי). Psalm 5 portrays the need for God to lead because the destination is life and harmony with God's way, and as in Ps 1, the Psalmist knows that the way of the wicked will perish. Even physiological imagery where the Psalmist associates the wicked with death (inward parts as destruction, an open throat as a grave) is used (v. 10).

Table 6. Lexical parallels between Psalms 6–7 (MT)

Psalm 6	Lexical Links	Psalm 7
6:2	באפך	7:7
6:5	ישׁע root	7:2, 11
6:5	חלץ	7:5
6:5, 11	שׁוב	7:8, 13, 17
6:6	מות	7:14
6:6	ידה	7:18
6:8	צוררי	7:5, 7
6:9	און	7:15
6:9	פעל	7:14
6:11	איב	7:6

In comparing Psalms 6 and 7, the tension of life and death and destiny continues, but the focus shifts here to God's justice in judgment as the answer to moral evil. A cursory reading might make one assume that judgment is done with anger (אף), as modern readers understand being mad. However, in other places in the Psalms, it is associated with divine disgust for sin and the impact of judgment.[54] Thus, anger is perspectival of the Psalmist's notion of how the negative consequences of God's judgment appear. It is the imagery of volcanic heat, an extremely explosive activity, that can erupt into destruction.[55] The cry for mercy from God's wrath brings the reader back to the tension between life and death (מות/ישׁע), for in death, there is no remembrance or praise (6:6, ידי), which are synonymous with life (cf. 150:6). In death, man is incapable of relating to God. In Ps 7, death, in the form of God's weapons of warfare, is seen as an enemy to those who do not repent (v. 13, 14). This death must be more than all humanity's lot, for it is the result of

---

53. The phrase עד־מתי, "how long," in its immediate historical context, refers to the Psalmist's plea for deliverance from his situation. However, in broader terms, it points to an unresolved end of sin and its effects, a traditional refrain in penitential literature. It is familiar from the Psalms (6:4; 79:5; 80:5; 90:13) and the Prophets (Isa 6:11; Jer 12:4) and recurs in apocalyptic literature (4 Ezra 6:59). Brueggemann commented, "Israel fully anticipates that the God of its core testimony must and will act decisively to intervene and transform unbearable circumstances. But the intervention and transformation are not on the horizon—hence the question. The question is not a request for information or a timetable. It is a restless insistence that amounts to a reprimand of Yahweh, who has not done for Israel what Israel has legitimately expected." Walter Brueggemann, *Theology of the Old Testament: Testimony, Dispute, Advocacy* (Minneapolis, MN: Fortress, 2005), 319.

54. Cf. Ps 18:16. Notice in Ps 18:8 the association with volcanic activity. Commenting on its use in Psalm 6, Wilson stated that "the two parallel words for 'anger' and 'wrath' suggest anger that is hot and poisonous in its intensity. Wilson, *Psalms*, 178.

55. Note in Psalm 6 how the Psalmist associates the impact of God's anger to the waves of chaos (v. 7). William Brown noted that "the psalmist envisions his bed submerged in a pool supplied by his tears. The second verb (*msh*) means to 'dissolve, melt,' as in the case of ice (cf. 147:18)." Brown, *Seeing the Psalms*, 118.

the judgment. The rest of the comparisons in these psalms continue to express the life/death tension which brings us to Ps 8.

Table 7. Lexical parallels between Psalms 7–8 (MT)

Psalm 7	Lexical Links	Psalm 8
7:5, 7	צרר	8:3
7:6	ארץ	8:2, 10
7:10, 13, 14	כון	8:4
7:18	שם	8:2, 10
7:6	כבוד	8:6
7:6	אויב	8:3

As noted earlier, Ps 8 plays a pivotal role as the pivot point between Psalms 3–7 and 9–14 and brings the two foci together. The כבוד,[56] and שם,[57] respectively one's glory and name or character/reputation, in their thematic import and varied contexts come to an apex in the creation hymn of Ps 8.[58] This psalm brings out more fully what exactly is involved only in part in each preceding psalm. Psalm 8 also helps the reader put into context the succeeding psalms, the tension of life and death. Up to Ps 8, the editor's organizing theme concerns the antagonist's attitude and action against the righteous, who are stated emphatically to be the glory of the Lord (3:4). In subsequent psalms, the honor or reputation of the Lord and the antagonists are the main emphases where God judges all and destiny is expressed (Pss 8:2, 10; 9:3, 6, 11; 14:5).

The tone shifts from describing the characteristics of the righteous and wicked to describing God's response to both entities.[59] Seen in its most immediate context of looking back at Ps 7 and forward to Ps 9, it is important to see that, inserted between these judicial laments, is a hymn of creation, of life.[60] Psalm 7 ends and Ps 8 begins by dealing with exalting the name of the Lord while moving from judgment in Ps 7 to creation in Ps 8. As Ps 8:17 closes on the exaltation of God's name, Ps 9:1–2 opens by exalting God for his wonderful deeds, which include Creation, and moves forward into another judgment context (cf. vv. 3–20) where the Psalmist vows to sing of the name of the Lord. The reader may ask why a creation hymn is placed here. In the lexical and thematic correspondence from texts outside the Psalter that deal with glory, a consistent pattern emerges from

---

56. Cf. Pss 3:4; 4:3; 7:6; 8:6.

57. Cf. Pss 5:12; 7:18; 8:2, 10; 9:3, 6, 11; 14:5.

58. These words are associated throughout the Psalter as well as the whole HB. Cf. Pss 29:2; 66:2; 72:19; 79:9; 96:8; 102:15; 115:1; Isa 59:19; 1 Chr 16:10, 29.

59. Consider that there are 61 indictments, in 29 verses, of the wicked person in Pss 9–14. Cf. Pss 9:5, 16, 17; 10:2, 3, 4, 5, 7, 8, 9, 10, 11, 13, 15, 18; 11:2, 5, 6; 12:2, 4, 7, 8; 14: title–1, 3, 4, 5, 6. Many of the indictments are predominantly in two forms: 1) why God judges them and 2) the result of God's judgment. God judges the wicked because they are arrogant (10:2). The result of God's judgment is that they perish, their name is blotted out forever (9:5), they are snared in the work of their hand (9:16; 10:2), and they return to Sheol (10:17).

60. The lexical and thematic parallels are apparent. Cf. Pss 7:9; 9:9 (דין), 7:7; 9:5, 17 (משפט), 7:9, 18; 9:5, 9 (צדק).

the text about the themes of creation, judgment, and salvation.[61] More frequently, the passages that deal with the name of God are about God's role as Sovereign and Vindicator and man's role and responsibility as an image-bearer of God.[62] In Pss 3–14, the understanding of justice encompasses humanity's relation to God as Sovereign and Creator, to humanity as co-image-bearer, and creation as the landscape upon which those relations traverse. These are all associated with life in the present. Where these themes intersect is in their relation to man's purpose in Creation: to live in harmony with the character of God. Thus, injustice is not an abstraction, but a tangible rebellion against God's created order; its association is with death. This also reveals the reality that the people of God are subject to suffering in their role of image-bearers and oppression is the destruction of the expression of that image as has been outlined in Psalms 3–7.[63]

According to the Creation account (Gen 1–2), humanity's rule is relational, not hierarchical (cf. 1:26–28; 2:24).[64] Psalm 8 tells the reader that mankind was given "glory and majesty," a phrase usually reserved for God (cf. Ps 145: 5, 12). This privilege, weighed in its manifold expressions, is to be doxological and service-oriented and not like the manipulation of power structures. This climactic focus grounded in several references to man, in general, makes it clear that justice and judgment are based on God as Creator and his purposes and plans for creation. The phrase "son(s) of man," used in varied contexts in this small grouping, has a common theme of expressing the finite, the limited, and the created.[65] Juxtaposed

61. For a more in-depth look at this concept in the Psalter, see Jerome Skinner, "The Locus and Activity of כָּבוֹד [Glory] in the Psalms" (unpublished Sanctuary Class paper, Andrews University, Spring 2011, available upon request). Psalm 4:3 speaks of man's glory regarding his position of kingship. Gerald Wilson stated that glory here has been understood in two ways—human dignity or—the Psalmist's God, Yahweh. Wilson, Psalms, 153. Goldingay argued, "Subsequent lines will suggest that v. 2 refers to Yhwh's honor rather than the suppliant's. Yhwh is Israel's (106:20; Jer. 2:11) and thus the one the suppliant honors." Goldingay, Psalms, 1:120. This insight does not conflict with the fact that the Psalmist is referring to the defamation of his position, which Yahweh has given (Ps 3:4). Glory here parallels a contrast with what is empty and false. Davidson noted that "his—honor (kābôd; cf. 3:3), his standing in the community is under threat. He is being subjected to—shame, humiliation at the hands of those who—love vain words and seek after lies." Davidson, The Vitality of Worship, 23. Contextually, "if this refers to the rebellion in Absalom's time (see introductions to Ps 3 and 4), the allusion most obviously would be to the fact that David was being robbed of his kingly dignity and reduced to virtual beggary and extreme want." Francis D. Nichol, ed., The Seventh-day Adventist Bible Commentary, rev. and electronic ed.; Logos Bible Software (Washington, DC: Review & Herald, 1978; 2002), 3:639. Psalm 21:6 also alludes to honor by describing the reality of how Yahweh's salvation affects him. (Pss 62:7; 112:9; 149:5). Psalm 7:5 can be called a psalm of judgment/vindication.

62. For a more in-depth look at this concept in the creation narrative, see Jerome Skinner, "Roles and Rulership in Genesis 1" (Old Testament Theology Class paper, Andrews University, 2010, available upon request). In that paper, I noted that "the Creator and created describe the relationship between God and man, and the rulers and the ruled describe the relationship between man (in the image of God) and the creation." Thus, the notion of dominion is not just a matter of power but of relationship and service as expressing the image of God.

63. McCann made the point that, in the juxtaposition of Psalms 4–7 to 8, "the 'glory and honor' of humanity (Psalm 8) are not incompatible with the distress, trouble, and weakness of humanity portrayed in Psalms 4–7." J. Clinton McCann Jr., A Theological Introduction to the Book of Psalms: The Psalms as Torah (Nashville, TN: Abingdon, 1993), 60–63.

64. Richard M. Davidson, Flame of Yahweh: Sexuality in the Old Testament (Peabody; MA: Hendrickson, 2007), 22–35. A central point is that both male and female were made in the image of God as co-rulers (Gen 1:27, 28).

65. Cf. Pss 4:3; 8:5; 11:4; 12:2, 9; 14:2.

to man's description, it is the name of God and his glory as the eternal Creator that distinguishes him from the creature and holds a man responsible in relation to his justice in a creation context (cf. vv. 3–4).[66] The structure of Ps 8 points this way as the interplay between heaven and earth points the reader back and forth between these two poles.[67] The attitude and actions of the antagonist are a denial and frustration of the image-bearing purposes of God. Thus, the "curses" are not curses typically understood in modern day vernacular, but are cries of the heart for God to restore what is being attacked, i.e., the glory and majesty of God as Creator.

The links between Pss 8 and 9 express the connection between creation, justice, and ethics. Meredith Kline captured this phenomenon by noting,

> Nuclear to the divine Glory is its official-functional aspect: it is the glory of royal-judicial office. In the Glory, God sits as King. This official royal glory comes to formal-physical expression in theophanic radiance; in the Glory, God is enthroned in majestic robes of light. There is also an ethical dimension to the Glory: the foundations of the cloud-veiled throne are justice and righteousness, and fidelity and truth go before it in royal procession (Pss 89:14; 97:2). It is a throne of holiness (Ps 47:8) and the enthroned King of glory is ever acclaimed as "holy, holy, holy" by the multitude of the heavenly host (Isa. 6:3).[68]

Table 8. Lexical parallels between Psalms 8–9 (MT)

Psalm 8	Lexical Links	Psalm 9
8:2, 10	שׁם	9:3, 6, 11
8:3	אויב	9:4, 7
8:4	כון	9:8
8:4	ראה	9:14
8:5	אנושׁ	9:20, 21
8:5	זכר	9:7, 13
8:7	שׁית	9:21

Moving into Psalms 9–14, lexical parallels are reduced in quantity, but the focus becomes sharper when looking at the thematic content. Structurally, these psalms are held together by a cache of terms that runs throughout and focuses on similar concepts including the judgment of God, the work of the wicked and the heart condition, and the verbal proclamations/testimony of the righteous and the wicked.

Justice for the Saints: The Thematic Perspective of Psalms 9–14

The thematic narrative of Psalms 9–14 is still grounded in the lexical parallels of adjacent psalms as Tables 9–13 show.

---

66. Cf. Meredith G. Kline, "Creation in the Image of the Glory-Spirit." *WTJ* 39.2 (1976): 250–72.

67. David Dorsey suggested an abba chiastic structure (vv. 2a, 2b–5, 6–9, 10 MT) followed here. David A. Dorsey, *The Literary Structure of the Old Testament: A Commentary on Genesis-Malachi* (Grand Rapids, MI: Baker Books, 1999), 177.

68. Meredith Kline, *Images of the Spirit*, repr. ed. (Eugene, OR: Wipf & Stock Pub,1999), 27.

122

Table 9. Lexical parallels between Psalms 9–10 (MT)

Psalm 9	Lexical Links	Psalm 10
9:6, 16, 18, 20, 21	גוי	10:16
9:2	לב	10:6, 11, 13, 17
9:16, 17, 18	רשע	10:2, 3, 4, 13, 15 (*2)
9:4, 6 7, 19	אבד	10:16
9:11, 13	דרש	10:4, 13, 15
9:13, 14, 19	עני	10:2, 9, 12
9:5, 8, 17	משפט	10:5
9:5, 8, 12	ישב	10:8
9:13, 18, 19	שכח	10:11, 12
9:6, 8	עולם	10:16
9:20, 21	אנוש	10:18

Table 10. Lexical parallels between Psalms 10-11 (MT)

Psalm 10	Lexical Links	Psalm 11
10:2, 3, 4, 13, 15 (*2)	רשע	11:2, 5, 6
10:6, 11, 13, 17	לב	11:2
10:17	כון	11:2

Table 11. Lexical parallels between Psalms 11-12 (MT)

Psalm 11	Lexical Links	Psalm 12
11:2, 5, 6	רשע	12:8
11:4	בני אדם	12:9
11:2	לב	12:3

Table 12. Lexical parallels between Psalms 12-13

Psalm 12	Lexical Links	Psalm 13
12:2 (verb)	ישע	13:6 (noun)
12:2 (adj.)	חסד	13:6 (noun)
12:3	לב	13:3, 6
12:6	שית	13:3
12:9	רום	13:3

Table 13. Lexical parallels between Psalms 13-14

Psalm 13	Lexical Links	Psalm 14
13:5, 6	גיל	14:7
13:3, 6	לב	14:1
13:6	ישועה	14:7

Psalms 9–14 pick up the theme of man and image bearing and its far-reaching claims inclusive of a worldwide scope. The personal and private now broadens to the corporate and universal. The line that runs through all these psalms is the focus on the heart (לב). By comparing man's actions with the divine design (creation covenant), injustice is seen as a tangible denial of, a going beyond the boundaries of, and a frustration of God's purposes of creation. Wilson noted that

> the psalmist's experience of oppression at the hands of the wicked is a result of the 'enoš gone wrong–an abuse of the power and authority given to humans by God in Psalm 8. This divinely given power has been misdirected because of an arrogant and prideful misunderstanding of how and why humans are to exercise that power.[69]

These psalms paint the picture of God's attitude towards righteousness, which he loves, and wickedness and the inner character of people regarding violence and evil. From the Psalmist's perspective, the only answer to the dilemma is the God of justice. "The book of Psalms presents many moods in dealing with aspects of the justice of God. A dominant note of the Psalter is the celebration of Yahweh's kingship over creation, and his exercise of justice is acclaimed in association with this sovereignty."[70] Here it is noted that juridical activity is associated with kingship in the spatial context of the heavenly sanctuary. In the Psalter, the heavenly sanctuary is the epicenter of God's judicial activity: his throne (9:4, 7; 11:4).

The People's Role as *Image Bearers*[71]

The people of God can be seen in two ways when it comes to the justice of God: an active and a passive role. Actively, in indirect agency, those in positions of authority or with positions of influence are to "use their power and influence to seek justice and equity, defending those in society who have no access to power and representation: the widows, orphans, needy, weak, and so on."[72] It is in this way that, for those less fortunate, the image of God can be nurtured and protected from the onslaughts of indifference. What is of import in the use of these descriptive terms is that it provides a rhetorical mode of ethical dialogue that allows suffering to speak, to hear the truth from the voiceless and powerless. Structurally, in most of these laments, the Psalmist uses motivation as a rhetorical device. That is, the Psalmist pleads his case as in court trials giving reasons for the intervention sought. As W. H. Bellinger noted "All expressions look toward the purpose of the psalm–to persuade God to deliver."[73] Based on previous revelation, the Psalmist and, in this grouping, the people of God are justified in seeking God's protection from an oppressor (Pss 5:4; 6:23; 10:18; 11:2), judicial vindication against unjust

---

69. Wilson, *Psalms*, 241–242.

70. J. Davies, "Theodicy," in the *Dictionary of Old Testament: Wisdom, Poetry and Writings* (Nottingham, UK: IVP, 2008), 811.

71. Words of the people of God are descriptive regarding their moral character. The lexical range encompasses the active and passive roles of those in the realm of God's justice which can be seen even in the use of the same word. Cf. צדיק (Pss 5:3; 7:10, 12; 11:3, 5, 7; 14:5).

72. Wilson, *Psalms*, 242.

73. Bellinger, *Psalms*, 59.

accusations (Ps 7:6, 8, 11),[74] and even social justice as it relates to the plan and purposes of God as outlined in the Bible, a pivotal issue in the Torah and for most of the prophets.[75]

Passively, the oppressed, defenseless members of society (10:18) are the beneficiaries of judgment. Psalm 2:8–12 makes it clear that a righteous kingdom will be established through the Messiah. More than just one's civic or socio-economic status of having no recourse against the aims of the perpetrators of injustice, what the Psalmist has in mind here as the defenseless are those who need the intervention of the Messianic king to establish true righteousness. Given the inherent nature of assaults (slander, lies, and false testimony; cf. Pss 3:2; 5:5; 6:8; 7:14; 10:7; 12:4), the Psalmist makes it clear he was not primarily dependent on political structures and social movements to right wrongs and saw the claims of divine justice beyond the judicial precedents of secular courts. The nature of injustice here is covenantal, religious. "Since Yahweh is the eternal righteous king, he will take the side of the weak, defenseless, and oppressed in society against the wicked so that the one 'who is of the earth [i.e. is mortal and of limited power and authority], may terrify no more' (10:18)."[76] This statement can be taken in an eschatological sense that points back to the two destinies marked out in Ps 1. The major focus is that the oppressed and downtrodden have no recourse to establish eternal justice and right wrongs beyond the confines of time and space. Moreover, one gets a sense that even in situations where they could, it would only be temporal, limited, and personal. This was true historically for the majority of Israel, even with a theocratic nation, and for the majority of God's people today, for in both cases, the source of oppression comes not just from those who have the resources and power to use to their advantage, but also in a deeper sense, those who say in their hearts, "There is no God" (cf. 14:2).

From the abundance of designations, the enemy of righteousness is not necessarily those outside the covenant community.[77] The discussion on exactly who the enemy is has concentrated on two main offenders: (1) those in the covenant community, including the post-exilic Jews and the faithless and (2) those outside the covenant community, including foreign powers. Within these groups, it is observed that there are even broader designations. However, as noted earlier, the issue at hand is not relative; that is, one cannot simply apply psalmic language to anyone who annoys or even antagonizes on a personal level, though that is not out of the realm of injustice. The objective criterion for distinguishing between the just and unjust, the righteous and the wicked, is their relationship to the authority of the Davidic king and the Word of God. What is clear is that the Psalmist's use of moral terminology is grounded on a covenantal foundation. Two points bring this out more clearly: (1) the descriptions of the antagonist and (2) and their attitudes and action towards God and man. The descriptions are of a

---

74. Mic 7:9.

75. Mic 3; 6:9–7:6. See works like Jeffries M. Hamilton, *Social Justice and Deuteronomy: The Case of Deuteronomy 15*, SBLDS 136 (Atlanta: Scholars Press, 1992); Julie Woods, "The West as Nineveh: How Does Nahum's Message of Judgement Apply to Today?" *Them* 31.1 (October 2005): 7–37.

76. Wilson, *Psalms*, 235.

77. See Creach, *The Destiny of the Righteous in the Psalms*, 7.

qualitative nature, seen in adjectival and participial designations: "wicked" (Pss 3:8; 7:10, 15; 34:22), "boastful" (Ps 52:2), "enemy/foes" (Pss 3:2, 8; 7:6; 18:4, 18, 38, 41, 49; 54:7, 9; 56:3, 10; 59:2, 11; 60:13, 14) "workers of iniquity" (Ps 59:2), and speaker of "lies" (Pss 7:15; 52:5).

The Tension of Justice: Crying for Justice by Living for Justice

Throughout these psalms, there is a consistent pattern of the plot. Though not in a specific paralleled order in these laments, statements of trust, questions of presence, appeals to justice, reasons for distress, the character of the wicked, the righteousness of God, and God as a refuge are evident. In a collective sense, all these factors convey something about the nature of justice. Moreover, each of these can be traced through this small collection to get a broader perspective of the justice of God and the ways in which that central theme addresses each of those factors. The language of justice from the Psalmist's perspective goes far beyond punitive justice, but has to do with human destiny. The appeals for God to act are not from a vengeful heart, but a deep commitment to God's covenant promises, especially in relation to 2 Samuel 7. They are prayers that God will act in harmony with his previous word and his eternal purposes for humanity.

To come back to the notion of indifference, the very nature of these psalms argues against passive acceptance of injustice (cf. Ps 11:1, 2). The Psalmist does not resign himself to accept the activity of evil as a given with no recourse. In the book of Psalms, the Psalmist resorts to divine intervention, rather than political maneuvering, yet the ways God answers those cries for intervention are in many cases manifested in historical circumstances of the times. Many psalms of thanksgiving make this point evident. By juxtaposing these laments in Book 1, the editor conflates several psalms that portray a deep sense of divine justice to give voice to this central theme of Israel's and the church's thinking and acting. The appeals to God are set in temporal ways. Connected to the notion of time and justice in Adventism's understanding of Daniel 7–9 is the Psalter's parallel focus on the eschatological nature of injustice and God's vindication of his people. The Psalmist asks "How long?" *ad mattai* until God acts (6:4, cf. Ps 13).

Destiny of the Nations

The Psalms give a comprehensive view of the destiny of the unrighteous which focuses on their personhood (annihilation), their plans and ambitions, and the end to their destructive actions (*lex talionis*) (Pss 9:4, 6, 7; 10:16; 11:6). Final destruction (9:5) is expressed as the ultimate destiny of the wicked. For example, it is the destiny of the enemies of righteousness (9:4), the wicked (9:6–7), and the godless nations (10:17). The Psalter presents the multifaceted nature of justice where the particular and personal judgments precede and anticipate the universal and corporate. By seeking justice, the people of God must learn to be just people. The ethical is not just an ideal, but a lived and shared experience of image bearing through the work of the Messiah and guided by the teachings of the Torah. For the Psalmist, judgment for the saints is not solely a matter of being the beneficiaries of God's grace and justice, but it is how that grace and justice pervade the sense of justice and judgment of the saints in their praying, thinking, and living. Faith in God's justice for the Psalmist is active. That the passive resignation of the Epicurean has no place in the life of faith is the cry of the Psalter.

PART 2: NEW TESTAMENT

The Issue of Divorce and Remarriage in 1 Corinthians 7:15 in the Light of the *Dominical Logion* of 7:10

Davide Sciarabba

Divorce and remarriage remains a controversial issue among Christian scholars. Although the gospels (Matt 19:1-12 and Mark 10:1-12), and Paul (1 Cor 7:10-16) present general guidelines on divorce and remarriage,[1] there is still no agreement on these matters when it comes to church discipline. While some tend to justify divorce and remarriage in certain cases, others consistently condemn these practices. According to Johnson Lim, there are currently four main Christian views on the issue of divorce and remarriage: (1) divorce and remarriage are not permitted; (2) divorce is sometimes permitted, but not remarriage; (3) divorce and remarriage are permitted on grounds of adultery or abandonment; and (4) divorce and remarriage are also permitted under other circumstances.[2] The theological and practical implications of 1 Cor 7:15 have been extensively debated in this controversy. Some scholars interpret this passage as permitting divorce while denying remarriage,[3] whereas others view this as a "Pauline privilege" that permits divorce and remarriage in certain circumstances.[4]

This paper contains an analysis of 1 Cor 7:15 in light of the dominical logion of verse 10.[5] Although many scholars concede that Paul is quoting a dominical

---

1. See also a very short statement in Luke 16:18 and Matthew 5:31-32.

2. Johnson Lim, "Divorce and Remarriage in Theological and Contemporary Perspectives," *AJT* 20 (2006): 271. See also H. Wayne House, ed., *Divorce and Remarriage: Four Christian Views* (Downers Grove, IL: InterVarsity Press, 1990).

3. For instance see Robert G. Olender, "The Pauline Privilege: Inference or Exegesis," *Faith and Mission* 16 (1998): 96. He suggested that the interpretation of I Corinthians 7:15 as a "Pauline privilege is more an inference than correct exegesis. Ibid., 94-117. Gordon D. Fee, *The First Epistle to the Corinthians* NICNT (Grand Rapids, MI: Eerdmans, 1987), 303.

4. See for instance the Catholic interpretation of the passage by Thomas Aquinas, *Super Epistolas S. Pauli Lectura* I, 299, paragraph 336, ed. R. Cai, 8th ed. (Paris/Rome: Marietti, 1953); Hans Conzelmann, *1 Corinthians: A Commentary on the First Epistle to the Corinthians*, trans. J. W. Leitch; Hermen (Philadelphia: Fortress, 1975), 123; Jean Héring, *The First Epistle of Saint Paul to the Corinthians* (London: Epworth, 1962), 53.

5. The expression *Dominical Logion* refers to the teaching that Jesus gave on the life of the Christian or the church that are reported outside the Gospels. They are also called *Commands of the Lord* or *Teachings of Jesus*. See for instance David L. Dungan, *The Saying of Jesus in the Church of Paul: The Use of the Synoptic Tradition in the Religion of the Church Life* (Philadelphia: Fortress, 1971); F. F. Bruce, *The Hard Saying of Jesus* (Downers Grove, IL: InterVarsity Press, 1983).

logion to present his point on the issue of divorce, many others overlook the theological and practical implications of this fact. I seek to demonstrate that verse 15 must be read as an explanation and extension of the dominical logion of verse 10, which constitutes the theological background of Paul's argumentation.

To understand the pronouncement of Paul in 1 Cor 7:15, "But if the unbeliever leaves, let him do so. A believing man or woman is not bound in such circumstances; God has called us to live in peace" (NIV),[6] it is first necessary to grasp the cultural and literary context of these important statements.

Paul worked in Corinth for approximately eighteen months.[7] At that time, the city was a flourishing cosmopolitan center of commerce.[8] In the Corinthian harbor, as in many other harbors, the mariners spent their time and money in bars and with prostitutes.[9] The Acrocorinth ("Upper Corinth"), or acropolis looming over ancient Corinth, housed a temple dedicated to Aphrodite. This temple was famous for its prostitution cult. Despite a good number of Jews, the lifestyle of the Corinthians clashed with Jewish culture and religion. "Old Corinth had gained such a reputation for sexual vice that Aristophanes (ca. 450-385 B.C.) coined the verb *korinthiazō* (to act like a Corinthian, i.e., to commit fornication."[10] It is understandable that Paul wrote so much about sexuality and marriage in the epistles to the Corinthians. Therefore, 1 Corinthians 7:10-16 is an important portion of the key passage (1 Cor. 5-7) regarding the way of life and ethics for marriage and sexuality preached by Paul to the first Christian believers in that city.[11]

Concerning the literary context of the passage, not all scholars agree on the section of the book to which it belongs. Roy E. Cimapa and Brian S. Rosner, much like Raymond F. Collins and Kenneth E. Bailey, included this text in the section 4:18-7:40, in which Paul condemned illicit sexual relations and sexual immorality, and affirmed sexual purity as a way of glorifying God in the body.[12]

6. In this article I will use the NIV version unless otherwise indicated.

7. Acts 18:11.

8. Corinth was located in a strategic place, in the neck dividing the Peloponnesus and the peninsula regions. The ships coming from Asia had to circumnavigate the Peloponnesus in order to bring their goods to Europe. Many ships wrecked because of the strong marine currents of the Aegean Sea and the Sea of Crete in the south part of the Peloponnesus. A safe solution was to harbor the ships at the level of the neck and to transport the goods by land from the Aegean to the Ionian Sea. This made an important contribution to the prosperity of both Corinth and its harbor. See further Charles K Barrett, *A Commentary on the First Epistle to the Corinthians*, HNTC (New York: Harper & Row, 1968), 2.

9. Anthony C. Thiselton, *The First Epistle to the Corinthians: A Commentary on the Greek Text*, NIGTC (Grand Rapids, MI: Eerdmans, 2000), 1-12; Raymond F. Collins, *First Corinthian*, SP 7 (Collegeville, MN: Liturgical Press, 1999), 21-24; Roy E. Ciampa, and Brian Rosner, *The First Letter to the Corinthians*, PNTC (Grand Rapids, MI: Eerdmans, 2010), 2-5;

10. Fee, *The First Epistle to the Corinthians*, 1-4.

11. Thiselton, *The First Epistle to the Corinthians*, 381-382, 483-484.

12. Ciampa, and Rosner, *The First Letter to the Corinthians*, 189-367; Collins, *First Corinthians*, 203-304; Kenneth E. Bailey, *Paul Through Mediterranean Eyes. Cultural Studies in 1 Corinthians*, (Downers Grove, IL: IVP Academic, 2011), 226. Garland reads the passage within chapter 7, which is an isolated section with respect chapters 6 and 8, dedicated to instructions about sexual relations, divorce and marriage. David E. Garland, *1 Corinthians*, BECNT (Grand Rapids, MI: Baker Academic, 2003), 243-346. J. A. Fitzmyer and Gordon D. Fee advocated that the passage belongs to a long section starting with chapter 7 and ending with chapter 14:40 or 16:12 where Paul answered the Corinthians' letter about moral, liturgical, and other questions. Joseph A. Fitzmyer, *First Corinthians: A New Translation with Introduction and Commentary*, AB 32 (New Haven: Yale University Press, 2008), 273-538. Fee, *The First Epistle to the Corinthians*, 266-825.

Anthony C. Thiselton read the passage in a section starting at chapter 7 and ending at chapter 11:1, where Paul replied to some questions from the Corinthians about a series of practical issues, including marriage and divorce, eating meat associated with idols, and the freedom and rights of the apostle.[13] This paper adopts the last interpretation, which views 1 Corinthians 7:10-16 within the broader context of section 7:1-11:1. As several scholars have observed, chapter 6 is a transitional unit or hinge, and therefore, a key chapter to understanding the following chapters.[14] After an initial orientation concerning celibacy and marriage in chapter 7, Paul dedicated chapter 8 to answering the Corinthians on the recommended attitude towards pagan customs in relation to meats sacrificed to idols. This is the broad context of chapter 7 and of our passage.[15]

Scholars have differing views on the structure of chapter 7. Ciampa and Rosner saw four sections: (1) counsels concerning various marital statuses (1-16), (2) the development of principle of "remaining as you were when called" (17-24), (3) counsels for single adults (25-38), and (4) counsels for wives and widows (39-40).[16] In my opinion, the view of Garland and Thiselton seems to respect better the natural flow of the chapter's argumentation. They detected the following parts in 1 Cor 7: the first section addresses the issues of sexual relations within marriage (7:1-5); the second section discusses celibacy and marriage for the unmarried and widows (7:6-9); and the third section presents Paul's counsel on divorce for those married to Christians and for those married to unbelievers (7:10-16). This is the immediate context of the passage in the research. The last section is followed by some guidelines related to the principle of "remaining as you are" (7:17-24), and then different counsels on the advisability of marriage for the betrothed and for widows (7:25-40).[17]

The analysis of 7:10-16

Verses 10-11

Paul addressed the issue of divorce after answering the Corinthians on matters of celibacy, marriage, and sexual relationships (7:1-9). Verse 10, which starts with the phrase Τοῖς δὲ γεγαμηκόσιν ("But to the married," NASB), introduces a new issue in the topic of marriage.[18] The passage starts with an order to those who are married.[19] This introduction raises several questions, well formulated by Jerome Murphy-O'Connor:

13. Thiselton, *The First Epistle to the Corinthians*, 493-797; *First Corinthians: A Shorter Exegetical and Pastoral Commentary* (Grand Rapids, MI: Eerdmans, 2006), 99-169.

14. See for instance Collins, *First Corinthians*, 239-251 and Garland, *1 Corinthians*, 219-241.

15. Chapter 9 changes subject and Paul treats the question of his apostolic freedom. In chapter 10, he warns the Corinthians against idolatry once again and develops the subject of the fair usage of Christian freedom. Max-Alain Chevallier, *L'exégèse du Nouveau Testament: Initiation à la Méthode* (Geneva: Labor et Fides, 1985), 24.

16. Ciampa and Rosner, *The First Letter to the Corinthians*, 266-366. See also Collins, *First Corinthians*, with a few variations.

17. Garland, *1 Corinthians*, 242-346. See also Thiselton with a few nuances, *The First Epistle to the Corinthians*, 483-606.

18. Jerome Murphy-O'Connor, "The Divorced Woman in I Cor. 7:10-11," *JBL* 100 (1981): 605.

19. "The perfect denotes the married state consequent on the act of marrying." Thiselton, *The First Epistle to the Corinthians*, 520.

Why does Paul begin *tois de gegamêkosin parangellö*, which he then has to qualify by *ouk ego alla ho kyrios*, when it would have been easy to write *tois de gegamêkosin ho kyrios parangellei?* Why does he introduce a dominical logion? Why does he mention the wife first when the reverse order (followed in 7:12-13 and in Mark 10:11-12) would have been more natural? How is *me chôristhênai* to be translated? Why is the refusal of remarriage introduced in a parenthetical clause and apropos of the woman when the synoptic form of the dominical logion (Matt 5:32; 19:9; Mark 10:11; Luke 16:18) contains this element as an integral part referring to the husband? Finally, how are we to understand the relationship between the prohibition in 7:10-11 and the permission in 7:15?[20]

The verb παραγγέλλω, literally "I command, I give order," reinforces a strong statement against divorce. Paul addressed this command first to women (v. 10) and then to men (v. 11). Even if the strength of the verb seems to imply a personal command,[21] Paul introduced this new issue under the authority of a dominical logion, quoting what the Lord had said about divorce.[22] In so doing, Paul reminded his readers that his teaching on divorce comes directly from Jesus,[23] thus differentiating it from the other teachings deduced by himself (7:12,25).[24] Thus, vv. 10 and 11 form a main statement that serves as the basis for understanding the rest of the text (7:12-16).

Herold Rey England interpreted 7:10-11 as a Christian *halaka* on divorce, and suggested that Christians should take these verses as a command to obey. In this case, if a divorce happens, "the believer is not to remarry another,"[25] leaving open the possibility of reconciliation with the spouse later on. However, if the divorce happens, the right of remarriage is offered.[26] The rejection of divorce formulated

20. Murphy-O'Connor, "The Divorced Woman in I Cor. 7:10-11," 601.
21. Murphy-O'Connor, "The Divorced Woman in I Cor. 7:10-11," 605.
22. For a deeper study of the saying of Jesus see David L. Dungan, *The Sayings of Jesus in the Churches of Paul* (Philadelphia: Fortress, 1971), xviii-xxix. In Corinthians 7:10-16 is Paul using material from the synoptic tradition? Did he know what Mark wrote in 10:1-12? The debate on the fact that Paul used Markian sources or not depends on the date given to the gospel of Mark. Murphy-O'Connor thought that Paul did not know Mark. Murphy-O'Connor, "The Divorced Woman in I Cor. 7:10-11," 605. Others date Mark around A.D. 40, see for instance James G. Crossley, *The Date of Mark's Gospel: Insights from the Law in Earliest Christianity* (London: T&T Clark, 2004), who recently again suggested this early dating of the book. A majority of scholars prefer dating the gospel of Mark around A.D. 70 (before or after). For a summary of the major interpretation see John S. Kloppenborg, "Evocatio Deorum and the Date of Mark," *JBL* 124 (2005): 419-450. That Paul knew Mark or not does not change very much the importance of Paul's quotation of the Dominican logion and of his command on divorce and remarriage in 1 Corinthian 7:10-16. For a further study on the relationship between Paul and Mark see Oda Wischmeyer, David C. Sin, and Ian J. Elmer eds., *Paul and Mark. Comparative Essays Part I. Two Authors at the Beginnings of Chrstianity*, (Berlin: De Gruyter, 2014); Eve-Marie Becker, Troels Engberg-Pedersen, and Mogens Müller eds., *Mark and Paul. Comparative Essays Part II. For and Against Pauline Influence on Mark*, (Berlin: De Gruyter, 2014).
23. W. D. Davies, *Paul and Rabbinic Judaism: Some Rabbinic Elements in Pauline Theology*, 2d ed. (London: SPCK, 1958), 138-139.
24. Fitzmyer, *First Corinthians*, 290.
25. Herold Rey England, "Divorce and Remarriage in I Corinthians 7:10-16" (PhD diss., Southern Baptist Theological Seminary, 1982), 174-175.
26. Cf. *Shepherd of Hermas*, Mandates IV, 1, 4-11; Carolyn Osiek, *Shepherd of Hermas: A Commentary* (Hermen; Minneapolis: Fortress, 1999), 109-112.

by Paul seems an absolute (according to Mark 10:9-12 and Luke 16:18) that does not mention the exception of *"porneia"* admitted in Matt 5:31-32 and 19:6-9,[27] nor the Mosaic legislation in Deut 24:1-4.[28] However, claiming the authority of a dominical logion echoes Mark 10:9 and Matt 19:6, particularly because it uses the same verb (χωρίζω).[29]

By paraphrasing the dominical saying, Paul put the question of marriage, divorce, and remarriage in the light of the Lord's logion. We assume that Paul was providing a supplementary, articulated explanation of the saying in the following verses (7:10-16) to expound upon Jesus' thought. This allowed Paul to deal with the problem of divorce and remarriage without looking for exceptions for divorce (Matt 19:6-9) or absolute prohibitions (Mark 10:9), but recalling the seriousness and at the same time, the fragility of marriage. In light of this assumption, we are better equipped to read contextually v. 15, the focus of this article.

The main issue in v. 10 is the translation of the verb χωρισθῆναι, an aorist passive infinitive, literally translated as "a wife *must not be separated* from her husband."[30] However, most English versions of the Bible[31] translate this verse as a present infinitive, χωρίσεσθαι. This is supported by several manuscripts,[32] and "is obviously a *lectio facilitans*,"[33] meaning that "a wife *should not separate* from her husband." The first translation (aorist passive) assumes the indirect responsibility of the woman in the separation from her husband. This reading finds its counterpart in v. 11, which says: "a husband should not separate from his wife" (NASB). This implies that if it is wrong for a man to separate from his wife, it is also wrong for a wife to agree to divorce from her husband.[34] Conversely, the second translation implies the wife's responsibility in separating from her husband.[35] This second reading relates the separation to the action of the wife.

In explaining this difference of tense in the manuscripts, Murphy-O'Connor argued that some copyists, seeing a problem with v. 13, tried to harmonize the χωρισθῆναι of v. 10 with the ἀφιέτω (present imperative) of v. 13 by transforming the former verb into a present infinitive, χωρίσεσθαι. This discrepancy

27. He probably did not know what Matthew wrote in his gospel. See J. C. Laney, "Paul and the Permanence of Marriage in 1 Corinthians 7," *JETS* 25 (1982): 283-294.

28. It is certain Paul knew what the Mosaic Law says about marriage and divorce (Acts 22:3). See also David Instone-Brewer, "1 Corinthians 7 in the Light of the Jewish Greek and Aramaic Marriage and Divorce Papyri," *TynBul* 52 (2001): 225-243.

29. David E. Garland suggested that the usage of the verb χωρίζω in the dominical logion of Mark 10:9 may have influenced Paul's usage. Fitzmyer saw clear connections between the gospels and 1 Corinthians: "Paul passes on the prohibition in indirect discourse, whereas the pronouncement in the Synoptics is presented as a dominical saying in direct discourse: "what God has Joined together, let no human being put asunder," and "Anyone who divorces his wife and marries another woman commits adultery." This also explains the shift from Paul's giving a command to the Lord's giving it; Paul does not quote the dominical saying, but paraphrases it in his own words. Fitzmyer, *First Corinthians*, 290-291.

30. NJB, see also J. A. Fitzmyer, "The Matthean Divorce Texts and Some New Palestinian Evidence," *TS* 37 (1976): 200, and W. F. Orr, and J. A. Walther, *1 Corinthians* (AB 32; Garden City, N.Y.: Doubleday, 1976), 211.

31. See for instance the KJV, KJG, NAS, NIV, NIB.

32. A, D, F, G, 1881, 1945.

33. Murphy-O'Connor, "The Divorced Woman in I Cor. 7:10-11," 601.

34. Murphy-O'Connor, "The Divorced Woman in I Cor. 7:10-11," 602.

35. Murphy-O'Connor, "The Divorced Woman in I Cor. 7:10-11," 601-602.

of tense induced Murphy-O'Connor to suggest that v. 10 might be read in the light of a Jewish background, in which the wife had no right to ask for a divorce, whereas v. 13 speaks to a Greco-Roman audience, in which the wife could initiate a process of divorce.[36] Fitzmyer observed that the aorist passive infinitive does not indicate that the wife should not allow herself to be divorced, but "that she should not be divorced (at all)," leaving no questions as to the wife's acceptance.[37]

Murphy-O'Connor justified his position by supposing that this passage refers to a specific couple in which the husband, adopting ascetic behavior, decided to divorce his wife.[38] England, disagreeing with this position, concluded that 1 Cor 7:10-11 does not contain enough information to refer to a specific couple, but that Paul is referring to Mark 10:11-12 here.[39] Fitzmyer, along with other scholars,[40] understood that Paul was writing about divorce in general, not addressing his solution to a specific case. They suggest that Paul was using the case of a woman in Corinth as a pretext to address the general issue of divorce, thus justifying his mention of women in the first place.[41] England believed that Paul mentioned women first because of the leadership and spiritual enthusiasm held by Corinthian women (1 Cor 1:11; 11:2-16; 14:33-36).[42] According to Brooten, a Jewish woman could divorce her husband in certain cases, initiating the action of divorce herself.[43] However, both of these interpretations seem weak.[44]

Verse 11 seems to leave only two options for those women who are separated: remain unmarried[45] or be reconciled[46] with their husbands.[47] There is no mention here of the possibility of divorce and remarriage stated in Deuteronomy 24:2. "He is not contemplating a future exception to the dominical command but is addressing a hypothetical situation: the possible divorce of a Christian woman, which should not happen, but which may happen."[48] Paul's opposition to the remarriage of believers was based on the possibility of their future reconciliation unless they decide to stay separated. After reading 7:10 and 11 with their reference to the dominical logion against divorce and remarriage, how do we understand verse 15?

Verses 12 and 13

After commenting on Christian matrimonies, in vv. 12 and 13, Paul addressed

---

36. Murphy-O'Connor, "The Divorced Woman in I Cor. 7:10-11," 602. England disagreed with this view-point, arguing that a woman in the Jewish context "had not right to accept or reject the bill of divorce," but he did not solve the problem of the different usage of the tense in the manuscripts. England, "Divorce and Remarriage in I Corinthians 7:10-16," 176-177.

37. Fitzmyer, *First Corinthians*, 293.

38. Murphy-O'Connor, "The Divorced Woman in I Cor. 7:10-11," 601, 604.

39. England, "Divorce and Remarriage in I Corinthians 7:10-16," 167-170.

40. See for instance Collins, *First Corinthians*, 269, and Garland, *1 Corinthians*, 281.

41. Fitzmyer, *First Corinthians*, 291-293.

42. England, "Divorce and Remarriage in I Corinthians 7:10-16," 175-176.

43. B. Brooten, "Konnten Frauen im Alten Judentum die Scheidug Betreiben" quoted by Fitzmyer, *First Corinthians*, 289.

44. See argumentations brought by Fitzmyer, *First Corinthians,* 288-290.

45. W. Schrage, *Der Erste Brief an die Korinther* (1Kor 6, 12-11, 16), EKKNT (Cincinnati, OH: Benziger, 1995), 102. Also cited by Garland, *1 Corinthians*, 283, and Fitzmyer, *First Corinthians*, 294.

46. Collins, *First Corinthians*, 269-270.

47. Fitzmyer, *First Corinthians*, 294.

48. Fitzmyer, *First Corinthians*, 294.

the issue of mixed marriages between believers and unbelievers.[49] The phrase Τοῖς δὲ λοιποῖς (to the rest) of 7:12 is referring to Christians married to unbelievers, not to all the Christians in Corinth, because the second part of the verse restricts the meaning of the word "rest."[50] In this verse, the clause λέγω ἐγὼ οὐχ ὁ κύριος is very similar to the one found in 7:10, οὐκ ἐγὼ ἀλλὰ ὁ κύριος except for the negation particle, which refers to the Lord and not to Paul. The argument presented in v. 12 by the phrase "I say, not the Lord" is no less authoritative than v. 10, where Paul quoted a saying of the Lord,[51] since in 7:40, the apostle affirmed that even in his judgment, he had the Spirit of God. At the same time, this text implies that Paul was not aware of any specific saying of the Lord concerning mixed marriages.[52] After paraphrasing the dominical logion, he admitted that his counsel regarding mixed marriages did not come directly from Jesus' mouth, but his paraphrases explaining the issue of divorce implied that his advice (7:12-16) on mixed marriages was inspired by the dominical logion.[53]

Paul initially addressed Christian husbands married to unbelieving wives (7:12), and living together, for the expression γυναῖκα ἔχει (has a wife) means to have a continuous marital union with a wife.[54] The verb συνευδοκεῖ translated by "she agrees" evokes her willingness to live together. In fact, the meaning of this verb, "to join in approval," "agree with," "approve of," "consent to," and "sympathize with"[55] describes the approved union of the husband with the wife[56] and "expresses the active willingness of the wife to share married life with a Christian husband."[57] This verb also assumes that the Christian husband has not coerced his wife into compliance.[58] Here, it is possible to see the principle of mutual agreement previously expressed in 7:5, which implies that marriage requires not only a legal signed document or just the continuation of sexual intimacy, but also a commitment and respect for the personal differences of the partner. The function of the verb συνευδοκέω (7:12, 13) implies a contrast between the approval of the unbeliever in keeping the right relationship in a mixed marriage (v. 12, 13) and the unwillingness of the unbeliever to maintain the right relationship in a mixed marriage (v. 15). Paul's counsel on marriage and divorce in vv. 12 and 15 took into account the conflicting attitude of the unbeliever, which is a determinant of the future stability of the marriage. If there is agreement, approval, and willingness, the believer is invited to continue the marriage with the unbeliever, understanding that even if his or her spouse is not a Christian, their marriage is

---

49. I understand that Paul is talking to people who became Christians after marriage. Now, after conversion, they were encountering the problem of a mixed marriage.

50. See Garland, *1 Corinthians*, 283-284; Fitzmyer, *First Corinthians*, 298.

51. Barrett, *A Commentary on the First Epistle to the Corinthians*, 163; Garland, *1 Corinthians*, 285.

52. Fitzmyer, *First Corinthians*, 297.

53. Garland, *1 Corinthians*, 285. Cf. Fitzmyer, *First Corinthians*, 297-298. He affirmed that these two verses must be considered as separate from the dominical logion in verse 10, and that they came from Paul's pastoral advice.

54. Fitzmyer, *First Corinthians*, 279.

55. See BDAG, 970.

56. Garland, *1 Corinthians*, 285. Cf. Luke 11:48; Acts 8:1; 22:20; Romans 1:32; 1 Maccabees 1:57; 11:24.

57. Fitzmyer, *First Corinthians*, 298.

58. Garland, *1 Corinthians*, 285-286.

not defiled, but holy.[59] Conversion to Christianity by one partner can favor the salvation of the unbelieving partner.

Although Paul used the verb χωρίζω to express the idea of divorce in vv. 10 and 11, he used ἀφίημι to express the same idea in vv. 11 (the last verb), 12, and 13. The verb ἀφίημι means "to release," "to let go," or "to dismiss" and is frequently used in extra-biblical literature with the legal meaning of "to discharge someone from a legal relationship, whether it be an office, marriage, custody, or punishment."[60] In the New Testament, this word is used in four senses: "to let or allow," "to pardon or forgive," "to leave," and "to divorce."[61] Paul only used the verbs ἀφίημι and χωρίζω for divorce.[62] Is the verb ἀφίημι a synonym of the verb χωρίζω or do they have significantly different meanings?

The verb χωρίζω originally meant "to divide," "to separate," "to depart," "to cause separation through use of space between," and "to separate by departing from someone."[63] The verb is not frequently used in the New Testament.[64] Throughout the entire Bible, if we also consider the LXX, it relates to the context of divorce only in Matt 19:6, Mark 10:9, and 1 Cor 7:10,11, 15.

England argued that Paul used the verbs ἀφίημι and χωρίζω interchangeably not to point out the Jewish and the Greek customs of divorce (if not, he would have used the verb χωρίζω consistently), but to emphasize their technical differences in the divorce procedure.[65] "Forms of χωρίζω would describe the action of departing from or leaving a spouse (see 7:15); forms of ἀφίημι would describe the action of divorce depicted in the legal action of putting away a spouse."[66] Charles K. Barrett argued that "Paul's reference to the unbeliever separating indicates probably more than the refusal of conjugal rights, but less than legal divorce."[67] Olender embraced the idea of distinction in the usage of the two verbs, affirming that "ἀφίημι describes marital disunion in a legal sense when referring to believers, whereas in verse 15 χωρίζω stresses special separation and is applied to the unbelieving spouse."[68] However, this viewpoint raises a question: Does the verb χωρίζω refer to the unbeliever in vv. 10 and 11? The text does not seem to support this reading. A point against differentiating between the meanings of these two verbs is the fact that Greek writers during the classical and Hellenistic periods used both verbs to mean divorce and in marriage contracts.[69] The verb χωρίζω meant "to divorce" in Greek marriage

59. Garland, 1 Corinthians, 286.

60. Rudolf Bultmann, "ἀφίημι," TDNT, 1:509.

61. In the Gospels, it means also "to leave," "to forsake," and "to abandon." England, "Divorce and Remarriage in I Corinthians 7:10-16," 11.

62. Other authors of the New Testament use the verb ἀπολύω in reference to divorce (Matthew 1:19; 5:31f; 19:3, 7-9; Mark 10:2, 4, 11f; Luke 16:18). Moreover, the term ἀποστάσιον in Matthew 5:31; 19:7, and Mark 10:4 means divorce. See I. H. Marshall, "Divorce", NIDNTT, 1:505-507.

63. BDAG, 1095.

64. Matt. 19:6; Mark 10:9; Acts 1:4; 18:1, 2; Rom. 8:35, 39; 1 Cor. 7:10, 11, 15; Phil. 1:15; Heb. 7:26.

65. England, "Divorce and Remarriage in 1 Corinthians 7:10-16," 182.

66. England, "Divorce and Remarriage in 1 Corinthians 7:10-16," 182, see footnote 79 below.

67. Barrett, A Commentary on the First Epistle to the Corinthians, 162.

68. Olender, "The Pauline Privilege," 96.

69. Joseph A. Fitzmyer, "The Matthean Divorce Texts and Some New Palestinian Evidence," TS 37 (1976): 211-212.

contracts,[70] and the verb ἀφίημι was also used for "divorce" in a legal sense during the same period.[71] The usage of the verb χωρίζω for marriage contracts in extra-biblical literature is well attested.[72] It is, therefore, not possible to say with certainty that Paul, by using the two verbs, was referring to two different realities (separation and legal divorce), for both verbs can be used as synonyms for divorce.[73] Collins, confirming this idea, remarked that if any distinction should be made, it would be the following: "It may be attributable to Paul's Jewish tradition that tends to use active verbs for man and passive verbs for woman."[74] Fitzmyer strongly affirmed that a distinction between the two verbs "is untenable, since both words are well attested in the sense of separation meaning divorce, and Paul does not show any awareness of the modern distinction of "separation" and "divorce.""[75] Given this evidence, I conclude in this article that Paul used these two verbs interchangeably, considering them as synonyms.

Verse 14

In v. 14, Paul introduced the idea of the sanctification of the unbeliever through the believing spouse.[76] Barrett and Will Deming asserted that this argument is not about salvation,[77] but about ritual cleanness.[78] In this case, it would be a reference to the Jewish norm that there should be no union between clean and unclean people.[79]

The sentences ἐν τῇ γυναικὶ or ἐν τῷ ἀνδρί[80] are generally translated as "through the woman or the husband," even though the Bauer-Danker Lexicon says that it should be read as a causal clause "on account of the woman or the brother."[81] Garland read this phrase with a locative sense: the Christian is the agent, and the unbelieving spouse obtains his or her holiness "in" the believer.[82]

Paul used the perfect passive of the verb ἁγιάζω to discuss the sanctification of the unbeliever. The tense of the verb implies a present condition resulting from sanctification that happened previously. This verb, meaning "to consecrate" or "to set aside for a cultic purpose" implies that God is the one who accomplishes the

---

70. Cf. Euripides, Fr. 1063:13; Isaeus 8:36; Polybius, *Hist.* 31.26.6.

71. Cf. Euripides, *Andromache* 973; Herodotus, *Hist.* 5:39; Plutarch, *Pomp.* 44.

72. BDAG, 1095.

73. England, "Divorce and Remarriage in I Corinthians 7:10-16," 11-16. Cf. James Hope Moulton and George Milligan, *The Vocabulary of the Greek Testament* (London: Hodder & Stoughton, 1949). On page 696, they stated that the term χωρίζω had become a technical term in connection with divorce.

74. Collins, *First Corinthians*, 269.

75. Fitzmyer, *First Corinthians*, 295.

76. For a further study on sanctification, purity, cleanness, and uncleanness in the social context of a Christian household, see Caroline Johnson Hodge, "Married to an Unbeliever: Households, Hierarchies, and Holiness in 1 Corinthians 7:12–16," *HTR* 103 (2010): 13-20; Will Deming, *Paul on Marriage and Celibacy: The Hellenistic Background of I Corinthians 7*, SNTSMS 83 (Cambridge: Cambridge University Press, 1995), 130-144.

77. Barrett, *A Commentary on the First Epistle to the Corinthians*, 165; Deming, *Paul on Marriage and Celibacy*, 132.

78. England, "Divorce and Remarriage in I Corinthians 7:10-16," 183.

79. Cf. M. Kaddushin 4:1; 4:2-8, in England, "Divorce and Remarriage in I Corinthians 7:10-16," 183-184.

80. Other manuscripts use the form ἐν τῷ ἀδελφῷ.

81. BDAG, 329.

82. Garland, *1 Corinthians*, 287.

sanctification of the unbeliever.[83] Some argue that sanctification happens simply through marriage with the believer,[84] whereas others suppose that sanctification comes through the baptism of the partner.[85]

Fee argued that maintaining the marital relationship increases the likelihood of leading the unbeliever to salvation.[86] Holiness is a characteristic of those who have accepted Jesus and have been baptized, but it is also a pattern of conduct, a way of life (see Rom 6:19-22 and 12:1-2).[87] In this sense, the unbeliever will be sanctified by adopting the same behavior as the believer by virtue of being under the influence of the Christian spouse and by keeping his or her commitment to the marriage.[88]

Garland added that the unbeliever, being one flesh with the believer and being under God's approval because marriage is according to God's will, can be sanctified by a willingness to remain married to a committed Christian.[89] For Fitzmyer, this text stresses three aspect of marriage: "First, it implies that a marital union brings holiness to the spouse... Second, the same extension of his argument would be valid for children born of two Christian spouses, who are also 'holy.' Third, Paul sees the husband and wife as the possible source of salvation to each other."[90] In conclusion, verse 14 clearly shows the reasons for maintaining the marriage and avoiding divorce with an unbeliever.

Verse 15

The key verse of our study is 15. This verse first affirms clearly that there are no grounds for divorce for a believer in mixed marriages if there is a willingness of the unbeliever to remain married. However, this verse also seems to present a certain openness to divorce and remarriage, which is the core of our topic. To grasp the meaning of this text, which seems to make an exception to the rule of no divorce and no remarriage in v. 10, it is important to determine the meaning of the four main terms of the statement: "unbeliever" (ἄπιστος), "to separate" (χωρίζω), "to be under bondage" (δουλόω), and "God has called you in peace" (ἐν δὲ εἰρήνῃ κέκληκεν ὑμᾶς ὁ θεός).

---

83. Fitzmyer, *First Corinthians*, 299.

84. Orr and Walther, *1 Corinthians*, 212.

85. Collins, *First Corinthians*, 266. See also J. C. O'Neill, "1 Corinthians 7:14 and Infant Baptism," in *L'Apôtre Paul: Personnalité, Style et Conception du Ministère*, ed. A. Vanhoye, BETL 73 (Leuven: Leuven University Press, 1986), 357-361. J. C. O'Neill insisted on the fact that the perfect, instead of referring to a past event, can refer to a future event. That event is the cleanness of baptism for both the unbelieving partner and the children.

86. Fee, *The First Epistle to the Corinthians*, 300-301. See also Laney, "Paul and the Permanence of Marriage in 1 Corinthians 7," 286-287.

87. J. Murphy O'Connor, "Works Without Faith in I Corinthians 7:14," *RB* 84 (1977): 355-356.

88. Thiselton, *The First Epistle to the Corinthians*, 530.

89. Garland, *1 Corinthians*, 288-289. Rosner explained the process of sanctification of the unbeliever, affirming that "Paul has been influenced by three biblical currents of thought which he has channeled into his teaching; the holiness of people in God's temple; the transferability of such holiness; and the interrelatedness of families." Brian S. Rosner, *Paul, Scripture and Ethics: A Study of 1 Corinthians 5-7* (Leiden: Brill, 1994), 169. Cf. I Corinthians 3:16, 17; 6:19; Exodus 29:37; 30: 29; Leviticus 6:18; contrast Numbers 4:15-20; Genesis 6:18; 17:7-27; 18:19; Deuteronomy 30:19; Psalm 78:1-7; 102:28; 103:17-18; 112:1-2.

90. Fitzmyer, *First Corinthians*, 298.

"Unbeliever"

The text in 1 Cor 7:10-16 argues that the believer should not initiate a divorce, but v. 15 raises the possibility of the unbeliever wanting to divorce. Olender, who is against divorce in all cases, affirmed that "Paul is not acknowledging the unbeliever's right to divorce. Rather he is acknowledging that the unbeliever does not feel constrained to act according to God's laws."[91] This passage (7:10-16) clearly states that marriage, even marriage to an unbeliever, remains sacred.[92] However, the holiness of the marriage does not solve the issue of divorce if the unbeliever, not respecting God's will, decides to divorce the Christian spouse. The apostle recognizes the liberty of an unbeliever to divorce, leaving the spouse without obligation.[93]

To clarify this point, we must answer the following question: who is the unbeliever in this context (7:12-15)? What does "unbeliever" (ἄπιστος) mean? In the New Testament, the word ἄπιστος can mean "faithless," "unbelieving," "non-Christian," "unworthy of credence," or if expressed through a verbal form, "to refuse to believe."[94]

Ed Christian suggested that the right translation of the term ἄπιστος is not "unbeliever," but rather "unfaithful," a possible interpretation emphasizing that divorce, even in the case of infidelity, is not mandatory because of a possible reconciliation.[95] If reconciliation happens, the bound of marriage is safe, but if reconciliation does not happen, this reading favors both consent for the promiscuity of the partner and the continuous humiliation received by the betrayal, adding a sense of guilt on the shoulders of the faithful partner if s(he) decides to divorce.

The term ἄπιστος includes in its meaning an atheist or a pagan or any person who has a different faith from that of the believer. Along with Fitzmyer, most scholars interpret the word ἄπιστος to mean "pagan person."[96] However, can ἄπιστος include the person who apostatized and rejected the Christian faith? May this include a person who, considering himself a Christian, no longer practices Christian behavior even if s(he) refuses to consider himself/herself an unbeliever?

According to Byron, ἄπιστος can refer to a person who received infant baptism and is Christian only in name, but does not have any true faith.[97] The word πίστις in Pauline writings has the meaning of "faith" in Jesus, not in other gods, but also of "acceptance of the Kerygma."[98] According to this interpretation, it is possible to include any person who does not believe in Christ or who decides to reject the faith in Jesus in the category of "unbeliever." According to this definition, the unbeliever can be any apostate, declared or undeclared (cf. 1 Tim 5:8).

91. Olender, "The Pauline Privilege," 112, see footnote 11 in this chapter.
92. Cf. A. T. Robertson, *Expository Lectures on St. Paul's Epistles to the Corinthians* (London: Smith, Elder, 1860), 125 in Olender, "The Pauline Privilege," 95, 96.
93. England, "Divorce and Remarriage in I Corinthians 7:10-16," 184; Olender, "The Pauline Privilege," 95.
94. R. Bultman, "πιστεύω," *TDNT*, 6:204-205.
95. See especially pages 52-55. Ed Christian, "1 Corinthians 7:10-16: Divorce of the Unbeliever or Reconciliation with the Unfaithful?" *JATS* 10 (1999): 41-62.
96. Fitzmyer, *First Corinthians*, 253, 298-299.
97. B. Byron, "The Brother or Sister is Not Bound: Another Look at the New Testament Teaching on the Indissolubility of Marriage," *New Blackfriars* 52 (1971): 519.
98. Bultman, "πιστεύω," *TDNT*, 6:217-219.

"To separate"

The verb χωρίζω, as we stated before, means "to separate" (7:15a), but was also used outside the New Testament with the meaning of "to divorce."[99] In the NT, the only other passages that use the verb χωρίζω in the context of divorce are Matt 19:6 and Mark 10:9, where Jesus teaches against divorce. In the context of 1 Cor 7:10-15, the meaning of the verb "is not just separation in 'bed and board' but of the legal dissolution of the marriage bond."[100] In v. 15, Paul used the indicative present middle/passive voice of χωρίζω (χωρίζεται), translated rightly by the majority of Bible versions as the middle (direct/reflexive) "leaves" or "separates/ separates himself," because the context (7:10-14) does not allow a passive translation. This is also the case of the following imperative middle/passive of the verb χωριζέσθω, "let him separate" or "let him be separated," which underlines the active sense of the first verb following the flow of the sentence.[101] The force of the indicative present middle clearly expresses the mindset of an unbeliever who is determined to separate definitively from the believer.[102] This present, highlighting the resolution of the unbeliever in breaking the marriage, parallels the verb συνευδοκεῖ (also an indicative present) in vv. 12 and 13, which expresses the attitude of the unbeliever in approving the marriage with a Christian. This shows that Paul's reasoning on the matter of marriage and divorce in mixed couples considers the will of the heathen spouse, who does not abide by God's law. This is supported by the subject ὁ ἄπιστος standing in an emphatic position.[103]

The second verb for divorce, χωριζέσθω, is an imperative middle that expresses a permission of separation/divorce.[104] This last imperative does not imply that the Christian spouse must resist the separation, but being an imperative of toleration or permission, rather implies that the act is a "*fait accompli*,"[105] and that the believer assumes that the unbeliever is free to make other choices.[106] This verb indicates that separation and divorce are beyond the believer's control and willingness. The continuation of marriage depends entirely on the approval[107] of the unbeliever because the Christian cannot start a divorce. This imperative

---

99. England, "Divorce and Remarriage in I Corinthians 7:10-16," 15; Isaeus 8:36; Polybius, *Hist.* 31.26.6.

100. R. L. Roberts, "The Meaning of *Chorizo* and *Douloo* in I Corinthians 7:10-17," ResQ 8 (1965): 180.

101. Cf. Olender, "The Pauline Privilege," 97.

102. Roberts, "The Meaning of *Chorizo* and *Douloo* in *I Corinthians* 7:10-17," 180.

103. Roberts, "The Meaning of *Chorizo* and *Douloo* in *I Corinthians* 7:10-17," 180.

104. Roberts, "The Meaning of *Chorizo* and *Douloo* in *I Corinthians* 7:10-17," 180-181. Cf. I Corinthians 7:36, where Paul also uses an imperative present of permission.

105. Deming, *Paul on Marriage and Celibacy*, 130. Garland, *1 Corinthians*, 290.

106. R. L. Roberts, "The Meaning of *Chorizo* and *Douloo* in I Corinthians 7:10-17," 180-181, suggested that the cause of separation of the unbeliever is given by the "faith" of the believer. This reading of the text seems not to be supported by the text in verse 15. In vv. 12 and 13, the approval of the unbeliever seems related to the choice made by the spouse in becoming a Christian, implying that the marriage is based on respect for diversity and willingness to be "one flesh." In v. 15, the willingness of separation/divorce of the unbeliever is not directly caused by the conversion of the partner, but by the inexistence of respect for diversity and by the unwillingness to be one flesh. Conversion can be only a pretext, not a direct cause for divorce.

107. By willingness and approval, I mean the consent to continue the marriage is a respectful way, which aims to be "one flesh" with the believer.

implies the tolerance of the Christian spouse and supposes that the believer already did everything in his or her ability to avoid the dissolution of the marriage. If the rupture of marriage is a *fait accompli* and the unbeliever wants a divorce, what can the Christian spouse do?

"To be under bondage"

The sentence οὐ δεδούλωται ὁ ἀδελφὸς ἢ ἡ ἀδελφὴ ἐν τοῖς τοιούτοις, "the brother and the sister is not bound in such cases" (7:15b), raises some questions concerning the translation of the verb δουλόω "to be under bondage" or "bind." The verb can be translated literally as "has not been enslaved" or "is not held in a state of slavery." What does this mean? This verb appears in 7:15 and in 7:17-24 concerning slavery. According to Deming, the reference to "slavery" is more the announcement of the next topic, than a conclusion of Paul's comments on marriage and divorce.[108] Fitzmyer suggested that the reference to slavery comes as the conclusion of the passage 7:12-16 because v. 16 is closely related to 7:12-15.[109] The association of marriage with slavery is not a topic that Paul developed in this chapter, even if in verse 15 he indirectly evoked a problem of interpreting the law on marriage and divorce, which can lead to slavery.[110] Instone-Brewer argued that divorce can be "compared to an emancipation certificate for a slave... this was not because they regarded marriage as slavery but the divorce legislation of Exodus 21:10-11 was based on the law of the slave wife, and they found many parallels between the release of a woman from marriage and the release from slavery."[111]

The verb δουλόω, like the verb δέω, is usually translated as "to bind" in vv. 7:27, 39, where Paul, talking about a marital relationship, explained that if a spouse is bound to a wife or a husband, he or she should be not unbound until the death of the spouse. Are these verbs synonyms, or are they used to describe two different realities? Olender, supporting the second option,[112] argued that δουλόω, "to bind," is a forensic term, also meaning "to enslave (losing his own autonomy)." In his opinion, this verb is not addressing remarriage in 7:15, but only separation, whereas δέω, "to bind in a metaphoric sense" with mutual commitment, opens up the possibility of remarriage in 7:27, 39.[113] Olender's argumentation was based on the fact that v. 7:39 also uses the word ἐλεύθερος, translated as

---

108. *Deming, Paul on Marriage and Celibacy*, 145, 147, 150. In fact Deming structured chapter 7 with a different organization of the topics in relation to the authors whom this research quotes above. He organized our passage in the following way: 7:10-15a "The Holiness of a Non-Christian Spouse as Grounds for Divorce" and 7:15b-24 "Marriage to an Unbeliever as a form of Slavery".

109. Fitzmyer, *First Corinthians*, 301.

110. Cf. Philo, Hypotetica 11.17. He related marriage with slavery: "For the man who is bound under the influence of the charms of a woman, or of children, by the necessary ties of nature, being overwhelmed by the impulses of affection, is no longer the same person towards others, but is entirely changed, having, without being aware of it, become a slave instead of a free man." Cf. also Deming, *Paul on Marriage and Celibacy*, 145-169; he thinks that the main topic of the section 7:15b-24 is slavery.

111. David Instone-Brewer, "1 Corinthians 7 in the Light of the Jewish Greek and Aramaic Marriage and Divorce Papyri," *TynBul* 52 (2001): 238-239.

112. See also Deming, *Paul on Marriage and Celibacy*, 145-146.

113. Olender, "The Pauline Privilege," 97.

"free" with clear social connotations, and implies that the person is free to remarry. In support of this view, Olender quoted Romans 7:2, 3, where Paul uses both δέω and ἐλεύθερος to state that a woman is free if the husband dies. According to Olender, Rom 7:2, 3 and 1 Cor 7:27 and 39 are addressing remarriage because the bind is not forensic, but metaphorical to mutual commitment, whereas 1 Cor 7:15 is not.[114] England, opposing Olender, concluded that the two verbs have a similar meaning and that δέω has a legal meaning instead of a metaphorical meaning.[115]

This leads to the following question: Does the phrase "not be enslaved" relate to marriage to an unbeliever or to the principle of "no remarriage" stated by Paul in v. 11? In other words, is the divorced Christian free to remarry, as in the case of the widow stated in 7:39? Roberts read the verb δεδούλωται as a perfect of an existing condition, implying that the believer should not remain a slave of the unbeliever's decision. He affirmed that the force of "οὐ δεδούλωται is that the believer is not obligated to prevent the divorce at the cost of losing all liberty, which is exactly what enslavement would be in this case."[116] Baumert, similar to Roberts, read that the believer is not under an "enslaving law" that obligates the maintenance of the marriage at all costs against the will of the unbeliever.[117] For Fee and Collins, 7:10-16 does not address the question of remarriage. However, Fee admitted that v. 15 does not prohibit remarriage,[118] whereas Collins affirmed that remarriage is likely possible, given the social circumstances at Paul's time.[119] Stein recognized that "one cannot be dogmatic and claim that the believer 'no longer being bound' (7:15) implies the right to remarry, but it would be equally wrong to be dogmatic and say that it excludes the right to remarry."[120] Kurt Niederwimmer suggested three possible interpretations because the verb in question is unclear: "'not bound' to the non-Christian spouse, 'not bound' to the marriage agreement, and 'not bound' by Jesus' prohibition of divorce" in 7:10-11.[121] Fitzmyer suggested that the verb δεδούλωται, a perfect passive, expresses the condition of a slave, the counterpart of the concept of freedom (ἐλεύθερος) in Rom 7:3.[122] From this perspective, the Christian spouse would be free from

114. Olender, "The Pauline Privilege," 97-98, 100. The problem with this interpretation (see for instance the context of Romans 3 to 7; in a special way verse 6:22 where Paul uses also the word "freedom") is that freedom in Christ cannot exclude, a priori, a forensic meaning of His sacrifice. If we keep only the metaphorical sense of mutual commitment, the liberating grace of Christ would be only a metaphor. The context of Rom 6 and 7 is against the interpretation of the verb δέω with just a metaphorical meaning, because nobody has a mutual commitment with sin. Sin cannot have a commitment with man; it enslaves man. This shows that Oleander's reading of the passages (Romans 7:2, 3 and I Corinthians 7:27, 39) is very weak and finally works in favor of the opposite thesis, advocating the similar meaning of the two verbs. On this issue, Garland affirmed that the two verbs in questions are not synonyms. Garland, *1 Corinthians*, 290.
115. England, "Divorce and Remarriage in I Corinthians 7:10-16," 186. See also BDAG, 221-222.
116. Roberts, "The Meaning of *Chorizo* and *Douloo* in I Corinthians 7:10-17," 181.
117. Norbert Baumert, *Woman and Man in Paul: Overcoming a Misunderstanding*, trans. Patrick Madigan and Linda M. Malonay (Collegeville, MN: Liturgical Press, 1996), 60-61.
118. Fee, *The First Epistle to the Corinthians*, 302-303.
119. Collins, *First Corinthians*, 272.
120. Robert H. Stein, "It is Lawful for a Man to Divorce His Wife?" *JETS* 22 (1979): 120.
121. Niederwimmer, quoted in Deming, *Paul on Marriage and Celibacy*, 145.
122. Fitzmyer, *First Corinthians*, 301-302.

any bond and could remarry.[123]   Hans Conzelmann supported the concept of remarriage here by affirming that the believer "is not subjected to any constraint because of the pagan's behavior."[124] A. Lindeman observed that the expression οὐ δεδούλωται does not make any sense if it means that the Christian spouse, after having being rejected and abandoned, has no right to remarry because he or she is still bound.[125] Instone-Brewer showed that the Jewish law perceives remarriage after divorce as a right:

> When Paul says they are 'no longer enslaved', any first century reader would understand him to mean that they can remarry, because they would think of the words in both Jewish and non-Jewish divorce certificates: 'You are free to marry'. If Paul had meant something else, he would have had to state this very clearly, in order to avoid being misunderstood by everyone who read his epistle.[126]

Nevertheless, he added that the usage of the image of slavery in marriage also meant that the marriage bound should not be treated lightly.[127]

"God has called you in peace"

Scholars have debated whether the clause, ἐν δὲ εἰρήνῃ κέκληκεν ὑμᾶς ὁ θεός (translated "but God has called you in peace"), belongs to what precedes or to what follows (7:15c). Baumert affirmed that "to be called in peace" means that, even if the unbelieving partner wants to leave, separate, or divorce, the believing spouse should do everything possible to save the marriage because he or she never knows if God will save the unbelieving spouse.[128] Garland read this sentence as an adversative or as a consecutive (but) as attached to what precedes, and not at all in a causal sense (for).[129] This reading of the text assumes that the believer should not contest the divorce decided by the unbeliever. According to Garland, Paul was not trying to comfort believers who were suffering from divorce or those who did not want to admit that the marriage was definitively broken and nothing else could be done against the choice of the unbeliever spouse. Paul's purpose was to make them understand that they must maintain their marriage with the unbelieving spouse as long as the unbeliever was willing to continue.[130] Robertson and Plummer stated the following:

---

123. Héring, *The First Epistle of Saint Paul to the Corinthians*, 153; Conzelmann, *1 Corinthians*, 123; Fitzmyer, *First Corinthians*, 302. England, "Divorce and Remarriage in I Corinthians 7:10-16," 186.

124. Conzelmann, *1 Corinthians*, 123.

125. A. Lindemann, *Der Erste Korintherbrief* quoted in Fitzmyer, *First Corinthians*, 302.

126. Instone-Brewer, "1 Corinthians 7 in the Light of the Jewish Greek and Aramaic Marriage and Divorce Papyri," 241. Keener suggested that after divorce remarriage was a normal. "No first century reader would have derived the meaning that some modern scholars have read into Paul's words." Craig S. Keener, *And Marries Another: Divorce and Remarriage in the Teaching of the New Testament* (Peabody, MA: Hendrickson, 1991), 61-62.

127. Instone-Brewer, "1 Corinthians 7 in the Light of the Jewish Greek and Aramaic Marriage and Divorce Papyri," 240-241.

128. Baumert, *Woman and Man in Paul*, 61, 62.

129. Garland, *1 Corinthians*, 292. Cf. Deming, *Paul on Marriage and Celibacy*, 153, who supports a casual close.

130. Garland, *1 Corinthians*, 291-292.

To what peace is opposed to? If to *bondage*, which seems natural, than the meaning will be that to feel bound to remain with a heathen partner, who objects to your remaining, would violate the peace in which you were called to be a Christian. If 'peace' is opposed to *separation*, then the meaning will be that you ought to do your utmost to avoid divorce. The former is probably right.[131]

Rosner read the sentence as valid for both "keeping the marriage bond in peace and allowing a determined unbelieving partner to depart in peace."[132] For Fitzmyer, the particle δὲ., "but" (adversative), introduces a restriction to the concession of 15a and introduces what follows in v. 16.[133] Peace is needed to maintain harmony in a relationship, but when the believer is divorced by the unbeliever and reconciliation is no longer possible, the term peace must be interpreted as referring to the fact that the believer is still "'called' by God to live in some sense in 'peace' (Rom 12:18; 14:19)."[134] Conzelmann saw that "the peace in question is valid independently of the behavior of the pagan partner," understanding that reconciliation or remarriage with the same partner is not the issue in this sentence.[135] Peace in this case should be understood as more than mere emancipation.[136] This concept implies that a divorce may occur "as an uncalculated and overhasty course of action."[137] If the problem cannot be solved, then the faithful partner is called in peace by God, which implies the possibility of a new phase in life with the possibility of remarriage.

Verse 16. The word "peace" is an important key to understanding the role of v. 16 in the passage. If the word "peace" is related to the attempt of the believer to reconcile with the unbeliever, considering divorce as non-definitive, then v. 16 would mean that the waiting of the Christian spouse for a future reconciliation with the heathen spouse may be helpful in saving the unbeliever.[138] In this way, Paul would have returned to the argument of v. 14, making the content of v. 15 incomprehensible.[139] If we read the word "peace" as referring to a condition of

---

131. Archibald Robertson and Alfred Plummer, *A Critical and Exegetical Commentary on the First Epistle of St. Paul to the Corinthians*, ICC; (Edinburgh: T&T Clark, 1955), 143.

132. Rosner, *Paul, Scripture and Ethics*, 170-171.

133. Fitzmyer, *First Corinthians*, 302.

134. Fitzmyer, *First Corinthians*, 302.

135. Conzelmann, *1 Corinthians*, 123-124.

136. Deming remarks that Paul has called the believer to "peace" and not to "freedom" as alternative to slavery. Deming, *Paul on Marriage and Celibacy*, 151.

137. Deming, *Paul on Marriage and Celibacy*, 152.

138. See Garland, *1 Corinthians*, 294. Verse 16 is also understood as the capstone of Paul's argument for the Christian not to initiate divorce against the unbeliever. This interpretation also does not respect the flow of Paul's argumentation. See England, "Divorce and Remarriage in I Corinthians 7:10-16," 187. Sakae Kubo, "I Corinthians 7:16: Optimistic or Pessimistic?" *NTS* 24 (1977-1978), 539.

139. We must say that attempts in reading verse 16 as related to vv. 12-14 have been made. J. B. Lightfoot read the expression τί γὰρ οἶδας, γύναι, εἰ not as a doubt but as a hope. He did that by quoting other passages (2 Sam 12: 22; Esth\ 4:14; Jonah 3:9; Joel 2:14), using similar expressions which emphasize hope, and not doubt. J. B. Lightfoot, *Notes on the Epistles of St Paul from Unpublished Commentaries* (London: Macmillan, 1904), 227. See also J. Jeremias, "Die missionarrische Aufgabe in der Mischehe" in Fitzmyer, *First Corinthians*, 303, who understood the expression to mean "perhaps," given that several extra biblical Greek writers used it: Epictectus, Diss. 2.20.30; 2.22.31; 2.25.2; *Joseph and Aseneth* 54, 12-13; Philo, *LAB* 9.6; 25.7; 30.4; 39.3; Homer, *Odys.* 3.216; Sophocles, *Antig.* 521; Plato, *Gorg.* 492e. This interpretation does not give justice to the function of v. 15 which seems out of place.

the believer to which God called him, whether or not he is able to reconcile with the heathen partner, v. 16 is stressing the idea that, after divorce (χωρίζω) from the unbeliever, one cannot know if the heathen spouse will be saved or not (only God knows and will provide other ways to call the unbeliever).

This is for two reasons: First, trying to maintain a marriage with somebody who does not want it does not grant that the unbeliever will be saved;[140] second, separating from the heathen spouse breaks the marriage, the bond that can sanctify the unbeliever.[141] This understanding justifies the position of v. 15 and indicates its role as a conclusion of the passage.[142] In fact, the expression τί γὰρ οἶδας, γύναι, εἰ (how do you know, wife, whether) at the beginning of v. 16 expresses a doubt about the future of the heathen partner that only God can take care of.[143]

Conclusion: How to read 1 Corinthians 7:15

After studying the issues at stake in 1 Corinthians 7:15, we can now propose an interpretation in the light of its immediate context.

As stated above, Paul introduced the topic of divorce in v. 10 by using the verb χωρίζω, which is also used in vv. 11 and 15. This verb links the three verses tightly, even though they present an apparent contradiction: in vv. 10 and 11, Paul seems to exclude the possibility of divorce, whereas he seems to allow an exception in v. 15. The Catholic interpretation,[144] based on Aquinas, solves the problem by differentiating between a marriage between two believers and a mixed marriage. The former is indissoluble because there is unity of faith, while in the latter, divorce and remarriage are possible because of disunity of faith.[145] If the Catholic interpretation is correct, Paul would have considered the dominical logion of 7:10-11 on divorce applicable only to marriages between two Christian believers, making his and Jesus' commands on divorce a principle applicable only to Christian believers and excluding a priori mixed marriages with unbelievers. This interpretation presupposes that Jesus' saying was addressed only to Jews and not also to Gentiles, and forgets that Jesus, recalling that marriage was instituted "in the beginning" as a blessing for all creatures,[146] was speaking to all of humanity.[147]

To resolve the apparent contradiction between Paul's "rejection" and "permission" of divorce and remarriage, we must step back and consider the value of the Jesus' sayings on divorce. Paul, because he was quoting Jesus' sayings, showed that the authority of his advice had to be found in Jesus' statement on divorce and

---

140. Fitzmyer, *First Corinthians*, 303.

141. England suggested that if the unbeliever divorced and left, he was probably rejecting salvation. ("Divorce and Remarriage in 1 Corinthians 7:10-16," 187).

142. Fitzmyer, *First Corinthians*, 303.

143. Fitzmyer, *First Corinthians*, 303.

144. The Catholic interpretation is officially the only unified interpretation of a church on divorce and remarriage. In fact, there is no Protestant reading of a possible "Pauline privilege." The only possibility for a Protestant to divorce is because of "*porneia*." See Pierre Dulau, "The Pauline Privilege: Is It Promulgated in the First Epistle to the Corinthians?" *CBQ* 13 (1951): 147.

145. Aquinas, *Super Epistolas S. Pauli Lectura* I, 299, paragraph 336.

146. See Matthew 19:1-12; Mark 10:1-12.

147. Cf. Murphy-O'Connor, "The Divorced Woman in I Cor. 7:10-11," 605.

remarriage.[148] Since Mark and Matthew also report Jesus' teaching on divorce and remarriage in an extended form, the meaning of the same key words employed by Mark, Matthew, and Paul is relevant. These key words are the following: γαμέω "to marry" (Mark 10:11, 12; Matt 19:9, 10; 1 Cor 7:10); γυνή, "wife" (Mark 10:2, 7, 11; Matt 19:3, 9; 1 Cor 7:10-12, 16); ἀνήρ "man" (Mark 10:2, 12; 1 Cor 7:10, 11, 13, 14, 16); and χωρίζω "to separate, divorce" (Mark 10:9; Matt 10:6; 1 Cor 7:10, 11, 15). Since there is little question as to the meaning of the words "to marry," "wife," and "man," the problem of interpretations must arise with the verb "to separate, divorce." As we have observed, some scholars read the verb χωρίζω with the meaning of separation. Others read both separation and divorce in this verb, but not remarriage. Still others read the possibility of separation, divorce, and remarriage.[149] Paul's statement, "not I but the Lord," seems to imply that he was actually giving to the verb χωρίζω the same meaning that Jesus gave, according to Mark and Matthew's accounts. This reading is supported by the fact that Paul used χωρίζω as part of the dominical logion and ἀφίημι as part of his own command or development on the issue: "I say, not the Lord" (7:10, 12). This suggests that when we find the verb χωρίζω, we should read "to divorce" with the meaning given by Jesus in the dominical logion, and when we find the verb ἀφίημι, we should read "to divorce" within the meaning that Paul intended in 1 Cor 7, which is a further application of the dominical logion. Consequently, the verb χωρίζω in verses 10, 11, and 15 (twice) should be read within the meaning of the dominical logion.

In Mark 10:9 and Matt 19:6, the verb χωρίζω is primarily translated as "separate."[150] In the synoptic Gospels, this verb means not only "to separate" with a spatial dimension, but, as stated above, may also mean "to divorce," which implies the breaking or dissolution and the end of the relationship.[151] If we take the verb with the meaning of just "spatial separation," we must also read the rest of the sentence, "what God joined together," in the same way, with the meaning that God joined man and woman only physically, without giving any deeper significaction to that union.[152] If this is the sense of what Jesus said, Adam and Eve would have been joined together only physically, fulfilling their marriage only when they met together. If we read the verb χωρίζω with the meaning of "to divorce," but with the impossibility or remarriage, this reading presupposes that the sentence, "what God has joined together," does not offer freedom of choice in marriage,

---

148. Cf. B. Byron, "General Theology of Marriage in the NT and 1 Corinthians 7:15" ACR 49 (1972): 1-10. He understood that the "Pauline Privilege" did not depend on the dominical logion, but rather from Paul's command, where v. 15 is a natural argument coming out of v. 12 where Paul says "not the Lord, but I …"

149. See above.

150. GNT, NIV, ESV, GDB, GW, CSB, LEB, BLA, LSG, NAS, NCV, NKJV. It is also translated, "put asunder" (ASV, RHE, KJV, RSV), "be parted" (BBE), "break or split apart" (CJB), "separate or tear apart" (HNV), and "cutting apart" (MSG).

151. H. G. Coiner, "Those 'Divorce and Remarriage' Passages (Matt. 5:32; 19:9; 1 Cor. 7:10-16)," CTM 39 (1968): 382.

152. In this way, the union cannot be called marriage. In my opinion, in Genesis 2:24-25 Moses used a legal term to talk about Adam and Eve's union. For a further study of this topic see Richard Davidson, The Flame of Yahweh: Sexuality in the Old Testament (Peabody, MA: Hendrickson, 2007), 15-54.

forcing two people to be united and not respecting their choice. Adam and Eve chose to join together and God blessed their union because of their free choice. If there is no consent in a marriage, that marriage does not reflect God's original design. To be "one flesh" implies not only sexual intimacy, but also a willingness to live in a marriage with the partner.

Verses 12 and 15 strongly support this concept. The verbs συνευδοκεῖ and χωριζέσθω respectively show a willingness or unwillingness to continue a marriage, creating the condition for not divorcing or for divorcing definitively. Jesus' sentence is eloquent: "Therefore what God has joined together, let man not separate." Jesus knew that humans can end a marriage through their behavior, which is why he said, "Let man not separate." The meaning of the verb "to separate" in Mark 10:9 and Matt 19:6 implies that a believer must not break a marriage. In giving this warning, Jesus recognized that human beings have the power to end their marriages. Jesus did not mean a partial rupture, but a total rupture of marriage. A marriage can be completely broken, not just partially broken with the prohibition of remarrying. If remarriage is not allowed, it means that the marriage is not completely broken. For this reason, Paul used the verb χωρίζω in vv. 10 and 11 to say that believers should not remarry because the verb implies a definitive rupture of the marriage with the possibility of remarriage. If this was not so, there would not be a reason to insist on this. Nevertheless, divorce between believers is not a fatality: God has the power to reconcile two believers who have a sincere desire to restore their marriage. If one of the two spouses does not share the same faith and breaks the marriage, God can no longer intervene in that marriage. In this case, the abandoned person is free.

Further support for this reading is given by the fact that the dominical logion to which Paul makes reference is quoted by Mark and Matthew in different ways: Mark puts it as an absolute, while Matthew leaves room for a specific exception (*porneia*). All three authors have been inspired by the same Spirit, and all three come to apparently different, but complementary conclusions.[153] This means first of all that the logion cannot be viewed as an absolute, and that the prohibition of divorce and remarriage, which is the rule for marital issues, may have exceptions.[154] Paul, even quoting the logion, recognized that the saying was not applicable when there was no longer any hope for the restoration of the marriage because the unbelieving partner refused it. "We believe that the Matthean (5:32; 19:9) and the Pauline (1 Cor. 7:15) exceptions are directed at those innocent parties and function to relieve them of the responsibility for the breakup of the marriage."[155]

Another relevant point in favor of this reading is that there is no clear mention that, in the case of a divorce provoked by the unbeliever, the believer should not remarry. Although Paul clearly stated in 7:11 that believers cannot remarry if they separate, he did not say that in mixed marriages, the believer cannot remarry if the

---

153. Fitzmyer, *First Corinthians*, 298; J. A. Fitzmyer, *To Advance the Gospel: New Testament Studies*, 2d ed.(Grand Rapids, MI: Eerdmans, 1998), 100.

154. Stein, "It is Lawful for a Man to Divorce His Wife?" 119; Keener, *And Marries Another*, 53-54.

155. William A. Heth, "Divorce and Remarriage: The Search for an Evangelical Hermeneutic," *TrinJ* 16 NT (1995): 64.

unbeliever divorces, but rather, suggested that the believer is no longer "enslaved" or bound.[156]

Finally, Paul confirmed God's rejection of divorce as Mark and Matthew did. This rejection is a rule aiming at goodness for all humanity, believers and unbelievers, regardless of whether they recognize and accept it. If the unbelieving spouse pays no heed to the Lord's command, he or she will only be under the marital civil law of the country.[157] Believers are called to listen to the dominical logion for several reasons. The most obvious reasons are that God can operate in their marriage to solve existing problems. Believers, when they are patient, can save their partners and their children through the sanctified bonds of a marriage.[158] Mixed marriages can also be an opportunity to aid in the sanctification of the spouse and children.[159] Believers who have tried everything to maintain their marriages with an unbeliever are called to peace if the unbelieving spouse wants to divorce. In this case, they are free and no longer under bondage, but this does not mean that they must remarry. They can stay single, as Paul suggests to the unmarried and widows (7:9).[160] However, if they decide that remarriage is good for them, they are free, before God, to remarry. It seems evident from this text that Paul read the dominical logion as a universal principle, yet admitted specific exceptions, respecting the freedom that God gives to all human beings.

---

156. England, "Divorce and Remarriage in I Corinthians 7:10-16," 185.
157. England, "Divorce and Remarriage in I Corinthians 7:10-16," 189.
158. Fitzmyer, *First Corinthians*, 297.
159. Garland, *1 Corinthians*, 279.
160. England, "Divorce and Remarriage in I Corinthians 7:10-16," 189.

Interpretations of the Metaphor "Spiritual House" In 1 Peter 2:4-10 and Their Implications for the Indwelling of Divine Presence

Cory Wetterlin

In the Old Testament, divine presence was a physical presence-to-physical presence relationship with God. If one wanted to come to God, he could approach his presence within the Sanctuary or Temple. Divine-human encounters before the construction of the earthly Temple were also presence-to-presence, such as Moses' meeting at the burning bush and Jacob's wrestling with the Angel of the Lord.[1] The New Testament begins with the same paradigm. The Messiah enters the world as Immanuel, "God with us" (Isa 7:14; Matt 1:23). Therefore, the followers of Jesus interacted with him on a face-to-face basis, which was a more tangible and visible type of interaction than some of the encounters in the OT. At the end of the New Testament, a similar interaction occurs with the fulfillment of the promise of the New Jerusalem in Revelation. The holy city will descend and God will once again dwell among his people; he will be their God and they shall be his people (Rev 22:3-4).[2]

However, a problem arises during the time between Christ's ascension and his second coming. Jesus promised that another Comforter, the Holy Spirit, would come (John 14:16, 26). This fulfilled his promise never to leave or forsake his people (Matt 28:20). In the New Testament, the Holy Spirit is manifested in real and visible ways (especially at Pentecost) and his power is displayed in the works of the church. However, the paradigm seems to shift; no longer is there a

---

1. "First, regardless of whether Gen. 32:31 (EVV 30) originally belonged to the account of Jacob's nocturnal wrestling-match or not, it is difficult to escape the conclusion that in its present context the verse identifies the God whom Jacob saw 'face to face' with the 'man' with whom he had wrestled. Secondly, in view of the reference to the descent of the pillar of cloud in Exod 33:9, it is generally considered that YHWH was present on those occasions when he is described as speaking to Moses 'face-to-face.' Thirdly, there are no indications of Divine Presence in the context of Deut 34:10. YHWH's 'face-to-face' knowledge of Moses is frequently understood as an expression of the intimacy of the unique relationship, which existed between them, but few if any scholars relate it explicitly to an experience of the Divine Presence." Ian Wilson, *Out of the Midst of the Fire: Divine Presence in Deuteronomy* (Atlanta: Scholars Press, 1995), 77.

2. Ranko Stefanovic, *Revelation of Jesus Christ: Commentary of the Book of Revelation* (Berrien Springs, MI: Andrews University Press, 2009), 600, 605, 609.

face-to-face relationship with God; now there is an indwelling, divine presence.[3] There are two primary interpretations of what indwelling actually means. First, the sacramental interpretation focuses on the Eucharist and the transformation of the form or substance of the bread into the actual presence of Christ.[4] Believers who receive the host once it has been transformed thus has the divine presence within them. It also remains within the tabernacle in the altar of the church as long as the host is there.[5] Second, pantheism suggests that all is God and panentheism suggests all is in God. Such beliefs extend the sacramental system to the cosmos. Everything is within God while God is also beyond all and cannot be contained in the creation.[6]

The biblical view of the indwelling of the Spirit, however, does not change the paradigm. The indwelling of the Holy Spirit is taking in the words of God and submitting the life of the individual believer to the authority of Christ in one's life (John 14:23). The Holy Spirit may come upon the individual and the power and providence of the Spirit can work within the life of the individual, but onto-logically, the divine presence remains outside the individual believer. Yet, God is still among his people, as ever he was. When Christian believers gather and call upon the name of Jesus, he is in their midst (Matt 18:18).[7] Corporately, the church is a temple of the Holy Spirit in which the Holy Spirit moves and dwells (1 Cor 6:19). Many passages in the New Testament make reference to the divine presence among the body of believers and there are many different interpretations imposed on those passages. One such passage is found in 1 Pet 2:4-10.

The face-to-face paradigm of divine presence found in the OT at the time of the first advent of Jesus in the NT and after the second advent of Jesus in the New Jerusalem poses a question regarding the divine presence for the waiting period between Jesus' ascension and Second Advent. The question for this research is in what way, if at all, the concept of the spiritual house of 1 Peter addresses the issue of divine presence.[8]

---

3. J. M. Hamilton, *God's Indwelling Presence: The Holy Spirit in the Old and New Testaments* (Nashville, TN: B & H Academic, 2006), 3-4, 54-55, 125.

4. "He is present in the Sacrifice of the Mass not only in the person of his minister, 'the same now offering, through the ministry of priests, who formerly offered himself on the cross,' but especially in the Eucharistic species." Catholic Church., *Catechism of the Catholic Church* (Mahwah, NJ: Paulist, 1994), 283.

5. Catholic Church., *Catholic Catechism*, 348.

6. Philip Clayton and Arthur Peacocke, eds, *In Whom We Live and Move and Have Our Being: Panentheistic Reflections on God's Presence in a Scientific World* (Grand Rapids, MI: Eerdmans, 2004), 8.

7. "Thus this presence of Jesus 'in their midst' is not just the regulation of disputatious church members, or a good feeling, or a practiced cultic expression, or religious acknowledgment of a cor-porate desire. It is real empowerment when God's little people gather in Jesus' name. It is the social and religious experience of his gathered people being filled with divine authority, focus and cohesion for the ordinary and extraordinary events in the life of their community." David D. Kupp, *Matthew's Emmanuel: Divine Presence and God's People in the First Gospel* (Cambridge, GBR: Cambridge University Press, 1996), 199, 183.

8. Jerry Truex clearly suggested that Peter does deal with questions of the presence of God along with questions of the atonement and identity and obedience. He also called out 1 Peter 2:4-5 as a "stunning response" the questions of divine presence. Jerry Truex, "God's Spiritual House: A Study of 1 Peter 2:4-5," *Direction* 33, (2004): 186.

The way in which to answer the question of whether the spiritual house in 1 Pet 2:4-10 addresses the issue of divine presence is first to define the term spiritual house (*pneumatikos oikos*). This study compares and contrasts the two major interpretations of this term as a temple or household.[9] These two options are strongly related to the interpretation of spiritual sacrifices; therefore, the second step of this research will to be to present the different views on the meanings of spiritual sacrifices. Finally, the arguments will be summarized and some conclusions drawn about how the concept of spiritual house and spiritual sacrifices help to answer the question of divine presence in the time of waiting.

This study will be limited to exegetical studies of 1 Pet 2:4-10. The questions of authorship, date of composition, audience, and literary genre of 1 Peter are not included in this study unless it becomes relevant for the exegetical information of the particular passage. While there is much more information within the verses of 1 Pet 2:4-10 regarding Jesus (for example Jesus as the cornerstone of the spiritual building), this study does not deal with all of the details of interpretation for the entire passage. Instead, it focuses on the interpretation of the terms "spiritual house" and "spiritual sacrifices," while only mentioning other exegetical details from the passage as they relate to these two concepts.

Interpretations of "spiritual house"

The word *oikos* in 1 Pet 2:4-5 is interpreted in many different ways, as John Elliott made clear; several examples include a physical house, a family or clan,

---

9. The authors supporting the temple interpretation are Francis D. Nichol ed, *Seventh-day Adventist Bible Commentary* (*SDABC*), rev. ed., 7 vols.; Washington, DC: Review & Herald, 1976), 7:560; R. J. McKelvey, *The New Temple: The Church in the New Testament* (London: Oxford University Press, 1969), 127-129, 131-132; Karen H. Jobes, *1 Peter*, BEC 21 (Grand Rapids, MI: Baker Academic, 2005), 148-149; Thomas R. Schreiner, *1, 2 Peter, Jude*, NAC 37 (Nashville, TN: Broadman & Holman, 2003), 105; J. N. D. Kelly, *A Commentary on the Epistles of Peter and of Jude*, TC (Grand Rapids, MI: Baker Books, 1989), 90; Edward Gordon Selwyn, *The First Epistle of St. Peter: The Greek Text with Introduction, Notes and Essays*, TC (Grand Rapids, MI: Baker Academic, 1981), 160; M. Eugene Boring, *1 Peter*, ANT (Nashville, TN: Abingdon, 1999), 98-99; Ernest Best, "1 Peter 2:4-10: A Reconsideration," *NovT* 11, (1969): 280; Truex, "God's Spiritual House," *Direction*, 189; Dennis E. Johnson, "Fire in God's House: Imagery from Malachi 3 in Peter's Theology of Suffering (1 Pet 4:12-19)," *JETS* 29, (1986): 290-293; John S. Marshall, "A Spiritual House an Holy Priesthood (1 Peter ii.5)," *AThR* 28, (1946): 227; David Hill, "'To Offer Spiritual Sacrifices' (1 Peter 2:5): Liturgical Formulations and Christian Paraenesis in 1 Peter," *JSNT*, (1982): 61. The authors supporting the household interpretation are J. Ramsey Michaels, *1 Peter*, WBC 49; (Waco, TX: Word, 1988), 100, 105; John Hall Elliott, *1 Peter: A New Translation with Introduction and Commentary*, AB 37B (New York: Doubleday, 2000), 415, 417; John Hall Elliott, *A Home for the Homeless: A Social-scientific Criticism of 1 Peter, Its Situation and Strategy: With a New Introduction* (Minneapolis, MN: Fortress, 1990), 168, 170-175, 180, 183-184, 189, 201-202, 207. While the weight of evidence would seem to be on the temple side, Elliott did such extensive exposition on the household position that most of the authors who choose the temple interpretation refer to and interact with Elliott's work. I did also find one author who specifically chose the middle way of saying it is both temple and household. Charles Bigg, *A Critical and Exegetical Commentary on the Epistles of St. Peter and St. Jude*, ICC (Edinburgh: T. & T. Clark, 1902), 414.

a household, and the metaphorical interpretation of temple.[10] Elliott argued that it is the context of the passage that provides the proper interpretation of the term, which he argued to be household. However, the modifier of *pneumatikos* leaves this interpretation up for debate. The scholastic literature abounds with the debate between two basic positions, temple or household. The vast majority of scholarship is on the side of temple, but Elliott's work is so extensive that most scholars address his conclusions. This study will start with the majority position of the spiritual house interpreted as temple.

Temple Interpretation

Spiritual House. The Seventh-day Adventist Bible Commentary simply states that because the house pertains to the spirit, it is therefore considered the temple of God.[11] The modifier "spiritual," added to *oikos*, is the primary connection for most scholars to call it a temple. The house is considered spiritual by R. J. McKelvey because of the cultic language and insinuations of worship seen in the rest of the passage. For example, there are the spiritual sacrifices that are to be offered, believers who are both living stones that make up the temple and who resemble the living stone, Jesus Christ; these believers are also made into a priesthood that offers the accompanying sacrifices. McKelvey moved away from the notion that the house is called spiritual because it is indwelt by the Holy Spirit. He stated that because the author of 1 Peter does not directly mention the divine presence, it is better to recognize the spirituality of the house because it is made up of "consecrated persons" who are spiritually dedicated and who offer their obedient lives as spiritual sacrifices.[12] For McKelvey, the spiritual interpretation is based on the cultic worship focus in the passage.[13]

The rest of the temple interpretation camp, on the other hand, suggests that Peter is referring to a spiritual temple precisely because of the indwelling presence of the Holy Spirit, as well as the idea of "a place of true worship and spiritual sacrifice."[14] Karen Jobes suggested that because the temple is made up of living stones, as Jesus is a living stone, this passage also suggests the close relationship with Jesus Christ as the cornerstone.[15] Jobes also emphasized the unity of the spiritual house, which is derived from "God's presence, the one Cornerstone, and

---

10. *"Oikos/oikia* designates, variously, a building, dwelling, residence; a room or chamber; a hall or meeting place; a storehouse or treasury; a palace; a building in which a divinity is thought to reside, a *temple*; a burial chamber or tomb; a *household*, family or lineage; household goods, substance, estate, inheritance; a reigning house or dynasty; a clan, tribe, tribal confederation, nation or state; and a social, commercial or religious organization or community." (Emphasis added) Elliott, *A Home for the Homeless: a Social-Scientific Criticism of 1 Peter, Its Situation and Strategy*, 182.

11. Nichol, *SDABC*, 7: 560.

12. McKelvey, *The New Temple*, 128-129.

13. McKelvey, *The New Temple*, 131. Elliott proposed that the direct response to worship is the focus of 1 Peter and suggested that "it is as the place of worship that 1 Peter is most interested in the new temple" (p. 131). However, this and similar interpretations fail to note that nowhere in the rest of 1 Peter is this supposed interest in worship made explicit. Elliott, *A Home for the Homeless*, 242. Marshall also emphasized the joint spiritual sacrifice made by the members of the spiritual house as an act of worship. Marshall, "A Spiritual House," 227.

14. Jobes, *1 Peter*, 148.

15. Jobes, *1 Peter*, 364.

a unity of purpose."[16] Divine presence clearly plays a significant role in Jobes' interpretation of spiritual house as the temple.

Thomas R. Schreiner followed along the same line, even discounting "some scholars" who are hesitant to use (or shy away from) the term temple. Following the LXX in using the verb *oikodomeo* in direct connection with *oikos* to speak of the OT temple, Schreiner believed the NT church represented in this passage by the term spiritual house is the new temple of God and said: "The house is 'spiritual' (*pneumatikos*) because it is animated and indwelt by the Holy Spirit."[17]

J. N. D. Kelly also suggested that Christians are God's temple "with Christ as the foundation and the Spirit dwelling in them."[18] He made reference to Jesus' speaking of raising a temple not made by hands to replace the physical temple in Jerusalem, suggesting that this new temple will be the Christian community. He also brought out the Qumran communities' understanding of the congregation and community being the house of God.[19]

Edward Selwyn took the interpretation of the temple a step further. He not only suggested the indwelling of the Holy Spirit, but also the sacerdotal nature of the temple.[20] Eugene Boring agreed; while some might suggest that *oikos* is a household, "the context indicates we have temple imagery."[21] Truex replaced the Jerusalem temple with the indwelling Christ of the Christian community.[22]

Dennis E. Johnson pointed to the OT language of sanctuary to suggest the temple imagery of 1 Pet 4 and uses 2:5 as further confirmation of the temple language within the book.[23] Johnson also tied Peter's language to the language of Paul in Eph 2:21-22 "... (Christ), in whom the whole building, as it is joined together, grows into a holy sanctuary in the Lord, in whom you also are being built together into a dwelling place of God in the Spirit."[24] Johnson clearly connected the temple language of 1 Peter to the indwelling of the Holy Spirit . Johnson also brought out the judgment parallels between 1 Peter and the judgment in the OT. Judgment in 1 Pet 4 starts with the house of God and Johnson referenced Ezek 9 and Mal 3:1-5 in which Yahweh comes to the temple to begin judgment. While Johnson recognized the language in Hebrews of the heavenly sanctuary, he suggested that Peter maintains that there is still an earthly temple composed of living stones.[25]

Within the passage of 1 Pet 2:4-10, v. 9 is often seen as a parallel to vv. 4-5. There is a significant word used in v. 9, which is significant to both parties of interpretation (temple and household). The use of *baseilion* is understood as a

16. Jobes, *1 Peter*, 149.
17. Schreiner, *1, 2 Peter, Jude*, 105. In his footnotes of this same page Schriener directly addressed Elliott's household position, stating that Elliott "underestimates the significance of the temple as God's house in the OT." Ernest Best also made the same tie between the verb *oikodomein* and *oikos* in the LXX and showed that *oikos* occurs ten times as often as *naos*, which is the next most common word used. Schreiner, *1, 2 Peter, Jude*, 280.
18. Kelly, *Peter and Jude*, 90.
19. Kelly, *Peter and Jude*, 90.
20. Selwyn, *The Epistle of St. Peter*, 160.
21. Boring, *1 Peter*, 98-99.
22. Truex, "God's Spiritual House," 189.
23. Johnson, "Fire in God's House," 290.
24. Johnson, "Fire in God's House."
25. Johnson, "Fire in God's House," 293.

substantive by both camps, rather than an adjective. That is, instead of *royal* modifying *priesthood*, they are seen in apposition. The believers are built into a spiritual house whose cornerstone is Christ, who is both a royal residence and the priesthood. Kelly, Selwyn, and Best all represented this translation on the side of the temple interpretation of spiritual house.[26] Best even admitted to an agreement with Elliott on this interpretation of *baseilion*. The main reason for this interpretation seems to be the enhancement of the indwelling of the Holy Spirit. If the Christian community becomes a royal residence, the divine presence among God's temple is more strongly represented.

The arguments for the temple interpretation of "spiritual house" have been presented. There are direct ties between the "spiritual house" and the "spiritual sacrifices." We will, therefore, turn to the temple camp's interpretation of spiritual sacrifices.

Spiritual Sacrifices. The major theme of what the spiritual sacrifices are in 1 Pet 2:5 is the surrender of life and conduct to the will of Christ. The SDA Bible Commentary suggests that the "sacrifices characterized by a spirit of love and devotion to God in contrast with the animal sacrifices of the ritual system had come to reflect little more than compliance with form. Only those who worship Him 'in spirit and in truth' (John 4:23, 24) can offer sacrifices that are 'acceptable to God.'"[27] McKelvey continued the theme of sacrifices being part of the cultic worship language of 1 Peter, listing some of the options as evangelism, good works, suffering, prayer, hospitality, and humility offered by the spiritual priesthood in line with the other themes of the epistle.[28]

Schreiner saw the modifier "spiritual" in relation to the work and influence of the Holy Spirit, as is the spiritual house. Schreiner brought in Elliott's interpretation of the sacrifices being the believer's holy life, Achtemeier's interpretation of the sacrifices evangelism, and Michael's reference to the sacrifices of both worship and conduct.[29]

Kelly agreed with the others that the spiritual sacrifices include the life and conduct of the believer. He referred to the Qumran recognition of the OT prophets' focus on prayer, praise, thankfulness, a broken and contrite heart, and a life of justice and compassion as spiritual sacrifices.[30] Kelly also included the interpretation, which is unique to the temple group, of the spiritual sacrifices as the Eucharist. He saw the Eucharist as the culmination of an offering of thankfulness.[31] Selwyn tied his interpretation of the spiritual house having sacerdotal connotations to the spiritual sacrifices having a proper sacerdotal sense as well: "Here the word is used in its proper sense of a sacerdotal act. It would be especially appropriate if the Eucharist were in the author's mind..."[32] Selwyn

26. Kelly, *Peter and Jude*, 97; Selwyn, *The Epistle of St. Peter*, 167; Best, "1 Peter 2:4-10," 288-289.
27. Nichol, *SDABC*, 7: 560.
28. McKelvey, *The New Temple*, 129.
29. Schreiner, *1, 2 Peter, Jude*, 107.
30. Kelly, *Peter and Jude*, 91.
31. Kelly, *Peter and Jude*, 92.
32. Selwyn, *The Epistle of St. Peter*, 161.

continued to express the Eucharist as the union of the Church's sacrifice with faith as an outward expression of God on one side and man on the other.[33] Boring and David Hill, who also interpreted spiritual house as temple, did not accept the Eucharist as part of the spiritual sacrifices because Peter does not make specific reference to the Eucharist in the passage, emphasizing instead the major theme in 1 Peter of the totality of Christian living.[34]

In summary, the temple interpretation understands Peter's use of spiritual house to be a transition, if not a replacement of the Jerusalem temple with the new temple of the Christian community indwelt by the Holy Spirit (with the exception of McKelvey who left out the component of divine presence). For some, both the temple and the sacrifices hold a sacerdotal meaning; for others, the sacrifices are simply those sacrifices influenced by the Holy Spirit and a part of worshiping God in both spirit and truth. After exploring the scholars who interpret spiritual house and temple and their understanding of spiritual sacrifices, this study will now move on to those who hold the household interpretation.

Household Interpretation

Spiritual House. The household interpretation is largely a sociological interpretation of the language in 1 Peter. This interpretation seeks to take in the entirety of the social structure and rule of life and conduct for the Christian believer in the whole book of 1 Peter. The emphasis is on the community formed, which is represented by the spiritual house, rather than any cultic temple language.[35] While Elliott acknowledged the possibility that *oikos* can be interpreted as temple, he saw the larger context of 1 Peter clearly showing household as the better option.[36]

Elliott was the primary voice of this argument; others who suggested this interpretation relied on Elliott. Elliott's argument was much too extensive for this paper and therefore, only the major points will be highlighted. The first of these points is the use of *oikos* outside of the Bible. *Oikos* is used by the Egyptians to express the whole land of Egypt as the household of Pharaoh. In other words, all that Pharaoh rules over is considered part of his household. According to Elliott, Philo shows the regular connection between politics and the household metaphor. The family is the place where *oikos* begins and then extends into the residence, land, property, and personnel, as well as the finances and economic management of the household.[37] The head of the household was seen as the *Pater Pariae* of all the members of the family; the servants of the household were also understood to be part of one large family unit under the *Pater Pariae*.[38] Elliott saw this language transfer into the language of 1 Peter and into the society of Bithynia.[39] Peter's use

33. Selwyn, *The Epistle of St. Peter*, 162-163.
34. Boring, *1 Peter*, 101; Hill, "Spiritual Sacrifices," 61.
35. Michaels, *1 Peter*, 100.
36. Elliott, *A Home for the Homeless*, 241.
37. Elliott, *A Home for the Homeless*, 172-173.
38. Elliott, *A Home for the Homeless*, 175.
39. Elliott, *A Home for the Homeless*, 180.

of *oikos* household would, therefore, reflect this social reality as he talks about the roles of servants, husband, wives, masters, elders, and younger men.[40]

The second point of interpretation for Elliott was demonstrated in the use of covenantal language. Elliott pointed out that throughout the OT, Yahweh made his covenants with the House of Jacob or the House of David: "This covenant established the basis of Israel's union with God as its exclusive kingly ruler, its collective identity as God's special elect and holy people."[41] Spiritual household, therefore, is to be understood as a house of the spirit through the new covenant with the Christian believers. The believers who make up the house of the spirit are those who accept the rule of Christ in their lives and recognize God as their *Pater Pariae*.[42]

Elliott then moved on really to discount the temple interpretation. For Elliott, temple was too narrow an interpretation for *oikos*; it limited the spiritual house only to the cultic rituals of worship, rather than an entire life encompassing surrender.[43] Elliott also explained the usage of *oikos* in the NT; he showed that the majority of times *oikos* was used, it referred to a home or domestic form of society. The terms *hieron* and *naos* are the conventional terms for temple in the NT.[44] While Elliott did recognize the usage of *oikos* with the verb *oidodomein* in the LXX to represent temple, he did not see the same usage in the NT, nor therefore, in the context of 1 Peter.[45] Elliott continued with a missional argument for household. The NT transitions from people gathering in the temple of God to households, which are filled with the Holy Spirit. The church moves and expands, based on households (*oikos*) and churches (*ekklesia*), which met in houses. Many households united together as the household of the Spirit.[46]

The divine presence was just as significant for Elliott as it was for the temple. The Holy Spirit now dwells in and among the community of believers, the household of God. This is seen in Elliott's interpretation of *basileion*. As mentioned before, the substantive interpretation of *basileion* as the royal residence is accepted both by those who interpret spiritual house as temple and by Elliott who proposed the household paradigm. Elliott considered the household as the divine residence.[47] He pointed to the same divine dwelling within the households of the OT in the tents (*oikos*) of Shem.[48]

Overall, Elliott developed the household interpretation of spiritual house extensively to include the social history of the time of the writing of 1 Peter, the context of the LXX and NT, and the immediate context of 1 Peter itself. It is important to look at Elliott's interpretation of spiritual sacrifices as well.

---

40. Elliott, *A Home for the Homeless*, 207.
41. Elliott, *1 Peter*, AB, 419.
42. Elliott, *A Home for the Homeless*, 186, 201, 207.
43. Elliott, *A Home for the Homeless*, 194.
44. Elliott, *A Home for the Homeless*, 197. Further down on this page Elliott made what I consider a weaker point of his argument, the dismissal of the spiritual modifier for *oikos*. He saw this as the only possible language that may link *oikos* to temple and simply brushes it aside for the significance of the rest of the context. There is clearly cultic language in this passage that needs to be connected: spiritual, sacrifice, priesthood, etc.
45. Elliott, *A Home for the Homeless*, 241.
46. Elliott, *A Home for the Homeless*, 222.
47. Elliott, *A Home for the Homeless*, 168-169.
48. Elliott, *A Home for the Homeless*, 170.

Spiritual Sacrifices. The interpretation of spiritual sacrifices by Elliott and others who held the household interpretation is not much different from the interpretation of those of the temple camp. As previously mentioned, those who held to the temple interpretation actually cited and agreed with Elliott's interpretation of spiritual sacrifices. Sacrifices include the possibility of praise and thanksgiving, holy and honorable conduct, upright behavior and the other household duties of the spiritual community. Elliott, while acknowledging the possibility of the Eucharist, also rejected it because of a lack of certain evidence in 1 Peter.[49] Elliott also included the declaration of "praise of him who called you out of the darkness into his marvelous light," from v. 10. This is the ground for the evangelistic interpretation of spiritual sacrifices.[50]

In summary, the household interpretation is focused on the spiritual house being the household of the Spirit. The household is still the royal residence of the Holy Spirit dwelling among his community. Elliott based this interpretation on the larger context of 1 Peter and interpreted the spiritual sacrifices accordingly as well performed household duties of the community.

Summary and Conclusions

It seems that both the household and the temple interpretations have merit. The "spiritual" modifier of house along with the other cultic or sanctuary language of sacrifices and priesthood seem too significant to ignore, which Elliott did in order to emphasize the household and reject the temple. Johnson's additional imagery of the judgment beginning in the temple for the OT and in 1 Pet 4 makes an even stronger case for the inclusion of temple for the interpretation of spiritual house. These evidences are found in the context of 1 Peter itself without over-laying Paul's understanding on Peter's writing to include all of Paul's temple imagery of the new Christian Community.

The household interpretation also has clear support in the context of 1 Peter. The sociological instructions for conduct and holy living within a system of community under Father God are very clear. Added to this is Elliott's evidence of the use of *oikos* in the NT to represent the domestic sense of household in both the societal structure of Egypt and the Roman household. I agree with Elliott that the NT shows a transition away from the building of the Jerusalem temple as the dwelling place of God to the households and communities of believers. The divine presence is no longer limited to the *shekinah* in the Holy of Holies, but is amongst the people wherever they may gather in the name of Jesus to worship in spirit and in truth. However, this shows temple transition to the community as temple as well as household.

---

49. Elliott, *1 Peter*, 422.
50. Elliott, *1 Peter*, 421.

This study agrees with Charles Bigg, Truex, and Nijay Gupta who accepted both interpretations, but who are also open to Elliott's criticism of such a position.[51] Essentially, it is unsound to disregard either interpretation.

Interpretations of "spiritual sacrifices"

The interpretation of spiritual sacrifices is the same on both sides of the argument, except concerning the understanding of the Eucharist. It makes sense that this argument would come from the side of the temple interpretation, especially from a sacramental system of thinking. The Eucharist is the very presence of Christ. Therefore, if the temple is to be indwelt by the presence of Christ, the Eucharist must be present. Christ's presence is what makes the house spiritual and is, therefore, directly referenced in such a system.

Because I do not subscribe to a sacramental system in the sense of transubstantiation and the real presence of Christ as being or embodied in the host, I do not see the Eucharist as a necessary part of an interpretation of the spiritual sacrifices. I am more inclined to connect it with the general context of 1 Peter concerning holy living and the conduct of the spiritual household, as well as the immediate context of the passage, which, in 1 Pet 2:10, includes offerings of praise to the one who has led believers out of darkness.

Implications for the understanding of divine presence

The theme of divine presence is considered to be a part of 1 Peter in reference to the spiritual house by each of the interpreters discussed, except McKelvey. Divine presence is made all the more significant by the interpretation of *baseilion* as the substantive divine residence. The answer to the research question for this study as to whether 1 Peter has anything to say about divine presence according to the scholars is an affirmative. Even though there is not a direct reference to the dwelling of the Holy Spirit in the community, the modifier "spiritual" infers the connection.

I believe the household/temple combination can give us some significant insight into how to interpret divine presence in the time between Christ's ascension and his second coming. The Bible supports an external face-to-face relationship with God in the OT temple and with the incarnated Jesus during his first advent and after his second. This is in contrast to an internal indwelling ontological relationship. To be a part of the household of Yahweh was to be in a

---

51. Bigg used the language of both the house and the temple. Bigg, *St. Peter and St. Jude*, 128. Truex suggested that "both then and now, the use of the metaphor 'spiritual house' (1 Pet. 2:5) is not limited to a single meaning or set of mental images. Thus we are not forced to choose either family or temple as its meaning. Both sets of images were within the cultural and linguistic grasp of the first readers, and both sets of images disclosed new realities for understanding the traumatic historical and social crises they faced. 1 Peter encourages its recipients not to be passive observers of traumatic events or powerless victims of other people's opinions. Rather, it empowers the readers to choose. They do not need to search for home; they can choose to be home and family for the homeless. They do not need to wonder where God is in all of this; they can choose to be the place of God's presence in the world here and now. In this way, they are the people of God." Truex, "God's Spiritual House," 190. Gupta also suggested that Peter may have meant to include both although he leans towards temple language. Nijay Gupta, "A Spiritual House of Royal Priests, Chosen and Honored: The Presence and Function of Cultic Imagery in 1 Peter," *PRS* 36 (2009): 71, 76. Elliott, however, called for a decisive alternative. Elliott, *A Home for the Homeless*, 194.

covenantal relationship with him and accept his rule over one's life. We find the same type of relationship described in 1 Peter through the household language and his emphasis on holy living. J. M. Hamilton made it clear that there was an internal working of the Holy Spirit for the regenerative work of salvation in the OT, rather than an ontological indwelling. However, rather than staying consistent with this understanding for the NT Church, he believed Christ establishes the ontological indwelling of the Holy Spirit.[52]

I see evidence in 1 Peter of what a continued external relationship with God would look like in this interim time. Rather than an individual indwelling, the community of believers is built up into a spiritual house of living stones in which the divine presence dwells. The believers then offer spiritual sacrifices of their lives in covenant with God as their head of household. They are empowered by the regenerative power of the Holy Spirit working in them to make them living stones just as their cornerstone (Christ) is also a living stone raised to life by the power of the Holy Spirit. 1 Peter 2:4-10 clearly offers significant insight into the question of the divine presence during this time of eschatological waiting for the second coming of Christ.

---

52. Hamilton, *God's Indwelling Presence*, 3-4, 54-55, 125.

PART 3: PSEUDEPIGRAPHA

SACRED TIMES: THE BOOK OF JUBILEES AT QUMRAN

J. Amanda McGuire

It is widely accepted that the Qumran community had an interest in matters pertaining to the calendar and the proper times to observe feasts.[1] Amongst the thou-
sands of manuscripts found in the Qumran caves, there are nineteen texts that are
primarily calendrical, as well as one sundial.[2] However, several other Dead Sea
Scroll (DSS) texts indicate an interest in, or even a preoccupation with, the calendar. One such example is the book of Jubilees.

The book of Jubilees holds a very distinct place in the Qumran library. It is
not regarded as a Qumran sectarian document because it lacks the characteristic
rejection of the established priesthood and because of certain dissimilarities in
theology and ritual.[3] Nevertheless, it is one of the most attested books in the
entire Qumran corpus.[4] At least fifteen manuscripts of Jubilees were found at
Qumran.[5] It is not, however, simply the number of manuscripts that indicates the
importance of Jubilees, but also the reliance of the sectarian writers on the book
itself. For example, the book is mentioned by name in the Cairo Geniza copy

---

1. For example, see James C. VanderKam, *Calendars in the Dead Sea Scrolls: Measuring Time*,
The Literature of the Dead Sea Scrolls (London: Routledge, 1998), 43-116; Sacha Stern, "Qumran
Calendars: Theory and Practice," in *The Dead Sea Scrolls in Their Historical Context*, ed. Timothy H.
Lim (London: T&T Clark, 2000), 179-186.

2. VanderKam, *Calendars in the Dead Sea Scrolls: Measuring Time*, 110. He defines "calendri-
cal" as "based on...the sequence of days, weeks, and months, whether for a year or a longer cycle."
Ibid., 71. For his analysis of the relevant texts, see ibid., 71-90. For a nice image of the sundial, see
James C. VanderKam, "Calendars in the Dead Sea Scrolls," *NEA* 63.3 (2000): 166.

3. O. S. Wintermute, "Jubilees: A New Translation and Introduction," in *The Old Testament
Pseudepigrapha*, ed. James H. Charlesworth (New York: Doubleday, 1985), 44.

4. Charlotte Hempel, "The Place of the *Book of Jubilees* at Qumran and Beyond," in *The Dead
Sea Scrolls in Their Historical Context*, ed. Timothy H. Lim (London: T&T Clark, 2000), 195-196;
James C. VanderKam, *The Dead Sea Scrolls Today* (Grand Rapids, MI: Eerdmans, 1994), 39-40. As
he notes, only Psalms, Deuteronomy, Isaiah, and Genesis equal or exceed Jubilees.

5. VanderKam, *The Dead Sea Scrolls Today*, 39-40. The manuscripts are 1Q17, 1Q18, 2Q19,
2Q20, 3Q5, 4Q176a, 4Q176b, 4Q216, 4Q218, 4Q219, 4Q220, 4Q221, 4Q222, 4Q223-224, 11Q12,
and possibly 4Q217; Stephen W. Marler, ed., "An Index of Qumran Manuscripts," OakTree Software,
Ver. 4.3, 2007.

of the Damascus Document (CD 16:2-4). In addition, Gershon Brin identified a linguistic connection between the sectarian documents and Jubilees.[6]

Given the evidence that Jubilees was so influential at Qumran, this article seeks to answer the following questions: How did the book of Jubilees understand sacred times in general, and the Sabbath in particular? How did its sacred time theology affect the theology of the Qumran community?

Background to the Book of Jubilees

The only complete version of Jubilees is written in Classical Ethiopic; however, fragments of the book also exist in Latin (approximately one-third of the book) and Greek (quotations only).[7] Before the discoveries at Qumran, it was hypothesized that Jubilees was originally composed in Hebrew, and the finds were able to prove it.[8] The earliest manuscript (4Q216) comes from c. 125-100 BCE, and thus was copied not long after the time the book was originally written.[9]

Current scholarship now dates the composition of Jubilees to c. 170-150 BCE. It was written in Hebrew and then, subsequently, translated into Greek and possibly Syriac. The book was translated from Greek into Latin and Ethiopic and thus, preserved.[10]

Jubilees was written during a fascinating time in Judaism's history. The Second Temple Period saw many different expressions and interpretations of Judaism. Despite the apparently united front, Judaism, like any family, had internal strife.[11] Diaspora Jews often endeavored to make their beliefs more palatable to their Gentile neighbors.[12] Palestinian Judaism was divided into various sects and groups following one teacher or another. It was the Maccabean Rebellion (c. 167-164 BCE), however, that set in motion a chain of events that led to the further splintering of Judaism. In the aftermath of the rebellion, the Maccabees made themselves a dynasty of kings and priests, but their authority was not universally acknowledged.[13] Josephus related that by the time of Jonathan the High Priest, the Pharisees, the Sadducees, and the Essenes were in existence.[14]

---

6. Gershon Brin, "Regarding the Connection between the *Temple Scroll* and the *Book of Jubilees*," *JBL* 112 (1993): 108-109. His short article points out that there is a unique linguistic connection between 11Q19 51:6-7 and 4Q216 1:12-13.

7. James C. VanderKam, *The Book of Jubilees*, 2 vols., CSCO 510-511/Scriptores Aethiopici 87-88 (Leuven: Peeters, 1989), 1:ix, 2:xi-xiv; Wintermute, "Jubilees: A New Translation and Introduction," 41-42.

8. Wintermute, "Jubilees: A New Translation and Introduction," 43.

9. James C. VanderKam and J.T. Milik, "Jubilees," in *Qumran Cave 4 VIII: Parabiblical Texts, Part 1*, ed. Emanuel Tov, Discoveries in the Judean Desert 13 (Oxford: Clarendon, 1994), 2.

10. VanderKam, *The Book of Jubilees*, 2:v-vi.

11. Shaye J.D. Cohen, *From the Maccabees to the Mishnah*, 2nd ed. (Louisville: Westminster John Knox, 2006), 12-14.

12. John J. Collins, *Between Athens and Jerusalem: Jewish Identity in the Hellenistic Diaspora*, 2nd ed. (Grand Rapids, MI: Eerdmans, 2000), 14-16.

13. Cohen, *From the Maccabees to the Mishnah*, 5, 22-23. The Essene sect is thought to have been loyal to another priestly family, the Zadokites, thus alienating them from the Temple cult. E. P. Sanders, "The Dead Sea Sect and Other Jews: Commonalities, Overlaps, and Differences," in *The Dead Sea Scrolls in Their Historical Context*, ed. Timothy H. Lim (London: T&T Clark, 2000), 16-17.

14. Josephus, *Ant.* 13.5.9 (*The Complete Works of Josephus: Complete and Unabridged*, trans. William Whiston, new updated ed. (Peabody: Hendrickson, 1987)).

Given this setting, Jubilees was most likely written by a Palestinian Jew of priestly background and Hasidic or Essene persuasion. His knowledge of Canaanite geography, as well as an intense interest in festivals and law give witness to this.[15] Though the book is well attested at Qumran,[16] it is generally thought to predate the site, as the Cairo Geniza copy of the Damascus Document refers to it as an authority.[17]

The book itself is a retelling of the events of Genesis 1 to Exodus 16. It begins with the Lord's calling Moses to the top of Mt. Sinai to receive a revelation.[18] The first chapter of the book clearly outlines the basic tenets of the author's theology and eschatology. The world and its events are running on a very strict calendar that was preordained and engraved on tablets in heaven.[19] God has scheduled the time from creation to the renewal of creation, and it is important for the children of Israel not only be aware of it, but also to follow it.

This is not the only tenet the book sets out to prove. Jubilees is also intensely interested in showing that the narrative accounts of Genesis 1-Exodus 16 establish the Mosiac law even before it is given on Sinai. The author reinterprets the events of Genesis, adding and subtracting material, expanding some stories, and shortening others.

Calendars

Jubilees has a very specific calendar. According to Jub. 6:32, the Israelites are only to recognize a 364-day (solar) year. Other texts throughout the book reflect this view, especially in the creation account. The author says, "And God appointed the sun to be a great sign on the earth for days and for sabbaths and for months and for feasts and for years and for sabbaths of years and for jubilees and for all seasons of the years."[20] This differs from Genesis 1:14, which indicates that both the sun and the moon (and possibly the stars) were "for signs and for seasons and for days and years."

The origins of the 364-day calendar have been much debated in the scholarly literature. The most important contributor is Annie Jaubert, whose work with the time scheme in Jubilees led her to apply its calendrical system to the entire Hebrew Bible and even to the New Testament. All of this was apparently with the end of figuring out what day of the week the Last Supper took place.[21] In essence, her theory is this: a 364-day calendar meant that every date of the year would always occur on the same day of the week. Since the heavenly bodies were

---

15. Wintermute, "Jubilees: A New Translation and Introduction," 45.

16. For the purposes of this study, I am assuming that the Qumran community was Essene, as has been generally assumed and recently defended in VanderKam, *The Dead Sea Scrolls Today*, 71-97.

17. Wintermute, "Jubilees: A New Translation and Introduction," 43-44.

18. Jub. 1:4, 26, 29.

19. An interesting summary of the predestination passages of Jubilees can be found in Florentino García Martínez, "The Heavenly Tablets in the Book of Jubilees," in *Studies in the Book of Jubilees*, eds. Matthias Albani, Jörg Frey, Armin Lange, TSAJ 65 (Tübingen: Mohr Siebeck, 1997), 247-250.

20. Jub. 2:9, Quoted from *Old Testament Pseudepigrapha*, ed. R. H. Charles (Oxford: Clarendon, 1913), OakTree Software Ver. 2.2

21. Her scholarly work on the subject culminates in her book: Annie Jaubert, *The Date of the Last Supper*, trans. Isaac Rafferty (Staten Island, NY: Alba House, 1965).

created on Wednesday, then the first day of the year started on a Wednesday.[22] She went on to argue that this calendar is in fact very ancient, and it is assumed throughout much of the Old Testament, though it was eventually replaced by the luni-solar calendar in the Second Temple Period.[23] Jaubert's theory is accepted or disputed to varying degrees, the chief argument against it being that the theory cannot be proved with any degree of certainty.[24]

Enoch, the mysterious figure from Gen 5:21-24, is mentioned in Jub. 4:17-25 as the first man who understood the heavenly calendrical system and wrote it down. This passage seems to presuppose the Astronomical Book of *1 Enoch* (ch. 72-82).[25] Though it appears that Jubilees depends on *1 Enoch* in some places, it certainly differs from *1 Enoch* on the specifics of the calendar. The Astronomical Book indeed mentions the 364-day solar year in chapter 72, but also makes use of the moon and intercalation of sorts in chapters 73-74.[26] Thus, though Jubilees appears to have great respect for the Astronomical Book, Jubilees does not agree with its use of the moon in addition to the sun.

There is a similar situation within the corpus of calendrical texts at Qumran. Though the community seems to have been preoccupied with the notion of getting the calendar right, their library was full of documents that contradicted each other. On the one hand, Jubilees mandates a strict 364-day solar year, while *1 Enoch*, 4Q317 and 4Q318 use a luni-solar model.[27] This has led Sacha Stern to conclude that the calendars were "purely theoretical models."[28]

Though the sect's documents do not entirely agree on the details, there are a few notable trends about the Qumran calendar. First, the liturgical year of the Temple Scroll included all the biblical festivals, plus the addition of three more festivals: Wine, Oil, and Wood.[29] Second, no Qumran text makes mention of Purim (instituted in Esther) or Hanukkah (1 Maccabees).[30] Third, the Qumran sect seems to have designated the weeks of the year according to the priestly rotations in the temple. There were 24 names mentioned in 1 Chr 24:7-18, and it has been speculated that the Qumran sect added two more names so that there would be 26

---

22. Jaubert, *The Date of the Last Supper*, 15-30.

23. Jaubert, *The Date of the Last Supper*, 31-52.

24. See, for example, James C. VanderKam, "The Origin, Character, and Early History of the 364-Day Calendar: A Reassessment of Jaubert's Hypotheses," *CBQ* 41 (1979): 390-411; Ben Zion Wacholder and Sholom Wacholder, "Patterns of Biblical Dates and Qumran's Calendar: The Fallacy of Jaubert's Hypothesis," *HUCA* 66 (1995): 1-40.

25. J. T. Milik, *The Books of Enoch: Aramaic Fragments of Qumrân Cave 4* (Oxford: Clarendon, 1976), 11; VanderKam, *Calendars in the Dead Sea Scrolls: Measuring Time*, 27-33.

26. VanderKam, *Calendars in the Dead Sea Scrolls: Measuring Time*, 20-26.

27. Milik, *The Books of Enoch*, 68; Matthias Albani, "Der 364-Tage-Kalender in Der Gegenwärtigen Forschung," in *Studies in the Book of Jubilees*, ed. Matthias Albani, Jörg Frey, Armin Lange, TSAJ 65 (Tübingen: Mohr Siebeck, 1997), 92-93; VanderKam, *Calendars in the Dead Sea Scrolls: Measuring Time*, 76, 88; For other texts and which camp they fall into, see ibid., 110-112.

28. Stern, "Qumran Calendars: Theory and Practice," 181-182.

29. 11QT 19:11-25:1; VanderKam, *Calendars in the Dead Sea Scrolls: Measuring Time*, 66-69.

30. VanderKam, *Calendars in the Dead Sea Scrolls: Measuring Time*, 71-72.

priestly watches, which would each fall twice a year.[31] With this understanding, the calendrical texts are somewhat easier to understand.[32]

It is unclear precisely what event led to such disunity over the calendar, but James C. VanderKam said:

> There is good reason for believing that a calendrical dispute was one factor that led the Qumran community to separate itself physically from the rest of Jewish society. For them the calendar was not simply a convenient tool; rather, the correct reckoning of time was divinely revealed, and conducting one's life according to it had been mandated by God himself in prediluvian times.[33]

In fact, there is very little information about the calendrical system of the Second Temple Period.[34] The Elephantine Papyri (c. 5th century BCE) combine Egyptian and Babylonian month names, but the Samaria Papyri (c. 375-335 BCE) use only the Babylonian month names. The Babylonian calendar was a lunar one, and the Egyptian was solar.[35] In Sirach 43:6-7 (written c. 175 BCE), the moon governs the seasons, months, and festivals.[36] The books of 1 and 2 Maccabees use the Greek month names, and Josephus uses Jewish, Macedonian, and Roman names.[37]

It is unclear to what extent these (and potentially other) calendars differed, but if they did differ substantially, it is easy to understand how Jews could become anxious about observing the festivals at the right time. Perhaps this confusion is what led the author of Jubilees to write:

> And command thou the children of Israel that they observe the years according to this reckoning– three hundred and sixty-four days, and (these) will constitute a complete year. ...But if they do neglect and do not observe them according to His commandment, then they will disturb all their seasons and the years will be dislodged. ...And all the children of Israel will forget and will not find the path of the years, and will forget the new moons, and seasons, and sabbaths. ...It is not of my own devising; for the book (lies) written before me, and on the heavenly tablets the division of days is ordained, lest they forget the feasts of the covenant and walk according to the feasts of the Gentiles after their error and after their ignorance.[38]

---

31. VanderKam, *Calendars in the Dead Sea Scrolls: Measuring Time*, 72-74, 48-50. 1Q2:2 is the basis for the assumption that the Qumran list had 26 names rather than 24; however, the War Scroll possibly hints at this idea as well.

32. See VanderKam's section entitled "Calendrical documents that incorporate the priestly courses," in *Calendars in the Dead Sea Scrolls: Measuring Time*, 77-86.

33. VanderKam, *Calendars in the Dead Sea Scrolls: Measuring Time*, viii.

34. While not denying the reality of calendrical concern at Qumran, Stern says of the limited evidence within wider Judaism: "...besides the Boethusians of the Mishnah and the book of *Jubilees*, there is nothing to suggest calendar sectarianism among the Jews of the Hasmonean or of the early Roman periods." Stern, "Qumran Calendars: Theory and Practice," 185.

35. VanderKam, *Calendars in the Dead Sea Scrolls: Measuring Time*, 15-16.

36. VanderKam, *Calendars in the Dead Sea Scrolls: Measuring Time*, 27.

37. VanderKam, *Calendars in the Dead Sea Scrolls: Measuring Time*, 34.

38. Jub. 6:32-35, Quoted from *Old Testament Pseudepigrapha*, ed. R. H. Charles (Oxford: Clarendon, 1913), OakTree Software Ver. 2.2

Verses 36-38 go on to say that a lunar calendar mixes up the times and causes the people to profane holy days and perform holy rites on profane days. Not all time is created equal, and the Israelites must be very careful not to confuse the days.

The Habakkuk Pesher indicates that the Teacher of Righteousness (likely the founder of the Qumran community) and the Wicked Priest (possibly the reigning high priest) used different calendars.[39] In The Rule of the Community, it reads:

> They are not to deviate in the smallest detail from any of God's words as these apply to their own time. They are neither to advance their holy times nor to postpone any of their prescribed festivals. They shall turn aside from His unerring laws neither to the right nor the left.[40]

VanderKam asserted that this is evidence of a difference in calendrical calculation because it would be unusual for Jews in the Second Temple Period to observe the festivals on completely different days than those mandated in the Torah.[41]

The Cairo Geniza copy of the Damascus Document, which is of much interest to Jubilees scholars because of its reference to the book in CD 16:12-14, is also of interest because the book warns that the children of Israel would go astray in regard to the Sabbaths and festivals.[42] This shows a similarity in thought and concern between the two works and perhaps, even dependence of CD on Jubilees.

Though the calendar of the book of Jubilees was not embraced whole-heartedly at Qumran, the ideology behind Jubilees' calendar was accepted. Jubilees drove home the concept that using the right calendar was imperative to the people of God. The Qumran community carried on this tradition, seeking to perfect their own calendar, for "it was incumbent on the members of the Qumran covenant to observe the sacred festivals at the revealed times. To do otherwise entailed violating the harmony of the universe and mixing the sacred with the profane."[43]

Jubilees presupposes a deterministic theology. The events of the world are inscribed on the tablets in heaven, and everything happens according to its time. This is another point in which the Qumran community agrees with Jubilees. Throughout their documents, the sect shows itself to be deterministic, even to the point of using astrology.[44]

It was crucial to the writer of Jubilees that everything happens in its proper time and that the festivals be observed using the 364-day calendar. It is time to look at its theology of the weekly Sabbath.

---

39. Shemaryahu Talmon, "Yom Hakkippurim in the Habakkuk Scroll," *Bib* 32 (1951): 549-563. See 1QpHab 11:4-8.

40. 1QS 1:13-15, quoted from "Qumran Non-Biblical Manuscripts: A New English Translation," based upon Michael O. Wise, Martin G. Abegg, Jr. and Edward M. Cook, eds., *The Dead Sea Scrolls: A New English Translation*, (New York: HarperCollins, 2005), OakTree Software Ver. 2.7.

41. VanderKam, *Calendars in the Dead Sea Scrolls: Measuring Time*, 45-46.

42. VanderKam, *Calendars in the Dead Sea Scrolls: Measuring Time*, 47-48. CD 3:14-15, 6:18-19, 12:3-6.

43. VanderKam, *Calendars in the Dead Sea Scrolls: Measuring Time*, 110-111.

44. 4Q318, 4Q186, 4Q561; VanderKam, *Calendars in the Dead Sea Scrolls: Measuring Time*, 88-89.

The Sabbath

It has been pointed out that the book of Jubilees essentially begins and ends with the Sabbath.[45] Chapter 2 of the book discusses the creation in great detail, including the Sabbath, and chapter 50 ends with the command to keep the Sabbath and prescriptions on how to do so. Doering noted that Jubilees follows the account of Gen 1-Exod 16 and models its overall structure on these portions of the Torah. Thus, though the Sabbath is not mentioned in the middle of the book, this is explained on the basis of its absence in the biblical text.[46]

Jubilees' treatment of the Sabbath is far more extensive than the corresponding biblical text. Jubilees 2 builds its theology of the Sabbath on creation.[47] Fortunately, chapter 2 of the book also occurs in the Qumran library, in fragments 4Q216 and 218.[48] VanderKam and J. T. Milik have concluded that these fragments resemble the Ethiopic versions more closely than that of the available Greek or Syriac fragments.[49] For this study, primary consideration will be given to the Ethiopic textual tradition, comparing it with the fragments of the surviving texts at Qumran.

The Sabbath is called "a sign for all His works"[50] at the beginning of the chapter. It is mentioned again soon after in 2:9 in connection with the sun, which was to be a "great sign"[51] for days, Sabbaths, months, years, feasts, and jubilees. As earlier noted, the solar calendar is vital to the book's time system, and so it is no surprise that the moon is neglected in this passage. It is, however, interesting that days and Sabbaths are mentioned in connection with the sun.

We know from the biblical text that the day and the Sabbath were calculated using the sun, most often from sunset to sunset.[52] It is appropriate for the sun to be the sign that governs the days and the Sabbath, as the moon has nothing whatsoever to do with the dark-light cycle of the passing days.[53] Perhaps it is because of Jubilees' interest in the Sabbath that the sun, not the moon, is the heavenly body that governs time.

---

45. Lutz Doering, "The Concept of the Sabbath in the Book of Jubilees," in *Studies in the Book of Jubilees*, eds. Matthias Albani, Jörg Frey, Armin Lange, TSAJ 65 (Tübingen: Mohr Siebeck, 1997), 179-180. For the end of Jubilees, see VanderKam, *The Book of Jubilees*, 2:325-327.

46. Doering, "The Concept of the Sabbath," 179-180.

47. And it has been said that the author builds his creation account based on his concern for the Sabbath. George J. Brooke, "Exegetical Strategies in Jubilees 1-2: New Light from 4QJubileesa," in *Studies in the Book of Jubilees*, eds. Matthias Albani, Jörg Frey, Armin Lange, TSAJ 65 (Tübingen: Mohr Siebeck, 1997), 47.

48. Marler, "An Index of Qumran Manuscripts"

49. VanderKam and Milik, "Jubilees," 4.

50. Jub. 2:1; Quoted from *Old Testament Pseudepigrapha*, ed. R. H. Charles (Oxford, GBR: Clarendon, 1913), OakTree Software Ver. 2.2. 4Q216 5:1-3 clearly shows the words ‫וישבת בים...מעשו‬ ‫הבריה‬. On the basis of VanderKam and Milik's reconstruction, the Qumran text matches the Ethiopic closely. VanderKam and Milik, "Jubilees," 13-14.

51. The use of the word "sign" alludes to Exodus 31:13, 17. Doering, "The Concept of the Sabbath," 181; For further allusions to Exodus 31 in Jubilees 2, see Odil Hannes Steck, "Die Aufnahme Von Genesis 1 in Jubiläen 2 Und 4. Esra 6," *JSJ* 8 (1977): 160.

52. For an analysis of the evening and morning theories see J. Amanda McGuire, "Evening or Morning: When Does the Biblical Day Begin?," *AUSS* 46 (2008): 201-214.

53. Jub. 2:10 says that the sun "divideth the light from the darkness [and] for prosperity, that all things may prosper which shoot and grow on the earth." Quoted from *Old Testament Pseudepigrapha*, ed. R. H. Charles (Oxford: Clarendon, 1913), OakTree Software Ver. 2.2.

The Sabbath is next mentioned in connection with the completion of creation (Jub. 2:17-33). The reader is informed that some of the heavenly creatures, the angels of the presence and the angels of sanctification, are commanded to keep the Sabbath with God. Just as a certain group of angels are elected to keep the Sabbath, so a certain class of humans will also keep the Sabbath.[54] This institution at the beginning of creation presupposes the coming of the children of Israel whom the Lord will set apart from among the peoples of the earth to keep the Sabbath (Jub. 2:17-24). Thus, though the Sabbath is created at the beginning of the world, it is not a universal commandment. In fact, the book prohibits Gentiles to keep the Sabbath (Jub. 2:31).[55]

This view is quite different from other authors of the Second Temple Period. Hellenistic Jews, who were necessarily more apologetic in nature,[56] may have had a tendency to see the Sabbath as a universal idea.[57] For example, Philo said: "For that day is the festival, not of one city or one country, but of all the earth; a day which alone it is right to call the day of festival for all people, and the birthday of the world."[58] Indeed, in *Moses 2*, Philo advocated the laws of Moses for all people, using the Sabbath as an example. He said of all classes of people, animals and even plants: "Everything is at liberty and in safety on that day and enjoys… perfect freedom…in obedience to a universal proclamation."[59] And before Philo, Aristobulus also saw the Sabbath as universally applicable, based on the seven-fold-order of the cosmos.[60]

Jubilees' theology of the Sabbath was not unacceptable to the Qumran community, however. The sect saw themselves as a "remnant" community,[61] and exclusivity was built into their worldview. Membership in the community required, among other things, strict observance of the Sabbath (CD 6:18; 10:14-11:18). Though no mention is made of Gentiles keeping the Sabbath, it is interesting to note that no one in the community could observe the Sabbath in a location near any Gentiles (CD 11:15). Ultimately, the Qumran community seemed more interested in separating themselves from other Jews than worrying about Gentile morality.

---

54. Interestingly, Jubilees also states that these two classes of angels are circumcised by nature, thus further legitimizing their election and the institution of circumcision. Jub. 15:27.

55. This verse is not attested at Qumran, although this is perhaps not surprising because 4Q218 is extremely fragmentary. This exclusive application of the Sabbath commandment is later echoed in Rabbinic writings, which taught that the Sabbath was for Israel alone, and Gentiles were forbidden to keep it on pain of death. Doering, "The Concept of the Sabbath," 189-191.

56. Collins, *Between Athens and Jerusalem: Jewish Identity in the Hellenistic Diaspora*, 14-16.

57. Doering, "The Concept of the Sabbath," 190.

58. Philo, *Creation* 89 (*The Works of Philo: Complete and Unabridged*, trans. C. D. Younge (Peabody: Hendrickson, 1993)).

59. Philo, *Moses* 2:19-22 (*The Works of Philo: Complete and Unabridged*, trans. C. D. Younge (Peabody: Hendrickson, 1993)).

60. Fragment 5. See A. Yarbro Collins, "Aristobulus: A New Translation and Introduction," in *The Old Testament Pseudepigrapha*, ed. James H. Charlesworth (New York: Doubleday, 1985), 834.

61. Sanders, "The Dead Sea Sect and Other Jews: Commonalities, Overlaps, and Differences," 16-17; Geza Vermes, *The Complete Dead Sea Scrolls in English*, revised ed. (London: Penguin Classics, 2004), 68-69. Vermes cites CD 5:2, 4Q266 f5i, f11, 4Q270 f7ii, 1QS 8:14-16, and 4Q265 f7ii as examples.

Jubilees 2:25-33 enumerates how to keep the Sabbath. Though much of this portion is not attested at Qumran, several parts of the Ethiopic text agree with the stipulations found in the Cairo Geniza copy of the Damascus Document. For example, on the Sabbath, one may not prepare food or drink, carry things in or out of the house, or draw water (Jub. 2:29-30; CD 10:22-11:1, 7-8).

Jubilees' most fascinating statement concerning the Sabbath regards its holiness. In 2:30, 32, the book declares that the Sabbath is the most blessed of all days, surpassing even the jubilee days. In essence, the Sabbath's supreme holiness is a result of its heavenly origins (Jub. 2:30-31). Again, though these verses are not attested at Qumran, similar sentiments can be found within the Qumran corpus. On the Sabbath day, only the Sabbath sacrifices and the daily sacrifices could be offered (CD 11:17-18), even if it coincided with a feast day.[62] Angelic participation in the Sabbath is also a major feature of the Qumran community, as is seen in the Songs of Sabbath Sacrifice.[63]

Jubilees 50:6-13, the end of the book, revisits the Sabbath. It gives more stipulations for how to keep the Sabbath properly. The list is longer than the list in chapter 2. The same prohibitions are enumerated, and others are added, such as the prohibition against sex, war, killing an animal, lighting a fire, riding an animal, or traveling by boat. This portion of the book is not attested at Qumran, but it bears an even stronger similarity to the Cairo Geniza copy of the Damascus Document than chapter 2 does. There are prohibitions against discussing business, working the field, making journeys, preparing food and drink, drawing water, and carrying things in and out of the house (CD 10:18-11:1, 7-8), all of which are present in Jubilees 50.[64]

The Sabbath's mention at the end of the book fulfills the institution of the Sabbath in chapter 2. Chapter 2 connects the Sabbath to creation; chapter 50 connects it to the Exodus.[65] Chapter 2 gives it to the elect angels, predicting that the children of Israel are destined to keep it; chapter 50 institutes the Sabbath for the Israelites. It is almost as if the entire book has been leading up to Israel's receiving the Sabbath.

Between chapters 2 and 50, the Sabbath is still present. Though the Sabbath was mandated for Israel alone, Jubilees has the patriarchs apparently keeping the Sabbath, and the author was careful to avoid mentioning travel on the Sabbath.[66] This is consistent with the book's method of grounding the Torah within the Patriarchal narratives. Other examples can be found with the laws of childbirth (Jub 3:8-14), covering one's nakedness (3:26-31), murder (4:1-6), retaliation (4:31-32), the Feast of Weeks (6:17-31), first fruits (7:34-39), circumcision (15:23-34),

62. Sanders, "The Dead Sea Sect and Other Jews: Commonalities, Overlaps, and Differences," 18-19. He points out that the community's calendar was set up to avoid such an occurrence, but this is not presupposed in CD.

63. Vermes, *The Complete Dead Sea Scrolls in English*, 329-330. For further references on this point see, Doering, "The Concept of the Sabbath," 188.

64. Another sectarian document, 1QM 2:8, mentions that war is prohibited during Sabbath-years.

65. Doering, "The Concept of the Sabbath," 183.

66. Annie Jaubert, "Le Calendrier Des Jubilés Et De La Secte De Qumrân: Ses Origines Bibliques," *VT* 3 (1953): 252-254; Jaubert, *The Date of the Last Supper*, 27; Doering, "The Concept of the Sabbath," 183.

tithe (15:25-27, 32:1-15), the Levitical priesthood (30:18-20), and incest (33:10-20; 41:23-26).

Jubilees constantly warns against forgetting the Sabbath, along with the feasts, months, and the commandments.[67] The author is clearly concerned about the laws that govern sacred time and the effects they have on Israel's covenant relationship with God. Jubilees 1 and 23 connect Israel's breach of the covenant, especially regarding neglecting sacred time and committing idolatry, to the exile. Chapter 6 ascribes Israel's evil deeds to failing to follow the solar calendar. By doing so, the profane and the holy are "mixed up,"[68] and the sacred times are not observed properly. The result is that Israel becomes like the Gentiles in their feasts and they violate the law by eating blood.

Conclusion

Though Jubilees was not written at Qumran, nor written for the sect specifically, the book was integral to the community. In fact, it has been suggested that the text be reclassified as a Dead Sea text, rather than a work of the Pseudepigrapha.[69] Though the Qumran sect did not accept the book's teachings unequivocally, it laid the groundwork for the community's theology of the Sabbath and the calendar.

The book of Jubilees sees time as fixed, ordained by God, and of cosmic significance. To alter the yearly calendar is to go against the order of heaven. If Israel does not follow the correct calendar, then they will be led astray, like the Gentiles. The Sabbath is the supreme expression of Sacred Time. Created at the beginning of the world, observed both in heaven and on earth, it is the most holy of the holy days.

The Jubilees framework for protecting and observing Sacred Time influenced the theology of the Qumran group, even if they did not agree on specifics such as whether a solar or luni-solar calendar was to be preferred.[70] Both schools of thought shared a unique view on the Sabbath as the ultimate expression of Sacred Time as seen in a comparison of Jubilees and the Cairo Geniza copy of the Damascus Document.

Like Jubilees, the Qumran sect wrestled with the concept of the divine order of time. In their minds, it seems, God's commandments were very clear and specific. In their attempt to follow the Law to the letter, they found themselves in opposition to the larger Jewish community on the issues of the temple, the priesthood, and even the calendar. Their retreat from society enabled them to follow the Law and observe the Sacred Times as they saw fit.

There is a lesson that the Seventh-day Adventist community can learn from the disputes of the Second Temple Period. The Adventist church believes that it has a special message about Sacred Time, specifically the Sabbath and the antitypical Day of Atonement. On this, Adventists differ from many other Christians.

---

67. Jub. 1:10, 14; 6:34-38; 23:19; Doering, "The Concept of the Sabbath," 183-184.

68. See the translation of the Ethiopic text 6:37 in Wintermute, "Jubilees: A New Translation and Introduction," 68. Compare with the note to the translation of 6:33 in VanderKam, *The Book of Jubilees*, 2:42.

69. Hempel, "The Place of the *Book of Jubilees* at Qumran and Beyond," 195-196.

70. VanderKam, *Calendars in the Dead Sea Scrolls: Measuring Time*, 111-112.

The church is not called, however, to follow in the steps of the Qumran community and withdraw from society in order to protect the sacred. Instead, it is admonished to share it through its churches, schools, and hospitals. Its message is not one of exclusion, but inclusion through the Gospel. The church is charged with sharing the message until such a time that it, too, may keep the Sabbath with God and His angels in heaven, just as Jubilees predicted.

PART 4: BIBLICAL ARCHEOLOGY

THE LEGACY OF INANNA

Michael Orellana

The Lady of Heaven is known by several names in the context of the Ancient Near East: Inanna (Sumerian), Ishtar (Akkadian), and Astarte (Canaanite). Other similar goddesses include Isis (Egypt), Tanit (Carthage), Aphrodite (Greece), and Venus (Rome). An excellent example of how the people of the ANE were aware of the different "versions" of this goddess is the Qudshu relief plaque, which is located in the Winchester College collection.[1] This relief portrays a naked female goddess standing on a lion, holding snakes, and wearing the "Hathor" wig. The accompanying hieroglyphs contain a very revealing list of her different names: Qudshu (Ashera), Anat, and Astarte (Dever 2005: 178; Edwards 1955: 49). This evidence has been widely discussed as a classic example of syncretism,[2] which probably merges two goddesses (Anat and Astarte) into a new type, Qudshu, or equates all three goddesses as the same (Cross 1997: 34). This relief has many iconographic correspondences with the Egyptian Qudshu plaque.

The cult of Ishtar is ancient, as is shown by the remains of Inanna's temple in Uruk (4th millennium B.C.E.), which is near the white temple dedicated to Anu. It is perhaps not inconsequential that the foundations of civilization were laid during this very time, suggesting that a religious motivation was the primary factor for the urban phenomenon known as the "Uruk revolution" (Stone 2000: 236).

Centuries later, the cult of Ishtar seduced the Assyrian Empire. The remains of Ishtar's temple in Aššur extend from the mid-3rd millennium B.C.E. to the end of the New-Assyrian Kingdom (Meinhold 2009: 48). Interestingly, Herman V. Hilprecht has suggested a connection between Nineveh and Nana, an old name for Ishtar (Barton 2007: 20). As an example of her relationship with Nineveh, there are some hymns written ca. 1800 B.C.E., where Assurbanipal I promoted her worship:[3]

---

1. This Qudshu relief plaque belongs to Winchester College and is known as the "Winchester College relief."

2. Syncretism is the amalgamation of different aspects of culture for several reasons, making the borders of identity diffuse.

3. This song is entitled "Prayer of Assurnasirpal son of Šamširaman" by Barton (Barton 2007).

2 To the mother of wisdom…[the lady of] majesty, 3 To her who dwells at Ibarbar, the goddess [who] made me renowned, 4 To the queen of the gods, into whose hands are delivered the command of the great gods, 5 To the lady of Nineveh…[of the gods], the exalted one. (Barton 2007: 133)

She seems to have played a variety of roles and exhibited several traits as the goddess of sexual love, fertility, war, rain, patroness of prostitutes and other independent women, and goddess of the morning and evening star –Venus (Abusch 1995: 848). Therefore, her influence extended from war to love and sensuality, from birth to death. She was usually depicted as a winged, voluptuous woman, naked or semi-naked, with exaggerated sexual organs, standing on lions, and wearing a tall mountain-shaped crown (Jones 2005).

Ishtar/Inanna's role within the Ancient Mesopotamian pantheon was preeminent and dominant. Its social and political configuration embraces her personality profoundly. Several scholars examined her traits both in anthropological and religious studies (Allen 2015; Frymer-Kensky 2006: 61-81; Margalit 1990). Since the study of Ishtar deals with the role of women in ancient societies (Bahrani 2001: 14-27),[4] it is necessary to obtain some comprehension of the role of women in both the religious and the sociological context.

Ishtar's Mythology

According to Sumerian-Babylonian theology, Ishtar or Inanna and her husband (Tammuz) were responsible for the seasonal shifts of summer and spring. These seasons are connected with the death and resurrection of Tammuz, thanks to Ishtar's intervention. Her sister Ereškigal, owner of the netherworld, was responsible for causing Ishtar's death. In consequence, Ea/Enki sent the water of life to Ishtar. She became alive again, producing seed germination and the beginning of spring. The core of this theology is found in the myth "Ishtar's Descent to the Netherworld," which emphasizes death and resurrection. This mortuary topic intertwines religious entities with the natural world.[5] It is remarkable that dying gods were very popular in Sumerian culture;[6] all of them were related to the cycles of nature (Wiggerman 1997: 41). This intricate fusion of nature and religion places Ishtar in the context of one of the most appealing religious motives that captivated the imagination of ancient people, and probably, especially women.

Her dual identity as mother and wife of Tammuz[7] may be confusing to the

---

4. Bahrani (Bahrani 2001: 14-27) mentions three movements that review the role of women in history: 1) documenting women in the historical record, 2) analyzing her oppressed role in the past, and 3) adopting a systematic approach to processes related to women's studies. The last one focuses on epistemological issues. In addition, she did a review of Ishtar in her book entitled "*Women of Babylon*," which seems to be part of the third movement.

5. Unlike the Jewish-Christian tradition, which stresses God as the Creator of nature, Mesopotamian theology made no difference between gods and creation, or made this difference very diffuse.

6. It is possible to distinguish at least four groups of Sumerian gods according to a specific region: the southern marshes, the farming regions, the herding regions, and the southern orchards. The latter group refers to the netherworld; dying gods belong to this group (Wiggerman 1997).

7. Or Dummuzi; In this case Ishtar is Inanna.

modern reader. However, this duality was very well understood in the ANE. There the female figure played an important role in the transmission of power,[8] especially in the early stages[9] (Langdon 1914: 25). In that case, to keep his royal lineage, the king had to marry his sister, or by default, his mother. Other parallels with this practice can be seen in the Osiris–Isis marriage. In addition, there is evidence that in the Early Dynastic II and III periods, queens were almost on the same level as kings, being depicted and mentioned in the royal tombs of Ur[10] (Rodin 2014: 59, 60). In consequence, Ishtar defined or at least, outlined the underlying concepts for hierarchy. She attached herself to the spine of the political order in a symbiotic relationship: the empire served Ishtar; Ishtar served the empire.

Fertility Theology

Although Mesopotamian deities seem to have been asexual at the beginning, they were in fact male-female couples that each reproduced another pair (Leick 1994: 19). Apsû and Tiāmat are masculine and feminine, grammatically speaking[11] (Leick 1994: 14). Even more interesting is the case of the Heaven-Earth couple. They are described as man and woman respectively. The sky pours out its vitality (semen) into the earth, which gives birth to divine heroes. In both couples, Apsû/Tiāmat and Heaven-Earth, the water is associated with fertility[12] since the Sumerian word for semen is equated with water[13] (Rodin 2014: 109). The following poem is a metaphorical description of copulation:

The great Earth (Ki) made herself glorious, her body flourished with greenery.
Wide Earth put on silver metal and lapis-lazuli ornaments,
Adorned herself with diorite, calcedony, cornelian and diamonds.
Sky (An) covered the pasture with (irresistible) sexual attraction, presented himself in majesty,
The pure young woman (Earth) showed herself to the pure Sky,
The vast Sky copulated with the wide Earth,
The seed of the heroes Wood and Reed he ejaculated into her womb.
The Earth, the good cow, received the good seed of Sky in her womb.
The Earth, for the happy birth of the plants of Life, presented herself (Leick 1994: 18)

One can see that the core of "fertility theology" in the Mesopotamian pantheon is animism. In this theology, all gods transmit their virtue by sexual reproduction. Therefore, it is reasonable to assume that sexual intercourse and giving birth replicate the divine nature. Hence, the woman embodies the "secrets" of divinity and Inanna is a natural development of this cosmic vision of life and religion.

8. This is the female lineage model.
9. Its antiquity can be supported by Semitic cults where the king often assumes the role of dying god (Langdon 1914).
10. Nibanda and Puabi are called "Queen," denoting their high status. On the other hand, the king Mesanepada is called "consort of the nu-gig priestess," denoting his inferior status before the "Queen." In addition, Puabi was buried in a rich tomb, similar to other royal tombs (Rodin 2014: 60).
11. Leick (Lieck 1994, 14) quoted part of the myth from Held: "When on high heaven had not (yet) been created, Earth below had not (yet) been brought into being, When Apsû primeval, their begetter, Primal Tia - mat, their progenitress, (Still) mingled their waters together...".
12. In this way "mingling waters" could be interpreted as a metaphor for sexual procreation.
13. It is especially true when it is connected to Enki and Ninḫursaĝa (Rodin 2014: 109).

Samuel Kramer (Kramer 1983: ix) suggested that the couple (Dumuzi/Inanna) evolved from the agricultural context of southern Sumer to the nomadic life of northern Akkad. The last version emphasized the arbitrary will and power of the gods instead of the force of grain in the earlier version.[14] It is probable that this shifting process took place along with the increasing attempts to centralize the various city-states, causing an amalgamation of local deities.

Therefore, the various relationships in Inanna's family tree change, depending on the stages of her evolution. For instance, she had several fathers[15] (Lapinkivi 2010: 35). Often, she was seen as the daughter of Anu, but other times her father was Sin (Jones 2005). Likewise, most of the time she and Ereshkigal, her sister, are different entities, but sometimes they seem to be the same. It is evident that the tradition, mythology, and depiction of Inanna grew and evolved. As will be commented on later, political forces played an important role in the unification of local versions of Inanna, using her symbol and personality as the glue for new emerging social structures.

Gender is the essence of this religious system that became intertwined with civilization at its very beginning. Although Sumerian-Babylonian theology seems to be genderless[16] because of some trinitarian patterns: heaven- earth-sea or Anu-Enlil-Ea, it works only on the assumption of female-male reproduction. Probably Inanna was a natural development or extension of the first female deity, mother earth.[17] As we have seen, mother earth female attributes were highlighted in opposition to sky male attributes.

It is clear that fertility is a main component of religion in Mesopotamia even before the historical period. Early references to the mother goddess are seen in several parts of the ANE. For instance, there are early depictions in the form of female figurines with overly-stressed sexual organs in Canaan (Garfinkel 2004). It is of particular interest for this article to mention a terracotta statuette from Çatal Hüyük (Anatolia) dated by archaeologists about 6500 B.C.E. (Bahrani 2001: 46) in Anatolia. This figurine could be a clear example of the "reign of the goddess" within a matriarchal society (Bahrani 2001: 46-47). She is depicted on a throne with two cat-like animals in the act of giving birth. Apparently, its association with womanhood, throne, and birth strengthens the idea of a matriarchal society, a time when the female figure was dominant. There is no evidence of an exclusive female cult in the archaeological record since male and female deities appear together. Nevertheless, the depiction of this mother goddess seems to emphasize

---

14. Kramer (Krammer 1983, ix) commented that Akkadian Dumuzi is characterized by the astral heavenly bull, and Inanna assumed directing and directive attributes as the Goddess of Love, which is different from her more peaceful earlier version.

15. An, Enlil, Enki/Ea, Nanna/Šin.

16. Genderless at least in appearance, since as we have seen, female and male characteristics are part of the fecundity notion inherent to gods.

17. The Sumerians called her Mother Vine-Stalk or Goddess Vine-Stalk (Lapinkivi 2010: 43). Even when there is no certainty of the first stage in Sumerian-Babylonian theology, the Sumerians seem to be very impressed by the natural connection between mother earth and grain, which corresponds with Inanna and her son. The reason for the link between religion and nature is because, in an agrarian society, everything depends on the constant cycle of the flooding of the Tigris and Euphrates rivers (Lapinkivi 2010).

the idea of female nudity in the ANE as an equivalent to power[18] (Bahrani 2001). From this example and others, it can be observed that the first mother goddesses were associated with power, sexuality, and motherhood, without clear limits between them (Murray 1934: 93-100).[19]

Sacred Marriage: Source of Power

The Greek term "*hieros gamos*," usually translated as sacred marriage, was initially addressed to the wedding of Zeus and Hera, which subsequently applies to alliances between a couple of deities or gods and humans when marked by ritual (Stuckey 2005). In the case of Inanna/Ishtar and Dumuzi/Tammuz, this ritual is attested to by some extant hymns that describe the human participants as personifying or incarnating them. From this union, divine power is transferred from Inanna to the king.

There is some speculation about whether the sacred marriage ritual actually took place and if this included sexual intercourse (Stuckey 2005). Evidence of the latter is given in poems that describe the rite in detail (Jones 2003: 291-302),[20] as well as other sources, like royal inscriptions and economic texts. It is probable that this rite took place on New Year's day in the palace of the king, known as "the house of life" (Kramer 1963: 490).

In this rite, Inanna prepared herself by taking a bath, and putting on perfume and special clothes (Stuckey 2005). Probably the sacred marriage is depicted in the second part of the Uruk vase. It seems there that Dumuzi is taking Inanna as his consort (Riddle 2010: 21). While worshipers are singing and sacrificing[21] themselves (Jones 2003: 292), Dumuzi approaches her door. Then, she greets Dumuzi and he gives her some gifts. Sexual intercourse follows, and finally both take their seat on the thrones.

In the hymn "The Courtship of Inanna and Dumuzi," their sexual intercourse is described in agricultural terms (Kramer 1983). The vulva of Inanna corresponds to a field needing to be plowed. "As for me, Inanna, Who will plow my vulva? Who will plow my high field? Who will plow my wet ground?" (Kramer 1983: 37). Along this line, other parallels are plants, grain, and the womb. Apparently, water, plants, and trees of various kinds are metaphors for sexual intercourse (Kramer 1972: 123). Some depictions of Inanna and Dumuzi make a connection between plants and fertility as well. One example is a Mesopotamian cylinder seal

18. The Baubo goddess was similar to Ishtar, with the difference that her cult was restricted to women while Ishtar was supported by men (Murray 1934: 93-100).

19. M. A. Murray (Murray 1934: 93-100) establishes three different kinds of female fertility figures: universal mother, divine woman, and personified yoni. This last one is Murray's technical term referring to figures whose genitalia are the essential part. These three categories correspond to child, virginity, and sexual functions. Murray identifies Ishtar with a "divine/woman."

20. Although there is little information about what happened during the rite, it can be understood partially by the Iddin-Dagan Hymn (Jones 2003: 291-302). There the ritual is two days long. She is invoked and worshipers execute a carnivalesque ritual accompanied by instrumental music. Inanna looks down from heaven on the cultic parade headed by the king. A great feast takes place. When the people go home to rest she appears in dreams, judging evil. An offering of food follows and the consummation of the marriage takes place.

21. This part of the rite is described in the Iddin-Dagan Hymn as carnivalesque: cross-dressing, bondage, and self-mutilation (Jones 2003: 292).

from about 2320-2150 B.C. (Stuckey 2005). There, Inanna welcomes Dummuzi, who is emerging from the base of a tree. Since similar metaphorical language is used in Song of Songs in the Hebrew Bible (Carr 1979: 103),[22] some scholars believe that this book belongs to the same literary genre. However, the book from the Hebrew Bible is not linked to a cultic context.[23]

In the execution of the sacred marriage rite, the king and Inanna/Ishtar´s priestess, *Nin-dingir/Entu*, were avatars in whom Inanna activated the fertile cycle of nature (Niehaus 2008: 43; Stuckey 2005). In consequence, particular power was transmitted from the divine to the human sphere through the king who acts as the mediator between them.

As we have mentioned, the female cult embodies most of the fertility theology of Ancient Mesopotamia. Consequently, Inanna/Ishtar introduced herself through the sacred marriage into the political scene.

Akkadian Syncretism of Inanna

Since culture and religion share a common ground in several aspects such as politics, the ruling society took both into consideration to maintain a sense of unity. In consequence, syncretism took place, amalgamating different myths to produce an official creed. For example, the Akkadian version of the Gilgamesh Epic seems to be a unified version of separate, independent Sumerian stories (Veenker 1981: 199). A similar process amalgamated the enormous corpus of Inanna stories during or about the time of the influence of Sargon of Agade (2300 B.C.). Other versions of Mesopotamian myths also went through the process of adaptation and syncretism.

Perhaps the most famous myth of Ishtar/Inanna is her descent in to the netherworld and resurrection. This is known in two different versions: Semitic and Sumerian. The Semitic version has been a part of the scholarly debate for about one century. On the other hand, the Sumerian version was translated and deciphered by comparing various extant copies[24] since 1940 (Kramer 1940: 18). Both versions are similar in general terms, but several details are different. Kramer (Kramer 1940: 20) suggested that the Semitic version is more emotional and intense than the Sumerian version, and their temporal distance is at least one millennium.

Kramer (Kramer 1940) summarized both versions as follows: In the Sumerian version, (1) Inanna has forsaken heaven and earth, and all her temples descend to the netherworld, (2) she adorns herself with her queenly robes; (3) she asks Ninshubur to plead for her to Enlil, Nanna, and Enki (Semitic Ea); (4) Inanna's

---

22. Some scholars have discussed to what extent Song of Songs is a reproduction or a sort of imitation of the Dumuzi-Inanna sacred marriage songs. However, the examination of some genres associated with Songs of Songs might suggest that although this Hebrew book reflects many motifs and topoi of Mesopotamian sacred marriage, it is, in fact, lyric love poetry, which distinguishes it from the others (Carr 1979: 103).

23. While some similarities are visible, there is no evidence for a cultic use of Song of Songs.

24. Kramer (Kramer 1940: 1) contributed to the deciphering of this Sumerian version by his discovery of two additional fragments in the Istanbul Museum of the Ancient Orient, and by comparing them with previous documents.

descent to the netherworld was supposedly an invitation by Ereshkigal to be present at the funeral of Gugalanna, the great bull of heaven; (5) she is admitted and
passes by the seven gates, naked; (6) once in front of Ereshkigal, she is judged by
the Anunnaki, the seven judges of the netherworld; (7) by their decree, she is put
to death; (8) after three days and three nights, Ninshubur pleads to Enlil, Nanna,
and Enki, being listened to only by Enki; (9) Enki sends sexless creatures, kur-
garru and galaturru, entrusting them with the "food of life" and "water of life;"
and (10) Inanna is revived and re-ascends to the earth, accompanied by the dead.
In the Semitic version, (1) Ishtar descends to the netherworld to mourn the death
of her husband and child; (2) she orders its keeper to open its doors; (3) when she
passes its seven doors, the keeper removes a bit of her apparel; (4) once she passes
the last door, Ereshkigal orders Namtar to bring forth 60 diseases against her; (5)
Papsukkal, fearing the extinction of life, hastens to Ea for help; (6) Ea sends to
Asnamir to intercede for her in front of Ereshkigal; (7) Ereshkigal orders to give
her the "water of life;" and (8) she is revived and re-ascends to the earth with her
apparel restored.

In the comparison of both versions, their differences in tone and orientation
are very clear, which implies a later adaptation of the earlier Sumerian version.
The netherworld in the Sumerian mind is related to a foreign land[25] in the mountains, which were a continuous threat for them (Kramer 1981: 154). In regard to
this aspect, it is observable how the Semitic version has a different attitude toward
the netherworld. While the Sumerian version describes Inanna as a hero in front of
Ereshkigal and the seven judges, the Semitic version emphasizes her aggressive
attitude toward the netherworld. In addition, attention shifts slightly from Inanna–
feminine–to Ea–masculine.

From Inanna to Ishtar

The earliest recorded mention of Inanna's name comes from the Late Uruk,
Jendet Nasr periods, about 3400 to 3000 B.C.E. (Collins 1994: 107). Some pic-
tographic signs read INANNA or MUS (radiant). The earliest cuneiform sign of
her name is a representation of a ring-post, which is the entrance door of a reed-
house. This Inanna symbol is depicted frequently. One example is a bearded man
holding stylized flowers and feeding sheep and goats. There, the ring-post of Inanna appears on each side of the man. Collins, (P. Collins 1994) suggested that it
symbolizes the "priest-king" of Uruk. Similar "city seals" from the Early Dynasty
I period represent a collaboration between cities to support the cult of Inanna at
Uruk. The disappearance of the ring-post symbol during the Early Dynasty II
period (2750-2600 B.C.E.) could reflect the decline of a centralized form of her
worship and increasingly independent cults in different cities (Collins 1994: 108).

An early portrayal of Inanna combines her motherhood and divinity and comes
from a trinket mold dated to the third millennium B.C.E., which was found in a
house at Titriş Höyük, Turkey (Laneri 2002: 14). It is possible to identify this
depiction with Inanna, thanks to the symbols surrounding her. She is depicted

---

25. The Sumerian word *Kur* "mountain" is equivalent to Hades (Greek) and Sheol (Hebrew).
Later on, this word came to mean "foreign land" (Kramer 1981: 154).

holding her breasts, a star with dots nearby, and a symbol of the bull of heaven to her right.[26] There are some parallels of some elements of this trinket mold in other contexts. For instance, the pendant with a pseudo-circular structure is seen at Kültepe (Central Anatolian) and in one tomb at the royal cemetery of Ur. In addition, the star with dots is the cosmological symbol of Inanna and is found in several other places (Laneri 2002: 26). On the other hand, two important characteristics are seen in this mold: Inanna naked holding her breasts and without her horned crown. Both differences make this representation closer to the mother goddess than some later ones.

Another early depiction of Inanna is on the Warka vase (3200-3100 B.C.E.). Here Inanna is represented as receiving an offering from naked priests. Apparently, the king is part of the initiation rite, facing the goddess (Stuckey 2005). This vase clearly distinguishes three social classes: the elite, controlling restricted temples; heads of houses, giving an offering; and the production force represented by herds and plants (Sundsdal 2008: 47-49). Even though only men constitute the elite class, Ishtar is above all social classes. The use of this kind of vase in a ritual context is attested to by other vessels found at Warka with the following inscription: "To Urru, the priest A-gid-ḫa-du for the son of Lugal-kisal-si born of his wife Mu-ḫar-sag has given (this vase)" (Banks 1904: 63).

It is under Sargon's influence that Inanna became Ishtar. The name Ishtar derives from Eshtar, which originated from Attar/Ashtart, a female deity from Ugarit (Collins 1994: 110). It is under this new name that Ishtar obtained male attributes, contrasting with her female attributes, as the goddess of war and love. Sargon intended a syncretism of Sumerian and Semitics deities[27] for the unification of his Sumer-Akkad empire (Collins 1994: 111). This Akkadian period is called the "Dynasty of Ishtar."

Perhaps the female-male characteristics represented on the Warka Vase in the form of a lion and a ram allowed the identification of Inanna with Ishtar, who seems to be clearly of double gender.

There are no extant sculptures of Ishtar coming down to us from Babylon (Ornan 2005: 63). This, however, does not mean that they did not exist.[28] It is likely that they were looted during countless upheavals, due to their precious materials.

Ishtar's connection with war and power is displayed in several depictions where she is standing upon a lion (Rodney 1952: 211-16). Some of the typical elements of these kinds of portraits are a staff (harp) in her right hand as a symbol of command; a ring and rod (land-measuring implements?) as symbols of her divinity; and a lion associated with several divinities (Rodney 1952: 213). In one carving depicted at Maltai, she and Shamash are heading a procession of mounted deities[29] (Ornan 2005: 64). Similar later Assyrian representations suggest that they

---

26. The double bull-headed pendant is considered as an idealized representation of a byre where the holy cattle was housed (Laneri 2002: 27).

27. Sargon made his daughter, Enheduanna, the high priestess at Ur (Collins 1994:11).

28. Their existence can be deduced from textual evidence of some rituals where divine statues were washed and we have some glyptic devotional themes from Assyria (Ornan 2005, 73).

29. Few depictions of human-shaped Shamash are also known (Ornan 2005).

were carved to commemorate the temple dedication (Layard 1852: 164; Rodney 1952: 214) or royal usage.

One example of this royal usage is a cylinder seal impression of Sennacherib (Winter 2010: 121). There the king is depicted facing two mounted deities: Aššur and Ishtar. In this political-religious portrait, he identifies himself as a vice-ruler of the chief gods. This seal quotes Aššur's words at the beginning: "Seal of Destinies, which Aššur, king of the gods, seals the destiny of …mankind: whatever he seals he will not alter" (Winter 2010: 122). Another example of this royal usage may be the White Obelisk, Side A, third panel from the top. Here Ishtar is depicted standing on a mountain.[30] It is known that this is Ishtar from the epigraph labeling "Bit naḫti," which is the sacred Ishtar temple at Nineveh (Ornan 2005: 30, 40). There is a close semantic relationship between temple and mountain, with the temples being microcosmic representations of the earth. In addition, floral imagery in Assyrian temples is symbolic of fruitfulness and riches coming from Ishtar (Ragavan 2010: 283-88).

It seems that when Inanna, the goddess of fertility, became Ishtar, the warrior goddess, her symbol became a binding force that legitimized the "state."[31] Then, the fertility theology permeated the transmission of authority from one generation to another. Because of that, animism as the essence of spirituality in Ancient Mesopotamia included the state in the realm of the gods in addition to the natural world. Therefore, the state became a new holy group of elements where the gods displayed their will.

Female Goddesses in Canaan

Several questions regarding religious phenomena at Canaan were raised since the publication of William G. Dever's book: *Did God have a Wife?* (Dever 2005: 181-84). He claimed that Yahwism, in its early stage of evolution, included the concept of sacred marriage between Yahweh and Asherah[32] (Dever 2005: 136, 212-14, 97; Wiggins 2007: 21). Later on, some reforms eliminated Asherah from the elitist theology, but not from the traditional or "folk" religion that was highly supported by women. This hypothesis supposes that the official cult or Yahwism was a reaction against folk religion; meanwhile, it admits some degree of evolution of the Hebrew God thanks to monarchic efforts and the necessity to create a new national identity after the exile. Dever supported the idea that these factors imposed a monotheistic version of Yahweh at the end.

One part of the archaeological evidence quoted by Dever is the discovery of the Judean Pillar Figurines (JPFs) coming from the 9th to 7th centuries B.C.E. These figurines, in accordance with Dever, are Asherah. Their existence might prove in some way that an early version of Yahwism in Israel appeared before the exile. Another argument presented by Dever is the discovery of the Kuntillet

30. Some parallels of deities above mountains are seen (Ornan 2005: 31).
31. If we can use the word "state" at all, since tribal origination was the main structure in Ancient Mesopotamia.
32. Some arguments in favor of this theory are (1) Asherah was the consort of the main god in ANE contexts, (2) deities were represented by symbols, as was Asherah, and (3) the deuteronomists' imprint is seen in its rejection of Asherah (Wiggins 2007: 21).

'Ajrûd inscriptions by Z. Meshel in 1975-76 (Dever 2005: 128, 62, 97; Wiggins 2007: 7). These inscriptions, dating from the 9th-8th centuries B.C.E., mention Yahweh and Asherah as a source of blessing: "...I bless you by Yahweh, [our guardian/of Samaria,] and by his/its ashera/Ashera" (Smith 1987: 333). Another similar inscription, dating from the 8th century B.C., was found on a wall of a tomb at Khirbet el-Qôm: "...May Urimayu be blessed by Yahweh my guardian (?), and his/its ashera/Ashera" (Smith 1987: 334). These inscriptions triggered several scholarly discussions dealing with early Israel's religion.

However, the main argument is not entirely new. Some critical scholars assumed that the deutoronomistic source rejected the idea of a divine couple (Asherah-Yahweh), so several passages would criticize Asherah, and this rejection would be instrumental in formulating the Israelites' rejection of images (Wiggins 2007: 21). In fact, J. Wellhausen reinterpreted Hosea 14.8 as follows: "I am his Anat and his Asherah" (Wellhausen 1898: 134), based on contextual connections already mentioned here previously. Even though this reinterpretation of Hosea 14.8 is not accepted by most scholars[33] (Doyle 1996: 85-86), it reflects the general tendency of critics to reinterpret biblical texts from an archaeological-historical perspective. Then, they conclude that Asherah was part of the official Yahwism during the 8th to 7th centuries (Doyle 1996: 86).

Asherah and Pillar Figurines

Let us take a look at one of the most common religious elements that is currently being discussed under "early religion" in Israel in connection with Dever's understanding of the Judean Pillar Figurines (Dever 2005: 176).

Several naked female pillar figurines were discovered in Israel from the very beginning of Palestinian Archaeology. W. F. Albright (Albright 1935: 96) led the identification of these Judean Pillar Figurines (JPFs) by identifying them with Astarte or Qadesh "beyond all cavil." Even when scholars did not make a difference between the pillar figurines and plaques at this early stage of research, Albright was aware that they were different in function[34] (Albright 1935: 98). Since more comprehensive information was needed, James B. Pritchard published a list of figurines and plaques, which was the first attempt to catalog all female figurines (Pritchard 1943). He recognized the inconvenience of identifying some of these figurines with specific goddesses based on the archaeological data available at that time, being reluctant to label them as Asherah or Ashterot. Later on, T. A. Holland made a broader study, coming to a provisional hypothesis, which suggested that some of these broken figurines symbolize a ritual of an expiatory offering, but he accepted that a full explanation of this phenomenon would require further research based on new data (Holland 1975b: 330).

On the other hand, some scholars, like Dever, attempted to explain the religious phenomena in Israel during the Iron Age, matching biblical Asherah and JPFs based on a supposed similarity between Asherah poles and her tree symbol

---

33. Mainstream scholars would disagree that a proper name could take a pronominal suffix (Doyle 1996: 86).

34. Albright supported the idea that Ashera/Qadesh may be a prototype for the pillar figurines, but this prototype may have been unknown. In the meantime, they may have been used as magical amulets for parturition, and this function could be the explanation for their similarity (Albright: 98, 110).

with the pillar bodies of these figurines (Hadley 2000: 4). Kletter (Press 2012: 17) agreed with Dever and concluded that JPFs were Asherah. M. Siebeck (Siebeck 2014) believed that Dever's equation, pillar figurines = fertility cult = Asherah, seems to be inconsistent with the rest of the archaeological information.[35] She also summarized all alternative interpretations of JPFs during the IA as follows: (1) JPFs as goddesses, (2) JPFs as religion, and (3) JPFs as female religion. However, she believed that any of these models are consistent with the current archaeological data.

Late Bronze Female Deities

As we mentioned above, at the beginning of the Bronze Age the fertility cult was firmly associated with divinities; this is also the case with Ishtar, according to several versions. For instance, a goddess with a plant emerging from the top of her head (Pittman 2014: 379) is depicted on a seal from Konar Sandal South on the Halil River, in the Kerman province of southeastern Iran. A horn on the front is portrayed looking forward. The context for this seal is a trash deposit on the side of a huge platform probably used in craft production (Pittman 2014: 390) dated to the Early Dynasty IIIB period in Mesopotamia, the mid-third millennium B.C.E. Another seal from the same area and about the same period portrays a horned goddess holding stalks and with vegetation emerging around her (Pittman 2014: 389). Several other examples could be quoted, but there seems to be sufficient evidence that female deities rooted in the Mesopotamian religious tradition were strongly associated with vegetation.

In this way, public or state female deities in Mesopotamia and the Levant were associated with power symbols such as horns, vegetation, or other conventional symbols associated with divinities during the Bronze Age (Wright 2007: 199-237). These kinds of representations are common on seals, refined ceramic wares, and official depictions on walls.[36]

Similar associations are found in Palestine during the Middle Bronze Age. A seal from Gezer portrays a naked woman who is apparently bold, with two plants on each side (Sugimoto 2014: 14). Her ears are longer than usual and seem to reflect a Canaanite version of Hathor, called "Hathor cow ears" (Ben-Tor 2007: 181). Since Palestine was under Egyptian control during most of the Middle Bronze Age, one would expect some association between Hathor and the local versions of Ishtar. For example, a tree growing out of the navel of a goddess, possibly Hathor, is shown on a gold pendant at Tell el-Ajjul (Hillers 1970: 606; Sugimoto 2014: 13). Sir William Matthew Flinders Petrie identified a similar piece as Asherah. Both have three dots under the face and share a common Egyptian Hathor style (Pritchard, and White 2003: 69). Another seal depicting her in a Levantine context shows her hands extending toward a tree with three dots

---

35. Siebeck discussed the pros and cons of current available interpretations.

36. The headdress relief of a male figurine from Hazor shows as its central component a stylized tree topped by a flower and two horned animals standing on their hind legs facing the tree. Ornan commented concerning this supposed Baal figurine that it is very clear that there were strong connections between trees, horned animals and either gods or goddesses during the Bronze Age. She claimed that this imagery was very common around fourteenth century B.C. in Egypt, and later, it became popular in Canaan (Ornan 2011: 266-270).

under it (Teissier 1996: 102). Astarte figurines were found dating from the Late Bronze Age in large numbers (Stuckey 2003: 137). These plaques were made with clay and follow the general Hathor style from MBA. Sometimes she is depicted holding snakes or stalks. Two other examples of this kind are two figurines found at Gezer, Stratum XIII, dated to the Late Broze Age (Dever, Lance, and Wright 1970: 108). One of them is holding stalks and appears to be a Hathor type. The other is partially broken and seems to depict a necklace, as well as a crown on her head. Her hair is slightly different from the more common Hathor look. Differences between these two artifacts that come from the same locus could be partially explained since they are from different periods (MB II and LB II). This particular difference can be described in terms of continuity, which could indicate a slow evolution of the same deity through different periods in the same location.

Other figurines from Megiddo portray a different style of Hathor. These female figurines are depicted holding their breasts and share some common characteristics, including the wearing of bracelets and having the pubic area represented by a triangle (Pritchard 1943: 5). One of them wears a crown, which would seem to link these figurines to royal deities. These similitudes have been explained as being made from the same mold (Guy 1938: 521) and may also indicate a common feature of domestic religion. In addition, nude female figurines holding their breasts are rarely found in Egypt, which would seem to indicate Asiatic influence (Holland 1975a: 133).

The transition to the Iron Age can be seen in a female figurine from Gezer (Dever 1975: pl. 40) with a tan surface, exhibiting a woman holding her breasts. These typical Iron Age figurines of the mother goddess seem to be more popular than the official female deity Hathor-type from Late Bronze Age. Handmade figurines and mold-made plaques became more widespread than official seal depictions. Another example of the mother goddess is a figurine from Kibbutz Revadim (Sugimoto 2014: 13). On this female figurine, two children are portrayed as hanging from her breasts, and the woman is wearing a necklace and bracelets and points to her vulva. Some common symbols from the Bronze Age are included, such as horned animals, trees, and explicit sexual organs. However, this figure seems to portray an ordinary woman without any identification in terms of divinity. An excellent parallel for this clay figurine would be a fragment of a nude female plaque figurine from Ashkelon. On this figurine are raised emblems: a horned animal next to a tree on the shoulder and a human figure around the neck area (Press 2012: 75).

D. T. Sugimoto (Sugimoto 2014: 11) studied the relationship between trees and horned animals. He reproduced in his article some seals listed by O. Keel (Keel 1998) and concluded that the tree is an Asherah symbol, which disappeared completely by the end of Iron Age and was replaced by the scorpion.

So far, it seems that gradual changes were introduced during the Iron Age in terms of female figurines. However, as often happens, some intrusive elements can distort the interpretation of the rest of the evidence. One example of this would be a Hathor pendant, 3.5 cm high and 1.3 cm wide, made in the Egyptian style. The goddess is depicted as standing and wearing an *atef* crown, with two cow-like ears. Since cow-headed depictions of Hathor are known from the 18th–26th Dynasties, it is hard to identify a chronological context for it. However, the depiction with a crown and scepter is more common in the 26th Dynasty and does not correspond chronologically to the context in which it was found (Currie and Hyslop 2009: 113).

Iron Age Female Deities

After the Sea People settled in Palestine during the 12th century at the beginning of Iron Age I, new forms of female deities were introduced. Philistine forms seem to resemble Mediterranean forms. Thanks to discoveries at Ekron, Tel Miqne, Tell es-Safi, and Ashdod, it is possible to have a better idea about early Philistine religious practices. Females are a central theme in the Philistine cult (Ornan 2011: 266-70). The Aegean Mother goddess is depicted in several ways by ceramic votives.

Michael D. Press has listed about 200 Iron Age figurines, grouping the female figurines in six categories: small standing, handmade figurines; large, seated handmade-figurines of Ashdoda type; composite figurines; plaque figurines; hollow, moldmade figurines; and miscellaneous forms (Ehrlich 2007: 47, 48). He argued that there are more types than Dothan had listed earlier and that apparently, the Philistines went through an acculturation process instead of assimilation. That means that while Philistine culture went through several changes, the underlying thought patterns remained distinct and they maintained their separate identity (Press 2012: 40).

For instance, some figurines known as mourning figurines resemble those of the Mycenean repertoire. They are standing female figurines and were found at Azor, Tell Jemmeh, Tell Jerishe, and Ashdod (Dothan 1982: 237). Most of them have both arms raised to the head in a mourning gesture. A 12th and 11th century B.C.E. context is assured for these figurines.

Ashdoda are female figurines in the shape of a chair. This is unparalleled in the coroplastic art of the Levant and is probably a variant of a Mycenaean female figurine seated on a throne (Landau 2010: 305). A close parallel to the "Ashdoda" is a painted figurine LHI-IIC of Tyryns (Greek), which has a polos hat, nose and ears, a long neck, breasts emphasized by circles, and a triangular pendant on the chest.

The Philistine cult persisted from the beginning of the Iron Age to the Babylonian destruction. Although there is just one complete example, many Ashdoda fragments have been found at Ashdod, Tell Qasile, Aphek, Gezer, Tel Miqne/Ekron, Ashkelon, and Tel Batash/Timnah. The discovery of this complete figure in the shape of a female chair shows a close connection to the Aegean cult of the Great Mother Goddess (Ehrlich 2007: 39). It is remarkable that during the first century following the migration, the Philistines remained faithful to the Great Mother Goddess of the Aegean world.

However, new figurine types seem to have been introduced by the 11th century B.C.E. after the Sea Peoples invasion (Press 2012: 192). Other forms, like the Philistine Psi, were more popular at the beginning of the Philistine occupation.

This type is a standing female figurine with pinched nose and incised eyes and mouth (Wright 2007: 226). Several examples of this type come from Ashkelon. For instance, a cylindrical female figurine with red-brown clay, cream slip, and black horizontal lines on the front, but not in the back, was found on the floor with occupational debris identified as Iron Age I (Press 2012: 43).

This "Philistine Psi" type contrasts with the "Composite Female Figurines" in detail and style. This type of figurine was very popular in Iron Age II, 8th to 7th century B.C.E. (Press 2012: 192). A typical composite female figurine had a tang, was made of brown clay, with traces of white slip, especially around the eyes, a moldmade face with some Egyptian features (Press 2012: 53). The Egyptian influence, particularly in this type, seems to be strong. Another similar type is a female head and torso, with a rounded veil as a headdress. Again, her face is moldmade and follows Egyptian features.

Another Philistine type is the "Plaque Type," some of which have been found at Askhelon dated to the beginning and end of the Iron Age (Press 2012: 192). This type represents different motifs. They are a naked woman, a woman holding her breasts, or a woman holding a baby. This last motif became popular during the Persian period at Dor (Stern 2010: 10-13). Stern suggested that they were connected with Astarte-Tanit based on textual evidence. Motherhood was strongly emphasized at that time with motifs representing babies, women holding babies, and women holding their breasts. This type differs from the Phoenician and northern Palestinian coast (Stern 2010: 11), where the bodies are round and wheelmade, their hair is pseudo-Egyptian, but their wigs are longer and sometimes curly.

In terms of continuity-discontinuity,[37] it can be said that the Sea Peoples' invasion introduced a new period affecting social structures in Canaan. It would be considered as discontinuity based on events influencing Canaan as indicated by Mediterranean fertility cults. This influence, plus the Phoenician impact, may have oriented a new conception of female deities. Judean Pillar Figurines seem to reflect this impact.

Judean Pillar Figurines (JPFs) were used in daily life as amulets[38] (Siebeck 2014), instead of resembling official female deities. Several of these figurines were crude and handmade, with an absence of power symbols such as horns or stalks. Their handmade heads were mostly orange or red with yellow, red, or white paint (Tushingham 1985: 361). Sometimes they had some fine white frits (Ben-Shlomo 2006: 195). Figurines representing motherhood, breasts, painting, and the absence of power symbols resemble Halafian types with similar characteristics, but were different in style. Earlier female figurines stressing motherhood can

37. The continuity-discontinuity model distinguishes between short, medium, and long-term periods. These three times can be affected by social, circumstantial, or event-based changes. While short-term periods affect only the individual (event-based), long-term periods are affected by changes in social structure. On other hand, circumstantial changes affect the medium-term period by introducing gradual changes (Roux, and Courty 2013: 187-93).

38. Siebeck, in her dissertation about the function of JPFs, compared textual and archaeological data to provide information about the meaning of this phenomenon in Israel and concluded that figurines were used in Assyrian texts as apotropaic amulets. In addition, she studied the context for these figurines and came to the conclusion that they were not associated with official, religious, and high residents (Siebeck 2014).

be found from third millennium B.C.E. contexts (Wright 2007: 220). Jordanian figurines from about the same time reflect similar characteristics as well (Pittman 2014: 379). Therefore, in function, JPFs are analogous to a very early version of handmade or wheel-made figurines existing earlier in Canaan.

In addition, these are clear differences between the two types of female religious representations—those that are connected directly with a deity by official seals and those that seem to have been used in domestic contexts. In terms of continuity and discontinuity of female deities, one can argue that women holding their breasts reflect northern influences, instead of Egyptian ones. Furthermore, figurines connected with vegetation motifs would seem to have been connected with deities, while those connected with motherhood might be connected with daily life.

While the Late Bronze Age was dominated by Ishtar symbols, whether in the Egyptian or Ugaritic style, her official depictions seem to have disappeared by the end of the Iron Age. Obviously, gradual changes in the religious climate took place between the LBA and the Iron Age (Press 2012: 10). Female deities strongly associated with Mesopotamian and Egyptian iconography almost became extinct, while family and domestic expressions such as the pillar figurines remained. The nude woman motif representing Ishtar with her upswept hair, holding stalks, with strong links to vegetation so common in LB are absent during the Iron Age. Apparently, the vegetation motif also disappeared, leaving horned animals alone on seals[39] by the end of the Iron Age (Sugimoto 2014: 16). This lacuna was filled later on with the scorpion. Transitional forms in between allowed certain sorts of symbols to pass on the essence of the old cults to next generations, with the scorpion being the last expression of divinity on seals of Iron Age II (Sugimoto 2014: 14). Evidently a lower class of female deities was also represented in clay. These kinds of goddesses are usually seen as protective spirits in the sphere of family religion (Siebeck 2014). Whether or not they were connected with the state religion, their function seems to have been apotropaic. In other words, their function was to protect and to heal family members (Siebeck 2014: 45). This shifting process may be the result of the monotheistic influence of Hebrew people.

In terms of Dever's equation of "Judean Pillar figurines = Asherah," it would appear that this is an oversimplification in relationship to the phenomenon of religion in Israel, which was more fluid and dynamic. The earlier concept of male-female divine couple from Late Bronze Age, as manifested at Ugarit, seemingly evaporated[40] during the Iron Age. Even though women are connected with several religious manifestations, their later function was not necessarily the same, nor does the social structure support this religious or spiritual symbol and the ideology behind it.[41]

---

39. Sugimoto (Sugimoto 2014: 14) reproduced in his article several Iron Age stamp seals listed by Keel from several places in Canaan (Ta'anach, Dor, Gezer, Megiddo, Beth Shemesh, Beth Shean) containing horned animals and trees, and stressing that eventually depictions of trees became less popular.

40. I use the term "evaporated" because of the lack of evidence to fully explain this discontinuity. New structures of power evidently affected Canaan, but they are not a sufficient explanation for this discontinuity.

41. While Inanna/Ishtar was a royal goddess during the Bronze Age, reflecting a strong fertility cult, during the Iron Age, female representations were connected with family.

A distinct point exists between the Bronze and Iron Ages in Canaan. The social structure seems to play a major role in the disappearance of a high-status goddess during the Iron Age. Several possible causes can be mentioned for this break, such as the Sea Peoples' invasion, the immigration of Hebrews, and the Phoenician influence. Therefore, it would seem that the assumption of Dever and others of a high female deity paired with Yahweh is unlikely. This assumption does not consider the discontinuity between the Bronze and Iron Ages, and it supposes that the divine couple from the Bronze Age was still vigorous during the Iron Age in Canaan.

Conclusion

We have seen that in earlier periods, Asherah had an official representation and was connected with signs of power, such as horns, plants, crown, and stalks. In contrast, another version of this deity, or what is sometimes called "domestic deity," was represented by a motherhood-oriented figurine typically made of clay.

The identification of Asherah with pillar figurines is based on the assumption that the column or post represented a tree trunk that is frequently associated with Asherah's "sacred tree" (Press 2012: 17). This connection links two elements that would seem to be mostly disconnected during the Iron Age: Asherah as a goddess and a tree as her symbol.

Since religious symbols change over time, they can also change their associations, depending on their interactions over that time. For instance, Inanna became Ishtar during the Uruk period. Then Ishtar was reinterpreted and assimilated into different cultures. In Egypt, she was often associated with vegetation during the Late Bronze Age, but at the beginning of the Iron Age in Canaan, her old connections with nature and horns faded. At that time, motherhood became a dominant focus for female representations. This phenomenon had some parallels in the early Mesopotamian religion.

Religious life in Ancient Mesopotamia allowed two spheres of divinities: the national or public, and the family or domestic. These two spheres were compatible, but they were represented in different ways. Figurines usually belonged to the family realm and were seen as protective spirits (Press 2012: 16). Did these same two levels of deities exist in Canaan, or were there more? (Siebeck 2014: 34-60). If so, it is possible that JPFs in Israel during the Iron Age belonged to the lower level.

It may be seen that Asherah did not succeed at the upper level of society during most of the Iron Age (1200–332 B.C.E.), as can be inferred from the archaeological record; nevertheless, the ancient fertility theology of Inanna was still evident in household religion. She succeeded at the family level. She never died for the common Israelite. The animism was vigorously preserved. Every pillar figurine is a silent witness that the spirituality of pantheism was the main reason for the victory of Inanna over Yahweh. For some reason, the idea of gods permeating nature was attractive to the human spirit.

The Torah describes this fact with mournful words: "The children are gathering wood, the fathers handle the fire, and the women knead the flour to prepare offerings for the queen of heaven, and make libations to foreign gods to provoke my indignation" (Jer 7:18, my translation).

194

References

Abusch, T.
1995 *Dictionary of Deities and Demons in the Bible*. eds. Karel van der Toorn; Bod Becking; and Pieter W. van der Horst. NY: E. J. Brill.

Allen, S. L.
2015 *The Splintered Divine: A Study of Ištar, Baal, and Yahweh Divine Names and Divine Multiplicity in the Ancient Near East*. Studies in Ancient Near Easter Records 5. Berlin: De Gruyter.

Albright, W. F.
1935 *The Archaeology of Palestine and the Bible*. NY: Fleming H. Revell Company.

Bahrani, Z.
2001 *Women of Babylon: Gender and representation in Mesopotamia*. London: Routledge.

Banks, E. J.
1904 A Vase Inscription from Warka. *The American Journal of Semitic Languages and Literatures* 21: 62-63.

Barton, G. A.
2007 *The Semitic Ishtar Cult*. NJ: Georgia Press.

Ben-Shlomo, D.
2006 Selected Objects. P. 511 in *Tel Miqne-Ekron Excavations 1995–1996, Field INE East Slope Iron Age I (Early Philistine Period)*, eds. Mark W. Meehl; Trude Dothan; and Seymour Gitin. Jerusalem: W. F. Albright Institute of Archaeological Research : Institute of Archaeology, Hebrew University of Jerusalem.

Ben-Tor, D.
2007 *Scarabs, Chronology, and Interconnections: Egypt and Palestine in the Second Intermediate Period*. Orbis Biblicus et Orientalis 27. Fribourg, Switzerland: Academic Press Fribourg.

Carr, G. L.
1979 Is the of songs a "Sacred Marriage" Drama? *The Journal of the Evangelical Theological Society* (JETS) 22: 103–14.

Collins, P.
1994 The Sumerian goddess Inanna (3400–2200 BC). *Papers from the Institute of Archaeology* 5: 103-18.

Cross, F. M.
1997 *Canaanite Myth and Hebrew Epic: Essays in the History of the Religion of Israel*. Cambridge, MA: Harvard University Press.

Currie, R., and Hyslop, S. G.
2009 *The Letter and the Scroll*. WA: National Geographic.

Dever, W. G.; Lance, H. D.; and Wright, G. E., eds.
1970 *Gezer I: Preliminary Report of the 1964–66 Seasons*. 1. Jerusalem: Hebrew Union College Biblical and Archaeological School in Jerusalem.

Dever, W. G., ed.
1975 *Gezer II: Report of the 1967–70 Seasons in Field I and II*. 2. Jerusalem: Hebrew Union College/Nelson Glueck School of Biblical Archaeology.

Dever, W. G.
2005 *Did God Have a Wife?* Grand Rapids, MI: Eerdmans.

Dothan, T.
1982 *The Philistines and their Material Culture*. Jerusalem: Israel Exploration Society.

Doyle, R.
1996 Baal, Ashera, and Molek and the Studies of the Hebrew Scriptures. Unpublished Ph.D. Dissertation, Hardvard University.

Edwards, I. E. S.
1955 A Relief of Qudshu-Astarte-Anath in the Winchester College Collection. *Journal of Near Eastern Studie*s 14: 49-51.

Ehrlich, C. S.
2007 Philistine Religion: Text and Archaeology. *Scripta Mediterranea* 27: 33-52.

Frymer-Kensky, Tikva
2006 *Studies in Bible and Feminist Criticism*. Philadelphia: The Jewish Publication Society.

Garfinkel, Y.
2004 *The Goddess of Sha'ar Hagolan: Excavations at Neolithic Site in Israel*. Jerusalem: Israel Exploration Society.

Guy, P. L. O.
1938 *Meggido Tombs*. Oriental Institute Publications 23, eds. John Albert Wilson, and Thomas George Allen. Chicago, IL: The University of Chicago Press.

Hadley, J. M.
2000 *The Cult of Asherah in Ancient Israel and Judah: Evidence for a Hebrew Goddess*. Cambridge, UK: Cambridge: University Press.

Hillers, D. R.
1970 The Goddess with the Tambourine: Reflections on an Object from Taanach. *Concordia Theological Monthly* 41: 606-19.

Holland, T. A.
1975a Appendix C: A figurine from Gezer. In *Gezer II: Report of the 1967 - 70 Seasons in Field I and II*, ed. William G. Dever. Jerusalem: Hebrew Union College/Nelson Glueck School of Biblical Archaeology.

Holland, T. A.
1975b A typological and Archaeological Study of Human and Animal Representations in the Plastic Art of Palestine. Unpublished Ph.D. Dissertation, Oxford University.

Jones, L. E.
2005 *Ishtar*. P. 760 in *Gods, Goddesses, and Mythology*, ed. C. Scott Littleton. China: Marshal Cavendish.

Jones, P.
2003 Embracing Inana: Legitimation and Mediation in the Ancient Mesopotamian Sacred Marriage Hymn Iddin-Dagan A. *Journal of the American Oriental Society* 123: 291-302.

Keel, O.
1998 *Goddesses and Trees, New Moon and Yahweh: Ancient Near Eastern Art and the Hebrew Bible*. Journal for the Study of the Old Testament: Sheffield.

Kramer, D. W.; Samuel N.
1983 *Inanna: Queen of Heaven and Earth, her stories and hymns from Sumer*. NY: Harper & Row Publishers.

Kramer, S. N.
1940 Ishtar in the Nether World According to a New Sumerian Text. *Bulletin of the American Schools of Oriental Research* 79: 18-27.

1963 Cuneiform Studies and the History of Literature: The Sumerian Sacred Marriage Texts. *Proceedings of the American Philosophical Society* 107: 485-527.

1972 Le Rite de Mariage Sacré Dumuzi-Inanna. *Revue de l'histoire des religions* 181: 121-46.

1981 *History Begins at Sumer: Thirty Nine Firsts in Recorded History*. Philadelphia, PA: University of Pennsylvania Press.

Landau, A. Y.
2010 *The Philistines and Aegean Migration at the End of the Late Bronze Age*. NY: Cambridge University Press.

Laneri, N.
2002 The Discovery of a Funerary Ritual: Inanna/Ishtar and Her Descent to the Nether World in Titriş Höyük, Turkey. *East and West* 52: 9-51.

Langdon, S.
1914 *Tammuz and Ishtar: A Monograph upon Babylonian Religion and Theology.* NY: Oxford.

Lapinkivi, P.
2010 *The New-Assyrian Myth of Ištar's Descent and Resurrection. State Archives of Assyria Cuneiform Texts* 6: The Neo-Assyrian Text Corpus Project.

Layard, A. H.
1852 *A Popular Account of Discoveries at Nineveh.* London: Harper Brothers Publishers.

Leick, G.
1994 *Sex and Eroticism in Mesopotamian Literature.* NY: Routledge.

Margalit, B.
1990 The Meaning and Significance of Asherah. *Vetus Testamentum* 40: 264-97.

Meinhold, W.
2009 *Ištar in Aššur: Untersuchung eines Lokalkultes von ca. 2500 bis 614 v. Chr. Alter Orient und Altes Testament* 367. Müster: Ugarit-Verlag.

Murray, M. A.
1934 Female Fertility Figures. *The Journal of the Royal Anthropological Institute of Great Britain and Ireland* 64: 93-100.

Niehaus, J. J.
2008 *Ancient Near Eastern Themes in Biblical Theology.* Grand Rapids, MI: Kregel Publications.

Ornan, T.
2005 *The Triumph of the Symbol: Pictorial Representations of Deities in Mesopotamia and the Biblical Image Ban. Orbis Biblicus et Orientalis* 213: Academic Press Fribourg.

Ornan, T.
2011 'Let Ba'al Be Enthroned': The Date, Identification, and Function of a Bronze Statue from Hazor. *Journal of Near Eastern Studies* 70: 253-80.

Pittman, H.
2014 Anchoring Intuition in Evidence: A continuing discussion of cylinder seals from southeastern Iran. Pp. 375-96 in *Edith Porada: zum 100, Geburtstag, A centenary Volume,* eds. Erika Bleibtreu, and Hans Ulrich Steymans. Leipzig: Academic Press Fribourg.

Press, M. D.
2012 *The Leon Levy Expedition to Ashkelon 4: The Iron Age Fogiromes of Ashekelon and Philistia*. Winona Lake, IN: Eisenbrauns.

Pritchard, J. B.
1943 *Palestinian Figurines in Relation to Certain Goddesses Known Through Literature*. *American Oriental Series* 24. New Haven, CT: American Oriental Society.

Pritchard, J. B., and White, L. M., eds.
2003 *The HarperCollins Concise Atlas of the Bible*. UK: Harper San Francisco.

Ragavan, D.
2010 The Cosmic Imagery of the Temple in Sumerian Literature, Harvard University.

Riddle, J. M.
2010 *Goddesses, Elixirs, and Witches: Plants and Sexuality Throughout Human History*. NY: Palgrave Macmillan.

Rodin, T.
2014 The World of the Sumerian Mother Goddess: An Interpretation of Her Myths, Uppsala Universitet.

Rodney, N. B.
1952 Ishtar, the Lady of Battle. *The Metropolitan Museum of Art Bulletin* 10: 211-16.

Siebeck, M.
2014 *Interpreting Judean Pillar Figurines: Gender and Empire in Judean Apotropaic Ritual (Forschungen Zum Alten Testament 2.Reihe)*. Nehren, Germany: Laupp & Göbel.

Smith, M. S.
1987 God Male and Female in the Old Testament: Yahweh and his 'Ashera'. *Theological Studies* 48: 333-40.

Stern, E.
2010 *Excavations at Dor: Figurines, Cult Objects and Amulets 1980-2000 Seasons*. Jerusalem: Israel Exploration Society.

Stone, E.
2000 *The Development of Cities in Ancient Mespotamia*. Pp. 235-48 in vol. 1 of *Civilizations of the Ancient Near East*, ed. Jack M. Sasson. MA: Hendrickson Publishers.

Stuckey, J.
2005 Inanna and the "Sacred Marriage," *Matrifocus* 4-2. http://www.matrifocus.com/IMB05/spotlight.htm

Stuckey, J. H.
2003 The Great Goddesses of the Levant. *Journal of the Society for the Study of Egyptian Antiquities* 30

Sugimoto, D. T.
2014 An Analysis of a Stamp Seal with Complex Religious Motifs Excavated at Tel 'En Gev. *Israel Exploration Journal* 64: 9-21.

Sundsdal, K.
2008 Ideology, social space & power in Uruk Societies: A comparative anlysis of North and South Mesopotamian Settlements in the 4th Millenniun B.C.

Teissier, B.
1996 *Egyptian Iconography on Syro-Palestine Cylinder Seals of the Middle Bronze Age*. Orbis Biblicus et Orientalis 11. Fribourg, Switzerland: University Press Fribourg Switzerland.

Tushingham, A. D.
1985 *Excavations in Jersusalem 1961-1967*. 1. Toronto: Royal Ontario Museum.

Veenker, R. A.
1981 Gilgamesh and the Magic Plant. *The Biblical Archaeologist* 44: 199-205.

Wellhausen, J.
1898 *Die Kleinen Propheten: Übersetzt und Erklärt*. Berlin: Verlag Von Georg Reimer.

Wiggerman, F. A. M.
1997 Transtigridian Snake Gods. *Cuneiform Monographs* 7: 33-55.

Wiggins, S. A.
2007 *A Reassessment of Asherah. Georgias Ugaritic Studies* 2, ed. N. Wyatt. NJ: Georgias Press.

Winter, I. J.
2010 *On Art in the Ancient Near East*. Of the First Millennium B.C.E., no. 1. Leiden: Brill.

Wright, K. I
2007 Women and the Emergence of Urban Society in Mesopotamia: Ancient & Modern Issues. Pp. 199-237 in *Archaeology and Women*, eds. Sue Hamilton; Ruth D. Whitehouse; and Katherine I Wright. Walnut Creek, CA: Left Coast Press.

Religious Syncretism in Transjordan during the Iron Age as seen in Tall Jalul and Khirbet Atarutz

Abelardo Santini Rivas

A constant element in Transjordan religion during the Iron Age is the prevalence of syncretism. The cultural mixture of different foreign and local sources produced different regional religious traditions practiced in Transjordan by different tribal groups. This paper aims to examine such syncretism as reflected in two sites: Tall Jalul, mostly domestic and administrative, and Khirbet Atarutz, mostly cultic. It examines cultic objects present in both sites that reflect different sources of cultic/cultural influence.

Tall Jalul

In the modern Hashemite Kingdom of Jordan, Tall Jalul is one of the most prominent features on the Madaba Plains. A large mound located next to the modern village of Jalul, about 5 km east of the modern town of Madaba, it is the largest archaeological site on the central Jordanian plateau. It is oblong in shape and about 18 acres in size. On the southwestern quadrant, and underneath a modern extant cemetery, is the unexcavated Acropolis. On the southeast side, a series of depressions seem to suggest the presence of a water (reservoir) system designed, it would seem, to cope with the dryness of the local climate. Excavations in Jalul since 1992 have yielded a number of architectural remains. Among the structures on the tell are paved streets, walls, houses, pillared buildings, a channel, and a water reservoir. A defensive system was built at Jalul consisting of well-built walls around the perimeter of the site. Tall Jalul's height provides an excellent vista of the surrounding plains in all directions; it even permits a view as far as Tall Hisban to the north. Beside the architectural remains, most of them showing the domestic occupation of the site since the acropolis is still unexcavated, a series of figurines indicative of perhaps domestic cultic activities have been found. These, in turn, point to a mixture of different religious influences that may have characterized the local religious practices of the inhabitants of Jalul.

Figurines of Jalul

Some of the several figurines found at Jalul seem to exhibit a mixture of local and Egyptian features or a local interpretation of Egyptian motifs. I have chosen some and divided them into female and male figurines, even though at least one of them seems to represent a primate instead of a human figure.

Female Figurines

While the female figurines may not represent direct Egyptian influences, they do share strong similarities with Egyptian features. In the 94 season in field A, which was classified as a burial place dated to the Late Iron II, a female figurine, J940053, shows several important features (Ray, Younker, Gregor, and Gane 2011: J0053). First, it presents a frontal view, almond-shaped eyes, and a headdress. The headdress seems to go behind the ears and extends to the upper part of the breast. At its extremes, it curves to the inside. While Hathor's headdress seems to curve to the outside, this style of curving the edges in a different direction also occurs in Egyptian art (Lange, and Max 1968:102). Another possible interpretation is that those are not curves but an adornment at the edges of the headdress. In the 2007 season in field D, a female figurine, J0532, almost identical, but better preserved than J940053, was found in a Late Iron II context. Indeed, the previous figurine must have come from the same mold as this one since the characteristics are identical. It has also almond-shaped eyes, frontal view, headdress curving at its ends, but this time, they seem to curve towards the outside (Ray, et al. 2011: J0532). Again, it is not identical to Hathor, but there is a similar artistic element.

Two figurines deserve special attention that were found during the 2009 season. J0730, found in field D during the removal of the North Balk, has unmistakably Egyptian features. The context dates to the Late Iron Age II/Persian period and the figurine has a frontal view, strong detailed emphasis on particular facial features, almond-shaped eyes, and hair going behind the ears and parted at the middle in the same way as figurines found in several Egyptian depictions (Ray et al. 2011: J0730). The lips seem to be wider than common Semite depictions and so does the nose, which more resembles Egyptian features. The contour of the face is well-delineated and the ears seem to be in frontal perspective. The second figurine, J0762, is more eroded, so its features are less distinctive than the previous one (Ray et al. 2011: J0762), yet, one can perceive a frontal view in the design and a headdress or hair that tends to curve in the same manner as the figurines described above.

These figurines show similarities with Egyptian artistic features, yet it would be difficult to assess whether there is direct influence. These similarities between the local portrayal of female features and Egyptian concepts tend to indicate syncretism between local and foreign style.

Male Figurines

The first group can be represented by figures J0455 and J0566 (Ray et al. 2011). Both figures wear a crown, which seems to resemble in form and detail the Tell Jawa male figure wearing a similar Atef crown representation (Daviau, and Paul 1994: 153–67). One major difference between the two figurines is the absence of ostrich feathers, perhaps broken off, in figure J0566. However, both crowns have the same conical form, also similar to the Tel Jawa's figurine, and have incised radiating lines from a central axis. Both figurines were made in a mold and have a frontal view. The facial features do not seem to resemble Egyptian influences except, perhaps, in the design of the lips and nose. These tend to have a more Egyptian aspect than local. The dating of both figures seems to be Late Iron II (Ray et al. 2011). These figures seem to have a modified version of Egyptian features and the incorporation of local artistic conventions.

The second type of figurine is represented by J0717 and J940036. While the dating of J0717 does not seem clear, it is most likely based upon the occupational faces of the site, an Iron Age dating. J940036 was found on top soil and the context suggested a LB/Iron II dating, a broad spectrum of time, but again, the figure most likely dates to somewhere in the Iron Age. Among the common characteristics are almond-shaped eyes with inlaid pupils. They were both also made in a mold and show a frontal view. However, the most distinctive feature, from an Egyptian perspective and from a common depiction, is the wearing of an Atef crown. In contrast with the previous type, they are more reminiscent of the Egyptian style and parallel the representation of the Atef crown found in the statue of the Amman Citadel (Bienkowski 1991: 41). The crown seems to be shorter than the typical Egyptian Atef crown. On the sides, the ostrich feathers are represented in both figurines. On the other hand, the emphasis in the eyebrows and an apparent depiction of a beard without a mustache seems to be more Semitic and definitely un-Egyptian.

The third type is represented only by one figurine uncovered during the 1996 season on field A and dated to the Iron II period, J0150. This figurine is unique because the Egyptian features represented in it are not common in Transjordan. The face has a frontal design. The eyes are almond-shaped with emphasis on the eyebrows with a "raised" type of carving. The borders of the mouth are much delineated and it seems to indicate some type of beard. The chin is over-emphasized with what seems to be a replica of a typical Egyptian beard at the chin, long and square at the bottom. The ears are in frontal view and are also disproportionally bigger in relation to other facial features. Based upon the right ear, three "rings" earrings seem to be depicted as attached to the ear. The left ear still seems to also have a similar depiction, although it is eroded and less certain. The figurine seems to have a crown or headdress. Such seems to be an attempt to depict a nemes headdress. At the top, a ribbon or lower border of the headdress is depicted in an Egyptian fashion (Lange, and Hirmer 1968: 47). It is also square and wide, which is also similar to Egyptian depictions (Lange, and Hirmer 1968: 16). At the top of the "crown," a depiction of what appears to be an uraeus snake is shown (Wilkinson 1994: 109). A small red dot on the right side (perhaps representing an eye) and a small incision in the front (perhaps a nose) make it also seem a plausible interpretation. However, it is eroded and a precise identification is difficult. The chest is flat and small in proportion as compared to the arms and the shoulders. No trace of clothing remains. It seems as if the chest is portrayed bare. The nose is quite wide, which seems to resemble certain Egyptian conventions (Lange, and Hirmer 1968: 107).

Hardly any features of this figurine seem to be un-Egyptian. The headdress, the uraeus, the width of the shoulders, the bare chest, the facial features, the square long beard at the chin, and the frontal perspective are all Egyptian artistic depictions. Perhaps the only aspect in this figurine that could be considered un-Egyptian is the end of the headdress, which does not fall on the frontal part of the chest. Similarly, the three-earring depiction in the ears may be a local feature.

A final type is also represented by one figurine excavated during the 2011 season on Field G, Square 12. Even though it is, as I will argue, a zoomorphic depiction, it is still included in the male representations because all the possible associations indicate a male Egyptian depiction (Wilkinson, 1994: 73).

J11.0879 is a zoomorphic figurine depicting perhaps a primate or more specifically a baboon. Its length is 6 cm. The width at its neck is 3.3 cm and at its headdresses, 2 cm. It seems to have been made using a mold to be seen from a frontal perspective. Its mouth is completely eroded, but it is portrayed longer as a snout, seemingly imitating a primate. On the sides, strident marks resemble similar attempts to portray facial hair, particularly that of a baboon. Its eyes are almond-shaped with exaggerated eyebrows. The ears are eroded or perhaps broken off at the top. It is wearing a headdress with perpendicular lines and a flat top. The nostrils are wide and significantly larger than normal depictions of humans. The nose is also very wide, which seems to correlate more with a depiction of a primate's nose. From a side view, the area from the nostrils to the mouth is brought forward more than the rest of the face, again resembling a primate. A parallel figurine of a primate carrying a sheep is in the Amman citadel which also dates to the Iron Age (Bienkowski 1991, 38).

Primates are not part of the natural fauna of Jordan. Thus, the idea must have come from foreign concepts. Obviously, Egypt is the most logical option. However, we must be careful not to associate every primate representation as a depiction of Thoth (Robins 1997: 190). Although a representation of Thoth would be the most logical choice, since it is largely depicted in Egyptian iconography, other possibilities cannot be discarded easily (Wilkinson 1994: 73). Yet, regardless of which deity is being depicted, the motif is without any doubt Egyptian. Not only is it Egyptian, but also seems to lack any local features.

Khirbet Atarutz

Khirbet Atarutz, located 3 km east of the Herodian fort Machaerus and 10 km west from Khirbet Libb, has been excavated during the last 12 years under the direction of Chang-Ho Ji (Chang 2012: 203). The site has yielded several cultic installations such as high places, temple installations, water cisterns, altars, and objects that speak of the cultic nature of the site. It continued to be occupied until the Islamic age, but its most prominent period was during the Iron Age II and the temple functioned until the Late Iron Age when it suffered a period of abandonment (Chang-Ho Ji 2012: 6-10). Later, the cultic role of the site was never to become as prominent. I have participated in the last two years of excavations, as well as in the study of the objects found in these cultic areas. It is important to mention that the site is not merely cultic and that several domestic areas remain unexcavated, some of which started to be uncovered during the last season. Naturally a series of cultic objects have been unearthed in Atarutz and these again reflect a combination of foreign and domestic religious/cultural influence during the Iron Age. For the purpose of our study, I am including those that precisely reflect the idea of religious syncretism and foreign influence.

Objects of Atarutz

Most of the cultic objects in this paper were uncovered during the 2001 season in Field A (Chang-Ho Ji defined the entire acropolis or cultic area as Field A). Field A constitutes the entire Acropolis of the Khirbet. A multi-chamber temple/ sanctuary has been excavated in this field. Chang-Ho dated this structure to what he defined as the temple phase II to the early mid-ninth century B.C.E. or the early Iron Age II. The artifacts themselves suggest the cultic nature of the building and the building's structure also suggests the cultic use of the objects. It seems that each object reflects local and foreign cultic parallels suggesting Hittite, Philistine, Canaanite, and partial Egyptian influence in the religion of Atarutz.

Kernoi

Three different hollow-ring libation vessels commonly known as kernos have been discovered at Atarutz. One of them is horizontal, while the other two are vertical. The horizontal kernos was also found during the 2001 season in Square 5, Locus 7. The pottery was also dated by the excavation team between the early to mid-ninth century B.C.E., early Iron Age II. The kernos was found over the offering table in the main court of the multi-room temple complex scattered in pieces. It is a circular-shaped ring. The ring area is hollow to keep the liquid used in the libation or ritualistic function of the vessel inside. Because of its openness and its width, it seems as if the front spout serves as the place where the liquid would be poured in and the smaller or side spout would serve as the place from where the liquid would be poured out. The two vertical kernoi were also found also during the 2001 season in Field A, Square 5. The first one was the whole form and was in Locus 7, while the second one was half-broken and was located in Locus 6. They seem to have very similar physical characteristics. They are 18 cm wide and 21 cm long from the spout to the bottom. The spout's diameter is 4.5 cm. At the mouth of the spout, there is a 1 cm inclination to pour out the liquid. The half-broken kernos has a round spout.

The kernoi seem to be associated with foreign cultures (Mazar 1980: 111), particularly those originating around the Aegean (Dever 2001: 119) and the Mediterranean (Dothan 1958: 22) seas. Two main cultures seem to be associated with the use of kernoi, predating the Late Bronze and Iron Age. In Palestine, they seem to be associated with the Philistines. "Most of the kernoi found in Palestine come from three contexts in the Iron Age: (1) twelfth-eleventh centuries B.C. levels of Philistine sites along the coast, especially Tell Qasile; (2) from later 'Neo-Philistine' sites of the ninth-seventh centuries B.C., such as Ashdod; and now (3) from a few tenth-seventh centuries B.C. sites in Israel and Judah" (Dever 2001: 119). William Dever argued that the kernos tradition was reintroduced in Canaan by the Sea People from Cyprus (Dever 2001: 125). Indeed, the horizontal kernos seems to resemble the rim of the "Philistine krater bearing cups," (Dever 2001: 248) namely, the kernos as a hollow vessel. However, kernoi also bear local Canaanite features. In regards to a group of kernoi found at Tel Miqne-Ekron, it has been argued that these "zoomorphic libation vessels (and kernoi) which, on the basis of their shape and decoration, do not display Philistine characteristics, but rather relate to local Canaanite traditions" (Ben-Shlomo 2008: 34). Besides Philistine and Canaanite parallels sustaining the argument of foreign influence, kernoi can be traced to Hittite culture with what scholars define as ring vase vessels (Kulakoglu 1998: 199). At Kutelpe, three of these ring-shaped vessels were found in what has been classified as a private domestic complex. While most of these were vertical, their description does closely resemble the one found at the Atarutz cultic structure. "They have ring shaped bodies with squat necks, simple rims and round orifices. A single handle connects the rim to the neck. Buff colored clay is levigated and fired. Over the micaceous pinkish cream slip, the outer part of the pipe is decorated with reddish brown colored lines forming irregular cross hatches" (Kulakoglu 1998: 200). The munsell chart of both horizontal kernoi found at Atarutz and the kernoi of Kutelpe reads 7.5YR/3 or 4. While the Kutelpe ring vessels are vertical, in contrast to most of the Philistine and Canaanite kernoi which are horizontal just like the one at Atarutz, the hollow form, the ring shape, the use of two spouts, the ware, the ritualistic function, and the lack of zoomorphic depictions along with a more simplistic model do resemble the Kutelpe ring vessels, or kernoi as they are known in Palestine.

The ritualistic function of these vessels is not only attested to by the direct context where they were found, but also by the inadequacy of its form for daily use and its parallels with similar vessels at other sites. The vertical ring vessels show a closer similarity with the Hittite ring vase libation vessels. A helpful classification of these vessels based upon ware and decoration has been proposed as follows:

Type one: round spout, footless, and plain ware or undecorated.
Type two: round spout, footless, and painted or relief decoration.
Type three: round spout, high pedestal base, and plain surface.
Type four: beak spout, high pedestal base, and plain surface (Kulakoglu 1998: 202).

While some variation or combination of these features can also occur, as indeed does happen with one of the kernoi from Atarutz, the proposer of the classification was able to indentify vertical kernoi in several important Hittite sites in Anatolia, as well as along the Aegean and the eastern Mediterranean sea coast, in sites like Byblos, Ugarit, Cyprus, and others (Kulakoglu 1998: 202). Therefore, it seems as if the origin of this type of ring-shaped vessels named kernos in Cisjordan and Transjordan archaeology can be traced back to Anatolia, which gained preeminence during the Hittite domination of the land (Bryce 2005: 48) and always fulfilled a cultic function, containing perhaps wine as a libation offering—a practice well attested to in the Ancient Near East (Pardee, and Theodore 2002: 216).

Standing Statue

A standing human statue carved out of limestone was uncovered on Square 5, Locus 6, Field A in the main sanctuary area during the 2001 season. The statue is broken at the torso or knees, which is unclear because the garment is not apparent. It seems to be in a walking position since the left foot is further towards the front than the right foot. It stands on a square vase 13 by 12 cm and its width is 3.5 cm. It is 11 cm tall from the base to the knees (assuming that such are the knees in comparison with the rest of the missing body). The garment covers the figure down to the ankle at the front and down to the ground at the back. A staff or part of the garment is over the left foot covering two toes. Furthermore, all the toes, as well as the lower part of the garment are carved in great detail. A carved design seems to be on both sides of the statue's square base and it appears to resemble palm branches. This statue was found as support for the large vase which included the bull motif typical of Atarutz. As stated above, the spatial context suggests a ritualistic purpose for the statue. It is difficult to determine if it represents a priest or a worshiper because all of the upper part is broken.

What is significant for this study of this statue is how it reflects a typical Egyptian building technique employed to avoid breaking it. It could be defined as standing/advancing.

Statues were normally made of stone, wood or metal. Stone statues were worked from single rectangular blocks of material and retained the compactness of the original shape. The stone between the arms and the body, and between the legs in standing figures or the legs and the seat in seated ones, was not normally cut away. From a practical aspect this protected the figures against breakage, and psychologically gives the images a sense of strength and power, usually enhanced by a supporting back pillar (Gay 1997: 119).

These standing/advancing statues, whether of wood or stone, seem to have the arms straight down or one down and the other up in an attempt to depict motion. A similar technique seems to be used with several standing statues found in the Amman citadel in the design of the feet, the intent of depicting forward motion, and the length of the garment seems to suggest a strong parallel. This seems to indicate foreign influence, whether Ammonite or indirect Egyptian influence.

Bronze Belt

In the area of the main sanctuary, a "belt" (Chang 2012: 197) was found having undeniable Egyptian origin. Ji described it as a "bronze belt-like plate decorated with serpents" (Chang 2012: 197) No chemical analysis has been performed on it and the material could also be copper. It is a two-part metal belt (it may not be a belt; it could also be a standard or some other type of cultic ornament) with back and front matching perfectly with each other. Ten cobras are represented in this belt. They are distributed in pairs or as twins (Wilkinson 1994: 109). Six of them are depicted as a reared-up cobra without any extra symbol. The other four are depicted as also reared up, but with the solar disk over their heads. All the ones depicted with the solar disk over their heads are in an upward position. Cobras paired with the solar disk are depicted in various Egyptian monuments and even in Egyptian crowns (Lange, and Hirmer 1968: pl. 51). Indeed, in some royal adornments such as pectorals, both depictions, with and without the solar disk, appear together (Lange, and Hirmer 1968: pl. 43). The artifact seems to be a direct import from Egypt since apparently no local features are present. If it is an import, then it demonstrates direct contact through trading with Egypt and the importance locals placed on Egyptian cultic material (Wilkinson 1994: 109).

Religious Syncretism

As seen in the description and analysis of the objects in these two sites, a series of local and foreign influences played a significant role in their fabrication and use. While the figurines at Jalul show a mixture of local and Egyptian features, there may be influence from other sources since the objects from Atarutz show Hittite, Egyptian, Canaanite, and even Philistine influence. More important, even though the influence of areas such as Mesopotamia is to be expected because of the political/historical context during the Iron Age, Egyptian or even Hittite influence is not expected. Most likely, such comes by the venues of trade or by older adopted traditions that remained in spite of the changes in the political climate of the time. In any case, the religious practices in these sites may have followed a similar path reflected in these objects, which included a mixture of local traditions, foreign influence, and local interpretation of older or recent foreign tradition through the eyes of local expressions.

References

Ben-Shlomo, David.
2008 "Zoomorphic Vessels from Tel Miqne-Ekron and the Different Styles of Philistine Pottery." *Israel Exploration Journal* 58, no. 1: 24–47.

Bryce, Trevor.
2005 *The Kingdom of the Hittites*. New ed. Oxford ; New York: Oxford University Press.

Bienkowski, Piotr.
1991 *Treasures from an Ancient Land : The Art of Jordan*. Stroud: Alan Sutton.

Daviau, P. M. Michèle, and Paul-Eugène Dion.
2002 *Excavations at Tall Jawa, Jordan*. Vol. 2. 2 vols. Culture and History of the Ancient near East. Leiden: Brill.

Daviau, P. M. Michèle, and Paul-Eugène Dion.
2002 *Excavations at Tall Jawa, Jordan*. Vol. 1. 2 vols. Culture and History of the Ancient near East. Leiden: Brill.

Daviau, P. M. Michele, and Paul E. Dion.
1994 "El. The God of the Ammonites? The Atef-Crowned Head from *Tell Jawa*, Jordan." *Zeitschrift des Deutschen Palästina-Vereins* 110, no. 2: 158–167.

Dever, William G.
2001 "Iron Age Kernoi and the Israelite Cult." In *Studies in the Archaeology of Israel and Neighboring Lands in Memory of Douglas L. Esse*, edited by Douglas L. Esse and Samuel Richard Wolff, 119–133. Chicago: Oriental Institute of the University of Chicago.

Dothan, Trude.
1958 "Philistine Civilization in Light of Archaeological Finds in Palestine and Egypt." *Eretz Israel* 5.

Ji, Chang-Ho.
2012 "The Early Iron Ii Temple at Hirbet Atarutz and Its Architecture and Selected Cultic Objects." *Abhandlugen des Deutschen Palastina - Vereins* 41: 203–222.

Ji, Chang-Ho.
2012 "Khirbat 'Ataruz: An Interim Overview of the 10 Years of Archaeological Architectural Findings." *Annual of the Department of Antiquities of Jordan*.

Kulakoglu, F. K. R.
1998 "Ring-Shaped Vases Discovered at Kultepe." *Essays on Ancient Anatolia in the Second Millennium BC* 10: 199.

Lange, Kurt, and Max Hirmer.
1968 Egypt: *Architecture, Sculpture, Painting in Three Thousand Years*. 4th revised and enlarged; ed. London, New York: Phaidon.

Mazar, Amihay.
1980 *Excavations at Tell Qasile : Part I. The Philistine Sanctuary: Architecture and Cult Objects* Qedem; 12. Jerusalem: Institute of Archaeology Hebrew University of Jerusalem.

2002 Pardee, Dennis and Theodore J. Lewis.
Ritual and Cult at Ugarit. Atlanta: Society of Biblical Literature.

Younker, Randall, Paul Ray, Paul Gregor, Connie Gane, and others.
2011 "Madaba Plains Project-Jalul." Berrien Springs: Andrews University Press.

Robins, Gay.
1997 *The Art of Ancient Egypt*. Cambridge, Mass.: Harvard University Press.

Wilkinson, Richard H.
1994 Reading Egyptian Art: A Hieroglyphic Guide to Ancient Egyptian Painting and Sculpture. Thames & Hudson.

PART 5: SYSTEMATIC THEOLOGY

An Ecclesiological Understanding of the Remnant: The Concept of Visible/Invisible Church and the Remnant

Adriani Milli Rodrigues

Even though Protestant Reformers did not begin the renewal of the church from a systematically developed ecclesiology, they had to elaborate theological ideas concerning the church in order to criticize the decadent condition of the late medieval church, and afterwards to explain the nature of the churches that were arising from this movement.[1] In opposition to Roman Catholicism, which emphasized the importance of the visible church, they supported that the church is, at the same time, a visible and invisible community.[2] According to that idea, the hidden aspect of the church implies the totality of the elect who are known only to God, whereas its visible aspect means the institutional body on earth.[3] This paradoxical concept engenders an intricate relationship between the notion of God's people and the institutional church.

This complex relationship is also found in Seventh-day Adventist theology, particularly in the central idea of its ecclesiological understanding: the remnant church.[4] Actually, the Protestant concept of visible and invisible church has been employed in diverse forms in the Adventist study of the remnant.[5] First, emphasizing visibility, Frank Hasel argued that "over the years, Sabbatarian Adventists

---

1. Kärkkäinen properly stated that "whenever Protestant ecclesiologies are studied, whether Lutheran or Reformed, it has to be acknowledged that these views represented at their best response to existing needs; they were occasional works rather than systematic theologies of the church." Veli-Matti Kärkkäinen, *Introduction to Ecclesiology: Ecumenical, Historical & Global Perspectives* (Downers Grove, IL: InterVarsity Press, 2002), 54.

2. See John Calvin, *Institutes of the Christian Religion*, trans. Henry Beveridge (Edinburgh: Calvin Translation Society, 1845), 4.1.7; Martin Luther, *Preface to the Revelation of St. John [II]*, Luther's Works, 35 (Philadelphia: Muhlenberg Press, 1960), 409-411.

3. For further information, see Kärkkäinen, *Introduction to Ecclesiology*, 40, 52.

4. According to Goldstein, "through the years, the word *remnant*, or the phrase *the remnant church*, has become the definitive, self-proclaimed mark of Seventh-day Adventists." Clifford Goldstein, *The Remnant: Biblical Reality or Wishful Thinking?* (Boise, ID: Pacific Press, 1994), 11.

5. For a useful historical overview about the discussion of the concept of the remnant among Seventh-day Adventists, see Samuel Garbi, "The Seventh-day Adventist Church as the Remnant Church: Various Views over 150 Years of Denominational History" (paper presented for CHIS 674 Development of SDA Theology, Andrews University, Berrien Springs, MI, December 1994), 13-50.

have considered themselves God's prophetic end-time remnant people."[6] This understanding is presented in many official[7] and representative[8] Seventh-day Adventist publications. Second, emphasizing both visible and invisible aspects, the significant work in the history of Adventist theology, *Questions on Doctrine*, states that "God has a precious remnant, a multitude of earnest, sincere believers, in every church,"[9] which seems to stress the idea of invisibility, but this text also affirms a visible remnant on the basis of Rev 12:17.[10] Third, there is an emphasis on the invisibility of the remnant. In this sense, regarding that God has "an invisible church or kingdom whose members cannot be numbered," S. Daily recommends that Adventists should cease to think about themselves as the remnant church and start to see themselves "as a part of God's larger remnant."[11] In another way, Jack Provonsha argued that the remnant of Rev 12:17, which is more than an institution, represents a prophecy that has not yet been fulfilled. It implies that the visible remnant is not a present reality.[12]

The various interpretations regarding the remnant church presented above indicate that there is no consensus about the visibility and/or invisibility of the remnant. This situation may lead to some questions. What is the relation between the concept of visible and invisible church and the remnant? Should it be applied to the remnant church? Is the remnant visible, visible and invisible, or invisible? What is the biblical understanding of its visibility and/or invisibility? How does this understanding impact the Adventist concept of the remnant church? Having these questions in mind, the purpose of this study is to explore the concept of the remnant in connection with the visible/invisible reality of the church.

---

6. Frank M. Hasel, "The Remnant in Contemporary Adventist Theology," in *Toward a Theology of the Remnant: An Adventist Ecclesiological Perspective*, ed. Angel M. Rodriguez (Silver Spring, MD.: Biblical Research Institute, 2009). For further information about the concept of the remnant among Adventist pioneers, see Alberto R. Timm, "The Sanctuary and the Three Angels' Messages: Integrating Factors in the Development of Seventh-day Adventist Doctrines" (PhD diss. Andrews University, 1995), 415-420; P. Gerard Damsteegt, *Foundations of the Seventh-Day Adventist Message and Mission* (Grand Rapids, MI: Eerdmans, 1977), 147, 164, 243-244.

7. Cf. General Conference of Seventh-day Adventists, *Seventh-day Adventist Church Manual*, 17th ed. (Hagerstown, MD: General Conference of Seventh-day Adventists, 2005), 33, 35; Ministerial Association of the General Conference of Seventh-day Adventists, *Seventh-day Adventists Believe: A Biblical Exposition of Fundamental Doctrines*, 2nd ed. (Boise, ID: Pacific Press, 2005), 181, 190-197.

8. F. D. Nichol, ed., *SDA Bible Commentary* (Washington, DC: Review & Herald, 1953-1957), 7:815; Hans K. LaRondelle, "The Remnant and the Three Angel's Message," in *A Handbook of Seventh-day Adventist Theology*, ed. Raoul Dederen (Hagerstown, MD: Review & Herald, 2000), 887-888.

9. George R. Knight, ed., *Seventh-day Adventists Answer Questions on Doctrine [QOD]*, Annotated ed., Adventist Classic Library (Berrien Springs, MI: Andrews University Press, 2003), 162.

10. The text seems to work with two different definitions of remnant: (1) "the church invisible," (2) the remnant of "Revelation 12:17." Knight, *QOD*, 159.

11. Steven Daily, *Adventism for a New Generation* (Portland, OR: Better Living, 1993), 315. Steven Daily labeled traditional Adventist remnant theology as an ethnocentric attitude, which does not acknowledge "that 'the kingdom of God on earth' transcends every religious movement of humankind." Ibid., 314.

12. Provonsha declared that the Adventist "claim to be a special people, the remnant, the people of God, seems almost perverse." In addition, he argued that the Adventist church may consider itself "a proleptic remnant," which "may one day be absorbed into a final remnant." Jack W. Provonsha, *A Remnant in Crisis* (Hagerstown, MD: Review & Herald, 1993), 35, 163.

In order to achieve this purpose, I will take three basic steps. First, I will begin with a historical reflection on the aspects of the visible and invisible church, especially covering the period of the Protestant Reformation. Second, I will describe the concept of remnant in the context of the Scriptures through a systematic approach, verifying how the idea of visibility and invisibility is presented or implied in the description of the remnant. Third, I will briefly summarize the discussion and indicate the main implications of this study on the Adventist understanding of the remnant church.

The Concept of Visible and Invisible Church in Historical Theology

In this section, I will briefly present the idea of visible/invisible church from the Patristic period until the Reformation. Despite the fact that the term *invisible* church was probably "first used by Luther,"[13] this notion seems to be rooted in some patristic writings. In addition, the Catholic emphasis on the *visible* church, and the subsequent Protestant reaction, cannot be fully grasped without a knowledge of the Patristic and Medieval periods.

The Patristic Period

Since the second century, "the rise of heresies made it necessary to designate some external characteristics by which the true Catholic Church could be known."[14] In this context, the Church Fathers stressed ever increasingly the visible church. By the third century, according to "his reputation for legalism and moralism,"[15] Cyprian "brought out, for the first time, with anything like clearness or distinctness, the idea of a catholic church comprehending all the true branches of the church of Christ, and *bound together by a visible and external unity*."[16] Strongly emphasizing the importance of being part of the visible church, he wrote:

> The spouse of Christ cannot be adulterous; she is uncorrupted and pure. She knows one home; she guards with chaste modesty the sanctity of one couch. She keeps us for God. She appoints the sons whom she has born for the kingdom. *Whoever is separated from the Church and is joined to an adulteress, is separated from the promises of the Church; nor can he who forsakes the Church of Christ attain to the rewards of Christ. He is a stranger; he is profane; he is an enemy. He can no longer have God for his Father, who has not the Church for his mother.* If any one

---

13. Reinhold Seeberg, *Text-Book of the History of Doctrines*, 2 vols. (Philadelphia: Lutheran Publication Society, 1905), 2:293.

14. Louis Berkhof, *The History of Christian Doctrines*, Twin Brooks Series (Grand Rapids, MI: Baker, 1975), 227.

15. Roger E. Olson, *The Mosaic of Christian Belief: Twenty Centuries of Unity and Diversity* (Downers Grove, IL: InterVarsity Press, 2002), 270.

16. William Cunningham, *Historical Theology: A Review of the Principal Doctrinal Discussions in the Christian Church since the Apostolic Age*, 2 vols. (Edinburgh: T&T Clark, 1863), 1:169 (italics mine). For further information about Cyprian and his ideas concerning the church, see John Alfred Faulkner, *Men of the Kingdom Cyprian the Churchman* (New York: Bibliolife, 2009); J. Patout Burns, *Cyprian the Bishop,* Routledge Early Church Monographs (London: Routledge, 2002); George Stuart Murdoch Walker, *The Churchmanship of St Cyprian* Library of Ecclesiastical History (London: James Clarke, 2002); Jane E. Merdinger, *Rome and the African Church in the Time of Augustine* (New Haven: Yale University Press, 2005), 36-42.

could escape who was outside the ark of Noah, then he also may escape who shall be outside of the Church.[17]

In short, his basic idea is that true Christians "will always obey and remain in the Church, outside of which there is no possibility of being saved."[18] Following this understanding, H. Milman pointed out that "Cyprian entertained the loftiest notion of the episcopal authority. The severe and inviolate unity of the outward and visible Church appeared to him an integral part of Christianity, and the rigid discipline enforced by the episcopal order the only means of maintaining that unity."[19]

However, "whereas for Cyprian the boundary between those who are 'outside' and those who are 'inside' coincides simply with the bounds of the visible church, Augustine distinguishes the visible church from the 'elect' whose number and limits are known only to the predestinating foreknowledge of God."[20] In his wrestling against the Donatists, Augustine was "compelled . . . to reflect more deeply on the essence of the Church."[21] In order to refute the Donatist argument that the true church is constituted by pious and holy believers,[22]

Augustine argued that the Church was a mixed community . . . made up of the truly pious, but also of the wicked and unfaithful. Its holiness did not lie in the holiness of its members but in its participation in Christ. Augustine conceived of the Church as both visible and invisible. The visible Church is the empirical and sociological reality that we can see and this is a mixed community. The invisible Church is known only to God and consists of those who are truly elect.[23]

With the Parable of the Wheat and the Tares (see Matt 13:24-30; 36-43) in mind, Augustine explained that, in this "mixed church," "hypocrites cannot even now be said to be in Him [i.e., in Christ], although they seem to be in His

17. Cyprian, *On the Unity of the Church*, 6, in *The Ante-Nicene Fathers*, eds. Alexander Roberts and James Donaldson,1885-1887, 10 vols., repr. (Peabody, MA: Hendrickson, 1995), 5:867-868 (italics mine).

18. Berkhof, *The History of Christian Doctrines*, 228.

19. H. H. Milman, *The History of Christianity: From the Birth of Christ to the Abolition of Paganism in the Roman Empire*, Baudry's Collection of Ancient and Modern British Authors, 1 (Paris: Baudry's European Library, 1840), 371.

20. Maurice F. Wiles and Mark Santer, *Documents in Early Christian Thought* (Cambridge: Cambridge University Press, 1975), 159.

21. Berkhof, *The History of Christian Doctrines*, 229.

22. For details about the history of Donatism and its ideas concerning the church, see David Benedict, *History of the Donatists: With Notes*, Memorial ed. (Providence, R.I.: Maria M. Benedict, 1875); James Alexander, "Donatism," in *The Early Christian World*, ed. Philip Francis Esler (London: Routledge, 2000), 2:218-236; W. H. C. Frend, *The Donatist Church: A Movement of Protest in Roman North Africa*, Oxford Scholarly Classics (Oxford: Oxford University Press, 2000).

23. Peter McEnhill and G. M. Newlands, *Fifty Key Christian Thinkers*, Routledge Key Guides (London: Routledge, 2004), 37. For additional information about the debate between Augustine and Donatists, see Geoffrey Grimshaw Willis, *Saint Augustine and the Donatist Controversy* (Eugene, OR: Wipf & Stock, 2005); Alister E. McGrath, *Christian Theology: An Introduction* (Oxford; Blackwell, 1994), 407-410.

Church."[24] Nevertheless, according to his writings against the Donatists, the separation between the pious and the wicked is not a human task:

> Nor will you separate yourselves by an impious secession, because of the mixture of the tares, from the society of that good wheat, whose source is that grain that dies and is multiplied thereby, and that grows together throughout the world until the harvest. For the field is the world, — not only Africa; and the harvest is the end of the world, — not the era of Donatus.[25]

Through this explanation, Augustine attempted to solve the contradiction between the traditional idea of visible church and the presence of impiety inside this church. Evidently, his solution included the idea of invisible church, which indicates that "the real unity of the saints and therefore of the Church is an invisible one."[26] However, at the same time that real and invisible unity "exists only within the catholic Church,"[27] the visible church is characterized mainly by the episcopal succession and the administration of the sacraments. Therefore, on the one hand, Augustine made "no hard distinction between a visible and an invisible church,"[28] since the notion of invisible church was used for the sake of the visible church.

On the other hand, there is an evident contradiction between the traditional emphasis on the visible church, particularly in its understanding of the church as the ark of salvation with its sacramental system, and the invisible church made up of those predestined by God. That contradiction may be expressed by questions such as the following: "Which is the true Church, the external communion of the baptized, or the spiritual communion of the elect and the saints, or both, since there is no salvation outside of either? . . . [and also,] what about the elect who never join the Church?" In any case, it seems that "Augustine's predestination views kept him from going as far as some of his contemporaries did in the direction of sacramentalism."[29]

The Medieval Period and the Roman Catholic Position

The scholastic development of the concept of the visible church can be basically depicted as the intensification of the Cyprianic understanding of the necessity of the church for salvation and the Augustinian notion of the church as the

---

24. Augustine, *Christian Doctrine* 3.32, in *The Nicene and Post-Nicene Fathers,* Series 1, ed. Philip Schaff, 1886-1889, 14 vols., repr. (Peabody, MA: Hendrickson, 1994), 2:1191. C. Hall argues that, in contrast to Augustine, "the Cyprianic model of the church pictures the church in this present age as a pure, holy community of only genuine believers." Christopher A. Hall, *Learning Theology with the Church Fathers* (Downers Grove, IL.: InterVarsity Press, 2002), 245.

25. Augustine, *Answer to The Letters of Petilian the Donatist* 3.2, in *The Nicene and Post-Nicene Fathers,* Series 1, ed. Philip Schaff, 1886-1889, 14 vols., repr., (Peabody, MA: Hendrickson, 1994), 4:1127.

26. Berkhof, *The History of Christian Doctrines,* 229.

27. Berkhof, *The History of Christian Doctrines,* 229.

28. Frederick Van Fleteren and Joseph C. Schnaubelt, *Augustine: Biblical Exegete* (Augustinian Historical Institute (New York: Peter Lang, 2001), 104.

29. Berkhof, *The History of Christian Doctrines,* 231.

kingdom of God on earth.[30] In this sense, medieval theology ascribed an "undue significance . . . to the outward ordinances of the church," because "all the blessings of salvation were thought of as coming to man through the ordinances of the church."[31] Moreover, there was a total "identification of the visible and organized church with the kingdom of God."[32]

This ecclesiological comprehension strongly emphasizes the visible nature of the church. Then, through this idea of visibility, Roman Catholic theology was able to explain its understanding of invisibility of the church, particularly in connection with its notion of Christ's incarnation and human soul. Assuming the church as a continuation of Christ's incarnation on earth, the church is described as

> the Mystical Body of Christ [which comprises] an external, visible, juridical element (i.e., the legal organization), and an inner, invisible, mystical element (i.e., the communication of grace), just as in Christ, the Head of the Church, there is the visible human nature, and the invisible Divine nature, and in the Sacraments, the outward signs and the inward grace.[33]

Likewise, employing the analogy of the dichotomous conception of human soul and body, the Holy Ghost is compared to the soul of the church, and this soul is considered the invisible aspect of the church: "While the Holy Ghost is the soul of the Church, the lawfully organized visible commonwealth of the faithful is the body of the Church. Both conjointly form a coherent whole as do the soul and the body in man."[34] Thus, "he who culpably persists in remaining outside the body of the Church cannot participate in the Holy Ghost." Exceptionally, those who do "not know the true Church of Christ, can receive the supernatural life given by the Holy Ghost outside the body of the Church. Such a person, however, must have at least an implicit desire to belong to the Church of Christ."[35]

As can be seen, the invisible church is basically discussed within the boundaries of the visible church. This means that "Catholics are willing to admit that there is an invisible side to the church, but prefer to reserve the name 'church' for the visible communion of believers,"[36] since "the visible church is first, then comes the invisible; the former gives birth to the latter."[37] Therefore, "the institute of the

---

30. P. Tillich pointed out that "the Catholic Church could use Augustine" to "identify the kingdom of God with the church to such degree that the church became absolutized; this was the one development which actually happened." Paul Tillich, *A History of Christian Thought: From Its Judaic and Hellenistic Origins to Existentialism*, ed. Carl E. Braaten (New York: Simon & Schuster, 1968), 121. For further information about the relation between the kingdom of God and the church in Augustine, see *Christian Doctrine*, 3.121-122; Hall, *Learning Theology with the Church Fathers*, 25; Henry Martyn Herrick, *The Kingdom of God in the Writings of the Fathers* (New York: Bibliolife, 2010), 78-91; Adolf von Harnack, *Outlines of the History of Dogma*, trans. Edwin Know Mitchell (London: Hodder & Stoughton, 1893), 358-360.

31. Berkhof, *The History of Christian Doctrines*, 233.

32. Berkhof, *The History of Christian Doctrines*, 23.

33. Ludwig Ott, *Fundamentals of Catholic Dogma* (Rockford, IL: Tan Books, 1974), 277.

34. Ludwig Ott, *Fundamentals of Catholic Dogma* (Rockford, IL: Tan Books, 1974), 294.

35. Ludwig Ott, *Fundamentals of Catholic Dogma* (Rockford, IL: Tan Books, 1974), -294-295.

36. Louis Berkhof, *Systematic Theology* (Grand Rapids, MI: Eerdmans, 1976), 562.

37. John Adam Moehler, *Symbolism or Exposition on the Doctrinal Differences between Catholics and Protestants as Evidenced by Their Symbolic Writings*, trans. James Burton Robertson (Whitefish, MT: Kessinger, 2003), 331.

Church logically precedes the organism, the visible Church precedes the invisi-ble."[38] As a result, "the order in the work of salvation is, not that God by means of His Word leads men to the Church, but just the reverse, that the Church leads men to the Word and to Christ."[39]

The Reformation Period

Even though von Harnack declared that the Protestant "reflections on the vis-ible and invisible church are indefinite and unclear,"[40] it seems evident that "the Reformation was a reaction against the externalism of Rome in general, and in particular, also against its external conception of the church. [In Protestantism,] . . . the essence of the church is not found in the external organization of the church."[41] Actually, "the church universal is spiritually united [which means an invisible unity,] rather than institutionally united."[42] According to W. Pauck,

---

38. Berkhof, *The History of Christian Doctrines*, 235. In opposition to the idea of an invisible church independent of the visible church, the First Vatican Council declared in 1870: "No one should ever believe that the members of the Church are united with merely internal, hidden bonds and that, therefore, they constitute a hidden and completely invisible society. For the eternal wisdom and power of the Godhead willed that, to these spiritual and invisible bonds by which the faithful through the Holy Spirit adhere to the supreme and invisible head of the Church, there should be corresponding external, visible bonds also in order that this spiritual and supernatural society might appear in ex-ternal form and be conspicuously evident. . . . Thus the Church of Christ on earth is neither invisible nor hidden; but it is placed in clear view like a city upon a mountain, high and brilliant, impossible to hide." Jesuit Fathers of St. Mary's College, *The Church Teaches: Documents of the Church in English Translation*, ed. John F. Clarkson, John H. Edwards, William J. Kelly, and John J. Welch (St. Louis: Herder, 1955), 89-90. R. Olson argued that "the Second Vatican Council (Vatican II) softened the perspective of the Catholic church somewhat with regard to Christians who are not members of the Roman Catholic Church, but it did not change the historic Catholic belief in the visibility and institutional hierarchy of the church. Even in the post-Vatican II era, in which the Catholic Church has reached out to 'separated brethren' (Protestants) as fellow true believers in Jesus Christ, the Roman Catholic belief in the church's visible and institutional unity under the pope around the bishops has remained intact. The Church of Rome throughout the world is the only true Christian church; all other groups of Christians are 'ecclesial communities,' religious clubs or parachurch organizations." Olson, *The Mosaic of Christian Belief*, 296.

39. Berkhof, *The History of Christian Doctrines*, 236.

40. Harnack, *Outlines of the History of Dogma*, 540. He also maintained that, at least at the be-ginning, the Reformers were concerned with the visible church: "Neither a communion of believers, nor an invisible church, as is falsely believed, did the Reformers have in view, but their object was to improve the old church of priests and sacraments by dissolving her hierarchic monarchical consti-tution, by abolishing her assumed political powers and by carefully shifting her priests according to the standard of the law of Christ, or of the Bible. On these conditions she was also esteemed by the Reformers as the visible, holy church, through which God realizes his predestinations." Ibid., 448-449.

41. Berkhof, *Systematic Theology*, 563-564. Stuart R. Jones indicated that even "on the Refor-mation's eve, John Wycliffe attacked the corruption of the church by defining the true church as the congregation of all who are predestined to salvation." Stuart R. Jones, "The Invisible Church of the Westminster Confession of Faith," *Westminster Theological Journal* 59 (1997): 71.

42. Olson, *The Mosaic of Christian Belief*, 296. S. Jones explained that the Reformation faced an "epistemological problem" in attacking Roman Catholic ecclesiology: "Rome, by claiming the four Nicene attributes (unity, holiness, catholicity, and apostolicity) defined in institutional terms, forced the Reformers to refine their understanding of those attributes. In rejecting the purely institutional approach of Rome, the Reformers emphasized a less institutionally tangible and visible notion of the church attributes. From this conception the formula 'invisible church' eventually developed." Jones, "The Invisible Church," 71.

the chief difference between Luther and [medieval] scholasticism was that, while scholasticism interpreted the *corpus Christi* in connection with the sacraments and the hierarchical order, Luther emphasized the Word. Within this new frame of reference, he declared the nature of the church spiritual and apprehendable only by faith. In so far as Christ renders his spirit efficacious through the preaching of the word and the administration of the sacraments, this invisible church undergoes a process of materialisation (W. Koehler) in becoming a visible cult congregation.[43]

Hence, contrary to Catholic teaching, Luther proposed that "from the invisible emerges the visible Church: and the former is the groundwork of the latter."[44] Following this idea, "the church of Christ is not a hidden reality in every sense of the word . . . [and] Luther does not distinguish a visible church from an invisible church but teaches that the one and the same church of Christendomis both invisible and visible, hidden and at the same time revealed – in different dimensions."[45] In its invisible aspect, the church is the "spiritual communion of those who believe in Christ." However, "this same church . . . becomes visible and can be known . . . by the pure administration of the Word and the sacraments." Therefore, "the really important thing for man is that he belongs to the spiritual or invisible church; but this is closely connected with membership in the visible church."[46]

Similarly, the Reformed tradition believes that the "universal Church, which is *invisible*, consists of the whole number of the elect, that have been, are, or shall be gathered into one, under Christ the Head thereof."[47] In fact, this invisibility is understood "in more than one sense: (1) as *ecclesia universalis*, because no one can ever see the church of all places and all times; (2) as *coetus electorum*, which will not be completed and visible until de parousia; and (3) as *coetus electorum vocatorum*, because we are not able to distinguish absolutely the true believers from the false."[48]

Although there is a direct connection between the invisibility of the church with its visibility, the Reformed tradition also admits that "in times of religious depression, as in the days of Elijah and the late medieval period, the true church

---

43. Wilhelm Pauck, "The Idea of the Church in Christian History," *Church History* 21 (1952): 209. About the invisibility of the church, Luther stated: "Because these mighty and imposing powers are to fight against Christendom, and it is to be deprived of outward shape and concealed under so many tribulations and heresies and other faults, it is impossible for the natural reason to recognize Christendom. On the contrary, natural reason falls away and take offense. It calls that 'the Christian church' which is really the worst enemy of the Christian church. Similarly, it calls those persons damned heretics who are really the true Christian church." Therefore, "Christendom will not be known by sight, but by faith. And faith has to do with things not seen." Luther, *Preface to the Revelation of St. John* [II], 409-410.

44. Moehler, *Symbolism or Exposition*, 331.

45. Paul Althaus, *The Theology of Martin Luther*, trans. R. C. Schultz (Philadelphia: Fortress, 1966), 293.

46. Berkhof, *The History of Christian Doctrines*, 236-237.

47. John Macpherson, ed., *The Westminster Confession of Faith* 25.1 (New York: Forgotten Books, 2007), 50 (italics mine). According to Calvin, the invisible church "is manifest to the eye of God only." *Institutes* IV.1.7, 1165.

48. Berkhof, *The History of Christian Doctrines*, 238. In this way, "it is possible that some who belong to the invisible Church never become members of the visible organization." "On the other hand there may be unregenerate children and adults who, while professing Christ, have no true faith in Him, in the Church as an external institution; and these, as long as they are in that condition, do not belong to the invisible church" Berkhof, *Systematic Theology*, 566.

is driven almost to invisibility."[49] In fact, this idea was radicalized by the Ana-
baptists in their belief that "the true church was in heaven, and its institutional
parodies were on earth," which means that the true church is totally invisible.
Such understanding denies that the church is a "mixed body" and affirms, like the
Donatists, that the church is a "holy and pure body." Hence, this invisible and pure
church is depicted "as a faithful remnant in conflict with the world." Certainly,
that notion is compatible "with the Anabaptist experience of persecution."[50]

Against the accusation that some scholars regard the Protestant concept of
invisible and visible church as being based on some kind of Platonism and its idea
of two worlds,[51] A. McGrath argued that this concept is not primarily philosophical, but eschatological:

> The former [invisible] consists only of the elect; the latter [visible] includes both
> good and evil, elect and reprobate. The former is an object of faith and hope, the
> latter of present experience. . . . The invisible church is the church which will come
> into being at the end of time, as God ushers in the final judgment of humanity.[52]

In short, in this historical section, I have provided a panoramic overview of
the idea of visible/invisible church in the Patristic Period, and in the Roman Catholic and Protestant traditions. Concerning the ancient Fathers, Cyprian stressed
that salvation is only possible in the visible church, and Augustine admitted that
there is an invisible church made up of the elected by God. Further, Roman Catholicism intensified the importance of the visible church through its sacramental
and hierarchical system and acknowledged the invisible church only within the
visible one. On the other hand, the Reformers underscored the invisible unity of
the church (the church as God sees it), which engenders a visible community (the
church as humans see it). However, the Protestant notion of invisible church is
based on the Augustinian concept of predestination.

My second step is to explore the visibility/invisibility of the remnant in Scripture.

The Visibility and Invisibility of
the Remnant in Scripture

In this section I will broadly describe the idea of visibility and invisibility of the
remnant in the Scripture, concisely examining the remnant motif in the OT and NT.

49. John T. McNeill, "The Church in Sixteenth-Century Reformed Theology," *Journal of Religion* 22 (1942): 268. Cf. Macperson, The Westminster Confession 25.4; Calvin, Institutes IV.1.2.
50. McGrath, *Christian Theology*, 415-416.
51. McGrath, *Christian Theology*, 413; McNeill, "The Church in Sixteenth-Century Reformed
Theology," 268. See for example the interpretation of Willard L. Sperry, "The Nature of the Church,"
The Harvard Theological Review 24 (1931): 155-196. It appears that this accusation was made in the
sixteenth century, since Philip Melanchthon wrote in the Apology of the Augsburg Confession (1531):
"We are not dreaming about some Platonic republic, as has been slanderously alleged, but we teach
that this church actually exists, made up of true believers and righteous men scattered throughout
the world. And we add its marks, the pure teaching of the Gospel and the sacraments." Theodore G.
Tappert et al., *The Book of Concord: The Confessions of the Evangelical Lutheran Church* (Sixteenth
Printing ed.; Philadelphia: Fortress, 1989), 171.
52. McGrath, *Christian Theology*, 413.

The Remnant Motif in the OT

In this study of the remnant motif in the OT, I will first indicate the terminology used for remnant in the First Testament, even though it must be noted that in both OT and NT "some passages that lack specific remnant terminology reveal remnant theology through related concepts."[53] Further, the notion of remnant will be examined in three main parts: (1) the period prior to the Israelite community;[54] (2) the pre-exilic Israelite community; and (3) the post-exilic community.

Terminology. The remnant theme is chiefly expressed in the OT by derivatives of six Hebrew roots (*š'r*[55], *plṭ*[56], *mlṭ*[57], *ytr*[58], *'šryd*[59], *'ḥryṭ*[60]), "which are employed over 540 times."[61] According to the meaning of these roots, remnant conveys the basic idea of a survivor of a great calamity. Overall, this concept describes three types of groups: (1) the "*historical* remnant," merely "made up of survivors of a catastrophe"; (2) "the *faithful* remnant," which carries the divine election promises and maintains a genuine relationship with God; and (3) "the *eschatological* remnant, consisting of those of the faithful remnant who go through the cleansing judgment and apocalyptic woes of the end time and emerge victoriously after the Day of Yahweh as the recipients of the everlasting kingdom."[62] Certainly, these three categories are not strict and there are areas of overlap between them. For instance, the eschatological and faithful remnants are also a historical remnant, since they can be survivors of physical calamities along with spiritual catastrophes. Although those categories are considered as "approximate labels,"[63] they will be useful for our study (specifically, the faithful and eschatological remnants).

The Period Prior to the Israelite Community. Taking into account the purpose of this study, the most relevant occurrences of the remnant motif before the estab-

53. G. F. Hasel, "Remnant," *The International Standard Bible Encyclopedia* (ISBE), ed. Geoffrey W. Bromiley (Grand Rapids, MI: Eerdmans, 1988), 4:130.

54. By using the term "Israelite community," this study simply means God's people of Israel, without distinguishing between Israel in the north and Judah in the south.

55. This root is used 266 times and its verbal forms "denote 'to remain' (*qal*), 'to be left over, remain (over, behind)' (*niph'al*), and 'to leave (over, behind), have left' (*hiph'il*). The nouns *š'r* and *'šĕ'erît* denote 'remnant, remainder, rest, residue'." In fact, *šĕ'ār* "is Isaiah's favorite word of his remnant theology with twelve of twenty-six usages in the OT (10:19-21; 11:11, 16)." G. F. Hasel, "Remnant," *The Interpreter's Dictionary of the Bible: Supplementary Volume* (IDBS) (ed. Lloyd R. Bailey Keith Crim, Victor P. Furnish, Emory S. Bucke; Nashville, TN: Abingdon, 1976), 735.

56. With 80 usages of this root, the verbal forms mean "'to escape, get away' (*qal*), 'to deliver, bring to safety' (*pi'el, hiph'il*), and as nouns *pālı̂ṭ* and *pallēṭ*, 'escape, fugitive,' and *p'lêṭâ* (often parallel to nouns of the root *š'r*), 'escape, deliverance'." Hasel, "Remnant," 735.

57. In its 89 usages, this root "appears only in verbal forms and denotes 'to escape, get oneself to safety, make for safety' (*niph'al*) and 'to deliver, save, let escape' (*pi'el*)." Hasel, "Remnant," 735.

58. "At least 110 usages of 248 forms of derivatives of this root (attested in cognate languages) contain the remnant idea. They contain the meanings 'to be left over, remain over' (*niph'al*), 'to leave over (behind), have remaining, have left' (*hiph'il*) in verbal forms, and in nominal forms 'remainder, rest, remnant'." Hasel, "Remnant," 735.

59. With 28 usages, it "describes the 'survivor' from military disaster (Josh. 10:20; Deut. 3:3)." Hasel, "Remnant," 735.

60. "Has clearly the meaning 'remnant' in Num. 24:20 . . . Amos 4:2; 9:1; and Ezek. 23:25 and possibly in Jer. 31:17." Hasel, "Remnant," 735.

61. Hasel, "Remnant," 735.

62. Hasel, *ISBE*, 4:130; see also LaRondelle, "The Remnant and the Three Angel's Message," 860-863.

63. Tarsee Li, "The Remnant in the Old Testament," in *Toward a Theology of the Remnant: An Adventist Ecclesiological Perspective*, ed. Angel M. Rodriguez (Silver Spring, MD: Biblical Research Institute, 2009), 27.

lishment of the Israelite community are found in the book of Genesis, particularly in the narratives of the Flood (Gen 6-9), the destruction of Sodom and Gomorrah (Gen 18:16-19:38), the encounter between Jacob and Esau (Gen 32-33), and Joseph as governor of Egypt (Gen 45).

The narrative of the Flood presents Noah and his family as the surviving remnant of the Deluge, as Gen 7:23 reads: "Thus He blotted out every living thing that was upon the face of the land . . . and *only Noah was left* [*niph'al* form of *'š'r*] *together with those that were with him in the ark.*"[64] In fact, that salvation of the remnant is clearly connected with Noah's faithfulness, since the narrative emphasizes that he was "righteous" (cf. Gen 6:8-9; 7:1).[65]

Furthermore, the narrative of the destruction of Sodom and Gomorrah depicts Lot and his two daughters as the sole surviving remnant. Such deliverance is described especially by the use of the root *mlṭ*. It appears five times in the *niph'al* form, stressing the necessity of "escape" from that destruction (Gen 19:17, 19, 20, 22). Once more, the idea of faithfulness is implied, inasmuch as the narrative is introduced by Abraham's dialogue with God, particularly his insistence that God could not slay "the righteous with the wicked" (Gen 18:23, 25).[66]

In his encounter with Esau, Jacob divided his people into two companies in order to preserve a remnant of his offspring. Thus, according to Gen 32:8 (32:9 MT), if Esau destroyed one company, the other one "which is left" (*niph'al* form of *'š'r*) would "escape" (derivative noun of *plṭ*).[67] Likewise, when Joseph revealed his identity to his brothers, he declared, "God sent me before you to preserve for you a remnant [derivative noun of *š'r*] in the earth, and to keep you alive by a great deliverance [derivative noun of *plṭ*]"[68] (Gen 45:7). On the one hand, there is no complete connection between the ideas of remnant and human faithfulness in these two situations, especially considering that in both cases Jacob and Joseph's brothers were conscious of their sins (cf. Gen 32:7, 11; 45:3, 5; 50:15). On the other hand, it seems that this consciousness was followed by repentance and forgiveness (cf. Gen 32:9-12, 26, 30; 33:4, 10-11; 45:3-5, 15; 50:15-21). In this sense, their faithfulness is implied and they can be regarded as faithful remnant, since they still were the depositories of the divine election promises (cf. Gen

---

64. Italics mine. Unless otherwise indicated, all English Bible references in this paper are to the New American Standard Bible (NASB) (La Habra, Calif.: The Lockman Foundation, 1995). The Masoretic Text (MT) used in this paper is the *Biblia Hebraica Stuttgartensia* (BHS) (4th corrected ed.; K. Elliger and W. Rudolph; Stuttgart: Deutsche Bibelgesellschaft, 1990).

65. According to G. Hasel, this faithfulness "is much more comprehensive than a narrow forensic or ethical notion." In other words, "Noah had no claim upon God on the basis of some intrinsic merit on his own." Rather, "by believing and trusting in God, Noah stands in the right relationship and thus finds favor in God's eyes." Therefore, "it is God's grace and mercy which brings Noah safely through the judgment of the flood." Gehard F. Hasel, *The Remnant: The History and Theology of the Remnant Idea from Genesis to Isaiah* (Berrien Springs, MI: Andrews University Press, 1980), 143-145.

66. G. Hasel also highlights that "the salvation of Lot is neither attributed to his own righteousness nor to that of Abraham." Rather, "the salvation of this remnant is due to the grace of Yahweh." Hasel, *The Remnant*, 151.

67. Cf. G. F. Hasel, "פָּלַט," *Theological Dictionary of the Old Testament* (TDOT) (ed. G. Johannes Botterweck, Helmer Ringgren, Heiz-Josef Fabry; Grand Rapids, MI: 2001), 11:562; Hasel, *ISBE*, 4:131; Hasel, *IDBS*, 735.

68. Cf. Hasel, *TDOT*, 11:562; Hasel, *IDBS*, 735.

32:11-12; 45:7). Therefore, "it reveals once more that the remnant can escape judgment only through God's grace."[69]

In summary, "we have up to this point four different kinds of threats in connection with which the remnant motif appears: flood [Noah], brimstone and fire [Lot], family feud [Jacob], and famine [Joseph]."[70] In all of them, the grace of God is the ground of their salvation, in contrast to any notion of human merit; but there is also a human faithful response to that grace.[71] Moreover, the faithful remnant community is clearly identifiable. However, the clear visibility of the remnant people does not mean total visibility, because those communities "often included members who were not completely faithful." For example, "although Noah and his family were a faithful remnant that survived the flood (Gen 6:9; 7:23), Ham later uncovered Noah's 'nakedness' (9:20-27)." Similarly, "Lot and his family were a faithful remnant that escaped Sodom. Yet, Lot's wife looked back and was turned into a pillar of salt (v. 26), and Lot's daughters gave birth to sons fathered by Lot (vv. 30-38)."[72]

The Pre-exilic Israelite Community. The most important occurrences of the remnant motif in the pre-exilic Israelite community, for this study, are found in the account of Elijah's persecution by Jezebel (1 Kgs 19) and in the prophetic writings.

Promoting a profound apostasy in Israel, Jezebel executed the prophets of the LORD" (1 Kgs 18:4) and "sought to make the cult of Baal the official religion of the court,"[73] with 450 prophets of Baal and 400 prophets of Asherah, who were eating at her table (1 Kgs 18:19). In this context, Elijah complained to Yahweh: "I have been very zealous for the LORD, the God of hosts; for the sons of Israel have forsaken Your covenant, torn down Your altars and killed Your prophets with the sword. And I alone am left [niph'al form of ytr]; and they seek my life, to take it away" (1 Kgs 19:10, 14).[74] However, according to Yahweh, Elijah is not the only remnant: "Yet I will leave [hiph'il form of 'š'r] 7,000 in Israel, all the knees that have not bowed to Baal and every mouth that has not kissed him" (1 Kgs 19:18).

G. Hasel indicated that "for the first time in the history of Israel [there is a . . .] promise of a future remnant that constitutes the kernel of a new Israel."[75] In that sense, there is a clear emphasis on the faithfulness of the remnant. "It is a remnant of believers, a group faithful to Yahweh, which represents the true Israel of God and maintains its existence," instead of "an historical remnant securing the future existence of the people."[76] Furthermore, this situation also indicates that in cases

---

69. Hasel, *The Remnant*, 145.

70. Hasel, *The Remnant*, 157.

71. As G. Hasel summed up, "there will be no remnant without God's grace just as little as there will be a remnant without man's return to God." Hasel, *The Remnant*, 206.

72. Li, "The Remnant in the Old Testament," 28-29.

73. Hasel, *The Remnant*, 163.

74. As G. Hasel pointed out, Elijah was "the only surviving prophet of Yahweh, who publicly stood up for Yahweh at the time when the life of each prophet of Yahweh was threatened. One hundred prophets of Yahweh had gone into hiding when Jezebel cut off the lives of the prophets of Yahweh [cf. 1 Kgs 18:4]." Hasel, *The Remnant*, 164. In this context, Elijah stated: "I alone am left [niph'al form of ytr] a prophet of the LORD, but Baal's prophets are 450 men" (1 Kgs 18:22).

75. Hasel, *The Remnant*, 172.

76. Hasel, *TDOT*, 11:563.

of deep apostasy, in which the faithful remnant is threatened, the invisibility of the remnant is strongly increased due to the necessity "to hide from the public eye. In those cases the emphasis seems to be placed on the individual rather than on the community."[77]

Nevertheless, even when there is not an extreme situation as in the case of Elijah, the faithful "invisible" (in the sense that they are occasionally apart from the visible remnant community) individual remnant cannot be overlooked. In effect, W. Brueggeman recalled the captive "little girl" who "waited on Naaman's wife" (2 Kgs 5:2-3), identifying her as "the Israelite remnant in Syrian society."[78] Despite all the "circumstance of her captivity and subservience, she is deliberately, resolvedly, unashamedly an Israelite," keeping her faith and "identity in an environment not hospitable to such faith and identity."[79]

The remnant motif is remarkably developed in the prophetic books. In fact, the connection between the notion of faithful remnant and eschatology (the Day of Yahweh) is first made by Amos.[80] The series of oracles against the nations (cf. 1:3-3:15) culminates in the pronunciation of judgment upon Israel. On the "dark" day of Yahweh (5:18-20) only a faithful remnant, "the remnant [derivative noun of $š'r$] of Joseph," will be spared (5:14-15).[81] In addition, "Amos sees the remnant not so much as an entity of national dimensions but as an entity of religious importance and destination," since he "enlarged the remnant motif to include also the 'remnant of Edom' [9:12] . . . as a recipient of the outstanding promise of the David tradition."[82]

In his turn, Isaiah is the first to speak of an eschatological "holy" remnant (4:2-3) or the "holy seed" (6:13), purified after Yahweh's cleansing judgment upon the nation (cf. 1:21-26).[83] Moreover, he mentions the gathering of "the remnant of His people" who is left over in various foreign nations (11:10-16) – referring to Is-raelites (cf. v. 12), and indicates that "the eschatological hope includes a remnant

---

77. Li, "The Remnant in the Old Testament," 27.

78. Walter Brueggemann, "A Brief Moment for a One-Person Remnant (2 Kings 5:2-3)," *Biblical Theology Bulletin* 31 (2001): 58. He highlighted that "her performance [in the biblical narrative] was so brief and so insignificant as almost not to be noticed, unless one is on the alert for a 'remnant' of Israel" ibid., 53.

79. Brueggemann, "A Brief Moment," 53, 57.

80. Whereas "in the Elijah tradition . . . the remnant is an entity that is already present," in Amos it "is an entity of eschatological expectation. Thus in Amos we encounter for the first time a connection of the remnant motif with eschatology." Hasel, *The Remnant*, 205.

81. This idea was against the popular identification of Israel (as a whole) as "the remnant of the nations to whom salvation would be granted on the Day of Yahweh when those around them would be destroyed." Hasel, *The Remnant*, 204.

82. Hasel, *The Remnant*, 394. "By 'remnant of Edom' the prophet refers to that part of Edom which is still independent, which is still to be 'possessed by the booth of David.' The 'remnant of Edom' as much as the other nations must again be brought under the rule of David [cf. Amos 9:11-12]." Ibid., p. 214.

83. Hasel, *The Remnant*, 395, 401. The purified remnant reveals "the vital link between judgment and salvation." Ibid., 253. The remnant terminology appears twice in 4:2-3: "the survivors [derivative noun of $plṭ$] of Israel" (v. 2) and "who is left [*niph'al* form of $š'r$] in Zion" (v. 3).

of the non-Israelites, 'the survivors of the nations' (45:20) who recognize Yahweh as the true God."[84]

Further, Micah connected the remnant of Israel with the Messiah (5:2-5), and other prophets used the remnant terminology to emphasize the eschatological salvation in the context of the Day of Yahweh (cf. Joel 2:32 [3:5 MT]; Obad 1:17; Dan 12:1).

The Post-Exilic Community. As L. Meyer pointed out, "the returned exiles of the Persian period" are portrayed in the OT "as a remnant left by Yahweh's favor, in spite of sins that merited total destruction"[85] (cf. Ezra 1:4; 9:8, 13-15; Zech 2:7 [2:11 MT]). However, "the post-exilic community is more than just an historical remnant;[86] it is also a faithful remnant" (cf. Jer 31:7-9; Ezra 1:2-5; Hag 1:12-14).

> The returnees are the ones who were moved by God's Spirit to return and rebuild God's temple in Jerusalem (Ezra 1:5), i.e., not all returned but only a remnant. In their work of rebuilding, they were encouraged by God's prophets (Ezra 5:1-2) and received God's blessing (Hag 2:19). Moreover, the genealogical lists establish a linkage between God's promises to Abraham and the post-exilic community (e.g., Ezra 2:1-70; 8:1-14; Neh 7:5-65; 1 Chron 1-9).[87]

The main contribution of the post-exilic writings for the development of the remnant motif is related to the distinction between faithful and eschatological remnant. T. Li argued that "the pre-exilic prophets did not always clearly distinguish between the faithful remnant who would return from captivity and the eschatological remnant." In order to support this argument, he mentioned Isa 11:6-13, which mixes promises of eschatological restoration (vv. 6-9) and promises of the return of the captives (vv. 10-13). In this sense, "the post-exilic experience of the Jewish people helped to further refine this important Old Testament motif by highlighting more clearly the distinction between the faithful and the eschatological remnants."[88]

There are some evidences that indicate that the post-exilic community did not consider itself as the final eschatological remnant, even though the post-exilic prophets regarded their community as the historical and faithful remnant.[89] J. McConville suggested that the books of Ezra and Nehemiah "express deep dissatisfaction with the exiles' situation under Persian rule, that the situation is perceived as leaving room for a future fulfillment of the most glorious prophecies of

---

84. Hasel, *ISBE*, 4:133. The translation of Isaiah 45:20 is from Hasel. The remnant terminology occurs 4 times in 11:10-16, specifically in vv. 11 and 16 (verbal form and derivative noun of *š'r*). Furthermore, the remnant terminology in 45:20 is a derivative noun of *plṭ*. Commenting on this passage, Hasel added that it "does not refer to Israelites who have escaped from the nations but to an eschatological remnant of the pagan nations that worship idols, who have escaped Yahweh's judgment. These survivors of the nations are offered salvation. . . . They are to turn to Yahweh, the only God (v. 22), for only in Yahweh are righteousness and strength (v. 24). Here the remnant concept becomes universalistic, transcending nationalistic particularism." Hasel, *TDOT*, 11:565.

85. Lester V. Meyer, "Remnant," *The Anchor Bible Dictionary (ABD)* (ed. David Noel Freedman; New York: Doubleday, 1992), 5:670.

86. Li, "The Remnant in the Old Testament," 35.

87. Li, "The Remnant in the Old Testament," 36.

88. Li, "The Remnant in the Old Testament," 34-35.

89. Li, "The Remnant in the Old Testament," 37.

Israel's salvation."[90] Following that idea, he stipulated three lines of evidence: (1) dissatisfaction with the Persian overlordship (probably implied in Ezra 4:6-23; 6:22);[91] (2) dissatisfaction with the temple/worship, implied in the deep lamentation of the elders when the foundation of the new temple was laid (Ezra 3:11-13); and mainly, (3) the problem with mixed marriages (Ezra 9-10; Neh 13), which was "an obstacle to the enjoyment of a right relationship with Yahweh."[92]

As T. Li concluded, in view of those problems, the post-exilic community could not identify itself as the eschatological remnant, since "a faithful remnant community could contain unfaithful individuals, whereas the eschatological remnant would be composed only of faithful individuals." Therefore, Zechariah pointed to the future and eschatological remnant (8:3-8; 11-12) in the context of the judgment of the Day of Yahweh (13:8; 14:1-15). He also included the remnant of other nations (14:6) among the Israelites who would worship the Lord (8:22-23), "thus hinting at the fact that the eschatological remnant will include individuals from outside the nation of Israel."[93]

The Remnant Motif in the NT

The remnant terminology in the NT comprises a few basic terms in comparison to OT terminology. Overall, the remnant specific vocabulary includes the derivatives of the adjective *loipos* (for the *rest*) and the noun *leimma* (for *remnant*).[94] Keeping in mind that "even in the absence of remnant terminology a remnant theology may still be present,"[95] our study of the remnant motif in the NT will focus more on the concept of remnant rather than its terminology. In this way, this investigation will be divided in three parts: (1) the remnant in the Gospels; (2) the remnant in Paul; and (3) the remnant in the book of Revelation.

The Remnant in the Gospels. According to G. Hasel, "though the noun 'remnant' is absent from the Gospels, the concept has a prominent place."[96] Actually, the remnant theme is implied even in the work of John the Baptist, especially due to the visible differentiation between those who "were being were being baptized . . . as they confessed their sins" (Matt 3:6), and those who were not bearing fruits worthy of repentance (v. 8). As "an eschatological prophet of repentance,"[97] John also announced the imminent judgment, namely the baptism of fire, which would separate the wheat from the chaff (vv. 11-12). Obviously, the notion of remnant is assumed in the metaphor of the wheat.

90. J. Gordon McConville, "Ezra-Nehemiah and the Fulfillment of Prophecy," *Vetus Testamentum* 36 (1986): 223.

91. "Although the book opens with Cyrus's decree, which includes an ascription of praise to Yahweh, there are also hints that Persian overlordship was a serious burden." McConville, "Ezra-Nehemiah," 208.

92. McConville, "Ezra-Nehemiah," 208-211. J. McConville also suggests that "the simple fact that both books end with the need to deal with the problem" of mixed marriages indicates that this problem was not completely solved with the reforms of Ezra and Nehemiah. Ibid., 211.

93. Li, "The Remnant in the Old Testament," 37-38.

94. See Hasel, *IDBS*, 735.

95. Clinton Wahlen, "The Remnant in the Gospels," in *Toward a Theology of the Remnant: An Adventist Ecclesiological Perspective*, ed. Angel M. Rodriguez (Silver Spring, MD: Biblical Research Institute, 2009), 62-63.

96. Hasel, *ISBE*, 4:134. See also Ben F. Meyer, "Jesus and the Remnant of Israel," *Journal of Biblical Literature* 84.2 (1965): 123-130.

97. E. P. Sanders, *Jesus and Judaism* (Philadelphia: Fortress, 1985), 92.

In regard to the remnant motif in Jesus' message, Clinton Wahlen delineated four important types of remnant imagery in Jesus' teachings: (1) the seed imagery; (2) the planting imagery; (3) the shepherd imagery; and (4) the quantifying terminology. First, using the seed imagery, Jesus contrasted two groups in the parable of the Wheat and Tares (Matt 13:24-30; 36-43). In the interpretation of the parable, He indicated that the good seeds "are the sons of the kingdom; and the tares are the sons of the evil one" (v. 38). However they will be separated only "at the end of the age" (v. 40). Second, in the context of the planting imagery, Jesus stated, "Every plant which My heavenly Father did not plant shall be uprooted" (15:13). "Similar language is found in a remnant context of Jeremiah (24:6-7), the larger context of which also contrasts 'good figs' with 'bad figs,' [cf. Jer 24:8] referring to two groups of people in Judah."[98] Third, in the shepherd imagery Jesus identified himself as a shepherd (Matt 25:32; 26:31; John 10:11, 14, 16), and described the disciples as the sheep (Matt 26:31; Luke 12:32). Further, He emphasizes the gathering of the "lost sheep of the house of Israel" (Matt 10:6; 15:24), "evoking a remnant image familiar from such Old Testament remnant passages as Jer 23:2-3 and Zeph 3:19-20." In addition, "Jesus' mention of 'other sheep' which are 'not of this fold' (John 10:16) points to an expansive notion of the remnant, drawing on prior prophetic hopes for the inclusion of Gentiles in the future kingdom (e.g., Isa 49:6; 56:6-8)." Nevertheless, He also used the shepherd imagery in the context of the final judgment: when "all the nations will be gathered before Him; and He will separate them from one another, as the shepherd separates the sheep from the goats" (Matt 25:32). Fourth, in His quantifying terminology, "Jesus refers to His followers with a variety of terms that suggest a small group. He refers to the 'few' . . . who find the way to life (Matt 7:14; cf. Luke 13:3) and affirms that, though 'many' are called 'few' . . . are chosen/elect (Matt 22:14)."[99]

On the whole, the remnant theme in the Gospels is discussed in terms of the eschatological judgment. In fact, there are here two significant implications for our study: (1) On the one hand, many groups are clearly identifiable in this discussion, such as the disciples as the sheep (Matt 26:31; Luke 12:32); the Pharisees as the plant which the Father did not plant (cf. Matt 15:12-14); and the Gentiles as "the other sheep" which are not of this fold (John 10:16). Actually, some ideas mentioned here seem to operate as visible marks of the true believers; for instance, baptism, confession of sins, fruits of repentance, and the idea of good figs in contrast to the bad ones. (2) On the other hand, it seems clear that the eschatological remnant will be completely identifiable only at the final judgment, since the separation between true and false believers is a divine task.

The Remnant in Paul. As L. Meyer indicated, "the most explicit NT references to the remnant are in Romans 9-11."[100] In those chapters, Paul dealt with the condition of Israel in the New Testament. In order to affirm that the word of God

---

98. Wahlen, "The Remnant in the Gospels," 74.

99. Wahlen, "The Remnant in the Gospels," 74-75.

100. Meyer, *ABD*, 5:671. See Rom 9:27 (*hupoleimma*); 11:5 (*leimma*). The Greek text used in this paper is *The Greek New Testament* (*UBS4*) 4th rev. ed.; Kurt Aland, Barbara Aland, Johannes Karavidopoulos, Carlo M. Martini and Bruce M. Metzger (Stuttgart: Deutsche Bibelgesellschaft; United Bible Societies, 2001).

has not failed (Rom 9:6), and that "God has not rejected His people" (11:1-2), he appealed to the OT concept of remnant, particularly Isaiah's prophecies (9:27, 29) and the persecution of Elijah (11:2-5).

Assuming the notion of faithful remnant, Paul distinguished the faithful Israel from the biological Israel:[101] "For they are not all Israel who are descended from Israel; nor are they all children because they are Abraham's descendants [*seed*]. . . . It is not the children of the flesh who are children of God, but the children of the promise are regarded as descendants [*seed*]" (9:6-8).

In this sense, he cited Isa 10:22-23: "Though the number of the sons of Israel be like the sand of the sea, it is the remnant that will be saved" (Rom 9:27). He also quoted Isa 1:9: "Unless the Lord of Sabaoth had left to us a posterity [*seed*], we would have become like Sodom, and would have resembled Gomorrah" (Rom 9:29).[102] Therefore, the use of remnant language in this context "presupposes that there has been a judgment, a division in Israel precipitated by the Christ event."[103] It implies that only "those Jews who accept this gospel constitute the remnant."[104] Moreover, in fulfillment of the OT promises concerning the inclusion of other nations, Paul "expanded the covenantal remnant of the faithful Jews by also calling the Gentiles (Rom 3:29-30; 9:24; 10:10-13; Gal 3:28-29)."[105]

In addition, he mentioned how Elijah pleaded with God against Israel—"they have killed your prophets, they have torn down your altars, and I alone am left"—and how God responded, "I have kept for myself seven thousand men who have not bowed the knee to Baal" (Rom 11:2-4). Paul's conclusion is that, in the same way, "there has also come to be at the present time a remnant according to God's gracious choice" (v. 5). In fact, two points are emphasized here: (1) "a part of Israel was apostate" and (2) "God had chosen a remnant." Therefore, in this sense, "all Israel will be saved" (Rom 11:26), since the faithful remnant "will stand as the ultimate witness to the covenant faithfulness of God."[106]

Overall, some ideas about the visibility/invisibility of the remnant can be seen in this Pauline discussion. On the one hand, he challenged the notion of visible (biological) Israel, opposing the concepts of *children of the flesh* and *children of the promise*, which allowed him to include the Gentiles in his conception of remnant. On the other hand, Paul was not speaking here about an *invisible*

---

101. Cf. Leslie N. Pollard, "The Remnant in Pauline Thought," in *Toward a Theology of the Remnant: An Adventist Ecclesiological Perspective*, ed. Angel M. Rodriguez (Silver Spring, MD: Biblical Research Institute, 2009), 77. George Eldon Ladd remarks that "the prophets saw Israel as a whole as rebellious and disobedient and therefore destined to suffer the divine judgment. Still there remained within the faithless nation a remnant of believers who were the object of God's care. Here in the believing remnant was the true people of God." George Eldon Ladd, *A Theology of the New Testament*, (rev. ed.; Grand Rapids, MI: Eerdmans, 1993), 106.

102. Thomas R. Schreiner commented that "Israel was no better than Sodom and Gomorrah and deserved the same fate as they. Nonetheless, this was not the fate of all of Israel, because the Lord 'had left' . . . a 'seed.' . . . As we saw in the exposition of 9:6-9, the term *sperma* refers to Israelites who are truly the children of Abraham, the genuine children of God. . . . It is merely another way of describing the remnant of verse 27." Thomas R. Schreiner, *Romans*, Baker Exegetical Commentary on the New Testament (Grand Rapids, MI: Baker, 1998), 534.

103. Pollard, "The Remnant in Pauline Thought," 82.

104. Meyer, *ABD*, 5:671.

105. Pollard, "The Remnant in Pauline Thought," 79-80.

106. Pollard, "The Remnant in Pauline Thought," 83-84.

remnant. His letter addressed a concrete church at Rome (Rom 1:7), comprising visible Jews and Gentiles members, and he used the concrete imagery of the olive tree, the branches which were broken off, the wild olive branches which were grafted (cf. Rom 11:17-24), insofar as he intended to represent specific groups of people.

The Remnant in Revelation. Generally speaking, the book of Revelation presents the remnant concept in its faithful and eschatological sense. Whereas the eschatological remnant designates those who will be saved at the Second Coming of Christ, the faithful remnant broadly points to God's people before the final judgment at that time. However, John also depicts the faithful remnant in a narrow sense, namely, the prophetic end-time faithful remnant (cf. Rev 12-14).

In a broad sense, the faithful remnant is discussed mainly in the letters to the seven churches (Rev 2:1-3:22). Each letter contains a promise of final reward "to him who overcomes" (cf. 2:7, 11, 17, 26; 3:5, 12, 21). As Richard P. Lehmann highlights, the overcomer is "is by definition a remnant, considering that not everyone is victorious and that only the conquerors will benefit from the promises."[107] On the one hand, the idea of invisibility of the remnant is emphasized, since "the promise is not offered to the church as a whole but to him/her (singular) who . . . is victorious by living according to the warning given to the church. The call is clearly given on a personal and individual basis." On the other hand, the visibility of the remnant is stressed by the fact that "the remnant is not made up of faithful ones who simply escaped the apostasy of the world. They are also those located within the Christian church who embraced the words of Christ in the midst of Christian apostasy."[108]

In a narrow sense, the prophetic end-time faithful remnant is described in Rev 12-14, particularly in 12:17: "So the dragon was enraged with the woman, and went off to make war with the rest of her children [*seed*],who keep the commandments of God and hold to the testimony of Jesus." As a matter of fact, several characteristics are mentioned in the description of the end-time faithful remnant, which strongly emphasize its visibility: (1) the time sequence, (2) the Commandments of God, (3) the gift of prophecy, and (4) the specific message.[109]

First, according to Rev 12:6, 14-17, the end-time faithful remnant appears after the 1, 260 years that the woman was hidden in the wilderness, that is, after

107. Richard P. Lehmann, "The Remnant in the Book of Revelation," in *Toward a Theology of the Remnant: An Adventist Ecclesiological Perspective,* ed. Angel M. Rodriguez (Silver Spring, MD: Biblical Research Institute, 2009), 90. Obviously, the book of Revelation emphasizes that this victory is achieved by the "blood of the Lamb" (7:14; 12:11). For further information about the concept of overcomer, see Kenneth A. Strand, "'Overcomer': A Study in the Macrodynamic of Theme Development in the Book of Revelation," *Andrews University Seminary Studies* 28 (1990): 237-254.

108. Lehmann, "The Remnant in the Book of Revelation," 90. Following this tension (visible/invisible), "the messages to the seven churches reveal that Christ focuses His attention upon all of His church, faithful or not. It is implied that in the church are both faithful and unfaithful persons (cf. Matt 13:24-30). However, salvation is not obtained corporately because it is not the result of belonging to a given community." Ibid., 91.

109. Cf. Ekkehardt Müller, "The End Time Remnant in Revelation," *Journal of the Adventist Theological Society* 11.1-2 (2000): 202; Gerhard Pfandl, "Identifying Marks of the End-Time Remnant in the Book of Revelation," in *Toward a Theology of the Remnant: An Adventist Ecclesiological Perspective,* ed. Angel M. Rodriguez (Silver Spring, MD: Biblical Research Institute, 2009), 140.

A.D. 1798.[110] Second, the end-time faithful remnant keeps God's Command-ments (Rev 12:17; 14:12, including the Sabbath commandment (Exod 20:8-11).[111] Third, the comparison of Rev 12:17; 14:17; 19:10; 22:9-10 indicates that the end-time faithful remnant possesses the gift of prophecy.[112] Fourth, the end-time faithful remnant is characterized by proclaiming the three angel's messages of Rev 14:6-12 around the world, which includes the biblical understanding of the Sabbath commandment and the judgment of God.[113]

In this sense, "the end-time remnant is a divine project in progress and will reach its ultimate expression shortly before the end of the cosmic conflict. Through their mission, God is reaching out to His people around the world, gathering the fullness of His remnant (Rev 14:6), and calling God's people to come out of Bab-ylon (18:4)."[114] Indeed, this "ultimate expression" or "fullness of His remnant" points to the eschatological remnant, the fully visible remnant. In its turn, the end-time faithful remnant is primarily (keeping in mind its visible marks), but not completely, visible, since it is not yet the eschatological remnant.

In short, the study of the remnant motif in the OT reveals that the faithful remnant community is generally clearly identifiable; however, those communities often included members who were not completely faithful. It implies that the rem-nant is primarily, but not fully, visible. Exceptionally, when the faithful remnant is in some way threatened, its invisibility increases significantly. Nevertheless, even in normal circumstances, faithful individuals who are occasionally apart from the

---

110. As Gerhard Pfandl summarized, "using the historicist method of interpretation, Seventh-day Adventists believe that the 1260 prophetic days refer to the period of papal supremacy from the sixth to the end of the eighteenth century (A.D. 538-1798), during which many of God's people were op-pressed, persecuted and killed. In Rev 12:17, after the fulfillment of the prophetic period of 1260 days, i.e., in the nineteenth century Satan is described as directing his attack at the remnant of the woman's seed–the end-time remnant people of God." Pfandl, "Identifying Marks of the End-Time Remnant in the Book of Revelation," 139. Cf. William H. Shea, *Selected Studies on Prophetic Interpretation* (Silver Spring, MD: Biblical Research Institute, 1992), 360; Alberto Timm, "Miniature Symbolization and the Year-Day Principle of Prophetic Interpretation," *Andrews University Seminary Studies* 42 (2004): 149-167; William Shea, "Time Prophecies of Daniel 12 and Revelation 12-13," in *Symposium on Revelation: Book I* (ed. Frank B. Holbrook; Silver Spring, MD: Biblical Research Institute, 1992), 67-110; Ranko Stefanovic, *Revelation of Jesus Christ: Commentary on the Book of Revelation* (Ber-rien Springs, MI: Andrews University Press, 2002), 395.

111. See Pfandl, "Identifying Marks of the End-Time Remnant in the Book of Revelation," 140-141; Johannes Kovar, "The Remnant and God's Commandments: Revelation 12:17," in *Toward a Theology of the Remnant: An Adventist Ecclesiological Perspective*, ed. Angel M. Rodriguez (Silver Spring, MD: Biblical Research Institute, 2009), 113-126; Mathilde Frey, "Sabbath Theology in the Book of Revelation," in *Toward a Theology of the Remnant: An Adventist Ecclesiological Perspective*, ed. Angel M. Rodriguez (Silver Spring, MD: Biblical Research Institute, 2009), 127-137.

112. "The spirit of prophecy, which energizes the remnant of the seed of the woman, is connected to the revelation of the true God as given in His Word, and is not only a manifestation of the spirit of prophecy in their midst. . . . This total reliance on Scripture allows the remnant to use it to identify the manifestation of the prophetic gift in their midst. Consequently, the Adventist Church has recog-nized that the ministry of Ellen G. White is a manifestation of the gift of prophecy." Lehmann, "The Remnant in the Book of Revelation," 104. Cf. Müller, "The End Time Remnant in Revelation," 202; Pfandl, "Identifying Marks of the End-Time Remnant in the Book of Revelation," 141-150.

113. Cf. LaRondelle, "The Remnant and the Three Angel's Message," 872-880; Lehmann, "The Remnant in the Book of Revelation," 104; Pfandl, "Identifying Marks of the End-Time Remnant in the Book of Revelation," 157; Müller, "The End Time Remnant in Revelation," 202-203.

114. Angel M. Rodriguez, "Concluding Essay: God's End-Time Remnant and the Christian Church," in *Toward a Theology of the Remnant: An Adventist Ecclesiological Perspective*, ed. Angel M. Rodriguez (Silver Spring, MD: Biblical Research Institute, 2009), 225.

visible remnant community (invisible in this sense) cannot be overlooked. In addition, OT prophets highlighted the holiness of the eschatological remnant, which included a remnant of the non-Israelites.

Likewise, in the NT the remnant is discussed in its faithful and eschatological forms. In the Gospels, the remnant is prominently described in its eschatological form, which will be fully identifiable at the final judgment, since the separation between true and false believers is a divine task. Similarly, Paul challenged the notion of visible (biological) remnant of Israel, which allowed him to include the Gentiles. However, those teachings (from the Gospels and from Paul) were addressed to concrete and identifiable individuals and communities, and they assume visible marks of the true believers. Particularly in the book of Revelation, there is an end-time faithful remnant with visible marks and a special mission. In fact, the faithful remnant is a project in process, whereas the eschatological remnant is its final form. It implies that the eschatological remnant is the fully visible remnant, and the faithful remnant is primarily, but not fully, a visible remnant.

Conclusions and Implications for the Adventist Understanding of the Remnant Church

Taking into account the ideas explored in this study, it is possible to conclude that, although the Protestant idea of visible/invisible church is originally based on the Augustinian concept of predestination, this idea is correct in stressing the tension between "the church as God sees it" (invisible) and "the church as humans see it" (visible). Indeed, the central point of this tension is the proper relationship of ecclesiology and soteriology. When a full visibility of the church is affirmed (outside the church there is no salvation), the main implication is that unfaithful individuals in the church will be saved. On the other hand, to focus on the invisible church means to disregard all the biblical teaching about the community of the body of Christ and the mission of the church. Therefore, the more appropriate solution seems to be a tension between the visible and invisible church.

The biblical description of the faithful remnant appears to imply this tension of visibility and invisibility. Overall, the faithful remnant is depicted as a visible community. However, considering that the conception of remnant is directly connected with the notion of judgment and salvation, to affirm that the remnant is completely visible means to assume that unfaithful members of this community will be saved, and that some faithful individuals who are not part of this community will be lost. Nonetheless, such division will be made by God in the final judgment: the visible eschatological remnant. Biblical data seems to suggest that the faithful remnant is basically visible in terms of community, leaving some room for invisibility in terms of individuals.

The association of the idea of remnant with soteriology, from the perspective of a Seventh-day Adventist ecclesiology, is not an easy task.[115] One attempt to overcome this difficulty is to consider that the universal church (faithful Christians in general) is the invisible aspect of the church of Christ, whereas the end-time

---

115. See, for example, the unclear position of *Questions on Doctrine*. Knight, *QOD*, 159-165.

remnant (Adventism) is its visible aspect, since "God is actively involved in the salvation of people outside the remnant. His people are larger than the remnant."[116] However, the understanding of Seventh-day Adventism as the full visible remnant brings soteriological problems associated with the idea of visible church. In addition, the Bible generally discusses the remnant in the context of salvation, and the OT remnant terminology is applied to faithful individuals from other nations.

In light of this complexity, I would suggest that the visibility-invisibility tension should be applied also to the concept of remnant, because the distinction between faithful (visible/invisible) and eschatological (visible) remnant is better than the differentiation between universal church (invisible) and remnant (visible). In this case, the Adventist movement would be seen predominantly as a faithful visible remnant community, while there is some room for invisibility in terms of individuals inside and outside this community, since the fully visible people of God will be the eschatological remnant. Nevertheless, this proposal is somewhat different from the traditional Protestant concept of visible/invisible church. Taking into account that this traditional concept is related to the notion of predestination, the visibility/invisibility of the church tends to be considered in a static manner, which emphasizes the difference between God's and human perspective. In contrast to that, the proposal of a visible-invisible remnant church in this study is not understood statically, but from the perspective of a process in history, something that is in movement. Certainly, there is still an important difference between God's and human perspective, but this is not the primary basis for the tension of visibility/invisibility of the remnant church. Rather, this tension is significantly related to the fact that the remnant is a community that is being dynamically formed in history, and it will end up as a fully visible eschatological remnant at the end of this history.

---

116. Rodriguez, "Concluding Essay," 216 n. 43. For further information about this explanation of universal church (invisible) and remnant (visible), see ibid., 217-224.

INDEX

Modern Authors

238

www.ingramcontent.com/pod-product-compliance
Lightning Source LLC
LaVergne TN
LVHW051043080426
835508LV00019B/1683